Greek Captives and Mediterranean Slavery,
1260–1460

Edinburgh Byzantine Studies

Innovative approaches to the medieval Eastern Roman empire and its neighbours

Edinburgh Byzantine Studies promotes new, theory-driven approaches to the empire commonly called Byzantium. The series looks at the literary, historical, material and visual remains of this long-living political order and its neighbours, often from a multi-disciplinary and/or cross-cultural vantage point. Its innovative readings highlight the connectivity of Byzantine culture as well as of Byzantine Studies.

Series Editors
Louise Blanke, The University of Edinburgh
Ivan Drpić, University of Pennsylvania
Niels Gaul, The University of Edinburgh
Alexander Riehle, Harvard University
Yannis Stouraitis, The University of Edinburgh
Alicia Walker, Bryn Mawr College

Books available in the series
Imperial Visions of Late Byzantium: Manuel II Palaiologos and Rhetoric in Purple
Florin Leonte

Identities and Ideologies in the Medieval East Roman World
Edited by Yannis Stouraitis

The Monotheisation of Pontic-Caspian Eurasia: Eighth to Thirteenth Centuries
Alex M. Feldman

Social Stratification in Late Byzantium
Christos Malatras

Sanctity, Gender and Authority in Medieval Caucasia
Nikoloz Aleksidze

Greek Captives and Mediterranean Slavery, 1260–1460
Alasdair C. Grant

Visit the Edinburgh Byzantine Studies website at edinburghuniversitypress.com/series-edinburgh-byzantine-studies.html

Greek Captives and Mediterranean Slavery, 1260–1460

Alasdair C. Grant

EDINBURGH
University Press

Edinburgh University Press is one of the leading university presses in the UK. We publish academic books and journals in our selected subject areas across the humanities and social sciences, combining cutting-edge scholarship with high editorial and production values to produce academic works of lasting importance. For more information visit our website: edinburghuniversitypress.com

We are committed to making research available to a wide audience and are pleased to be publishing a Gold Open Access ebook edition of this title.

© Alasdair C. Grant, 2024, 2025, under a Creative Commons Attribution-NonCommercial-NoDerivatives licence

Grateful acknowledgement is made to the sources listed in the List of Illustrations for permission to reproduce material previously published elsewhere. Every effort has been made to trace the copyright holders, but if any have been inadvertently overlooked, the publisher will be pleased to make the necessary arrangements at the first opportunity.

Edinburgh University Press Ltd
13 Infirmary Street
Edinburgh EH1 1LT

First published in hardback by Edinburgh University Press 2024

Typeset in 10.5/13 Warnock Pro by
IDSUK (DataConnection) Ltd

A CIP record for this book is available from the British Library

ISBN 978 1 3995 2383 7 (hardback)
ISBN 978 1 3995 2384 4 (paperback)
ISBN 978 1 3995 2385 1 (webready PDF)
ISBN 978 1 3995 2386 8 (epub)

The right of Alasdair C. Grant to be identified as the author of this work has been asserted in accordance with the Copyright, Designs and Patents Act 1988, and the Copyright and Related Rights Regulations 2003 (SI No. 2498).

Contents

Maps	vii–viii
Acknowledgements	ix
Preface	xii

Introduction: A Crisis of Captivity	1
Previous Scholarship	6
Aims, Evidence and Approaches	8
Ethnic Categories	14
Religious Categories	19
Categories of Unfreedom	22
Chapter Outline	23

Part I: Historical Contexts

Chapter 1: Political Changes in Asia Minor	27
The Late Medieval Romanía	27
The Collapse of Byzantine Asia Minor	30
Evidence of Crisis (1): Cyprus	34
Evidence of Crisis (2): Crete	38
Catalans in the Romanía	44
Conclusions	52
Chapter 2: Slave Trading in the Mediterranean and Black Sea	53
The Slave Trade	53
Greek Captives in Context	58
Genoa and the Trade in Greek Captives	61
Byzantine Relations with the Mamlūk Sultanate	68
Greek Captives, Cyprus and the Mamlūk Sultanate	72
Conclusion	81

Part II: Social Dynamics

Chapter 3: Captives, Slaves and Refugees	85
Captives or Slaves?	85
Experiences of Captivity	91
Experiences of Slavery	98
Captives or Refugees?	104
Trends in Forced Mobility	109
Conclusions	114
Chapter 4: Methods of Redemption	115
Ransom as Religious Duty	115
Captives' Letters of Clerical Advocacy (*Aichmalotika*)	119
The Distribution of Testimonials	124
Further Evidence for Itinerant Alms-Seeking	126
The Individual as Ransomer	128
Prisoner Exchanges	133
Military Orders	135
Conclusion	139

Part III: Cross-Cultural Relations

Chapter 5: Christian Masters, Christian Slaves?	143
Religion and Slavery	143
Ethnicity and Slavery	152
Subjecthood and Captivity	160
Conclusion	164
Chapter 6: Turkish Conquests, Conquered Greeks	166
Greek Clergy and Captives under Islamic Rule	166
Greek Captives and Slaves in Islamic Asia Minor	173
Raiding and Depopulation	179
Conquest and Deportation	186
Conclusions	192
Conclusion: A Mediterranean Phenomenon	194
Bibliography	199
Index	232

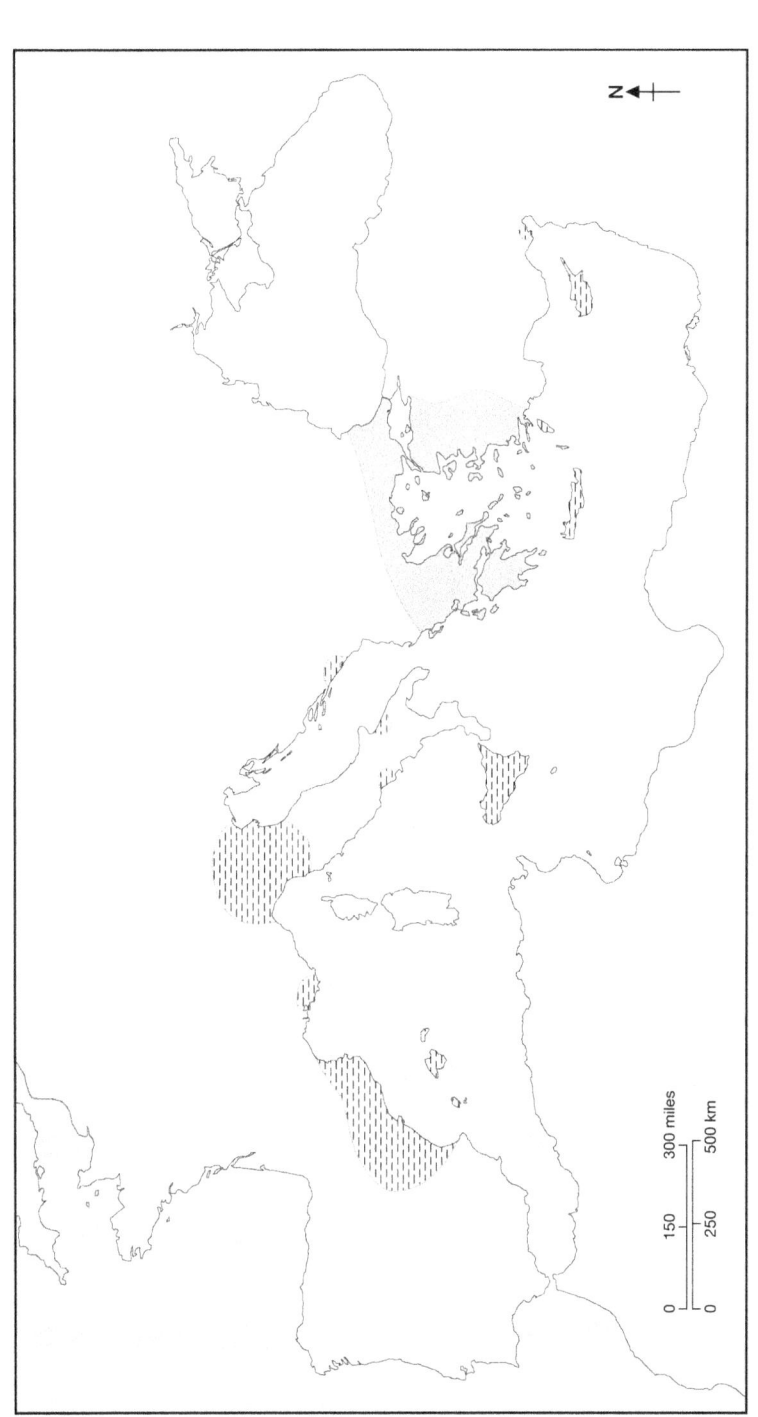

Map 1: The Trafficking of Captive Greeks from Latin Archival Sources, c. 1260–1460

* For the underlying data, see *infra*, 11, n. 13 and Grant, 'Cross-Confessional Captivity', 2.314–706. © Stephen Ramsay Cartography; Basemap: 'Blank Map of Mediterranean Sea Region', TheDastanMR via Wikimedia Commons; Licence CC0 1.0: Public Domain.

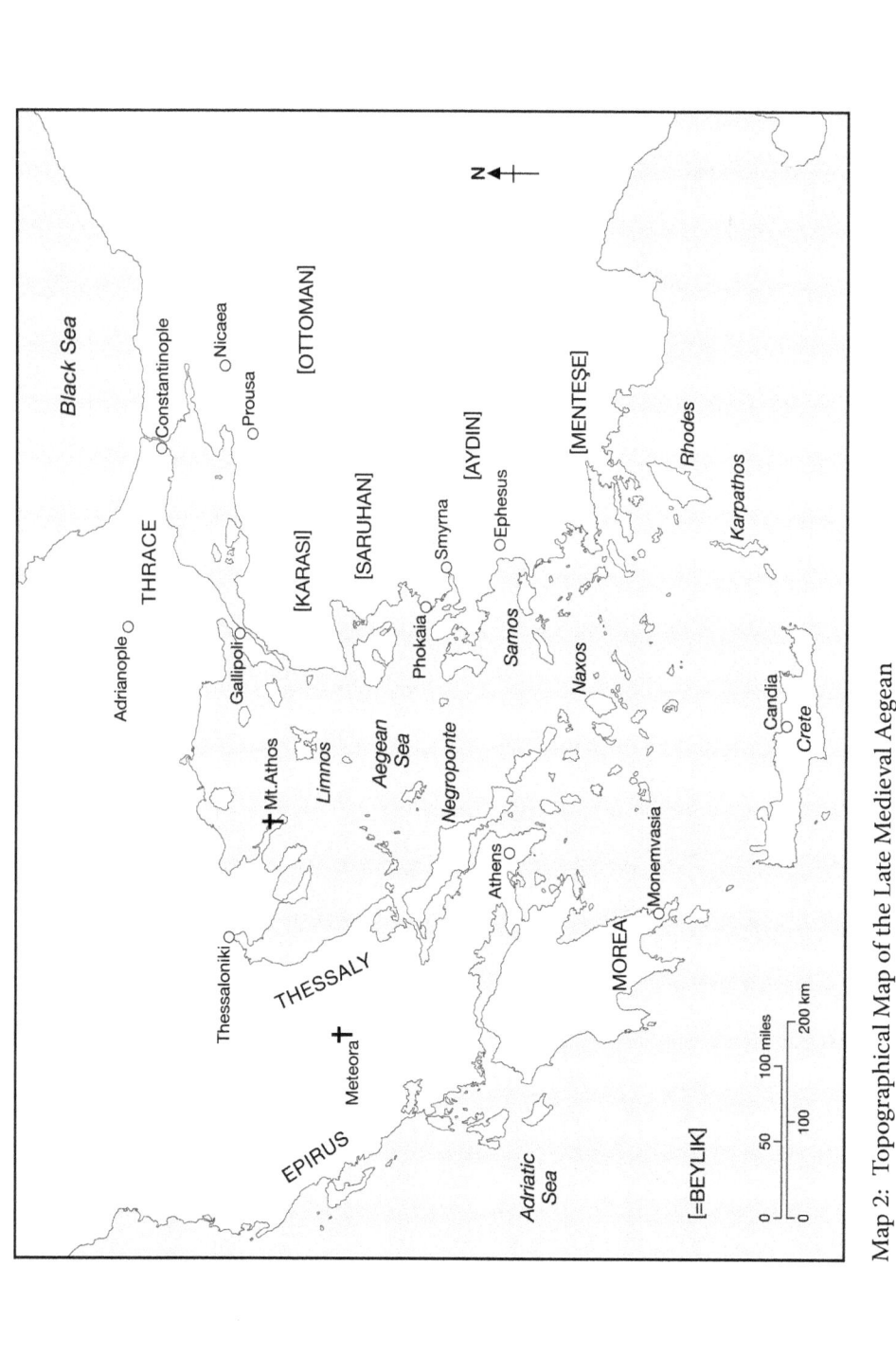

Map 2: Topographical Map of the Late Medieval Aegean

Acknowledgements

The preparation of this book has incurred many and varied debts of gratitude. Any errors, misjudgements or infelicities remain firmly mine alone, however.

Most immediately, I thank Dr Yannis Stouraitis, Rachel Bridgewater, Isobel Birks, Grace Balfour-Harle, and the rest of the editorial board of Edinburgh Byzantine Studies for bringing this book to publication. The two reviewers of my initial proposal gave me the most helpful advice I have ever received from any review, and for that I am most grateful. The final manuscript was much improved by the superb copy editing of Ioanna Mihelaki, and the excellent index was compiled by Zoe Ross. This book appears in Open Access thanks to the generous support of the Open Access Publication Fund of the Universität Hamburg.

I thank the Scottish Graduate School for Arts and Humanities for their leap of faith in my doctoral proposal, and for supporting me financially with a Doctoral Training Partnership studentship in Scotland and a Visiting Doctoral Researcher award in Germany, as well as helping me to indulge my interests in music through an internship. For paying for my year of master's study and thus setting me in good stead for doctoral applications, I thank my grandparents Bill and Margaret. The latter stages of preparation of this book were undertaken under the aegis of the Emmy Noether Junior Research Group 'Social Contexts of Rebellion in the Early Islamic Period' (SCORE) at the Universität Hamburg, funded by the Deutsche Forschungsgemeinschaft, project number 437229168.

I thank my doctoral supervisors, Prof. Niels Gaul, Dr Dimitri Kastritsis and Dr Mike Carr. Without Niels's recommendation at the start of my PhD that I consult the model letters of the manuscript Paris. gr. 400, I would likely never have lighted upon the subject of captivity, and instead persisted with my naïvely ambitious aims to write a total history of cross-confessional interaction in Byzantium from the Komnenoi to the Ottoman conquest. Without

Dimitri's nurturing of my interests throughout his superb special subject at St Andrews back in 2014–15, 'From Byzantium to the Ottoman Empire', I might have chosen to focus on a different area of medieval history in my postgraduate studies. Mike has been a supportive mentor, colleague and friend, opening up many opportunities to me.

I am much indebted to the wisdom and formidable Greek of Dr Mark Huggins, my friend and fellow student at Edinburgh.

I thank warmly the Byzantinists of the Johannes Gutenberg-Universät Mainz, who generously hosted me during the second year of my studies. Prof. Johannes Pahlitzsch, Prof. Günter Prinzing and Dr Zachary Chitwood welcomed me into their thriving department. The stretch of the Rhine between Mainz and Wiesbaden is as special to me as the banks of the Braid or Wartle Burns.

In the spring of 2020, I spent an all-too-short sojourn at Dumbarton Oaks as a Junior Fellow in Byzantine Studies. I thank Prof. Anna Stavrakopoulou for being such a supportive leader of our department, and Prof. Costas Constantinides for his kind mentorship. I also benefited much from conversation with Prof. Anthony Kaldellis during this time.

I thank the examiners of my PhD thesis, Dr Gianluca Raccagni, Prof. Dimiter Angelov and Prof. Andrew Peacock, for a thorough and stimulating examination. They will find aspects of our discussion on many pages of this book.

To my colleagues at Hamburg, Dr Hannah-Lena Hagemann, Natalie Kontny-Wendt and Alon Dar, I give my heartfelt gratitude for their friendship and conversation. Our research group SCORE has taken me far away from the world of this book, but their fresh perspectives have helped me to communicate its findings much more clearly.

Dr Audrey Scardina is due my considerable gratitude for advising me how to interpret and process my quantitative data, and no less for her friendship in the most critical times of thesis-writing. If I have done far less with that data than I could, that is my failing.

I thank the archivists and all staff of the archives of Genoa, Palermo, Venice and Dubrovnik, who indulged my dubious Italian and non-existent Croatian and helped me to consult a rich range of documentation. I hope to return soon.

I am forever in the debt of three people who supported and guided me long before I embarked upon this project. My former Latin and Greek teacher, Allan Bicket, taught my first class at secondary school in Aberdeen back in 2006; fourteen years later, he patiently proofread a prolix draft of my thesis. Prof. Frances Andrews of St Andrews supervised my first research project, which I began as a clueless eighteen-year-old; I always aspire to work with the rigour and high standards she exemplifies. Thirdly, I was extraordinarily fortunate as an undergraduate to live a few doors away from the late and much-missed Dr Ruth Macrides; although I was never her student, I certainly count myself among the many who benefited from her expertise and generosity.

Penultimately, Ann-Marie, Robert and Findlay, and my partner Marie Helen are owed a gratitude, the depth of which, they alone will appreciate.

Lastly, this book emerged from the context of the COVID-19 pandemic. I am forever grateful for my overwhelmingly good fortune during those difficult years, and as I write this, I think of all those friends and colleagues who have not been so lucky.

I lost my father and grandfather while this book was in press. It is dedicated to their memory: Robert Grant (1964–2023) and Bill Grant (1933–2023).

Preface

This study, like presumably many others, was originally meant to be something quite different. The PhD on which this book is based began its life in 2016 under the title 'Cross-Confessional Interfaces in the Later Medieval Eastern Roman World' and completed its gestation in 2021 under the title 'Cross-Confessional Captivity in the Later Medieval Eastern Roman World, c. 1280–1450'. The rather subtle change of wording belies a dramatic shift in subject matter: what is now unambiguously a study of captivity and slavery across two centuries was originally conceived as an attempt to write a study of lived religion between Greek Christians, Latin Christians and Muslim Turks across a period of half a millennium. Thankfully, in or, perhaps, even before the first week of my PhD in September 2016, my primary supervisor Prof. Niels Gaul suggested to me that I look into some unpublished manuscript letters written to help captives ransom themselves; what began as a small case study to get things started then expanded exponentially to fill the full thesis. The abandonment of the original and rather ambitious project was the right decision at the time, but I still hope to write that study in some form or other one day.

This book supersedes the thesis and should be cited in its stead. It is, however, neither simply a burnished version of the thesis nor a one-to-one replacement for it, but rather a substantially revised text. Indeed, the book is only half the length of the thesis, and it is important to explain here why that is, and what has changed. Firstly, I should make clear what the thesis did that the book does not. Most immediately obvious is that the book does not include the prosopography of captured and enslaved people drawn from Latin archival sources, which comprises the second volume of the thesis. The prosopography was a vital part of the original research process, 'showing my working' as it were, and allowing me to observe and visualise some quantitative trends. This data set is, however, very much incomplete, and it would require years of archival research – and preferably a team of specialists – to complete it. At the moment, this data set also focuses only on people I identified as Greeks, and any published prosopography would surely struggle to justify exclusion of other groups, especially when my identifications are often quite speculative. Similarly to the 'Cross-Confessional Interfaces' project, the prosopography might be published in some form one day, but for now I feel it is better simply to cite my sources where appropriate and to explain their limitations. The raw data is simply too raw.

The second way in which the book takes a step back from the thesis is conceptual. The original project was couched in terms of 'cross-confessional' relations, that is to say, captivity and slavery as social phenomena that brought people of different religious groups together. As more than one person who reviewed my book proposal pointed out, this book is not primarily about cross-confessional interaction, and captivity and slavery cannot be described in the same terms as the social relations formed through, say, shared saints' cults or places of worship. I have therefore dropped the term from the title, although the third part of the book (Chapters 5 and 6) does tackle this theme, asking what impact captivity and slavery had on wider relations between Greeks, Latins and Turks.

The book also offers the reader many things that the thesis does not. First of all, I do think that it is simply easier to read: once I had drafted the thesis in full, I then rewrote it from top to bottom; since then, it has been comprehensively rewritten once more, with considerably less complicated annotation and no unnecessary digressions. I was never especially happy with the structure of the thesis, which was divided up by geographical area, and have instead here selected a thematic structure, which I feel better serves the argumentation. For this structure I gladly thank the Very Revd Dr Derek Browning, who recommended that I approach the project as if I were writing up a series of evening lectures; this suggestion not only helped me to order my thoughts but also to express them in suitable language. I hope the result is something that will be simultaneously approachable to the non-specialist as well as rewarding to the specialist.

The 'evening lecture' approach demanded not just that I streamline my text, but also that I contextualise my arguments more fully; luckily, the first process naturally left room for the second. Readers will find a substantially new chapter – Chapter 2 – that sets out the wider picture of late medieval Mediterranean slavery in a way that the thesis did not. This complements Chapter 1, which offers context specific to Asia Minor and the Aegean and which, of all segments of the book, reflects most fully the original thesis (in which it was also Chapter 1). Chapter 6 of the book focuses on the Ottoman conquests and relates closely to Chapter 4 of the thesis, but it includes a substantial discussion of demography upon the helpful advice of a reviewer of the book proposal. The remainder of the book largely reorders material found in the thesis, such that Chapters 3–5 are new packages, even if their content is generally older. The book is therefore a substantially changed and, I trust, better work in numerous important respects.

Hamburg, August 2023

Introduction: A Crisis of Captivity

Ὑπὲρ πλεόντων, ὁδοιπορούντων, νοσούντων, καμνόντων,
αἰχμαλώτων καὶ τῆς σωτηρίας αὐτῶν, τοῦ Κυρίου δεηθῶμεν.

*For sailors, for wayfarers, for the infirm, for the suffering,
for captives, and for their salvation, let us pray to the Lord.*[1]

In the later thirteenth century, the Greek-speaking Christian communities of the Aegean region began to experience a new and disruptive chapter in their history. The disruption began in western Asia Minor where, following decades of relative stability, Turkish groups began pushing back the borders of the Empire of Nicaea (Nikaia) from 1259–60. In 1261, the emperor of Nicaea, Michael VIII Palaiologos, took the city of Constantinople from its crusader conquerors and thus recentred the East Roman (Byzantine) world on its historic capital. Despite repeated attempts over the following decades to reassert imperial control over western Asia Minor and to court military aid from the Christian West, a general trend of territorial fragmentation and loss had now begun that would end with the conclusive eclipse of all East Roman lands by the most successful Turkish polity, that of the Ottomans, by the 1460s.

This process of Turkish conquest had a drastic effect on the population and demographics of the region. Over various stages of raiding and conquest, the Greek-speaking Christians of Asia Minor and the Balkans were killed, displaced, deported, captured and enslaved. These phenomena were so widespread that they may be described as characteristic experiences of the period 1260–1460, and their severity was so great that they may be

[1] *Euchologion*, 3.1 and 9, ed. Goar, 52 and 56. I thank Dr Jamie Reid Baxter for this reference. Translations are mine unless indicated otherwise.

described as constituting a social and demographic crisis. This was a compound crisis, since in the fourteenth century this process of conquest and displacement coincided with Byzantine civil wars, serious droughts and the arrival of the Black Death. Captivity and enslavement, situated in these wider demographic contexts, form the focus of this book.

The capture and enslavement of Greek Christians and, later, of other Balkan peoples, generated labour and wealth for their Turkish conquerors.[2] Captured people were exploited for domestic (including sexual) labour, military service and administrative work, but they also had an immediate monetary value if ransomed by members of their community or sold as slaves.

The monetisation of Greek captives through ransom was facilitated, above all, by clergymen and the Christian communities that they served. Since Late Antiquity, canon (Church) law had made the ransom of captives an important duty of the institutional Church. In the late Medieval Period, this obligation was given further weight by the disintegration of the Byzantine Empire and hence also of its provincial administration: as the imperial bureaucracy retreated, the clergy took on more and more social responsibilities, especially in the fields of justice and charity. Senior clergymen (bishops, metropolitan bishops, patriarchs) wrote testimonials for captives and their family members to help them gather charitable donations from coreligionists in order to meet ransom costs.

The monetisation of Greek captives through enslavement was made possible by the existence of trading networks dominated by western European colonists known as 'Latins' or 'Franks'. These people had come to the eastern Mediterranean in the context of the crusades, and some of them had conquered formerly Byzantine lands in Cyprus and the Aegean region as a consequence of the Third and Fourth Crusades (1187 and 1204, respectively). From about 1300, Turks and Latins traded enslaved people alongside commodities such as grain or alum in the emporia along the western coast of Asia Minor, recently conquered from the Byzantine Empire and now under Turkish control. These Latins, usually Venetians or Catalans and sometimes Genoese, then transported these enslaved Greeks by ship to their mother cities and other places in the western Mediterranean, often via the large slave market in the Cretan capital Candia (modern Heraklion), then under Venetian rule. Through this export trade, the crisis of captivity became a pan-Mediterranean phenomenon, touching all coasts of the inner sea except perhaps for

---

[2] For this book's use of the term 'Greek (Christians)', see the section 'Ethnic Categories', *infra*, 14–19.

the Maghreb (North Africa). While a general trend of Turkish captors and Latin traders prevails, there were numerous exceptions to this rule: Turks also engaged in trade, and Latins in raiding, especially at sea.

It is often thanks to the book-keeping of these Latin traders that the phenomenon of captivity can be studied. Greek-language sources illuminate many qualitative aspects of the phenomenon, particularly the experience of the moment of captivity itself and the processes through which captives were redeemed. For quantitative aspects, however, Latin and western European vernacular documents are more useful. Through notarial acts recording the sale and freeing of thousands of enslaved people and through the minutes of governmental institutions, it is possible to trace the geographical and chronological emphases of the crisis of captivity. Broadly, this phenomenon began in western Asia Minor and the Aegean islands in the later thirteenth century, exploded through Latin trade around 1300, and then spread through Thrace, Macedonia, Thessaly and the Peloponnese, an anticlockwise motion through modern western Turkey and Greece broadly reflecting the paths of Catalan and Turkish invading armies. By the last quarter of the fourteenth century, Greek captives are less evident in Latin sources and their concentration hence trickier to measure; Greek and Turkish sources, meanwhile, suggest that their trafficking may have become a phenomenon largely internal to the expanding Ottoman Empire.[3]

This broadly triangular relationship between Greek captives, Turkish captors and Latin traffickers formed a distinct regional phenomenon with trans-regional significance. It involved the capture and enslavement of, overwhelmingly, members of one group – Greeks – and it emerged from the territorial breakdown of the Byzantine Empire, the political entity most closely associated with this group. In this sense, the crisis of captivity had local causes and affected an area concentrated around the Aegean Sea.

On the other hand, these captives soon entered much longer-distance slave-trading networks. These were the networks that brought enslaved people from the north coast of the Black Sea to the Mediterranean, where some were trafficked west to Italy and Iberia and others east to the Mamlūk Sultanate in Egypt and Syria. These networks were particularly vital for the survival of the Mamlūks, whose ruling class comprised manumitted (freed) military slaves drawn primarily from Turkic and Caucasian populations.

---

[3] This book follows Paolella, *Human Trafficking*, in its use of the term 'trafficking': it is a useful term because it encompasses a wider range of involuntary exploitative movement than 'captivity' and 'slavery' and reminds modern readers of the prevalence of sexual exploitation in medieval slavery.

Many Greeks were sold or ransomed within the Aegean region; others were trafficked along the westward arm of the Mediterranean slave trading network; only a few, however, seem to have been taken to Mamlūk Egypt and Syria. These two phenomena were thus connected but different in both origin and character.

In the West, the enslavement of Greeks had particular moral and political implications. This period gave rise to multiple crusades against Turks, sometimes ostensibly launched or at least discussed as being for the benefit of the shrinking Byzantine Empire. Yet here were members of these very same crusader groups trading with Turks – not only in material commodities, but also in captured Christians. On the other hand, the Greeks were seen as schismatics – 'splitters' from the Latin Church: they did not acknowledge the supremacy of the pope, nor did they have a doctrine of purgatory; they also adhered to other practices of which the Latins disapproved, such as the use of leavened bread in communion and the omission from the creed of the *Filioque* clause – the clause that states that the Holy Spirit proceeds through God the Father as well as through His Son, Christ. In Constantinople, meanwhile, the use of unleavened bread was equally rejected and the *Filioque* clause considered an objectionable innovation. So long as these disagreements persisted officially, however much they really mattered to the person on the street, the Latins could threaten to withhold military aid from the 'schismatic' East. Moreover, the Latins could justify to themselves the enslavement of these 'schismatics', whose Christianity was thus sufficiently compromised to exclude them from the widespread moral taboo against enslaving one's coreligionists. Such justifications, however, were evidently troublesome, since various Latin polities enacted legislation and concluded diplomatic agreements that sought to delimit the captivity and enslavement of non-Latin Christians, and of Greeks in particular.

Despite the widespread captivity and enslavement of Greeks by Latins, and despite religious repression, Greeks seem on the whole to have preferred living under Latin rather than Turkish rule. Though they were allowed to continue worshipping in the Greek language, Greek Christians had to make concessions to Latin regimes in their everyday religion, in some places including the loss of their bishops and the obligation to acknowledge the pope. It is clear that Latin regimes, and Venetian Crete in particular, saw Greek clergy as potential focal points for Greek discontent and as agents of a Church based in (and hence representing the interests of) the imperial capital of Constantinople. But even at times when Greek clergy were being imprisoned or subject to surveillance, Greek refugees were nonetheless frequently found moving west or south to avoid Turkish advances, or else further afield to Cyprus in the southeast, and often coming ultimately to areas under Venetian rule.

This apparent paradox is further borne out by the evidence for redemptorist practices among Greek-speaking communities.[4] In the early fourteenth century, this evidence comes almost entirely from Cyprus, then under the rule of the French Lusignan dynasty. Some captured Greeks were trafficked from the Aegean region to Cyprus, where many were enslaved but many others were ransomed by fellow Greek-speaking Christians. It is probable that some of these enslaved people were meant to be destined for sale in the Mamlūk Sultanate. Then, in 1373–4, Cyprus was invaded by the Genoese and the island's economy and society were severely disrupted; at this point, the evidence for redemptorist practices moves to Crete, where Greeks were widely enslaved, exploited and exported, and where both free and unfree Greeks were subject to harsh political and religious repression.

If Greeks appear, on balance, to have preferred alternatives to life under Turkish rule, the situation later changed. In the sixteenth century, the population of the Aegean region seems to have suffered comparatively far less disruption and to have recovered considerably. After the Ottomans had conquered new lands and thereby brought an end to war there, it was in the conquerors' interests to restore prosperity: accordingly, they resettled these lands strategically with farmers and artisans through incentives and, when necessary, deportations. While Greeks continued to be among various groups susceptible to the raids of North African ('Barbary') corsairs in the early modern period, their security and socioeconomic situation had improved by comparison with the decades prior to the Ottoman conquests, whether they had lived under the rule of Latins or of other Greeks. The period of the crisis of captivity therefore emerges as largely coterminous with the period of Turkish (latterly predominantly Ottoman) conquests, which was characterised by raiding and the forced movement of people. The maritime element of this forced movement was in turn catalysed by Latin traders. While captivities continued in the following centuries, the crisis was past.

The story summarised here is told in this book for the first time. The book's aim is to establish the causation, chronology, geographical reach, demographic impact and cultural significance of the crisis of captivity. Its approach is empirical and social-historical, its evidence based on a substantial tableau of literary and documentary texts mostly in Greek and Latin but also in western European vernaculars, Arabic and Turkish. The

[4] I use the term 'redemptorist' to refer to activities relating to the ransoming of captives.

result is a new social history of the late medieval Mediterranean, from a primarily Greek perspective, which puts ordinary people front and centre.

Previous Scholarship

In examining the political and economic history of the Aegean region in the fourteenth and earlier fifteenth centuries, Elizabeth Zachariadou inevitably touched upon the questions of captivity and slavery in her book *Trade and Crusade*. Although she devoted only a few pages to the subject – her chief concern was with contextualising a series of treaties between Venetian-ruled Crete and Turkish principalities in western Asia Minor – she made an incisive observation about the role of captivity and slavery in the later medieval Aegean. In a couple of sentences, she summarised the subject of the current study:

> The great Medieval Levantine slave trade was carried out between the Black Sea regions of Southern Russia and Egypt or Western Europe. From the early fourteenth century a subsidiary trade was established from the coasts of Asia Minor to Crete and thence to Western Europe, with the Turks raiding the Aegean islands and territories and carrying off the inhabitants who were then sold as slaves to the Latins.[5]

Zachariadou did not pursue these themes much further, and so their elaboration has been left to others. The 'great Medieval Levantine slave trade', called in this book the 'transregional slave trade', is the subject of a recent book by Hannah Barker, *That Most Precious Merchandise*. Barker examines Arabic and Latin documentation side by side to make a convincing case for the existence of a 'common culture of slavery' in the late medieval Mediterranean; not only were the same peoples, often from the Black Sea region, enslaved in both Italy and Egypt, but the ideas and practices surrounding slavery were common to both Christian and Muslim contexts: all across the Mediterranean, slavery was considered to be legal, justified by religious differences between the enslaver and the enslaved (for example, Christian and Muslim, Muslim and pagan), and posed a constant threat to people of all backgrounds.[6]

Barker's book is now the starting point for anyone, expert or newcomer to the field, who wants to know about the transregional slave trade. It is, however, far from the only recently published work on the topic, as

---

[5] Zachariadou, *Trade and Crusade*, 160.
[6] For a longer appraisal, see my review of Barker's book.

two lengthy multi-author volumes have appeared in recent years, both of which have informed the present book.⁷ These build on important studies by scholars who specialise in the study of Italian and Spanish archives, where much evidence for medieval Mediterranean slavery is to be found: the most important of these is Charles Verlinden, whose two-volume work on medieval slavery, and the many articles and book chapters on which it draws, remains the most important empirical contribution to the subject.⁸

What Zachariadou identified as the 'subsidiary trade' between the Aegean and Western Europe has, until now, not been studied comprehensively. Its existence is familiar to Byzantinists and scholars of the Latin East thanks to a number of studies, most of them brief, which address captivity and slavery from a Byzantine perspective. The problem with this scholarship, however, is that it has tended to regard this subsidiary trade as merely one aspect of the transregional trade, without analysing its own causes or characteristics. As a result, the buying, selling and exploitation of enslaved people within the Byzantine Empire, at that time a part of the transregional trade, is routinely conflated with the captivity and enslavement of Greeks within the subsidiary trade.⁹

Only a handful of studies have treated the subsidiary trade on its own terms, but these have been focused on the limited themes of either the ransom of captives or specific geographical contexts for the enslavement of Greeks. The first is a seven-page article in *Byzantinische Zeitschrift* for the years 1929–30, by the great Catalan historian Antonio Rubió i Lluch, entitled 'Mitteilungen zur Geschichte der griechischen Sklaven in Katalonien im XIV. Jahrhundert' ('Notices Regarding the History of Greek Slaves in Catalonia in the Fourteenth Century'). This article summarises, translates or partly edits various archival documents, many of which he would later print in full in his monumental collection of primary texts, the *Diplomatari de l'Orient Catala* ('Collection of Documents of the Catalan East'), published posthumously in 1947).

Rubió's ground-breaking work was taken up by Charles Verlinden in the second relevant study, the chapter 'Orthodoxie et esclavage au bas Moyen Âge' ('Orthodoxy and slavery in the late Middle Ages'). This is arguably still the most important and influential study of the status of captured and enslaved Greeks in medieval Latin societies ever published, and it has been drawn

---

⁷ Amitai and Cluse (eds), *Slavery*; Roşu (ed.), *Slavery*.
⁸ Verlinden, *L'esclavage*; for other works, see the bibliography.
⁹ Examples of this conflation include Köpstein, *Sklaverei*; Constantelos, 'Slavery'; Moschonos, 'Sklavenmarkt'; Pahlitzsch, 'Slavery'; Barker, *Most Precious Merchandise*.

upon extensively in most subsequent literature. Verlinden's study made it clear that non-Latin Christian slaves, and especially Greeks, were subject to important mitigating legislation in various western European contexts, and that some were able to regain freedom before tribunals on account of their Christianity. Verlinden's use of the category 'Orthodox' to embrace Greeks, Bulgarians, Russians and Vlachs has arguably led scholars of the Mediterranean slave trade who are not Byzantinists to underestimate the exceptional status of Greeks among the groups subject to enslavement by Latins – something elaborated below.

The third study of central importance is Johannes Pahlitzsch's 'Zum Loskauf von griechischen Gefangenen und Sklaven in spätbyzantinischer Zeit. Formen und Akteure' ('On the Ransom of Greek Captives and Slaves in the Late Byzantine Period. Forms and Actors', 2015). This study is largely, though by no means exclusively, focused on Greek sources, and as such constitutes a complement to Verlinden's chapter, which is entirely focused on Latin and western European vernacular evidence. Pahlitzsch has studied aspects of slavery in a late Byzantine context on multiple occasions, but it is here that the distinction between captivity and slavery becomes clearest, since he is focused on the question of ransom.[10] This study provides a robust overview of the salient evidence for the topic, drawing on the patriarchal register, historiography, clerical correspondence and a number of Latin documents.

The fourth and final study to note is the recent dissertation of Lorenzo Saccon on the redemption of captives in late medieval Cyprus, 'Ransoming Activities in the 14th Century Eastern Mediterranean'. This is primarily a study of unpublished texts in a single Greek manuscript written on Cyprus around 1343 (Paris. gr. 400), contextualised with wider remarks on the contemporary slave trade and practices of ransoming. This dissertation was undertaken at the same time as the research that led to the current book, though independently from it. Much of the evidence considered by Saccon is also considered here.

Aims, Evidence and Approaches

The limited scope of the existing scholarship has left much groundwork as yet undone, and it is the aim of the present book to complete that work and provide the first sustained and comprehensive study of the captivity and enslavement of Greeks in the late medieval period. Its research questions are therefore at a fundamental level: Why were Greeks taken captive and

---

[10] Pahlitzsch, 'Slavery' and 'Byzantine Saints in Turkish Captivity'.

enslaved? Where were they captured, and by whom? Where were they taken, and by whom? What were their experiences of captivity and slavery? What was the significance and impact of captivity for, and upon the Greek Christian population of the time? And how did these aspects change over the years?

The approach taken in this book is empirical. The strength of its argumentation rests not on literary analysis or theory-driven interpretations but on the aggregation of a large body of documentary evidence.[11] The process of aggregating this evidence was simple, but its scope ambitious: I checked every piece of scholarship I could find written on late Byzantine history or Mediterranean slavery for references to captured and/or enslaved Greeks; I did the same for all published sources I could find in all the languages of the region – Greek, Latin, western European vernaculars, Turkish and Arabic; I searched catalogues and digitisations of the major collections of medieval Greek manuscripts for any unpublished texts relating to captives; and I supplemented my reading of published Latin sources with brief and targeted visits to the archives of Venice, Palermo, Genoa and Dubrovnik. I built up a spreadsheet of the data I could find for individuals and identified trends in distribution over time and space. I then sought to place this evidence in its social and political contexts, in settings ranging from the Black Sea to the Balearics, and from Syria to Sicily.

This synthetic, empirical approach has necessitated the inclusion of a large and wide range of textual evidence. Broadly speaking, the Greek-language evidence (and the smattering of Arabic and Turkish evidence) provides qualitative insights. It is a varied mosaic of historiography, saints' lives, letters, homilies, and monastic and patriarchal records – a mosaic familiar to anyone who has read or written scholarship on Byzantine history. These texts have been approached through close reading, with individual narratives or statements being analysed and evaluated on their own terms before being deployed to illuminate one or other aspect of the topic under consideration. Generally, such texts have been introduced individually when they are first cited.

It is, however, worth introducing one particular type of Greek-language evidence already here. This is the captive's alms-seeking testimonial, sometimes called an *aichmalotikon* in the manuscripts: a text 'pertaining to a captive'. These texts are considered at length in Chapter 4, which focuses on methods of redemption, but as they are deployed as evidence starting in Chapter 1, it is helpful to become familiar with them straight away. These

---

[11] For a literature-driven study of Byzantine texts dealing with themes of captivity and displacement, see Goldwyn, *Witness Literature*.

testimonials are short, formulaic texts that survive across a range of late medieval and early modern manuscripts, sometimes as part of letter collections but other times as isolated instances. They were issued by senior clergymen to Greek Christians who needed help in raising ransom money, either for themselves or for family members. These testimonials describe the circumstances of captivity, sometimes specifying a ransom cost, and request charity to be shown by fellow Christians towards the bearer and/ or their family. The alms-seeker would carry this letter around from place to place, showing it to potential donors as an assurance of good faith. Some such alms-seekers had their causes championed in sermons in front of congregations. None of these letters survives in its original form, and most of the surviving texts were anonymised in the process of copying them into manuscripts; this was because the copies were to be used as reference templates for composing other such letters, and the person-specific details were thus no longer deemed important. Several of the examples used in this book are new discoveries, but as those that have been published have attracted scant attention, the substantial deployment of the corpus here thus represents as much of a new departure as the inclusion of the hitherto unknown material.

While the main asset of the Greek sources is their descriptive depth, the primary asset of the Latin sources is their quantity. The sale or manumission of an enslaved person, when enacted in a Latin-dominated social milieu, would routinely result in the drafting of a notarial document, many of which have been preserved. Notarial documents are formulaic texts that gave legal force to transactions between two or more parties. If someone decided to challenge a transaction at a later date (for example, who was to pay how much, or who was to receive what), then there existed an official record that should clear up any dispute. These usually specified the names of the buyer and seller or the manumitter (freer), the slave and the witnesses. The contracting parties might be described in these documents as *cives* ('citizens', for example of Venice or Genoa), or as *habitatores*, that is, people residing temporarily in a certain place (such as Candia on Crete). Such notarial sources comprise a subset of the enormous volumes of texts drawn up in Latin and western European vernacular languages (for example, Italian and Catalan) to record governmental and private business, and preserved today in the archives of Venice, Genoa, Palermo, Barcelona, Palma and Dubrovnik (among others).

By considering such factors as the names and places of origin noted in these sources for individuals, it has been possible to identify around 2,400 references from the period 1260–1460 to individuals who may plausibly be identified as captured and/or enslaved Greeks. This number excludes notices of mass captivities, found mainly in governmental documents, which can be hard to verify; were these numbers to be included, the total would rise by hundreds.¹² The primary criterion for identifying these people has been the inclusion of a taxonomy designating them as Greek; the secondary criteria, lacking this indicator, have been a person's place of origin, and/or their name. These secondary criteria are not always reliable: for example, someone whose name is given as 'Demetrius', and whose origin is stated to have been in Asia Minor or one of the Aegean islands, might fairly confidently be assumed to have been Greek; if the name alone is given, however, he cannot confidently be assumed to have been Greek, since this name was also common among Slavs and Vlachs. In addition to such problems of interpretation, some statements of ethnicity or origin may have been incorrectly given in the sources. Even accounting for such problems, however, the c. 2,400 references on which this book substantially relies remains a robust data set by the standards of Byzantine Studies. Future research in Italian and Spanish archives is likely to increase this number yet further.¹³

[12] E.g., the Byzantine claims against naval raiders under Venetian colours, 1319–20, where numbers range from 1–500: *Diplomatarium*, ed. Thomas, 1.124–7, No. 72; tr. Lopez and Raymond, *Medieval Trade*, 314–17.

[13] For a visualisation of this data, see Map 1, vii, *supra*. The data set comes from the following sources: all items listed in the Bibliography under 'Archival Sources', plus D'Amia, *Schiavitù*; Antonio di Ponzò, ed. Balard; Argenti, *Chios*; Balard, 'A propos de la bataille du Bosphore'; Balletto, 'Presenze bulgare' and 'Schiavi e manomessi'; Batlle i Gallart, 'Esclaus domèstics'; Blumenthal, *Enemies and Familiars*; Benvenuto de Brixano, ed. Morozzo della Rocca; Nicola de Boateriis, ed. Lombardo; Moretto Bon, ed. De' Colli; Bongi, 'Schiave orientali'; Stefano Bono, ed. Pettenello and Rauch; Brutails, *Roussillon*; Angelo de Cartura, ed. Stahl; Raffaele de Casanova, ed. Balletto; Cateura Bennasser, 'Cautivos griegos'; Čremošnik, *Spisi*; Delort, 'Quelques précisions'; *Diplomatarium*, ed. Thomas; *DOC*, ed. Rubió; 'Documents', ed. Sakasov; Duran Duelt, 'Companyia' and 'Ducados'; Epstein, *Speaking of Slavery*; Ferrer, 'Monedatge'; Ferrer i Mallol, 'Després de la mort'; Fleet, *Trade*; Gioffrè, *Mercato*; Dominicus Grimani, 'Documents', ed. Tsougarakis; Hillgarth, 'Greek Slave'; Juan, 'Cofradías'; Krekić, *Dubrovnik*; Livi, *Schiavitù*; Llompart, 'Pere Mates'; López i Bonet, 'Un fruit'; Luttrell, 'Slavery at Rhodes'; Luttrell and O'Malley, *Countryside*; Manousakas, 'Η πρώτη εμπορική παροικία'; Marcos Hierro, 'Catalan Company'; McKee, 'Greek Women', *Uncommon Dominion* and *Wills*; Miret, *Esclavitud*; Mortreuil, *Moeurs*; Felice de Merlis, ed. Sebellico; Mummey, 'Mallorca' and 'Women, Slavery and Community'; Musso and Jacopino, *Navigazione*; *Notai genovesi*, ed. Roccatagliata; 'Neobjavljene isprave i akti', ed. Lučić; Otten-Froux, 'Représentation' and 'Deux consuls'; Pietro Pizolo, ed. Carbone; Domenico Prete, ed. Tiepolo; Richard, 'Psimolofo'; Giovanni da Rocha, ed. Balard; Rubió, 'Mitteilungen'; Lamberto di Sambuceto, ed. Balard (1983), ed. Balard (1984), ed. Balard, Duba and Schabel, ed. Pavoni, ed. Polonio; Santschi, *Régestes*; Sastre Moll, 'Notas'; Sciascia, 'Schiavi in Sicilia'; Sevillano Colom, 'Demografia'; Simeone di San Giacomo dell' Orio, summarised Otten-Froux; Tria, 'Schiavitù'; Verlinden, 'Baleares', *L'esclavage*, 'Frédéric', 'Naples', 'Orthodoxie', 'Recrutement' and 'Sicile'; Vincke, 'Königtum und Sklaverei'. It has not been possible to complete my partial survey of Venice, Archivio di Stato, Notai di Candia, B9, Andrea di Belloamore, but I include the acts I have processed. Toponyms have been identified with the help of Markl, *Ortsnamen*.

Notarial sources are some of the best available sources for medieval Mediterranean demography and society, but they too have their limitations. Many notaries' names are known whose registers have not survived. Notaries primarily, but not exclusively, attracted business from their own socio-political community (Genoese, Venetian, and so on), and they also specialised in certain types of transactions to the exclusion of others (indeed, sometimes the sale or manumission of enslaved people). The same transacting party's name might be given differently in different acts, even on the same day. A person's ethnicity or place of origin was not necessarily given for private transactions. Toponymic surnames (that is, those based on places) had become hereditary in the Latin world in the thirteenth century, and therefore cannot be taken as firm indicators of the origin of Latins mentioned in these texts.[14]

Another important consideration with regard to these sources is their uneven survival. Notaries for Venetian Crete, for example, have survived particularly well: notarial registers were lodged with the government in Candia, and upon the Ottoman conquest of Crete in 1669 this archive was transported wholesale to Venice. Documents drawn up by Genoese notaries working overseas, on the other hand, have not survived nearly so well, because there was no compulsory central depository for them. For Greek notaries, the situation is far worse still, with only a few examples preserved by chance. The extant documentation is therefore not a representative sample of what once existed, but a series of historically contingent survivals. The number of 'unknown unknowns' makes any quantitative analysis highly unreliable.[15]

In addition to survival bias, these sources have been unevenly published, and the published sources disproportionately heavily studied. Once again, the most striking example is Venetian: many of the early fourteenth-century notarial registers from Crete – the *Notai di Candia* – have been edited, meaning that it is possible to study the demographics of Cretan slavery more robustly for this period than it is possible for others. Specialists in this series of documents have, however, often summarised the later registers or derived figures from them, and this book largely relies on such work for the period after the one covered by the published notaries. In a Genoese context, the documents of one particular notary, the prolific Lamberto di Sambuceto (also writing around the turn of the fourteenth

---

[14] Jacoby, 'Famagusta', 151–2.
[15] Notaries: Saint-Guillain, 'Venetian Archival Documents'; Barker, *Most Precious Merchandise*; Laiou, 'Collective Portrait'. Crete: McKee, *Uncommon Dominion*; Greene, *Shared World*.

century), have been edited and have thus also been studied in considerable depth. Gaps in survival and documents as yet inedited thus constitute a compound problem for the quantitative study of notarial documents.[16]

With regard to the study of enslaved people specifically, several more limitations of such documents should be highlighted. First, acts of sale or manumission reveal next to nothing about an enslaved person apart from the few pieces of information deemed necessary for the relevant transaction: in the case of acts of sale, that might (at best) include an ethnic taxonomy and place of origin, and sometimes a précis of a previous act of sale or (very occasionally) the circumstances of capture; acts of manumission generally contain less, as there was in this case no buyer requiring this kind of background information. Building a back-story of any of these enslaved individuals thus usually becomes a matter of circumstantial speculation, for which it is necessary to turn to literary sources. Notarial acts are like the *aichmalotika* insofar as their subjects enter the written record because at some point in their lives they were captured and/or enslaved; anything that occurred previously or subsequently in their lives is usually invisible unless it had or came to have direct bearing on the concerns of that document (for example, a previous sale). The experiences of the people mentioned in notarial sources are thus usually irrecoverable. Sometimes, if a person came before a tribunal to claim that they had been unlawfully enslaved, a document was drawn up that gave or purported to give their testimony; otherwise, their experiences survive only through the summary words of a Latin notary, a Greek clergyman or a historiographer. Notarial acts do, on the other hand, have certain benefits over other sources: these include the precision in their dating and the number of place names and personal names given – enslaved persons, vendors, buyers or witnesses.

Bringing together all this evidence and the perspectives of scholars from a range of disciplines – Byzantine, Crusader, Western Medieval and Ottoman Studies – has allowed this book to set forth some substantial new arguments about the social history of the late medieval Mediterranean. The new departures of this book may be summarised as follows:

1. The establishment of the mass captivity and enslavement of Greeks as a distinct phenomenon of the period c. 1260–1460;
2. The differentiation of this phenomenon from the Mediterranean trade in enslaved people from the Black Sea, both in terms of origins and characteristics;

[16] The published early fourteenth-century notaries are studied in Chapter 1, with references.

3. The outlining of the chronological and geographical emphases of this crisis of captivity through the use of archival documentary evidence for around 2,400 captured and/or enslaved individuals;
4. The contextualisation of this evidence for captivity with other demographic evidence for processes such as depopulation and migration, therefore also facilitating a holistic approach to population and demographics during the period of Ottoman conquest;
5. The positing of a new understanding of Greek–Latin and Greek–Turkish relations, emphasising Greek preferences for Byzantine or Latin over Turkish rule, despite Latin repression, but also emphasising demographic recovery in post-conquest Ottoman-ruled areas;
6. The establishment of the previously obscure *aichmalotikon* as an important mechanism for the redemption of captives in the late medieval (and indeed early modern) Greek Christian sphere.

Ethnic Categories

This book employs a number of labels for the groups that inhabited the late medieval Aegean. Primarily, these include 'Greeks', 'Turks' and 'Latins'. Each of these terms is problematic, so it is worth explaining how they are intended to be understood here. This explanation must tackle two points simultaneously: first, the use of terms in the sources; second, the question of which terms the scholar should use.

According to Roman law, the *natio* of an enslaved person had to be declared when they were sold. This term literally means 'nation' or 'people', but it does not carry the political implications of the modern term 'nation state'. The relevant law justifies this on the basis that the person's *natio* allowed the buyer to reach some conclusions in advance about their likely character. This would be understood today as a racialised framework: people were divided into groups according to origin, and each of these groups was believed to have certain fixed and thus predictable characteristics. Several other words were used by medieval notaries interchangeably with *natio* and its variant form *nacio*, primarily *genus* and *progenia* (also spelled *proienia*), both meaning 'descent' or 'origin'. In the late medieval Mediterranean, the *nationes* or *genera* recorded by Latin notaries generally corresponded to ethnic groups: for example, a person *de genere Cercasiorum* was a Circassian, *de nacione Blacorum* a Vlach, and *de genere Grecorum* a Greek. Some categories were less precise: someone *de genre Saracenorum*, a 'Saracen', was likely a Muslim of non-Turkish (for example, Arab) origin, since Turks were taxonomised separately, though it is sometimes difficult to interpret the evidence with confidence.[17]

There were various terms used to identify and taxonomise Greeks in notarial documents. As well as *de genere Grecorum*, these included *de nacione Grecorum* and the adjectival forms *Grecus/-a*. Also found is *Griffonus/-a*, a Latinisation of a vernacular Romance term blending *Griu* ('Greek') with *grifon* (gryphon), which smeared Greeks with the connotations of thievery considered characteristic of gryphons. Notaries sometimes recorded information about the origin of the enslaved person in addition to, or instead of, a taxonomy; this was most often expressed simply as *de . . .* ('from . . .'), but also with the formula *de loco qui dicitur . . .* ('from the place that is called . . .'). Often, the place of origin was given simply as the *Romanía* (pronounced with the emphasis on the penultimate syllable): this was the conventional term for the 'Roman land' of the Aegean region, though it was also applied to regions no longer under Roman (Byzantine) control.

Notaries did however often specify the town or village from which the enslaved Greek came. Many of the Greeks for whom a place of origin was given were sold in Candia on the Venetian-ruled island of Crete, and it is likely that the parties involved in the sale were familiar with the place in question, making it meaningful to include that information. Secondly, the origins of a slave were sometimes disputed; in these instances, the slave's own testimony might be called upon, suggesting that slaves might have been asked at the point of sale to state their place of origin. In these instances, there was less of a language barrier between a Greek and a Venetian than between, for example, a Tatar and a Venetian; while there are acts in which an interpreter between Greek and Italian was required, many Latins on Crete knew Greek, and plenty Greeks knew Italian.[18] The information that this familiarity generated is valuable for plotting the geographical emphases of the crisis of captivity. It also emphasises an important aspect of the crisis of captivity that distinguishes it from other systems of slavery such as the modern Transatlantic trade: these groups lived side by side in the same spaces and were already familiar with one another, culturally if not personally, before the point of captivity or enslavement.

---

[17] *Digesta* 21.1.31.21, ed. Mommsen, 275; Grant, 'Latin Categories of Greekness'; Barker, *Most Precious Merchandise*, 56–9.

[18] Taxonomies: Grant, 'Latin Categories of Greekness'; *Griffoni*: Livingston, 'Griffon "Greek"'; interpreters: Epstein, *Purity Lost*, 70; knowledge of other languages: McKee, *Uncommon Dominion*, 115–19.

The term 'Greek', used by these Latin notaries, is adopted in this book, but it is important to acknowledge that it is a problematic label. The medieval Greek-speaking population did not generally call itself 'Greek', so far as can be ascertained from the surviving texts produced by these people; rather, they called themselves 'Romans' (*Romaioi*), in the later Middle Ages sometimes the classicising term 'Hellenes' (*Hellenes*), and only occasionally 'Greeks' (*Graikoi*). It was rather the Latin world that called these people 'Greeks' (*Graeci* or *Greci*); especially in the early Medieval Period this had pejorative connotations, above all, a denial of their (ancient) Roman heritage and a corresponding claim for that heritage in the Latin West. The term *Greci* was nearly universal in the Latin texts studied in this book, and it is probable that in this context of constant cross-cultural interaction across the eastern Mediterranean this term had become normalised and lost some of its polemical edge. It is difficult to know what *Greci* under Latin rule called themselves, since evidence pointing towards both *Romani* and *Greci* exists. At any rate, it is likely that Greek-speakers had been compelled to accept Latin labels in order to negotiate the power structures of Latin regimes.[19]

The term 'Byzantine', by which the medieval empire of these people is generally known, is a category that emerged in early modern Western Europe. It is derived from the original name for Constantinople – Byzantion – and used to describe the world of Christian East Rome and distinguish it from its pagan past. Because of the way that Christian Roman society has been 'othered' and essentialised by antiquarians and other scholars as decadent and superstitious, the term 'Byzantine' has pejorative connotations, which more recent scholarship has interrogated and deconstructed. To talk of a 'Byzantine' Empire or of people called 'Byzantines' is therefore both anachronistic and potentially problematic for the preconceptions it may call forth.[20] These connotations may seem to recall the attitudes of the medieval Latins towards their eastern neighbours, but then the medieval Romans in turn viewed the Latins as barbarous. The construct of 'Byzantium' is rather a product of Enlightenment-era ideals that sought to trace the 'progress' of civilisation from Greco-Roman antiquity to the emergent ideal of (western) Europe. Medieval East Rome was deemed to have been a site of cultural decline and thus to have played a peripheral role in this process; as such, it could not be a true successor to the Greco-Roman past.[21] Despite these problems, however,

---

[19] Grant, 'Latin Categories of Greekness', with references.
[20] For recent discussions, see Cameron, *Byzantine Matters* and Aschenbrenner and Ransohoff (eds), *Invention of Byzantium*.
[21] Stouraitis, 'Is Byzantinism Orientalism?'

the term 'Byzantine' remains a useful and widely understood shorthand for an empire, its people and its culture, and hence it has not disappeared.

With these caveats in mind, the present book uses the term 'Greeks'. Here, that term should be understood as a shorthand for the clumsier compound label 'Greek-speaking Christians'. It should not be understood as implying that something resembling the modern Greek nation state existed in the later Middle Ages. There are several advantages to choosing the term 'Greeks' over the possible alternatives. First, it is immediately clear to the non-specialist which group is being discussed, where 'Romans' could be ambiguous. Second, 'Greeks' is arguably a more accurate designation than 'Byzantines' for the people discussed in this book, since many of them did not come from the lands of the polity we call the Byzantine Empire. The overwhelming concentration of evidence for 'Roman' self-designation among urban literate elites and its ambiguous status outside the empire are two factors adding additional weight to the choice of 'Greeks' over alternative terms.[22]

The argument in favour of using the term 'Latins' is more straightforward. In contrast to 'Greeks', there is good evidence for both emic and etic use of *Latini/Latinoi* – that is to say, people used the term about themselves as well as having it applied to them by others. In this context, the term 'Latins' signifies people of western European descent who were active in the eastern Mediterranean. The spread of the term is closely connected to the crusading movement in the twelfth and thirteenth centuries, which created crusader polities in Syria-Palestine, Cyprus and the Aegean, the colonisers of which came from areas of western Europe, principally France and Italy, where the written language was Latin. In the fourteenth and fifteenth centuries, Catalans also came to form an important fraction of this group. Other names were used for these groups, both specific names such as *Veneti* ('Venetians') and general terms such as *Franci* ('Franks'), but it is the term 'Latin' that has become standard in secondary literature, and as such it is adopted here.[23]

The term 'Turk' is also problematic in this context. As with 'Greek', perhaps its most immediate problem is its association with a modern nation state, which should not be conflated with the range of Turkish-speaking groups present in medieval western Asia Minor. Readers familiar with later periods may wonder why the term 'Ottoman' is not used here,

---

[22] Grant, 'Latin Categories of Greekness', with references.
[23] Jotischky, 'Ethnographic Attitudes'; axiomatic uses: Laiou, *Constantinople and the Latins*; Necipoğlu, *Byzantium between the Ottomans and the Latins*.

since that dynastic label is able to absorb ethnic and political plurality to an extent that 'Turks' cannot. The answer is that the Ottomans were the dominant Turkish dynasty of the region only in the latter half of the period under study here, and even by the end of that period they still had powerful Turkish-speaking competitors in Asia Minor in the form of the principality of Karaman. The *beyliks* (principalities) of Menteşe and Aydın, situated to the southwest of the Ottomans on the Aegean coast of Asia Minor, were at least as important as the Ottomans in the fourteenth and early fifteenth centuries, and were at times perhaps even more so.

People in late medieval Asia Minor did use the term 'Türk' in their literature to describe themselves, though the precise meaning of the term varied depending on the text. Sometimes, 'Türk' was distinguished from 'Mongol', though sometimes it was not. The label could refer to speakers of a language identified as Turkish, and it could also be used synonymously with 'Muslim'.[24] Sometimes, this book uses the term 'Turkmens' to describe the nomadic or semi-nomadic groups that formed important elements of the Turkish principalities of Asia Minor, including the nascent Ottoman polity. *Tourkoi* was one of the terms used in Greek texts for Turks, usually without precision, though more polemical terms such as 'Ishmaelites' or 'Hagarenes' were also used – after the tradition of Muslims' descent through Ishmael, son of Hagar – and even designations such as 'godless tribes' (*athea ethne*). In Latin, *Turci* is commonly found, as is *Teucri*, a homophonic humanist term alluding to the Turks' supposed Trojan origin, as the Trojans' ancestor was identified in ancient mythology as Teucer. In Italian documents recording trade, the geographical area of western Asia Minor is often called *Turchia*, though again without differentiating areas under different dynasties.[25]

Slavery in the medieval Mediterranean involved racialising elements, but with our modern understanding of the association between racialisation and slavery it would be misleading to suggest that these elements were of primary importance. The transatlantic slave trade is likely to be the most immediate context that comes to mind when the topic of slavery is discussed, on account of the immediacy and enormity of its legacy in the American supercontinent and western Afro-Eurasia today. Slavery in the medieval Mediterranean was a very different phenomenon in multiple

---

[24] Bayrı, *Warriors, Martyrs, and Dervishes*, 180–3.
[25] Ishmaelites/Hagarenes: Savvides, 'Some Notes'; Runciman, 'Teucri and Turci'; *Turchia*: Fleet, *Trade*; Grant, 'Latin Categories of Greekness'; conspectus of terms in Grant, 'Gottlose Korsaren', 52.

and important ways. First and foremost, it was not based on the opposition of the racialised categories of White and Black. This does not mean that the colour of people's skin went unremarked, since 'Blackness' and 'Whiteness' were already racialised in the Middle Ages. What it does mean is that slavery was not defined or justified primarily on this basis: instead, religious difference was the most important factor for circumscribing an 'enslavable' group. Religion, too, can be understood as a racialised category, just like skin colour or language, something seen most clearly in the persistent medieval Christian stereotypes of Jewish physiognomy and myths of their ritual killings, and in Christian violence against Jews and expulsion of them from places such as England or Iberia. On the other hand, Christians, Muslims and Jews held members of the other religious groups in slavery; there was, therefore, no dynamic comparable to that of the Transatlantic world, since anyone from any group might potentially fall victim to a raid by land or sea and subsequently be trafficked into slavery. While it contained elements that may be described as racialised, slavery in the medieval Mediterranean was neither primarily nor systematically racialised. Moreover, due to the absence of systematic segregation and centuries of mixed relationships, medieval slavery does not today have any tangible social, political or demographic legacy like that of transatlantic slavery, and it is now discussed almost exclusively by historians.[26]

Religious Categories

The practice of medieval slavery was underpinned by an 'us-and-them' binary of religion. Broadly, this meant that Muslims should not enslave other Muslims, Christians should not enslave other Christians, and Jews should not enslave other Jews. Governments might then try to limit this further: for example, Christian governments legislated against Jews or Muslims holding Christians as slaves. Perhaps unsurprisingly, this broad rule was often broken: people from Muslim communities were trafficked into slavery in the Muslim-ruled Mamlūk Sultanate, while Christians from the Aegean, Caucasus and Black Sea regions were trafficked into slavery in Western Europe and Byzantium. Once a person was enslaved, there was then generally an expectation that they would convert to the religion of

---

[26] Religion and slavery: Fynn-Paul, 'Empire, Monotheism and Slavery'; Barker, *Most Precious Merchandise*, 39–60; racialising ideas: Epstein, *Speaking of Slavery*; Heng, *Invention of Race*; comparison with the Transatlantic trade: Kołodziejczyk, 'Slavery in the Atlantic and the Black Sea'.

their masters; this might eventually, though by no means necessarily, lead to their manumission.[27] This religious binary naturally created problems when confronting groups that lay on the threshold of a religious community's perceived boundaries, such as Greeks enslaved by Latin masters.

There is a problematic tendency in scholarship to speak of enslaved 'Orthodox' Christians under 'Catholic' masters, with a capital 'O' and a capital 'C'.[28] This labelling seems at first sight to make a lot of sense, since the ethnic groups at stake correspond broadly to those encompassed by those terms today: on the one side, 'Catholic' Latins in or from Italy, Iberia and France; on the other side, Greeks, Bulgarians, Russians, Georgians and other 'Orthodox' Christians. This grouping is not meaningless, as Latins differentiated themselves from these other groups both within the institutional Church and in norms relating to slavery. It is however an arguably anachronistic binary, assuming a level of denominational differentiation and definition that was articulated clearly only from the time of the Counter-Reformation of the sixteenth century. While Greeks were often labelled 'schismatics' by Latin Christians, the attempts to reunify the two Churches, for example, in 1274 and 1439, suggest that this rupture was not considered conclusive or final, but one that could be healed by the mutual agreement of Church leaders.

What made Church reunification difficult was arguably less matters of doctrine and more cultural attitudes and their political ramifications. What made the Byzantine confessional position different from the Latin was chiefly the absence of the *Filioque* clause and the doctrine of Purgatory, the use of leavened bread in communion, and the rejection of papal supremacy. On the other hand, the differences that mattered in everyday life seem to have been cultural rather than confessional: language, traditions or rite, for example. These differences were deeply rooted thanks to a long history of anti-Latin discourse in the Greek world, and anti-Greek discourse in the Latin world. In this sense, it is doubtful that individual confessional issues mattered much on a day-to-day basis: rather, confessional issues were probably singled-out to justify culturally-ingrained, habitual positions.[29] The most useful terms for scholars to use would

---

[27] Barker, *Most Precious Merchandise*, 19–26. See also the various studies in Amitai and Cluse (eds), *Slavery*.

[28] Verlinden, 'Orthodoxie' and (largely under his influence) Blumenthal, *Enemies and Familiars*; Barker, *Most Precious Merchandise* and (to a greater extent) Barker, 'Christianities in Conflict'.

[29] See Kaldellis, *Hellenism*, 259–60; Kaldellis, *Ethnography*, 140–83, and further private communication with the author; Demacopoulos, *Colonizing Christianity*. Late arrival of confessional differentiation: Daniel, 'Coping with the Powerful Other'.

therefore be those that capture these cultural differences without assuming at this early date the existence of a monolithic 'Orthodox Church'.

The most useful terminology comes, in this instance, from medieval Latin sources, which speak of a 'Greek rite' and of 'Greek usages'. A rite is thus neither the same thing as a Church, nor as a religion, but a set of established practices for worship. The *aichmalotika* speak only of 'orthodox Christians', in the sense of Christians 'of correct doctrine' rather than members of the modern Orthodox Church. On the other hand, the Greek text of a treaty from Crete dated to 1299 speaks of 'Roman' bishops, while the Latin text of the treaty calls them 'Greek'; this suggests that Greeks and Latins alike might use comparable categories for clergy.[30] In Latin wills from Venetian Crete, terms to describe this Greek rite abound: *usum grecorum, ordo grecorum, mos grecorum, consuetudo grecorum*: 'Greek usage', 'Greek order', 'Greek custom' and – again – 'Greek custom', respectively.[31]

On Crete, a policy of 'one Church, two rites' was pursued. This was an ideal propagated by the Latins, who allowed Greeks to worship in their own language, but expected them to gloss over their confessional differences in favour of the Latins. The Greek Church, suppressed at episcopal and archiepiscopal levels, was led instead by 'first priests' (*protopapades*) and 'first cantors' (*protopsaltai*), who had to recognise Rome's supremacy and were drawn from the island's pro-unionist clergy, that is, those who supported official rapprochement with the Latin Church. In spite of this, the Cretan Greek Church continued to play a significant societal role quite separately from the Venetian regime, and to maintain links with Constantinople. This perception of Greek clergy as a possible imperial 'fifth column' prompted repressive and controlling measures from both Latin and Turkish rulers.[32]

The term 'Greek rite' was also applied to non-Greek Christians who were understood to adhere to these practices. A papal bull (a decree with a lead seal) of 1425, for example, demanded that Christians and Jews stop selling local Christians as slaves in Caffa on the north coast of the Black Sea: the victims were identified as Caucasian and Slavic groups from the Black Sea region, including Russians, Ossetians, Georgians, Abkhazians and Zygians, who had been baptised 'according to the rite of the Greeks'. Not all these groups will have used Greek as a liturgical language, and indeed perhaps few of them did; while it is possible that the papacy simply

---

[30] 'Ἡ συνθήκη Ἑνετῶν-Καλλέργη', ed. Mertzios.
[31] *Wills*, ed. McKee.
[32] Crete: Maltezou, 'Historical and Social Context', 26–9 (and references); Manousakas, 'Βενετικὰ ἔγγραφα'. On Turkish rulers, see Chapter 6, *infra*.

did not have good knowledge of this region, it is also possible that 'Greek rite' was a term that could be applied to any group worshipping according to the cultural patterns known mainly from the Byzantine world.[33]

The most helpful way to conceive of the religious difference between Latins and Greeks in the later medieval eastern Mediterranean is therefore to think in terms of a way of worshipping in Greek, which was closely associated with Constantinople and hence with the Byzantine Empire. Various groups were identified as following this rite, some of whom suffered repression from regimes with other religio-cultural identities, such as that of Venetian Crete. The relationship of this rite with Latin Christianity was elastic, and at times when Church union was being considered, habitual and cultural differences were imbued with heightened confessional and political significance. Accordingly, this book uses the terms 'Latin Christians' and 'Greek Christians', rather than 'Catholics' and 'Orthodox'.[34]

Categories of Unfreedom

This book deals with two major categories of unfreedom: captivity and slavery. The difference between these categories, both in terms of how medieval sources use them and in terms of how scholars might usefully apply them, is the subject of Chapter 3; accordingly, only the salient aspects of that discussion will be preempted here, to set out how these terms are used in this book.

In the medieval and early modern Mediterranean, captivity and slavery were largely overlapping but by no means coterminous categories. Many people became enslaved following an act of captivity, but not all captives were subsequently enslaved and not all enslaved people became enslaved as a consequence of being captured. The vast majority of enslaved Greeks did, however, lose their freedom as a result of capture. The large number of surviving manumission deeds indicate that enslaved Greeks were often, though not always, freed, and evidence for Greeks who were enslaved from birth or into old age is limited. The point at which captivity turned into slavery can be difficult to define, though in general captivity can be understood as a temporary state during which time there was hope that the

---

[33] *Bullarium Romanum*, ed. Franco et al., 4.718–21, Nos. 16–17. The claim that Jews were involved in enslavement in Caffa is perhaps inaccurate: Barker, *Most Precious Merchandise*, 202–3.

[34] The evidence cited in these paragraphs is discussed at greater length in Grant, 'Latin Categories of Greekness'.

person would be ransomed and released. Enslavement, on the other hand, can be understood as a longer-term state, often initiated by an act of sale.[35]

The main motive for taking someone captive may therefore be assumed, in most cases, to have been profit. In cases where the captive and/or captor had contact with members of the captive's family or wider community, it might be possible to secure their ransom. In cases where the captive held some sort of prominence in their community, they might raise a ransom price far higher than the market value of an enslaved person of similar attributes. A long captivity, however, might become costly to the captor, and therefore a quick ransom was desirable. Selling a captive into slavery would at times have been a faster way of making money, since it could be done at one of the major slave markets without waiting to establish contact with the captive's relatives or friends.[36] Moreover, an enslaved person could still sometimes be redeemed by others or through their own labour, emphasising once again that the lines between captivity and enslavement could be blurred.

The difference between captivity and slavery appears to have been to some extent a matter of perspective. Greek sources tend to talk of 'captives', while Latin sources talk of 'slaves'. The moment of dislocation is also a major theme of the Greek sources, especially the *aichmalotika*, since their concern tends to be with explaining how someone was seized from their community, as well as with the process of redeeming them and hence of bringing them back to that community. For the Latin sources, however, most of which are notarial documents recording transactions with legal and economic significance, the main concern is with the enslaved person as a chattel, to be bought, possessed, sold or freed. The historian is therefore left to draw the inference that these two groups of sources describe different sides of the same coin: the captives of the Greek sources are those who ended up enslaved in Latin and Turkish contexts and thus appear as such in Latin documents.

Chapter Outline

The book is thematically structured: it has three parts, each dealing with an overarching framework for the study of Greek captives and their Mediterranean contexts; the three parts in turn contain two chapters apiece, each

---

[35] See Hershenzon, *The Captive Sea*, 1–30, for a similar discussion relating to the early modern Mediterranean.
[36] Also discussed in Grant, 'Gottlose Korsaren', 62–4.

addressing a specific topic. Each chapter builds on groundwork laid by the preceding chapters, though the reader should be equipped to tackle any one chapter on its own terms after reading the Introduction.

The first part of this book orients the reader by laying out the wider historical contexts, both geopolitical and economic, in which the mass captivities of Greeks occurred. Chapter 1 considers how Byzantium's collapse in Asia Minor from c. 1260 brought Turkish groups to the Aegean and facilitated by c. 1300 a trade in Greek captives conducted with the collaboration of Latin merchants. These Greek captives thus became caught up in the larger slave trading route that ran from the Black Sea through the Aegean and into the wider Mediterranean, where it branched off towards Italy and Iberia in the west, and Egypt and Syria in the east. This larger structure and its relationship to the captivity and enslavement of Greeks is the topic of Chapter 2.

Part two examines in detail the social dynamics of the phenomenon of mass captivities. Within the structures outlined in Part I, it is often challenging to distinguish between captives, slaves and refugees. Chapter 3 addresses these ambiguities from lexical and social-historical perspectives, and in doing so also explores some of the major features of lived experiences of these circumstances. Chapter 4 considers how captives were ransomed, focusing especially on the practice of itinerant alms-seeking with *aichmalotika* and the growing social responsibility of the Church.

The third, and final, part of the book examines how the captivity of Greeks influenced cultural relations with Latin Christians and Turkish Muslims and their respective polities. Greek–Latin relations are addressed in Chapter 5, which considers how Latin regimes dealt with the moral ambiguity of enslaving fellow Christians both in domestic legislation and in foreign policy, particularly with regard to Church union and crusades against the Turks. The sixth, and final, chapter considers the conquest of Byzantine territory by the Ottomans and other Turkish groups and the implications of these conquests for Christian–Muslim relations. Particular attention is given to patterns of conquest, migration, depopulation and repopulation to contextualise the phenomena of captivity and enslavement.

Part I

Historical Contexts

> *Oh, what things I hear!...*
> *What sins have we committed,*
> *That we should live to see such misfortunes?*
> *Let no one harbour any hopes,*
> *Since the Romans hold the City again.*

(George Pachymeres, *Relations*, ed. and tr. Failler, 1.204–5; English tr. Laiou, 'Palaiologoi', 804.)

Words attributed to the imperial notary Kakos Senachereim upon Michael VIII's conquest of Constantinople, 1261.

Chapter 1
Political Changes in Asia Minor

This chapter lays out the geopolitical developments of the thirteenth and earlier fourteenth centuries that precipitated a crisis of captivity among Greek communities. It charts how Turkish groups gradually conquered Byzantine Asia Minor between the 1260s and the 1330s and established themselves in emporia on the Aegean coast, in which they traded captured Greeks with Latin merchants. Byzantium engaged Catalan mercenaries to stem this Turkish advance, but these mercenaries themselves soon became a hostile force that captured and enslaved Greeks across the regions of Macedonia, Thessaly and Boiotia. Having outlined this process of disruption, this chapter turns to notarial evidence from Cyprus and Crete that testifies to the trafficking of captured Greeks via long-distance Mediterranean slave trading routes. This last development, which appears to have begun in the late 1290s, resulted within only twenty or so years in the presence of enslaved Greeks as far afield as Mallorca. The crisis of captivity therefore took only a few decades to emerge from the borderlands of western Asia Minor and become a phenomenon visible across the Mediterranean.

The Late Medieval Romanía

The turn of the thirteenth century was a watershed moment in the history of the Byzantine world. The years of the imperial dynasty of the Angeloi (1185–1204) were a time of instability, characterised by tax abuses and sales of offices. It was dynastic in-fighting, however, that ultimately triggered catastrophe for Byzantium: in 1195, Alexios III supplanted his brother Emperor Isaac II; in turn, Isaac together with his son Alexios appealed to his nephew-in-law Philip of Swabia for support.[1] In 1202, the

[1] Chrysostomides, 'Eleventh to Fifteenth Century', 22.

Fourth Crusade was proclaimed, its destination Ayyūbid Egypt; the Venetians succeeded in diverting it first to Zara (today Zadar, Croatia) and then to Constantinople, though many crusaders abandoned the cause.[2] The disparity between Byzantium's diplomatic bravado and its flailing dynastic politics, coupled with the Latins' realisation of the empire's potential as a reservoir of manpower for the defence of the Holy Land, created an incentive for those who remained to take full advantage of this situation.[3]

The ousted emperor Isaac was to be restored. After a first siege of Constantinople in 1203, Isaac and his son Alexios reneged on the costly promises they had made to their crusader backers: there would be no Church union with Rome, no tribute, no provisions, and – crucially – no soldiers to support an expedition to the Levant.[4] The crusaders considered their hopes of reconquering Jerusalem dashed; the Greeks, treated with suspicion since the First Crusade and regarded as Muslim sympathisers during the Second and Third Crusades, were immediately deemed traitors.[5] The population of Constantinople rebelled against Latin influence and yet another Alexios, 'the monobrowed' (Mourtzouphlos) was proclaimed emperor and the old Isaac and his son murdered. The Venetians agreed to divide up the empire with the other Frankish crusaders, and on 13 April 1204 they took the city and subjected it to a devastating three-day sack.[6] The pope, Innocent III, legitimised the venture by permitting the crusaders to stay in Constantinople.[7]

The crusaders may have divided up the Romanía on paper, but now they had to conquer it on the ground. The new Venetian-backed emperor, Baldwin of Flanders, was given land on both the European and Asian sides of the straits of the Bosporus and Hellespont. In opposition to him, Boniface of Montferrat, who had been a strong contender for the imperial throne, built up a kingdom around Thessaloniki. These two men granted various parts of their lands in fief to other Franks. The primarily maritime Venetians found their various land-based claims to be a misjudged aspiration and set their

---

[2] Queller, Compton and Campbell, 'Neglected Majority'. Recent scholarship on the Crusade includes Angold, *Fourth Crusade*, Madden (ed.), *Fourth Crusade*, Laiou-Thomadakis (ed.), *Urbs Capta* and Queller, *Fourth Crusade*.

[3] Harris, *Byzantium and the Crusades*, esp. 154–5.

[4] Villehardouin, *Conquête*, tr. Smith, 50; Chrysostomides, 'Eleventh to Fifteenth Century', 22.

[5] Brand, 'Byzantines and Saladin'; more cautionary: Neocleous, 'Byzantine-Muslim Conspiracies'.

[6] Chrysostomides, 'Eleventh to Fifteenth Century', 22.

[7] Harris, *Byzantium and the Crusades*, 177.

sights instead on the Aegean islands, retaining only the strategic mainland ports of Modon/Methoni and Coron/Koroni in the southern Peloponnese. In addition to their promised three-eighths of Constantinople, the Venetians purchased the claim to Crete and spent the next seven years establishing control there. They further took Negroponte/Euboea, while a cadet house took Naxos and the surrounding islands. Venice would not be fully expelled from the region until the eighteenth century.[8]

Several regional Greek claimants also emerged. In the city of Nicaea in northwest Asia Minor, Theodore Laskaris established a new polity and had himself crowned emperor by the Patriarch of Constantinople, Michael IV Autoreianos. He soon brought to heel the aspirations of the Greek Christian Empire of Trebizond – a small polity founded along the Black Sea coast of eastern Asia Minor shortly before the capture of Constantinople – and thereby asserted Nicaea as the leading Roman power in Asia. Another Greek leader, Michael Angelos, established a polity known as the Despotate of Epirus, centred on the city of Arta in the northwest of today's Greece. Epirus was for many years a serious contender for Byzantine hegemony in the region, especially following its capture of Thessaloniki under Theodore Angelos in 1224.[9]

In 1259, at Pelagonia in the north of historic Macedonia, the Nicaeans under Michael VIII Palaiologos resoundingly defeated a coalition of Sicilians, Epirots and Achaeans. The coalition's Serbian allies consequently withdrew from Macedonia. Michael was thus in control of much of the Balkan Peninsula as well as western Asia Minor, and poised to take Constantinople itself. At Nymphaion/Kemalpaşa (western Asia Minor) in March 1261, Michael signed a treaty with the Genoese in order to protect himself against the latter's foremost rivals, the Venetians; he offered to the Genoese the Venetians' old economic privileges within the empire and asked them for manpower in return. In July of that year, Michael's general Alexios Strategopoulos took Constantinople: its Latin garrison had set out on campaign in the Black Sea and thus left the city so unprotected that Genoese help was not in the end required. The Latin Empire was thus reduced to an empty imperial title, to be passed between hopeful claimants but never to be materially revived, while the Byzantine world, however fragmented it remained, had at least regained its ancestral capital.[10]

---

[8] Van Tricht, *Renovatio*, 44–59; Chrysostomides, 'Eleventh to Fifteenth Century', 22–3.
[9] Chrysostomides, 'Eleventh to Fifteenth Century', 23–6.
[10] Ibid., 27–8.

Michael used diplomacy to manage the complex threats his empire faced from the West. He tried courting the Venetians in the first decade of his reign in Constantinople, but ultimately ended up privileging the Genoese yet further by granting them the neighbourhood of Galata. This helped the Genoese in their efforts to assert commercial dominance over the maritime trade of the Black Sea. Over the next centuries, Galata, or Pera as it was often known, would come to compete with Constantinople itself in economic importance.[11]

Meanwhile, Manfred of Sicily and Charles of Anjou successively contested the Latin imperial title. Accordingly, in July 1274, Michael agreed at the Council of Lyons to the proclamation of Church union with Rome. This, he hoped, would neutralise the threat Charles posed: if the Byzantine Empire could not be considered 'schismatic', Charles would not receive papal sanction for an invasion. The union, however, was unpopular in Byzantium and never properly observed, and in 1281 Pope Martin IV decided that Charles had a valid claim on the Romanía after all. But Charles had his own problems, and as the bells rang out for Vespers on Easter Monday, 30 March 1282, the population of Palermo rebelled with chants of 'Death to the French' – that is, Charles's Angevin regime. Peter III of Aragon invaded upon the invitation of the Sicilian rebels and took control of the island; Peter in turn enjoyed the backing of none other than Michael VIII. With Charles thwarted, the resurrection of the Latin Empire thus retreated into fantasy.[12]

By the late thirteenth century, the Aegean region and its hinterland was thus politically extremely fragmented. This political fragmentation matched the region's physical fragmentation, with its innumerable islands and craggy coastlines. In this world, coastal communities were vulnerable and naval raiding thrived.[13]

The Collapse of Byzantine Asia Minor

While much of Michael's attention was drawn westwards to Charles of Anjou and the papacy, his Asian frontiers were suffering, hence the significance of Kakas Senachereim's words in Pachymeres's *History*, quoted on the title page to Part I: once Constantinople was in Byzantine hands again,

---

[11] Ibid, 29. On his diplomacy: Geanakoplos, *Michael Palaeologus*. On Genoa in the Black Sea: Balard, *Romanie génoise*.

[12] Chrysostomides, 'Eleventh to Fifteenth Century', 29–30; the classic account is Runciman, *Sicilian Vespers*.

[13] In addition to the remarks in this chapter, see Grant, 'Gottlose Korsaren'.

Asia Minor would be relegated to a secondary concern.[14] In the middle of the thirteenth century, Mongol Īl-Khānid presence in eastern and central Asia Minor caused the displacement of significant numbers of Turkmens (nomadic or semi-nomadic pastoralists who spoke Old Anatolian Turkish), who were pushed ever closer to the Byzantine frontier; this disrupted what had been in the Nicaean era (1204–61) a near-enough equilibrium with the Seljuks of Rūm (c. 1081–1308). These Turkmens effected notable conquests, but their advance was forestalled by a number of countermeasures on the part of Michael VIII Palaiologos and, to a lesser extent, of his son Andronikos II. In 1259/60, a certain Muḥammad Beg came to control a Turkmen confederation centred on Denizli/Lādhiq; in 1262, he sought legitimacy for his rule through the recognition of the Mongols, the Seljuks' overlords. Muḥammad Beg's polity has sometimes been identified as an early manifestation of the principalities (beyliks) that would characterise Asia Minor in the fourteenth century, although there is an argument for understanding the rebellion undertaken by him and his successor, ʿAlī Beg, still in a Seljuk context.[15]

Either way, it was not long before the unambiguous fragmentation of Seljuk Asia Minor under multiple local lords began. The Empire of Nicaea and the Seljuk Sultanate of Rūm had enjoyed relatively close relations cemented by a series of dynastic marriages; after the imposition of Mongol overlordship in 1243, the two polities had followed trajectories that led them to look in opposite directions rather than to confront one another, and neither appeared to aspire to control the lands of the other. From 1211–c. 1260, the frontiers of Asia Minor thus retained a degree of stability that would see no parallel in the fourteenth century.[16] Once the Byzantine presence in Asia Minor had collapsed and Turkmens established control over ports on the western coast, the many small islands of the Aegean would also become vulnerable to attack. The disruption of the Byzantine–Seljuk *modus vivendi* was necessary before the number of captivities would increase dramatically.

The early fourteenth century was not the first time that a Turkish group had established a maritime polity on the Aegean coast of western Asia Minor. The victory of the Great Seljuks against Byzantium at the Battle of

---

[14] Laiou, 'Palaiologoi', 804.
[15] Uzunçarşılı, *Anadolu beylikleri*, 55–7; revision: Peacock, 'Frontier', 285. See also Korobeinikov, 'Formation'.
[16] Peacock, 'Frontier', 270; Korobeinikov, *Byzantium and the Turks*, 217–81; for an overview of the events and personalities, see Korobeinikov, 'Raiders and Neighbours', 717–27.

Manzikert in eastern Asia Minor (1071) dramatically inaugurated a period of headlong conquest, which to some extent foreshadowed the events of two hundred years later. By the time of the First Crusade (1096–9), Turkish groups controlled much of Asia Minor, including the far west. Within a decade after the Battle of Manzikert, a Turkish prince called Çaka (the Tzachas of Byzantine sources) had begun to launch naval raids in the region of Mytilene and Chios. The substantial threat that he posed to Byzantium may have prompted Emperor Alexios I Komnenos to offer Venice unprecedented commercial privileges within his domains, probably in 1082; in return for these privileges, Alexios could hope to harness Venetian seapower to his advantage and to Çaka's detriment. Çaka died in either 1093 or 1106, and his polity and raiding activities were consequently short-lived.[17]

During the following century and a half, Turkish maritime interests in the region turned away from the Aegean. In the early thirteenth century, the Seljuks of Rūm took control of the Black Sea port of Sinope/Sinop and the Mediterranean port of Antalya and consequently styled themselves 'lords of the two seas'.[18] In 1219 and again in 1220, Venice and the Seljuks of Rūm concluded treaties to allow for mutual maritime trade, thus in some respects foreshadowing the commercial treaties signed between Venetian Crete and the Turkmen beyliks in the fourteenth and early fifteenth centuries.[19] In the 1220s, the sultanate even undertook an expedition to establish control over the Crimean Peninsula and thereby assert their presence in the Black Sea at large.[20] On the other hand, there is no evidence for the Seljuks of Rūm ever having aspired to the establishment of control over any part of the Aegean coast, which was seemingly left to the Empire of Nicaea. The establishment of Turkmen maritime principalities in the period between roughly 1260 and 1330 was therefore a fundamentally new geopolitical development, and Çaka and his raids by that time a figment of the distant past.

Byzantium resisted the expansion of Turkmens in western Asia Minor. With the exception of a hiatus between 1267–80, when Michael VIII was preoccupied with the threat posed by Charles of Anjou and his claims to the defunct Latin Empire of Constantinople, imperial expeditions made robust attempts to strengthen the frontier. In the southwest of his lands,

---

[17] The most recent critical account is Beihammer, *Muslim-Turkish Anatolia*, 272–5, 281–3; for his death date: Savvides, 'Concerted action'; for the treaty with Venice: Frankopan, 'Byzantine Trade Privileges'.
[18] Redford and Leiser, *Victory Inscribed*.
[19] Martin, 'Venetian–Seljuk Treaty'; Chrysostomides, 'Privileges'; on the later treaties, Zachariadou, *Trade and Crusade*.
[20] Peacock, 'Saljūq Campaign'.

Michael streamlined the military holdings of the marcher lords (*akritai*) and pushed back substantially against Turkish expansion. He led campaigns against the Turkish confederation of Lādhiq/Denizli in 1260–1 and in the land along the Maeander in 1263–4; his brother, the despot John, then commanded the imperial forces there until 1267. After a hiatus, the future Andronikos II, Michael VIII's son and co-emperor, was once again sent to commence hostilities in the latter region. During the first half of the reign of Andronikos II, however, the headlong loss of Byzantine Asia Minor began, starting with the fall of Tralles (Aydın) in 1284.[21]

A captive's alms-gathering testimonial (*aichmalotikon*) has survived that appears to have emerged from the context of these late thirteenth-century Byzantine campaigns. It is preserved in a manuscript primarily of theological texts, now held in Vienna. The letter immediately follows a short chronicle for the eleventh century, though the hand that copied the letter is datable to the last quarter of the thirteenth century on palaeographical grounds. There are reasons to believe, both on the strength of the letter's narrative and on the basis of the fourteenth- and fifteenth-century dates of most of the other *aichmalotika*, that the text was likely composed only shortly before this copy was made. The letter itself has been partially anonymised: no personal names survive, though the copyist has retained the detail of where the events of the letter occurred: Mylasa/Milas in southwestern Asia Minor.

The text can be summarised as follows: There was a failed Byzantine campaign in the region of Mylasa against the Turks, who are polemically described as 'Ishmaelites' from among the ranks of the 'godless and barbarian heathens'. This campaign, described as a 'great war', was followed by a Turkish plundering expedition in the same region, leading to the captivity of the Christians in a once specified place, the name of which has been removed. The family of an unnamed man was taken captive, and this man later found out that he could redeem his family. He therefore approached the bishop (perhaps of Mylasa) and asked him for a testimonial in order that he might gather alms to redeem his family. The letter then turns to pious admonitions exhorting charity.[22]

It is possible that the 'great war in the region of Mylasa' was one of the Byzantine campaigns of the 1260s–80s. Two male figures are mentioned in the letter, though neither is named in the text as it survives; the first was

---

[21] Korobeinikov, *Byzantium and the Turks*, 217–81; Arnakis, 'Anatolian Provinces'; Geanakoplos, *Michael Palaeologus*; Runciman, *Sicilian Vespers*.
[22] Text and translation in Schreiner, 'Eine Schlacht', 612.

probably the Byzantine commander. One scholar, Efe Ragia, has suggested that the campaign described in the text could plausibly be placed in 1264; this would make the commander in question the *despot* John Palaiologos, who travelled that year from the Balkans to Asia Minor and died sometime in the years 1272–4. She interprets the text as implying that John was already dead by the time the letter was drafted.[23] While Ragia's reconstruction remains hypothetical, placing the letter's composition and the events it describes in the reign of Michael VIII (or Andronikos II) would make sense, given its contents. This is the one and only *aichmalotikon* to survive from an Asian context, and it is almost certainly representative of the transitional period of c. 1260–1302, as Byzantium lost its grip on the region.

These decades were, however, not a continuous period of headlong disaster. Andronikos toured the region of the Sangarios/Sakarya river in late 1283 and early 1284. He then rooted himself in Asia Minor in 1290–3, during which years the situation along the Maeander was safe enough for the emperor to grant a chrysobull (a document of privilege with a golden seal) confirming the possessions there of the Monastery of St John the Theologian, on the Aegean island of Patmos. The campaigns of 1292–3 were led by the general Alexios Philanthropenos, who subsequently came to grief after rising up against the emperor on the basis of concerns over loot and soldiers' pay. At the end of the decade, from 1298–1302, the general John Tarchaneiotes and Andronikos II's son and co-emperor Michael IX Palaiologos led Byzantium's Asian armies. Tarchaneiotes was one of numerous people who retained sympathies for the former patriarch Arsenios, deposed by Michael VIII; fearing that these sympathies would turn the establishment Church against him, Tarchanaiotes soon fled to Thessaloniki in an attempt to escape danger. In 1302, Michael was defeated at Magnesia and another general, George Mouzalon, suffered the most famous Byzantine defeat of this period, at Bapheus in Bithynia, where, on 27 July 1302, the Ottomans under Osman vanquished his army.[24]

Evidence of Crisis (1): Cyprus

The coalescence of Turkish raiding and Latin trading on the west coast of Asia Minor was a prerequisite for the precipitation of a crisis of captivity in the

---

[23] Ragia, 'Turcs'. Her argument for placing the text after John's death is that the text refers to the first anonymous figure, whom she identifies as the commander, with the pronoun 'that' (*ekeinos*); it is not clear to me why that must imply a deceased person rather than simply differentiating him from the second anonymous figure.

[24] Korobeinikov, *Byzantium and the Turks*, 257–61, 269–73; Lindner, 'Anatolia', 119.

Aegean region. The evidence for this precipitation comes from a large, albeit highly uneven, body of Latin notarial evidence. By the fourteenth century at the latest, Latin traders – especially Venetians – had become established in Turkish-ruled areas of western Asia Minor at emporia such as Ephesus (the Latin Altologo/Theologo), Anaia further south (today's Kadıkalesi, a neighbourhood of Kuşadası), Palatia (Balat), and Smyrna (İzmir).[25] These merchants began to buy Greeks who had been captured by Turks, and bring them to Latin-ruled emporia, above all Candia (Heraklion), Crete and Famagusta (Ammochostos), on Cyprus. This was a situation that emerged in the context of the collapse of Byzantine Asia Minor, and one that would hardly have been possible while these emporia were still under imperial rule.

From the end of the thirteenth century, enslaved Greeks from western Asia Minor are found in Famagusta, and from the very beginning of the fourteenth century they are found in Candia. The silence of the evidence for the period between the destabilisation of c. 1259/60 and the beginning of notarial evidence in Famagusta in 1295 does not necessarily mean that Greeks were not being trafficked into slavery in large numbers at that time as well. The land routes running east through Asia Minor and then south into Syria and Egypt are invisible in Latin notarial records, which are largely restricted to maritime trade; it may be that these routes did carry Greek captives, but that the transactions involved were not documented, or the documents do not survive. This observation stands, by and large, for the whole period under study. There is nevertheless an unambiguous upswing in the evidence for enslaved Greeks in multiple locations at precisely the same time, that is to say, the few years either side of 1300. This upswing in attested cases of captivity and enslavement plausibly reflects reality rather than being merely an accident of source survival, but the picture might look less dramatic were comparable evidence to survive from mainland Asia Minor, especially for the decades immediately before 1300.

At various points in its history, Cyprus has by virtue of its position become a crossroads of vital importance between the eastern and western Mediterranean regions.[26] Cyprus was the first Byzantine land to come under Latin rule, in 1191, and it would remain so until its conquest by the Ottomans in 1571. The island was captured by Richard I of England from a local pretender (possibly initially a legitimate imperial appointee), Isaac Komnenos, and sold twice – firstly to the Knights Templar,

---

[25] On the complex nomenclature of Ephesus in the later Middle Ages, see Hopfgartner, 'Altologo'; for Anaia, and discussion of some sources employed here, see Ch. Maltezou, 'Άναία'.

[26] Mango, 'Carrefour'.

secondly to the Frenchman Guy de Lusignan. The Lusignan dynasty remained in control of the island beyond the extinction of the Byzantine Empire, ultimately yielding to Venice in 1473.[27] With the collapse of the Crusader States of the Holy Land in the later thirteenth century, Cyprus took on additional economic and strategic significance due to the loss of mainland port cities. Huge numbers of refugees poured into Cypriot coastal centres, many arriving before the Mamlūk conquest of Acre in 1291. This reorientation and the migration that accompanied it drove the expansion of the Cypriot port of Famagusta in particular, and it is there that some of the earliest evidence for Greeks trafficked from the Romanía emerges.[28]

The Genoese notary Lamberto di Sambuceto, active in Famagusta and Pera at the turn of the fourteenth century, is undoubtedly one of the most well-known of all medieval Italian notaries. Some of his acts were first published in the late nineteenth century, and since then various leading scholars of the Genoese who were active overseas have completed the process of editing his complete output.[29] These documents have been well studied as sources for slavery,[30] but when placed in a pan-Mediterranean context, and especially when set in parallel with documents from contemporary Crete, they have the potential to yield fresh insights about the captivity of Greeks.

In February 1297, the first explicitly identified Greek slaves were manumitted at Famagusta. Iacoba, wife of the late Iohannes Balistarius, freed her slave Anna, while Leo, son of papa di Mirano of Paralime (Lemnos), freed Cali and her unspecified children.[31] Both are taxonomised as *Griffonie* – a perhaps pejorative term for Greeks – and described as 'of the Romanía', but no other details about these women are recorded. As for the contracting parties, Leo's father may himself have been a Greek priest (*papas*). Nicola, Cali and Catalina, due to be manumitted according to the will of Petrus Pilosus of 28 October 1296, were likely Greeks but may also have been

---

[27] Edbury, *Kingdom of Cyprus*; Hill, *History*, vol. 2; Mas Latrie, *Histoire*.
[28] Jacoby, 'Famagusta'.
[29] For those acts drawn up at Famagusta, the relevant editions are: Balard, *Gênes et l'Outre-Mer 1*; Balard, *Notai genovesi . . . Lamberto di Sambuceto*; Balard, Schabel and Duba, *Actes*; Pavoni, *Notai genovesi*; Polonio, *Notai genovesi*.
[30] Arbel, 'Slave Trade'; Usta, 'Famagusta'; Dincer, 'Enslaving Christians'; Preiser-Kapeller, 'Liquid Frontiers'.
[31] Lamberto di Sambuceto, ed. Balard (*Notai genovesi*), 40–2, Nos. 30–1. When quoting Latin notarial documents, I reproduce the – often – eccentric name forms given in the text.

baptised slaves with Christian names but of non-Christian backgrounds, as their origins are unspecified.[32]

The sales recorded for March and April 1301 speak to trends that are also evident on Crete. The slaves Eleni, Savasti, Patriarchi and Michali, all sold in a single transaction, are described as being Greek (*de proienie Griffona*) and as having lived in western Asia Minor (*que habitabant in Turchia*).[33] Twelve-year-old Augusta, who had already been sold at least once by the time her name was entered into Lamberto's register, was from Samos.[34] Echifor, sold just one day later (1 April), was a young boy of ten descried as 'white', and is one of only a few individuals attested as being Turco-Greek (*de proienie Turca et Greca album*).[35] These locations – *Turchia* and Samos – are two of those most amply attested in documents drawn up contemporaneously at Candia. These parallel trends probably reflect the same reality: the growth of Latin–Turkish emporia along the coast of western Asia Minor.

Lamberto's acts raise questions about two changes in the trade in Greek slaves in Famagusta, the first specific and the second general. First, until 1301, the relevant acts all comprise manumissions, either as distinct certificates or in wills, and not sales. This means that the people in question had been enslaved for some time already. It is uncertain whether the appearance of sale documents from 1301 represents a qualitative and quantitative change versus the 1290s, or whether this was simply an incidental reflection of which clients asked Lamberto di Sambuceto to record what business. Second comes the question of whether Lamberto's evidence for slaves may be back-projected before the 1290s – or even, in the more specific context of Greek captives, into the years before 1297. On balance of probabilities, it does seem likely that these acts record the beginning of a more intensive slave trade that reflected Famagusta's new-found commercial ascendancy.[36] The parallel case of Crete around the turn of the fourteenth century circumstantially corroborates the idea that this trade was a new phenomenon. While it is possible that a few Greeks might have entered slavery in Lusignan Cyprus in the period before the 1290s for local reasons,

---

[32] Ibid., 17–19, No. 13. The meaning of *Griffonie* is discussed *supra*, 15.
[33] Lamberto di Sambuceto, ed. Polonio, 320–1, No. 269.
[34] Ibid., 397–8, No. 332.
[35] Ibid., 396–7, No. 331. Other examples: Cateura, 'Politica', unpaginated appendix (s.a. 1388; unnamed slave of Pere Ses Eres); Državni Arhiv u Dubrovniku, Liber Dotium 2, fol. 39v (s.a. 1389; summary in Krekić, *Dubrovnik*, 395, No. 228).
[36] Arbel, 'Slave trade', 152.

the trafficking of Greek captives from the Romanía appears to have begun in the 1290s.

Evidence of Crisis (2): Crete

The demographics of the Greek population on Crete in the later Middle Ages were complex. First, there was a class of peasants who had been inherited by the Venetians from the Byzantine social order, and so these were labourers endemic to Crete. Sometimes, free Greeks are found giving themselves or their children into contracts of bondage, whether voluntary enslavement in return for basic life necessities, or in return for learning a trade or skill. The category that this study is chiefly concerned with comprised enslaved people, who appear to have been people trafficked to Crete rather than natives of the island.

In the early fourteenth century, Greeks seem to have made up the majority of Crete's enslaved population. By the end of the century, this had changed to a predominance of people from the Black Sea region.[37] In the first decade of the 1300s, these people were overwhelmingly Greeks from Asia Minor captured by Turks and then sold to Latin traders as slaves, with a number of Greeks from the Dodecanese too, captured either by Turks or Latins. By the 1330s, this demographic had shifted to a focus on central Greece due to the establishment of a major slave emporium at Thebes soon after the arrival of Catalan mercenaries there in 1311. Because Candia was a trading emporium linked with many other parts of the Mediterranean, particularly Catalan trading centres, it is probable that a significant number of the slaves documented in sale deeds were destined for further exportation, and information about the buyer can sometimes allow inference regarding where these slaves might subsequently have been resold.[38]

The crisis of captivity that came about from 1300 is by far most evident on Venetian Crete. It is possible that bias of evidence is a distorting factor in this picture: the number of notarial chartularies surviving from fourteenth-century Candia is probably disproportionately large compared with the rest of the eastern Mediterranean at that time, or compared with Candia itself in the previous century. It is probable, however, that a more representative sample would bear out the trends already in evidence, since the types of notarial acts, not just their frequency, changed c. 1300.

---

[37] Summary in McKee, 'Inherited Status', 40.
[38] Based on data from sources cited *supra*, 11, n. 13.

In the late thirteenth century, sales of Greeks on Venetian Crete concerned villeins (tied agricultural labourers) rather than domestic slaves. For example, one of the earlier Candian notaries whose acts survive, Leonardo Marcello (fl. 1278–81), preserves note of four transactions involving Greek villeins: Costa Pachorina, son of the late Iohannis Pachorina; Georgio Sculopodhy; an unknown villein (name erased) *in casali de Archy*; and Vaxilli *de pertinenciis casalis Girgari*, who would also learn his new master's trade of goldsmithing.[39]

The smattering of such evidence from the later thirteenth century shares in common the facts that it is limited, disparate and it does not concern captives. The circumstances that led to the mass captivity and enslavement of Greeks had not yet come about. Arguably, the evidence in the series of Cretan notaries is sufficiently robust for this to be understood as representative of a trend, rather than simply absence of evidence – in contrast, for example, with Famagusta. This changed dramatically for Crete early in 1301, a rupture clearly visible in the notarial acts of Benvenuto de Brixano. At this time, Venice had only recently signed the Treaty of Milan (1299), ending the War of Curzola, fought between Genoa and Byzantium on the one side, and Venice on the other. This stymied Byzantium's efforts to reconquer territory in the Aegean region and solidified Venice's presence on Crete, as well as in the Archipelago (Cyclades), Negroponte/Euboea and the twin ports of Coron/Koroni and Modon/Methoni in the southern Peloponnese. In Asia Minor, the Byzantine military presence was all but over, and would collapse following the Ottoman victory at the Battle of Bapheus in 1302.[40]

Of the notarial evidence for Greek captives employed in this study, the series dating from April 1301 to September 1308 comprises acts drawn up almost exclusively in Candia.[41] The only exceptions are a handful of cases from Famagusta, a single case from Genoa and a single case from Marseille.[42] The first twenty-seven relevant acts of Benvenuto de Brixano

---

[39] Leonardo Marcello, ed. Chiaudano and Lombardo, 70–1, No. 194; 77, No. 211; 82, No. 226; 159, No. 463. Cf. Verlinden, 'Crète', 595–6.
[40] Balard, 'Latins', 826.
[41] On the acts for these years, see Wright, '*Vade, sta, ambula*', *passim*, but especially 201–2.
[42] The exceptions are: Lamberto di Sambuceto, ed. Polonio, 396–7, No. 331 (which in fact comes before the Candian sequence, which begins on 8 April); 418–20, No. 351; Lamberto di Sambuceto, ed. Pavoni, 284–6, No. 239; Verlinden, *L'esclavage*, 2.463 (Genoa); Lamberto di Sambuceto, ed. Balard (*Notai genovesi* [1984]), 39–40, No. 19; 134, No. 63; 162, No. 92; 202, No. 134; Mortreuil, 'Moeurs', 159 (Marseille).

for the year 1301 concern twenty-eight individuals who may have been Greeks. Only ten of these are explicitly designated as such (all *de genere Grecorum*),[43] with a further one said to be formerly of Samos;[44] eleven are said to have been bought from Turks or in *Turchia*,[45] and two explicitly to have been captured.[46] In these acts there is no overlap between those who are explicitly said to have been Greeks and those who are said to have been bought from Turks, although such an overlap may probably be assumed for most cases. The case of Leo, sold by Filipachis de Caristo of Negroponte to the doctor George of Mallorca, is notable for stating that he was a Greek captured by the vendor on Samos.[47] This evidence clearly attests to a change of fate among the Greeks of the Romanía from 1301 at the latest: they were now being trafficked to Crete, something not apparent in the thirteenth century.

By the middle of the decade 1300–10, the notarial documents begin to show a fairly consistent flow of Greek slaves being brought from western Asia Minor (*Turchia*), where they had been bought, to Candia, where they were resold. Variants of the phrase *quem/quam emi a Turchis* ('whom I bought from the Turks') are common in these acts, with seventy-eight people from this period acquired in this way. The acts of Pietro Pizolo, Stefano Bono and Angelo de Cartura, all notaries in Candia, record 188 Greek or very likely Greek slaves being sold or manumitted in the years 1303–6.[48] In the acts of these three notaries, two distinct captivity zones are discernible: the first is western Asia Minor in the region around Ephesus; the second comprises the islands, particularly the Dodecanese; Samos, often attested, lay between the two.

Venetians and Turks alike operated in both zones, and while the number of purchases from Turks suggests that it was largely the latter who did

---

[43] Benvenuto de Brixano, ed. Morozzo della Rocca, 207–8, No. 575; 51, No. 133; 81, No. 220; 102, No. 277; 11, No. 302; 115, No. 315; 122, No. 333; 172, No. 478; 177, No. 494; 180, No. 502.

[44] Ibid., 83, No. 226.

[45] Ibid., 5, No. 1; 6, No. 4; 8, No. 10; 8, No. 11; 27, No. 63; 29, No. 68; 46, No. 119; 46–7, No. 120; 65, No. 172; 82, No. 222; 95, No. 256.

[46] Ibid., 60–1, No. 160; 81, No. 220.

[47] Ibid., 81, No. 220.

[48] By my count, 188 in number. Pietro Pizolo also mentions seven individuals in 1300 (ed. Carbone, 1.85, No. 173; 1.207–8, No. 447; 1.208, No. 448; 1.209, No. 449; 1.299, No. 657); all but the first are manumissions made after redemption payments. It seems clear that the true upswing in numbers did not occur until a couple of years later.

the capturing, there is some suggestion that Venetians raided for Greek captives, too. In 1303 Phylippus Bocontolo freed Nichita, son of the late Theodorus Sidherocasti of Rhodes, whom he had 'captured in *corso*' – whether at Rhodes or elsewhere is not certain.[49] Soy (Zoë), whose origins are not recorded, was sold in 1301 by Angelus de Riço and Biachinus Belo, both residents of Candia, having similarly been 'captured in *corso*'.[50] *Corso* was probably a general term for naval raiding at this time, perhaps not so clearly distinguished from opportunistic 'piracy', as 'corsairing' or 'privateering' would become in the early modern period and were already becoming in the western Mediterranean.[51] It is probable that many others engaged in similar raids, though did not declare it before a notary when selling those whom they captured.

These acts suggest the existence of a pincer movement involving the integration of Latins and Turks in raiding and trading networks. The marked prevalence of the Dodecanese among the captives' places of origin could reflect raiding from Crete itself as well as from Asia Minor. Cretan traders not only bought Greek slaves in *Turchia* for resale, but also for ransom farming. In 1304, Phylipo de Millano rescued Iohannes and Nicola. Originally from Leros, the pair had been enslaved by Turks before being conditionally ransomed by Phylipo; at the end of May, the pair recognised their obligations to pay Phylipo a total of two *hyperpyra* (gold coins) annually.[52] Exactly one century later, the Castilian Ruy Gonzalez de Clavijo wrote of Leros that it was frequently raided by the Turks of 'Palacia' (Palatia/Balat); a series of captivities of sheep and farmers had occurred immediately before his visit.[53] The islands were particularly vulnerable. In July 1304, the same notary, Pietro Pizolo, recorded the similar case of Nicola Gripioti: originally from the Dodecanese island of Kalymnos, Nicola had been bought by Phylipo, to whom he consequently owed one *hyperpyron* each year. Nicola's case is notable for an additional reason: the act states that there had been no notary in *Turchia* to whom Phylipo might turn for the recording of the sale; since this might cast doubt on the legality of Nicola's enslavement, Nicola professes in the deed that he was indeed Phylipo's slave, and that Phylipo might do with him as he saw fit.[54] Once

---

[49] Stefano Bono, ed. Pettenello and Rauch, 251–2, No. 568.
[50] Benvenuto de Brixano, ed. Morozzo della Rocca, 172, No. 478.
[51] Grant, 'Gottlose Korsaren', 54–7.
[52] Pietro Pizolo, ed. Carbone, 2.35, No. 764.
[53] Ruy Gonzales de Clavijo, *Narrative*, tr. Markham, 20.
[54] Pietro Pizolo, ed. Carbone, 2.58, No. 814.

such a statement had been taken down in writing by a notary, it would be difficult to deny it or retract it.

Lamberto di Sambuceto recorded a similar case in Famagusta. On 2 February 1300 he drew up an inventory of the possessions of the late Salvetus Pezagnus, Genoese. The goods were to be shipped to Genoa and to be taken into the possession of his sons and heirs there. Among his possessions were 'two Greek slaves of Monemvasia who are <intended> for redemption'.[55] It is likely that Salvetus expected, for reasons now lost, that he could raise more money from these men than they were worth on the slave market; otherwise, he surely would have sold them. Perhaps he was in contact with their relatives, or was in business with an agent involved in the repatriation of captives.

Some Latins like Phylipo acted as effective ransom farmers, speculating on the redemption of Greeks captured in the Dodecanese; others engaged in more straightforward trading, sometimes selling groups of Greek captives. For the year 1304, Pizolo records five occasions when a number of Greeks were sold together by a single trader. The sellers were Andreas Lupino of Candia,[56] Pantaleo de Spiga of Candia,[57] Angelus Gostatera of Stimpalia,[58] Raymundinus Barsume of Candia,[59] and Franciscus of Candia, the emancipated son of Georgius the Catalan of Stimpalia (that is, he was legally autonomous from his father);[60] of the buyers, the most prolific was Iohannes Mudacio of Candia, who purchased no fewer than nineteen of a total of thirty-eight Greek slaves sold by these five men.[61] These Greeks came not only from locations near *Turchia*, but also from northern Greece: Andreas Lupino, for example, sold individuals from Ierissos on the Athos peninsula and the Chersonesos (in this case, likely meaning the region of Gallipoli);[62] these individuals were probably led into captivity as a consequence of the Catalan presence at the Bosporus at this time. The involvement of Franciscus, a Catalan trader settled in Candia, is also prophetic of the substantial role that Catalans would play throughout the fourteenth

---

[55] Sambuceto, ed. Balard, Duba, and Schabel, 52–5, No. 42: *sclavi duo griffoni de Marvasia qui sunt pro redemptione*.
[56] Pietro Pizolo, ed. Carbone, 2.39, No. 772.
[57] Ibid., 2.78, No. 857.
[58] Ibid., 2.84, No. 870; 2.86, No. 873; 2.116, No. 941; No. 943.
[59] Ibid., 2.159–60, No. 1040; 2.161, No. 1042; 2.162–3, No. 1046; 2.171, No. 1066.
[60] Ibid., 2.194–5, No. 1119; 2.197–200, Nos. 1125–38.
[61] Ibid., 2.39, No. 772; 2.78, No. 857 (also 2.78, No. 858: Costa, sold by Michael Massamurdi = Maçamurdi), 2.116, No. 941.
[62] Ibid., 2.39, No. 772. For *Stilari* as Ierissos, see Markl, *Ortsnamen*, 60.

century in the trafficking of Greeks across the Aegean and further afield over the Mediterranean. Otherwise, the origins of the Greek slaves sold in 1304 are mostly places in the Dodecanese or western Asia Minor, reflecting Turkish expansion in the region.

The captivities on the smaller Aegean islands are another part of this bleak story. These islands are remote and prone to shortages of drinking water; in the later Middle Ages, many were completely abandoned. Astypalaia (the Stimpalia of Latin notaries) may have been home to a number of slave traders in the early fourteenth century, but it had also been home to Georgius Musseri, released from slavery by Constantinus Saclichi of Candia in 1303,[63] and was an island no doubt prone to raids. One century later, the local ruler Giovanni Quirini had to resettle the depopulated island with some of his subjects from Mykonos and Tinos. Just twenty of over one hundred Cycladic isles were settled in the fifteenth century, 85 percent of the archipelago being unfit for cultivation.[64] Of the islands, Thira/Santorini was apparently particularly vulnerable to captivity.[65] Furthermore, many of the members of the already small group of noble Venetian families that ruled over these archipelagoes seem to have preferred to reside in Candia and to participate in the political life of Crete, making it likely that these islands were often without a resident lord.[66] These islands were thus environmentally impoverished and controlled by absentee colonial lords, as well as being vulnerable to Turkish raiding and apparently varying levels of compassion, enterprise or exploitation from Latin interlopers.[67]

Most of the trends evident in the acts drawn up by Pietro Pizolo and Stefano Bono are more amply attested in the acts of Angelo de Cartura. Over one hundred Greek slaves and captives are attested in his register, recorded over a space of only one year (May 1305–May 1306). At this time, Gallipoli was of central importance as a place of exchange. Starting late in March 1306, various Greeks were purchased from Catalans and two from Turks at Gallipoli.[68] While Gallipoli had also been an important slave

---

[63] Stefano Bono, ed. Pettenello and Rauch, 187–8, No. 400.
[64] Luttrell, 'Latin East', 797 and 806.
[65] Pietro Pizolo, ed. Carbone, 2.39, No. 772; 2.210, No. 1160; Angelo de Cartura, ed. Stahl, 94, No. 244; 112, No. 295; 133, No. 352; Verlinden, *L'esclavage*, 2.831 (notary Stefano Bon).
[66] McKee, *Uncommon Dominion*, 45.
[67] The depopulation of the Aegean islands is discussed further in Chapter 6.
[68] Catalans: Angelo de Cartura, ed. Stahl, 190, No. 490; 201, No. 516; 202–3, No. 520; 207, No. 532; 208, No. 536; 211, No. 543; Turks: ibid., 211, No. 544; 215, No. 553.

market in the thirteenth century, it now assumed particular importance with the arrival of Catalan mercenaries, who generated wealth through the trafficking of captives.[69] A number of their Greek captives ended up being brought to Crete. The contours of the crisis of captivity, therefore, largely follow the contours of the fate of the late empire more broadly.

Sometime in 1306, probably in May (the date sequence is disrupted due to damage in the manuscript), Cartura drew up an act recording Hemanuel Virino's manumission of his Greek slave Iohannes, son of the late Georgius Glafchyrno. Iohannes had been received from Marcus Belliparo, who had taken Iohannes captive during a raid employing three Turkish galleys. Marcus was evidently a Latin, and this act reveals a characteristic of the trafficking of Greek captives that is seldom stated so clearly: that Latins collaborated with Turks in the crisis of captivity, fulfilling not only the roles of ransom farmer and trader, but also of raider – even aboard a Muslim-controlled ship. Iohannes' freedom was conditional upon his labouring for Hemanuel every August for the rest of his life.[70] Freedom and unfreedom thus existed in shades of grey in a society like fourteenth-century Candia, something especially visible in the acts of Marino Doto in the next decade: on 3 April 1313, for example, a manumission contract drawn up for a family group of three had to state explicitly that they had the right to leave Crete, suggesting that this was not a right routinely given to slaves when freed.[71]

Catalans in the Romanía

In 1303, in the aftermath of the Ottoman victory against Byzantium at the Battle of Bapheus, the former knight Templar Roger of Flor offered Andronikos II the service of a force of mercenaries in the form of the recently constituted Grand Catalan Company. This marked the climax of a Byzantine tradition of employing mercenary groups and complemented the engagement of Turkish mercenaries at around the same time. The core of this company comprised infantry of low social rank known by the sobriquet *almogàvers* after their border-raiding predecessors in Iberia. Their name probably came from the Arabic *al-maghāwīr*,

---

[69] George Akropolites, *History*, 35, ed. Heisenberg, 54, tr. and comm. Macrides, 199–200 (I thank Prof. Dimiter Angelov for the reference). Setton, 'Catalans in Greece', esp. 169–70.
[70] Angelo de Cartura, ed. Stahl, 221, No. 570; cf. Wright, '*Vade, sta, ambula*', 215.
[71] Verlinden, *L'esclavage*, 2.829 (notary Marino Doto).

referring to their boldness or their practice of raiding, and it is often by this name that the whole company is called in scholarship. Roger had served Frederick III, the Catalan king of Sicily, in the war against the Angevins (1282–1302), and was now in a position to seek a new paymaster. As the Byzantine presence in Asia Minor was in dire straits, Andronikos was in little position to refuse his offer. In order to keep the company on side, Roger and the other important Catalan leaders, Berenguer of Entenca and Ferran Ximenes of Arenos, were rewarded with some of the empire's highest honorary titles and with marriages to imperial princesses. The company made considerable progress in Asia Minor, pushing back the Turks and taking many of them captive. Relations between the company and the empire were always strained, however, and in April 1305 Roger of Flor was assassinated at Adrianople/Edirne, apparently on Byzantine orders. The company now had to take its immediate provisioning and its future prospects into its own hands and attempted to carve out a polity in mainland Greece. Greeks had already been subject to pillage in the course of the Catalans' Asia Minor campaigns, but from this point onwards they were copiously captured and enslaved, too.

The Catalans began at Gallipoli, where they had established themselves. In June 1307 they moved through Thrace to Macedonia, then to Chalkidiki where they raided until their move to the Thessalian plains in earlier 1309, including destroying the Athonite monastery of St Panteleimon and unsuccessfully besieging Chilandar. They were then briefly employed by Gautier of Brienne, Duke of Athens; but Gautier ran up arrears, and his promises of limited rewards were seen as insufficient by the Catalans, who had made significant gains in Thessaly in his name. On 15 March 1311, the Catalans defeated Gautier at the Battle of the Halmyros, and settled in the Duchy of Athens, centred on Thebes. In 1319, they added Neopatras/Neopatria to their composite domain. The Duchy was to last until its occupation by the Navarrese in 1388. By 1303, therefore, all the major actors of the crisis of captivity were present in the Romanía: Greeks, Turks, Venetians, Genoese and now also Catalans. It was this coalescence – or, perhaps, collision – of Turkish and Latin interests at Byzantium's expense that was unprecedented in the thirteenth century, and which precipitated the new triangulation of raiders, captives and traders.[72]

---

[72] Carr and Grant, 'Catalan Company'; Setton, 'Catalans in Greece'; Laiou, *Constantinople and the Latins*, 147–57 and 220–9; Marcos, 'Catalan Company'; Catalan and Turkish ('Anatolian') mercenaries in context: Gheorghe, *Metamorphoses*, 93–140.

Catalans were established actors in Aegean trade before the arrival of Roger of Flor and the Grand Catalan Company. In 1296, Andronikos II granted privileges within his empire 'to the inhabitants of the lands of Barcelona, Aragon, Catalonia, Mallorca, Valencia, Tortosa, and other lands of the most excellent king of Aragon and Sicily [James II]', setting import and export customs duties at three percent. According to the text of the privileges, the Catalans already had a consul in Constantinople, Dalmau Sunyer, indicating that this was by no means a new market for them.[73] A mere five years later, in the city of Candia on 9 July 1301, Filipachis de Caristo of Negroponte sold to Georgius, a doctor of Mallorca, a Greek man called Leo whom he had captured on Samos.[74] Georgius thereby became the earliest known Catalan to buy a Greek captive as a slave.

The period between Roger's assassination and the conquest of the Duchy of Athens is known as the 'Catalan vengeance' for its violent reprisals, and the captivities of Greeks perpetrated during these years are likewise visible in notarial acts from Candia. The notary Angelo Cariolo drew up acts between 1307 and 1309 that record the sale of thirty-seven captured Greeks as slaves. The origins of these Greeks are mainly Macedonian locales including Thessaloniki, Kassandreia and Veroia, but they also include Anaia, the Karamenderes and the Chersonesos in western Asia Minor. This spread of locales clearly reflects the movements of the Catalan army, and indeed some of the acts explicitly state this fact, mentioning the army's presence at both Kassandreia and Thessaloniki, from which the captives were trafficked to Candia. Twenty-nine of these captives are noted to have been sold at auction. The sellers were mostly residents of Candia; some are noted as being Venetians, and one was a Catalan of Venice, who resided in Venice. Some of the buyers' names appear to be Greek, and one is explicitly noted to have been Greek: these included priests, a villein (peasant) and a Greek of Mantua who lived in Candia. It is uncertain whether these Greeks bought the captives in order to free them or to exploit their labour.[75]

---

[73] Marinesco, 'Notes' (text at 508–9).
[74] Benvenuto de Brixano, ed. Morozzo della Rocca, 81, No. 220.
[75] Duran Duelt, 'Companyia' and Marcos, 'Catalan Company', 338–9 (notary Angelo Cariolo). Possibly Greek buyers: Papati (the priest) Antonius Angelidni of Candia, Emmanuel Agiostefaniti of Pavosnico, Nicolao Gerano, the villein (peasant) of Gabrieli Barba of Sassiti, Papati Theofilacto Paputo of Delese, Vassili Agiostefaniti of terma Apanosiuriti, a Greek of Mantua who lived in Candia, (perhaps) Iohani Russogerii of Axo, Papati Georgius Cafato of Veni. Others may also have been Greeks, though with more Latin-sounding names.

The Catalans' evolution from a wandering mercenary force to the settled rulers of central Greece did not diminish the importance of slavery to their economic survival. Greeks were being trafficked from the Duchy of Athens at least as early as 1317, a mere six years after the Catalans' conquest and settlement there. On 18 February, a male slave originally from Nafplio was sold by a Genoese trader at Candia; the act notes that the vendor 'led him from the Catalan Company of Athens'.[76] He was surely a captive of the Catalans'. Nafplio remained in the hands of the Brienne family, former rulers of the Duchy of Athens, but the city lay close to Catalan domains.[77] There would be a great deal more whose fate, like his, took them from their homes to Athens–Neopatria and thereafter into slavery, often by way of the slave market of Candia.

As is often the case with the various late Byzantine theatres of captivity, the presence of the Catalans and their slave trading activities are reflected in a saint's life, on this occasion that of Athanasios of Meteora.[78] Athanasios was born in 1305 at Neopatras (Neopatria to the Latins), southern Thessaly, and baptised as Andronikos. On the death of John II of the Greek principality of Thessaly, the Catalans took the area and annexed Neopatras to their Athenian duchy (1319). Andronikos was raised and educated by his uncle, since his parents were both long dead. The Catalan invasion resulted in Andronikos's captivity, while his uncle was compelled to flee. Andronikos was apparently desired as a page by the Catalan governor, whom the author perhaps intended to be understood as the vicar general Alfonso Fadrique. 'Once the city had been taken by the Italians [= Catalans]', the *vita* continues, 'the child was taken hostage (*omera*) by them; but the *exarch* of the Franks, seeing this boy, charming in his looks, wanted to escort him home as a piece of loot, wherefore the boy, having perceived this, delivered himself by flight.' Accordingly, he set out to re-join his uncle, and the pair made for Thessaloniki. His uncle died a monk of Akapniou, while Andronikos took up a job assisting a scribe of the imperial bureaucracy and continued his education.[79]

---

[76] Verlinden, *L'esclavage*, 2.831 (notary Stefano Bon).
[77] Luttrell, 'Argos and Nauplia', 34.
[78] More examples in Chapters 2 and 6, *infra*. Rotman, *Byzantine Slavery*, employs numerous examples from the first millennium.
[79] Ed. Bees, 'Συμβολή', 237–60 (= *BHG* 195); English summary of the text, with notes, in Nicol, *Meteora*, 88–91; quotation from Bees (ed.), 'Συμβολή', 240: Τοῦ ἄστεως δὲ ἁλόντος ὑπὸ τῶν Ἰταλῶν, ὅμηρα ὑπ' αὐτῶν ὁ παῖς λαμβάνεται· ἰδὼν δὲ τοῦτον ὁ Φράγγων ἐξάρχων ἀστεῖον τῇ ὄψει, ἐβουλήθη οἴκαδε ὥς τι λάφυρον παραπέμψαι, ὅπερ διαγνοὺς ὁ παῖς φυγῇ τὴν σωτηρίαν ἐχρήσατο. The term 'Italoi' means Catalans, but may reflect the company's earlier phase on Sicily.

Following a preliminary trip to Athos and visits to Constantinople and Crete, Andronikos returned to the Holy Mountain by 1325, and became a disciple of Gregory of Sinai at the monastery of Iviron's *skete* (dependent house) of Magoula. Magoula was sacked during a Turkish raid in about 1325 and its community dispersed; Gregory made for Thessaloniki, but Andronikos remained on Athos and moved to the secluded hermitage cell of Melaia, where his companions were the holy men Moses and Gregory. In 1335, Gregory tonsured Andronikos, now thirty years of age: as a novice he was called Antonios, and then, as a monk, Athanasios.

At Melaia, a remarkable instance of captivity purportedly occurred. One of the many raids launched by 'the Hagarenes (those commonly called "Turks")' targeted the cell. While some escaped, the old hermit Moses was tied up and carried away, saved only by the intercession of St Nicholas. Moses and a disciple of his called Stephen moved to the monastery of Iviron, but Gregory took Athanasios and another disciple, Gabriel, towards the west.[80]

Following this disruption, Athanasios left for Meteora, where he founded the monastery on the Broad Rock dedicated to the Metamorphosis (Transfiguration) of Christ, the Great Meteoron. Athos was attacked regularly by Turks throughout the fourteenth century,[81] though it is likely that this episode is a narrative device asserting the holiness of the Melaian community over the barbarism of the Turkish raiders, set in a fictive but entirely plausible context.

Athanasios's *Life* is symptomatic of the circumstances of central Greece at that time, victim to both Turks and Catalans. Captivity and forced dislocation were central to Athanasios's story as they were to the experience of many around him. However literally one takes his *vita*, as a wanderer from Thessaly to Constantinople to Crete to Athos to Thessaly, once captive and twice more nearly captured along the way, his story is emblematic of its time.

The Turks and Catalans cooperated for a period in the early fourteenth century. In 1318, Alfonso Fadrique allied with the beyliks of Aydın and Menteşe against Venice and Naples as he wished to secure control over the island of Negroponte, which lay adjacent to his duchy. Alfonso was soon compelled to sign and subsequently renew a treaty with Venice, which was designed to prevent him from employing Turkish proxies. In 1328, Turks landed on Negroponte/Euboea; in 1329, the Catalan–Turkish

---

[80] Ed. Bees, 'Συμβολή', 243–4.
[81] Živojinović, 'Turkish Assaults'; cf. Nicol, *Meteora*, 91 n. 6.

pact dissolved, and the Turks had their vengeance by attacking Athens and leading off captives. The Catalans were consequently brought to heel, and seem once again to have made terms with Venice.[82] While notarial acts from Crete dating to the years 1300–6 strongly suggest that western Asia Minor was the most prominent centre of captivity at that time, Thessaly and central Greece assume prominence immediately thereafter.[83] This change coincides with the movement of Catalans from Gallipoli, through Thessaly, to Boiotia and Attica. It is clear that the instability the Catalans brought to Greece while on the move from 1305–11, followed by the instability they brought to the Aegean after Alfonso Fadrique's establishment of relationships with Aydın and Menteşe from 1318–29, fundamentally shaped the extent of the crisis of captivity.

It is at this time that evidence begins to appear attesting to a diaspora of unfree Greeks on Mallorca. This island was an independent monarchy until its annexation by the Crown of Aragon in 1343–4.[84] Mallorca would, over the course of the fourteenth century, become home to one of the largest communities of diasporic Greeks in the Mediterranean, many of whom were also born into slavery in the western Mediterranean – something unusual for enslaved Greeks at that time.[85] While Mallorcans are first attested trading on Crete in 1301, the earliest evidence for transactions on Mallorca itself comes in 1318, with the sale of the two slaves Stana and Arena. Both women appear to have been the property first of Italians: Andreu (= Andrea) Fontanella in the case of Stana, and Ferrari de Colle in the case of Arena, on whose behalf his relative Guillem Drescoll sold her. The buyers, Jaume Fornells of Tarragona and Gerarda, widow of Ramon Fullana, appear to have been Catalans.[86] If these people were indeed a mixture of Italians and Catalans, then these transactions suggest an integrated trade network that joined the Romanía, Italy and the Crown of Aragon, embracing traders from multiple sides. Several years later, in 1324, another Greek was sold in Manresa, from two merchants to a painter.[87]

---

[82] Zachariadou, *Trade and Crusade*, 13–16; for the captives of Athens, Zachariadou, 'Σχετικά'.
[83] This turning point is particularly visible at Candia between 11 May 1306 (Angelo de Cartura, ed. Stahl, 215, No. 215: the end of a series of purchases at Gallipoli) and 18 July 1308 (Duran Duelt, 'Companyia', 568, summarising the notary Angelo Cariolo).
[84] Bisson, *Aragon*, 106–7.
[85] This demographic claim is substantiated in Chapter 3.
[86] López, 'Un fruit', 1474 and n. 70.
[87] Verlinden, *L'esclavage*, 1.326.

Catalan merchants are known to have travelled continuously from the duchy to the West in the service of trade. In 1351, for example, Ferrer d'Oms, a burgher of Thebes, appointed Jordi Virgili, a merchant resident in Thebes, to bear five male and three female Greek slaves to Mallorca and to sell them on arrival. Virgili died upon reaching Mallorca, which led to a complex series of negotiations regarding the disposal of his property.[88] Some other Greek slaves are documented on Mallorca in 1361 having been purchased in Thebes earlier the same year.[89] This is evidence that Catalans on both sides of the Mediterranean engaged directly with one another in the trafficking of Greek captives.

On the other hand, notarial evidence from Venetian Crete suggests that Candia played a major role as a clearing house in the exportation of Greek captives by Catalans of Athens–Neopatria. This is particularly evident in the acts of the notary Giovanni Similiante, whose register contains 111 notices, most dating from 1332–3, referring to enslaved people who are either designated Greek or specified as coming from parts of Greece. Many of these were traded by Catalan merchants active in Candia.[90]

The relevant acts reveal a series of large-scale sales by people either explicitly called Catalans, or else active in the Catalan Duchy of Athens and Neopatria. Guillelmus Simon, a Catalan from Perpignan residing in Thebes, was the most prolific slave trader in this series of acts, selling thirty-four slaves, some of whom are explicitly said to have been of Greek birth or *nacio*, and almost all of whom are recorded as coming from Corinth, Thebes or the 'Despotate'. Among the buyers, the priest Baxili Cartero, probably a Greek, stands out:[91] as noted above, clergy are attested buying Greeks from Catalans in 1308 – whatever their motives and intentions in doing so. In December 1332, another Catalan, Franciscus de Brurbin [sic] of Barcelona, together with his business partner Bernard de Castigelo, sold sixteen people from the regions of Corinth, Athens and the Despotate, none of whom is given an ethnic description. Jacobus Raynaldus, yet another Catalan, sold ten; Nicola de Corron of Thebes (perhaps a Venetian of Coron/Koroni or the descendant of one, resident at Thebes, rather than a Catalan) sold eight, while Johannes Çoli, a Catalan of Perpignan, sold one. Thebes

---

[88] Duran Duelt, 'Ducados', 111–12, with details of the property disposal at n. 74.
[89] Ibid., and n. 73.
[90] Archivio di Stato, Venice, Notai di Candia, DIII Busta 244 (Giovanni Similiante): 111 by my count. The notary has been the subject of an incomplete survey by Verlinden, *L'esclavage*, 1.397, 2.833–5.
[91] Giovanni Similiante, fol. 121r, No. 12; Verlinden, *L'esclavage*, 1.397, 2.835.

was not only a centre of export, but a point of departure for merchants, too.[92] It is Candia, however, that emerges as the slave trading emporium of greatest transregional importance.

The *despotatus* that features prominently as the origin of many of the Greeks sold in these transactions is almost certainly the Despotate of Epirus, at this time under the control of the Orsini family. In 1311, Gautier II of Brienne, count of Lecce, obtained crusading status from John XXII for an expedition against the Duchy of Athens, lost by his family to the Catalans in 1311. If successful, he hoped that he would win the submission of Giovanni Orsini. Orsini was compelled to submit to Gautier's backer, Roberto of Naples, but the expedition against the Catalans failed. Walter left for Italy in 1332, having taken Leukas and Vonitsa, but having achieved little else.[93] The sale of many of these Greeks into slavery may be a reflection of instability in Epirus and central Greece caused by these hostilities.

It was at this time, too, that the last Byzantine campaigns in Asia Minor were being undertaken by Emperor Andronikos III Palaiologos, son of Michael IX and grandson of Andronikos II. By the death of Andronikos II in 1328, all but a couple of Asian cities were lost to the Byzantines. Prousa/Bursa surrendered in 1326 after an Ottoman siege lasting perhaps fifteen years, during which time the inhabitants had been obliged to pay tribute to the enemy. In 1329, Andronikos III attempted to prevent the Ottomans from laying siege to Nicomedia/İzmit; the Byzantine army confronted them at Pelekanon and successfully withstood the Ottomans' mounted archers until the emperor himself was injured and his men consequently routed. This battle also testifies to the waning numbers of pastoralists in the Ottoman polity and hence to the waning importance of steppe-style warfare for its army: in the following years, the Ottomans began to develop the use of infantry and to move towards a more sedentarised mode of warfare. The cities of the northwest were soon lost: Nicaea/İznik fell to the Ottomans in 1337 and Nicomedia in 1337; the sole Byzantine stronghold remained Philadelphia, situated to the south, which remarkably survived until 1390.[94]

It is a synchronicity worthy of note that Andronikos III, the last emperor to campaign in Asia Minor, was also the emperor who established a new general judicial court in 1329, comprising one bishop and three laymen. This court sat initially in Constantinople, with authority conferred by means of a ceremony in Hagia Sophia, but iterations of this institution

---

[92] On Thebes as a slave market: Setton, *Catalan Domination*, 87; Rubió, 'Mitteilungen'.
[93] Nicol, *Despotate*, 97–8.
[94] Lindner, 'Anatolia', 121–2.

subsequently convened in Thessaloniki, the Peloponnese, Trebizond and probably the island of Limnos. This establishment is illustrative of the trend of clergy taking an ever-greater role in traditionally lay capacities, notably the judiciary and charity, as the empire and its bureaucracy were diminished by Turkish advances.[95] Just as Turkish expansion in Asia Minor had led to the hiring of the Catalan Company, so it contributed to the increasing role of the Church in all areas of Greek Christian social life.

Conclusions

In order to understand how a crisis of captivity among Greeks had arisen by around 1300, it is necessary to look at the geopolitical circumstances of the region in which this crisis began: Asia Minor. Under the first two Palaiologan emperors, Michael VIII and Andronikos II, Turkish groups made substantial conquests in western Asia Minor at Byzantium's expense; defensive military campaigns achieved occasional reprieves, but by the 1330s only the city of Philadelphia remained in imperial hands. The towns and cities conquered by these Turkish groups included the important trading emporia on the Aegean coast; there, Turks traded Greeks – whom they had captured in raids, sieges or battles – with Latin merchants, mostly Venetians and sometimes Catalans. By the turn of the fourteenth century, notarial evidence from Crete and Cyprus shows the arrival of the first waves of these captives trafficked from Asia Minor, who were then exploited as domestic slaves. At this point, Byzantium contracted Catalan mercenaries to help stem the advances of these Turkish goups; when the contractual relationship between Byzantium and the Catalans broke down, the Catalans in turn captured and enslaved people in mainland Greece. These captives were also traded via Crete, and slave trading became one of the major sources of income for the Catalans once they had settled in Athens, Thebes and Neopatras.

[95] Laiou, 'Palaiologoi', 812. This trend is explored further in chs 4 and 6, *infra*.

Chapter 2
Slave Trading in the Mediterranean and Black Sea

In the Introduction, the two major slave-trading structures of the late medieval Mediterranean were described: a transregional trade running from the Black Sea to Egypt and Italy, and a more localised trade emanating from the Aegean region. It was also emphasised that scholars have tended to conflate these two slave-trading structures; in response, this chapter undertakes the task of comparing, contrasting and framing them. As the emergence of the Aegean trade and its wider ramifications in the eastern Mediterranean have already been addressed in Chapter 1, the present chapter focuses on the transregional trade. It considers first the geopolitical circumstances under which this trade emerged and then analyses the range and interests of the various actors – Mamlūks, Mongols, Genoese, Byzantines and Cypriots – that were involved in it, highlighting areas of overlap or contrast with the Aegean trade. While the slave trade undertaken between the Mamlūks, Genoese and Mongols has been the subject of a number of excellent recent studies,[1] Byzantium's role in this nexus has received far less attention,[2] and the discussion of the Cypriot context presented here is a new departure; the result is a substantial reframing, largely from a Greek perspective, of a seemingly familiar phenomenon.

The Slave Trade

The period 1259–61 was a turning point in the geopolitical history of the whole of western Eurasia, not just of western Asia Minor. The ultimate cause for both these changes, local and transregional, was the arrival of

---

[1] Notably, Barker, *Most Precious Merchandise* as well as the various studies in Amitai and Cluse (eds), *Slavery* and Roşu (ed.), *Slavery*.
[2] Amitai, 'Diplomacy and the Slave Trade'; Jacoby, 'Byzantine Traders in Mamluk Egypt'; Mansouri, *Recherches*; the subject is far from exhausted.

the Mongols. The disruption of the balance of power between the Empire of Nicaea and the Seljuk Sultanate of Rūm can be attributed to a domino effect of westward migrations of Mongols and Turkmens. In 1260 at the Battle of ʿAyn Jālūt – 'Goliath's Eye' – near Galilee, the Mamlūk Sultanate stemmed the seemingly unstoppable advance of the Mongols when it defeated an army of the Īl-Khānate, the Mongol polity in Iran.[3]

In 1261, Michael VIII Palaiologos, emperor of Nicaea, took Constantinople from its Latin conquerors. The Latin Empire of Constantinople, established as a consequence of the Fourth Crusade in 1204, thus ceased to exist, even if western European rulers still kept alive the imperial title and its aspirations. Over the following years, the consequences of this development coalesced with the consequences of the Battle of ʿAyn Jālūt to create two of the largest power blocs of the pre-modern world.[4]

To the north of Michael VIII's empire, in vast swathes of land surrounding the Volga River, lay another great Mongol polity: the Khanate of the Golden Horde. In the later thirteenth and fourteenth centuries, the Golden Horde was the source of huge numbers of enslaved people. Many of these ended up in domestic slavery in Italy, the Crown of Aragon and southern France; many others ended up in domestic or military slavery in Mamlūk Egypt and Syria. The Mamlūk Sultanate was ruled by an elite of manumitted military slaves, who provided its soldiers, generals and sultans.[5] This was an elite that could not reproduce itself, insofar as each generation had to be recruited directly from imported enslaved people. Access to the Black Sea slave trade was thus integral to the continued survival of the Mamlūk polity. This, in turn, necessitated cordial diplomatic relations between the Mamlūk Sultanate and the Golden Horde. In the winter of 1262–3, the Īl-Khānate (under the command of Hülegü) and the Golden Horde (under Berke) went to war; for the Mamlūk Sultan Baybars, this development offered a clear diplomatic opportunity to tighten relations with his enemy's enemy.[6] Over a period of a little under two hundred years (to c. 1440), the powers exchanged perhaps eighty diplomatic missions; although there was not a continuous alliance between them, their relationship was regularly maintained and generally cordial.[7]

Bilateral relations between the Golden Horde and the Mamlūks required the cooperation of the power that controlled the straits separating the Black

---

[3] Saunders, 'Mongol Defeat'.
[4] Ibid.: this is Saunders's major thesis.
[5] The classic study of the mamlūk system is Ayalon, *L'esclavage du Mamelouk*.
[6] Saunders, 'Mongol Defeat', esp. 73.
[7] Favereau, 'The Golden Horde and the Mamluks'.

Sea from the Mediterranean. Until 1261, this power had been the Latin Empire of Constantinople; the Latin Empire, however, was a territorial embodiment of the crusading movement, and the biggest threat to the territorial integrity of the crusader states of the Syro-Palestinian coast was the Mamlūk Sultanate. After the crusader states lost Jerusalem to the Ayyūbid Sultan Ṣalāḥ al-Dīn Yūsuf (Saladin) in 1187, a cornerstone of crusader strategy was the plan for a pre-emptive strike against the Ayyūbid and later Mamlūk heartlands in Egypt before the launch of a general expedition aimed at Jerusalem. This happened with the Fifth Crusade of 1217–21, launched against Ayyūbid-controlled Damietta. The arrival of the Mongols and the emergence of the Īl-Khānate presented the Latins, especially the English and French, with a potential ally for any expedition against the Mamlūks; this alliance was repeatedly championed by crusade propagandists in the late thirteenth and early fourteenth centuries, but although the subject was broached multiple times, its aspirations were never realised.[8]

From 1261, however, the power that controlled the straits was not a crusader state but the empire of Michael VIII Palaiologos. Michael's political and economic interests sat well with those of the Mamlūk Sultanate, while the Golden Horde posed a far more immediate military threat to his empire than the Īl-Khānate. Michael was a consummate diplomat and managed to conclude marriage alliances with both the Īl-Khānate and the Golden Horde by two illegitimate daughters: in 1265, Maria married the Īl-Khān Abaqa (reigned 1265–82), and in 1266, Euphrosyne married Nogai, nephew of Berke (died 1299), khan of the Golden Horde (reigned 1257–66). The capture of Constantinople in 1261 had thus facilitated the formation of a geopolitical configuration that stretched from the British Isles to Central Asia, and Michael VIII trod carefully between its two major blocs.[9]

In 1261, Michael VIII signed the Treaty of Nymphaion with Genoa and thus made the Genoese his most favoured commercial partner. This was reinforced by the concession of the Constantinopolitan neighbourhood of Galata/Pera in 1267, and more or less set the tone for Genoa's relationship with Byzantium for the rest of the empire's existence. It was not long before the Genoese had received permission from the Golden Horde to establish a commercial colony at Caffa in the Crimean Peninsula (the old Byzantine Theodosia), from which they could exert a strong

---

[8] On this alliance: Schein, *Fideles crucis*; Leopold, *How to Recover the Holy Land*; Grant, 'Mongol Invasions', 150–61.
[9] Dashdondog, 'Black Sea Slave Trade', 285.

influence over the Black Sea mercantile economy. For some time now, scholars have identified the Mongol–Mamlūk–Byzantine configuration as immediately placing Genoa in prime position to monopolise the Black Sea slave trade on which the Mamlūk Sultanate existentially relied.[10] While this is a plausible inference, there is however limited evidence to support it, while other evidence is available that demands the revision of this hypothesis in various ways.

First, there is no direct evidence for Genoese traders supplying the Mamlūk Sultanate with slaves in the thirteenth century. The agreement that Sultan Baybars concluded with Michael VIII in 1261–2 took the supply of enslaved people from the Black Sea as a key concern, but it is, in fact, only Muslim merchants that are mentioned: there is not the slightest hint that third parties, Genoese or otherwise, were involved. It is only in 1281 that indirect evidence that may point to the involvement of Genoese traders arises: in that year, Sultan Barqūq concluded a treaty – technically an undertaking under oath – with (the now elderly) Michael; one of the clauses stipulated that the passage of traders from Sudak (the Greek Sougdaia, west along the Crimean coast from Caffa) would not be hindered, nor that of Muslim merchants, assuming they paid their dues to the Byzantine authorities on their way past Constantinople. While this reference is non-specific, it is on balance of probabilities likely that it refers to Genoese traders established in the Crimean Peninsula. That said, the possible involvement of Venetians – something equally obscure at this early date – should also be borne in mind.[11]

Second, even in the fourteenth and fifteenth centuries, by which time the participation of Genoese traders is beyond doubt, it is clear that the Genoese did not exercise a monopoly. Of c. 170 slave traders attested in Caffa for the years 1410–46, thirty-four were from Genoa or Liguria and a further forty from other or unspecified areas of Italy. Others are identified as 'Saracens' (twenty-seven; perhaps Arabs from the Mamlūk Sultanate, or perhaps Persians), some were from the southern Black Sea, while others may have been of Armenian, Tatar or Bulgarian origin. Thirty-eight have been identified as Greek: while this does not inherently imply imperial subjects, it does nonetheless attest to the substantial participation of Greeks in this trade at a time when the empire was

---

[10] Starting with Ehrenkreutz, 'Strategic Implications'; for further bibliography, see Amitai, 'Diplomacy and the Slave Trade'.

[11] Amitai, 'Diplomacy and the Slave Trade'; for the texts of the agreements, see Holt, *Early Mamluk Diplomacy*, 118–28.

severely reduced. In general, it is clear that the Genoese far from dominated this trade.[12]

Third, the Caffa–Constantinople trade artery was by no means the only maritime slave trading route in the Black Sea. Constantinople is rarely recorded as the destination of shipments of enslaved people, and other ports along the southern coast of the Black Sea such as Simisso, Sinope and Trebizond also feature. There is also evidence for Muslim figures trafficking enslaved people between the Īl-Khānate and the Mamlūks. Altogether, this evidence suggests that overland slave trading networks persisted from the Ayyūbid into the Mamlūk period despite the ongoing war with the Īl-Khānate. These three qualifications thus reduce the Genoese to the position of one among a number of important economic stakeholder-groups in the trade in Black Sea slaves. They were nevertheless among the most important, and it is likely that Genoese ships at times bore non-Genoese traders.[13]

Part of the reason Genoa has loomed so large in scholarship on the Black Sea–Egypt slave trade is the role attributed to one man: Segurano Salvaygo. He was an early fourteenth-century Genoese merchant who converted to Islam and served the interests of the Mamlūk Sultanate. The crusade propagandist William of Adam picked him out as the ultimate 'bad Christian', abandoning the faith for material gain and selling enslaved people to Muslims. In fact, the evidence for Salvaygo engaging in the mamlūk trade is limited outside William of Adam's polemic, and even if his characterisation were accurate, Salvaygo was now a Mamlūk subject with an Arabic name, Sakrān, rather than flying the Genoese colours. Salvaygo/Sakrān cannot, therefore, be taken as axiomatic of a Genoese trade in mamlūks.[14]

William of Adam was engaging in wider discourses that deplored Christians who materially aided Muslims. In the later Middle Ages, this was put into practice by the papacy in the form of trade embargoes. While embargo often appears strongly linked to the aims of the crusading movement, it is perhaps better understood as a broader framework for the interaction of Latin Christians with the religious 'other', especially Muslims. Embargo theory was composed of two major strands that developed separately, though in the period under study tended to come together.

---

[12] Stello, 'Caffa'.
[13] Ibid.; Yudkevich, 'Slave Traders'.
[14] William of Adam, *Tractatus*, ed. and tr. Constable; Kedar, 'Segurano-Sakrān Salvaygo'; Cluse, 'Role'; Yudkevich, 'Slave Traders'; Barker, *Most Precious Merchandise*, 186–208.

The first strand comprised the indictment of selling enslaved people to Muslims – here, in practice, meaning the Mamlūk Sultanate. This prohibition reflected a wider phenomenon, which Hannah Barker has aptly termed 'the competition for slave souls' – that is, that enslavement was in itself a type of proselytisation, and selling people to Muslims (or Jews) would only swell the ranks of that other religion. In this framework, slavery per se was not condemned.[15]

The second strand was the indictment of the sale of materials that might support the waging of wars against Christians, such as raw iron, weapons, horses or ships. Depending on the state of Byzantine–Latin Church relations, Greek Christians were also sometimes included in the category of prohibited trading partners alongside Muslims. In the Mamlūk case, these two strands were further connected by the fact that many of the males among these enslaved people became soldiers.

Embargo was variously promulgated, particularly in the decades after the loss of the crusader states in Syria-Palestine in 1291, but it was possible to secure papal licences that exempted particular ventures from the embargo. One possible justification for making exceptions to embargo was the ransom of Latin Christian captives from the Mamlūk Sultanate; this too was part of 'the competition for slave souls', as conversion to Islam was a possible outcome in cases where such captives were not redeemed.[16]

Those people who were not trafficked to the Mamlūk Sultanate were mostly transported west, to Italy and Iberia. While Italian scholars first began uncovering archival evidence for Black Sea slaves back in the nineteenth century,[17] it is only recently that the connection between the western and eastern Mediterranean arms of the slave trade has been comprehensively demonstrated: the traders in both arms of this trade included many from northern Italy, while many of the enslaved people came from the same areas in the lands of the Golden Horde and the Caucasus.[18]

Greek Captives in Context

The study of the experiences of Greeks, however, emphasises some of the ways in which the western and eastern arms of the transregional

---

[15] Barker, *Most Precious Merchandise*, 14.
[16] The leading study of embargo is Stantchev, *Spiritual Rationality*; see also Barker, *Most Precious Merchandise*, 186–208.
[17] Starting with Bongi, 'Le schiave orientali'; for a full overview of this scholarship, see Epstein, *Speaking of Slavery*, 1–15.
[18] Demonstrating this relationship is one of the most important achievements of Barker, *Most Precious Merchandise*.

Mediterranean slave trade were distinct. Greeks are found trading enslaved people in the eastern arm of this slave trade while being themselves trafficked in the western. In this respect, the regional Aegean slave trade as described by Zachariadou was only partially integrated into the Mediterranean's larger slave-trading structures as elucidated by Barker. This chapter seeks to sketch out the nature of the relationship between the Aegean and transregional slave trades and the reasons behind this relationship.

The ethnic groups who composed the enslaved populations of the Mamlūk Sultanate and the Latin West varied over time. Generally, it is clear that one or two particular groups dominated at any given moment, the causes of which included both supply and demand. In Genoa, the majority of enslaved people came from Iberia in the thirteenth century; this was a consequence of the expansionist campaigns of Christian kingdoms in the peninsula. By the later fourteenth century, this emphasis had changed to the region north of the Black Sea; this was due primarily to Genoa's increasing role in the slave trade of the region from the later thirteenth century onwards.[19] Civil war in the lands of the Golden Horde, coupled with the effects of the Black Death, seem to have encouraged impoverished families to sell their children into slavery; when the civil war ended in 1381, this trend consequently declined.[20]

In Italy, the demographics of slavery moved gradually and unevenly away from Tatars to Circassians and Russians, who faced raids and their own civil wars. This change took place over the course of the later fourteenth and (more precipitously) early fifteenth centuries. In the Mamlūk Sultanate, military slaves were overwhelmingly of Turkic origin such as Kipchaks until Sultan Barqūq began promoting the purchase of people from his own ethnic group, the Circassians, from 1382. When Genoa started to tax Muslim travellers and traders in the Black Sea, another development of this time, Mamlūk merchants began looking for trading routes further east to evade the charges.[21] Demographic shifts in Mediterranean slavery were thus products of both 'push' and 'pull' factors.

Notarial documents from Sicily for the period 1280–1460 offer a clear illustrative example of how these ethnic and geographical emphases of slavery changed over time. From 1280–1309, the dominant group were Muslims from North Africa or Iberia ('Saracens'). In the period 1310–59,

---

[19] See the many works of Balard listed in the bibliography; Delort, 'Quelques précisions'.
[20] Barker, 'Shift'.
[21] Ibid.

Greeks comprised 54% of taxonomised enslaved people, thus reflecting the effects of the crisis of captivity in the Aegean; a further 39% were almost evenly split between black Africans and 'Saracens'. The figures for the last four decades of the century demonstrate the prevalence of peoples from north of the Black Sea, as explained above: these comprise 91% of those enslaved people whose origins are considered to be known and 76% of the overall total. In the decades 1400–39, for those people whose origins are given, there was a fairly even split of black African (36.5%), 'Saracen' (25%) and Black Sea (31.1%) peoples, while in the period 1440–60 the predominant group was black Africans (43.7%).[22] A comparative reading of these various trends reveals that the demographic emphases of medieval Mediterranean slavery moved in cycles, each of which was brought about by its own nexus of causes, related to both supply and demand. The Greek crisis of captivity was one of these cycles, largely concentrated in the early fourteenth century from a western European perspective, but largely focused in the later fourteenth and earlier fifteenth centuries from an Ottoman perspective; in any case, from a Greek perspective this was a full two centuries of hardship.[23]

On the other hand, it is important that Greeks should not be understood solely as the victims of human trafficking. Certainly, far more of the evidence from the thirteenth to fifteenth centuries attests to trafficking of Greek Christians than trafficking by Greek Christians, but the second category of evidence should not be overlooked. Notarial evidence demonstrates the participation of Greeks in the trafficking of enslaved people along the Black Sea–Egypt trading axis. Because hardly any Greek notarial evidence survives, these references are chance survivals preserved in the context of Latin registers, usually because one or more Latins were involved in the transaction. Given the evidence for Greek slave traders in the official records of Caffa, it is unsurprising that notarial evidence also attests to Greeks buying and selling enslaved people there.

Here are a few illustrative examples: In 1289, Nichete Tana bought the Bulgarian (presumably Christian) woman Kressana and her two sons from Ugolino of Piacenza.[24] The next year, Michael Chidonios of Sinope sold the Circassian woman Archona.[25] Then, in 1351, the tavern-keeper and burger of *Solchatus* (likely Sugdaia/Soldaia) sold Borolat, of Cuman origin,

---

[22] Bresc, *Un monde méditerranéen*, 1.439–75; see also Barker, *Most Precious Merchandise*, 121–51.
[23] The Ottoman context is considered in Chapter 6, *infra*.
[24] *Actes*, ed. Brătianu, No. 143.
[25] Ibid., No. 238.

to Anthonius Donatus.[26] To the east, in the Greek quarter of the largely Venetian-dominated port of Tana, Georgius, son of Georgius, sold the Circassian Cotlu to the Venetian Petrus Barbo.[27] In Chilia/Licostomo on the Danube Delta, the Constantinopolitan Manoli Offilimas bought the Tatar woman Taytana from her father, Daoch – a transaction that provides anecdotal evidence for the sale of children by parents in the Black Sea economy.[28] In Alexandria at the other end of the trading axis, Nicolas Chiona of the Aegean island of Karpathos sold a black man called Barch to the ship's captain Manoli di Giorgio, himself a man with a Greek name, who was then in port.[29] There can therefore be little doubt that Greeks both from inside and outside the Byzantine Empire were not just the victims of trafficking but also themselves involved in the transregional Black Sea and eastern Mediterranean slave trade.

Genoa and the Trade in Greek Captives

One of the most striking factors differentiating the Aegean slave trade from the transregional slave trade is the comparative absence of Genoese actors in the former. Even when the role of the Genoese in the Black Sea trade is qualified as above, it nevertheless remains clear that Genoese were both important and numerous actors in the trafficking of enslaved people from the region into the Mediterranean. By comparison, evidence for Genoese trafficking or owning captured and/or enslaved Greeks is slim, and much of this evidence concerns diplomatic negotiations or legal proceedings intended to prevent or end enslavement.

It seems beyond dispute that the Venetian Cretan capital of Candia was consistently the single largest market for the trafficking of Greek captives, standing at the crossroads of trading networks reaching to Mallorca in the west, and Cyprus and Egypt in the east.[30] In the later fourteenth century, when Sicily was moving away from enslaving Greeks to enslaving people from the Black Sea region, the enslaved population on Crete remained perhaps around one-third Greek, having been overwhelmingly Greek in the early years of the century.[31] The high numbers on Crete can be explained in part by contrasting Venice's position in the Black Sea with Genoa's: while

---

[26] Verlinden, 'Mer Noire', 11–12 (notary Antonio Capello).
[27] Verlinden, 'Tana', 19 (notary Benedetto Blanco).
[28] Antonio di Ponzò, ed. Pistarino, 175–7, No. 97.
[29] Verlinden, *L'esclavage*, 2.658 (notary Vittore de Bonfantinis).
[30] See Verlinden, 'Crète'.
[31] Verlinden, *L'esclavage*, 2.870.

Venice did maintain predominance in the port of Tana on the Don Delta in addition to trading in Caffa, Genoa's dominance over not just Caffa but also Chilia–Licostomo on the Danube Delta, and Galata/Pera near Constantinople gave it the upper hand in the Black Sea slave trade.[32] Venice contested this position by obtaining the island of Tenedos by concession from the Byzantine Empire; this led to the Venetian–Genoese War of Chioggia, fought mainly in the Adriatic in the years 1376–81.[33] Venice, which controlled the Aegean's largest islands, Negroponte and Crete, competed with Genoa for access to the Black Sea slave economy. Thus, it had greater incentives than Genoa to exploit the labour of captured Greeks; this was especially the case in its most significant overseas city, Candia, where domestic and artisanal labour was sought by Latin colonists.[34]

In fourteenth-century Genoa, by contrast, only fifty-one Greek slaves have been identified among a total sample of 2,369 taxonomised slaves, thus comprising a mere 2.15%.[35] For the period 1400–60, that is, to the end of the period covered by this book, that number may (on current knowledge) be supplemented by only a further eight.[36] There were also free or freed Greeks who lived in Genoa at this time and are found working as marines or shipbuilders.[37] There was also a confraternity of manumitted Greeks, though this is not attested until 1486, later than the remit of the current study.[38]

In published fourteenth- and fifteenth-century notarial sources drawn up in Genoese communities overseas, it is likewise possible to identify only a few enslaved Greeks: five on Chios, one in Chilia on the Danube delta, one in Pera, one in Mytilene on Lesbos, and none in the important Black Sea

---

[32] Barker, *Most Precious Merchandise*, 121–51 (ch. 5); on Genoese interests in the region, see the works of Balard listed in the bibliography; on the Venetian trade, see Quirini-Popławska, 'Venetian Involvement'.
[33] Balard, 'Latins', 827; Thiriet, 'Ténédos'.
[34] McKee, *Uncommon Dominion*, 'Inherited status', 'Domestic Slavery' and 'Familiarity of Slaves'.
[35] Balard, *Romanie génoise*, 2.799 (table No. 53). Greeks are all but absent from Delort, 'Quelques précisions' (analysis of Genoese notaries of the late fourteenth century).
[36] Six in Gioffrè, *Mercato*, unpaginated tables (the two people called Margherita who appear in 1459 and 1460 are probably one and the same), which includes Catalina alias Passa found in the document ed. Tria, 'Schiavitù' 167–8, No. XXXVIII; one in Fleet, *Trade*, 52; and one in Otten-Froux, 'Représentation', 102.
[37] Harris, *Greek Emigres*, 32 (Genoa), 169–75 (naval officers and shipbuilding).
[38] Gioffrè, *Mercato*, 105.

slave-trading port of Caffa.[39] (There was, though, one dramatic exception to this trend in the Genoese capture of Byzantine Herakleia near Constantinople in 1351–2, considered below.) To these figures, it is possible to add a further thirty-one Greek – or probably Greek – individuals who were trafficked by Genoese in or to places dominated by other groups: twenty-four in Famagusta (all before its conquest by the Genoese), six in Candia and one (perhaps) in Valencia. The number of Genoese individuals involved is difficult to assess, as sometimes unspecified groups are mentioned.[40]

Unlike the Venetians, the Genoese therefore do not seem to have trafficked many Greeks into slavery, either in their metropolis or in places where they exerted a hegemony or strong commercial interest. This sharp disparity, already immediately visible even with provisional figures such as those presented here, does not appear to have prompted comment in previous scholarship. The explanations for this disparity may be sought in Genoa's diplomatic relationship with Byzantium and, corollary to this, its economic and political position beyond the Bosporus in the Black Sea.

The first example of relevant diplomacy comes from the list of stipulations issued by Andronikos II on 22 March 1308 to the Genoese of Pera/Galata, of which a Latin translation survives in Genoa. One of Andronikos's priorities in these stipulations was to protect the interests of his own subjects, many of whom lived just opposite Pera in Constantinople. Andronikos began by demanding that people identified as Greeks (*greci*) should enjoy the same kinds of tax immunities in Genoa as the Genoese did in the 'Empire of the Romanía'. He then lodged a more specific complaint: he had heard rumours that Greek children were being led from Constantinople

---

[39] Chios: Raffaele de Casanova, ed. Balletto, 120–1, No. 12; 105–6; Argenti, *Chios*, 3.570, No. 86/113; Balletto, 'Schiave e manomessi', 672; ibid., 689–90; Chilia: Antonio di Ponzò, ed. Balard, 2.83–6, No. 41; Pera: *Notai genovesi*, ed. Roccatagliata, 1.138–9, No. 53; Mytilene: ibid., 2.100–1, No. 46.

[40] Famagusta: Lamberto di Sambuceto, ed. Balard (1983), 17–19, No. 13 (three enslaved Greeks); Lamberto di Sambuceto, ed. Balard, Duba and Schabel, 52–5, No. 42 (two enslaved Greeks); Lamberto di Sambuceto, ed. Polonio, 93, No. 80; 196, No. 168; 198–9, No. 170 (two enslaved Greeks); 198–9, No. 176 (two enslaved Greeks); 320–1, No. 269 (four enslaved Greeks); 396–7, No. 331; 418–20, No. 351; Lamberto di Sambuceto, ed. Balard (1984), 39–40, No. 19; 134, No. 63; 162, No. 92; 202, No. 134; Nicola de Boateriis, ed. Lombardo, 52–3, No. 48; 70–1, No. 66; Simeone di San Giacomo dell' Orio, summarised Otten-Froux, 96, No. 167; Candia: Angelo de Cartura, ed. Stahl, 97–8, No. 253; Verlinden, *L'esclavage*, 2.831 (four people) (notary Stefano Bon); Duran Duelt, 'Companyia', 571 (notary Angelo Cariolo); Valencia: Blumenthal, *Enemies and Familiars*, 36, 38 (a woman who declared that she was a Greek, but the authorities declared to be a Circassian).

and other parts of the Romanía to Genoa with deceitful promises of good treatment and sold there as slaves. Andronikos accordingly demanded that Greek children who had gone to Genoa of their own will but had not been sold into slavery by the Genoese should be recognised as free and allowed to go where they pleased.[41] This passage thus implies that Greek children were being taken captive by the Genoese of Pera by the early fourteenth century. This ordinance was promulgated only a decade or so later than the date of the earliest extant notarial evidence from Cyprus and Crete for the crisis of captivity. The lack of evidence for enslaved Greeks in Genoese sources suggests that the Genoese of the Romanía took this demand seriously. It is probable that the physical proximity of Pera to Constantinople and the inseparability of Genoese and Byzantine commercial interests contributed to the continued observance of this principle.

In terms of captivity, the outstanding event in Genoa's relationship with Byzantium was the Bosporus campaign of Paganino Doria in 1351–2, during which 766 Greeks are recorded as having been captured by the Genoese; these were put up for sale as slaves in Pera from 6 November 1351, but some were still unsold by the following spring. Many of these were purchased *en masse*, some of whom were children: Bartolomeo Lercario bought 290, Antonio Pallavicino 216 and Enrico di Rustico of Messina 150. They cost an average of fifteen *hyperpyra* each. A handful of acts drawn up in early 1352 by Tommaso Ottone, Doria's own notary, however, reveal what seem to have been private transactions involving individual enslaved Greek captives, and therefore the official number of 766 given in the records of the Genoese War Office may well be too low.[42]

Philotheos Kokkinos, at that time metropolitan of Herakleia and later patriarch of Constantinople, records in his 'Historical Speech' (*Logos Historikos*) the destruction caused and the captives taken by the Genoese. The captives fell broadly into two groups: firstly, those held by the Genoese in Galata/Pera (whom Kokkinos calls 'the barbarians'), and secondly, those Genoese who had been left behind to sack Herakleia, purportedly spending as much as two months turning the city over and digging up the ground in search of buried loot. Kokkinos records how the population of Constantinople gave alms to the captives, often at his own encouragement. The result of these efforts was that most of those taken captive were redeemed. The only reason that some people had not been redeemed was that the Genoese fleet had encountered some merchant ships near the

---

[41] 'Prima serie', ed. Belgrano, 113.
[42] Balard, 'A propos de la bataille', 441–2.

Bosporus and forced them to give up the Greek captive men and boys on board, and then had them sold into slavery once they reached port; presumably, these merchant ships had been taking these captives back to Byzantine Constantinople, only to be diverted to Genoese Galata.[43]

The treaty of 6 May 1352 that ended the Bosporus campaign, concluded between Emperor John VI Kantakouzenos and Admiral Paganino Doria, distinguished between Greeks who were entitled to release and those who were not. Greeks who had been captured by the Genoese from enemy Catalan or Venetian ships could be retained by the Genoese if those Greeks had been part of the enemy forces or joined them of their own volition. By contrast, Greeks who had been on those ships because they had been captured and taken there by force were to be released by the Genoese. This clause therefore drew a distinction between prisoners of war and non-combatants caught-up in the conflict.[44] This clause would become a reference point for decades to come, as two legal cases involving contested slave status, preserved in the Genoese State Archive, attest.

The first case sheds light on the immediate ramifications of the attack. It is a record of a dispute held in the presence of the vicar of the *podestà* (chief magistrate) in Genoa regarding the status of the enslaved Greek woman Lucia, captured during the Bosporus campaign. The document is dated only to 4 and 6 February, and not to any specific year, but its editors have suggested that it may be placed in 1365. Lucia claimed that she had been unjustly enslaved: the case rested on the question of when she had been sold, and how the timing of that sale related to the treaty concluded between John VI and Paganino Doria.

The text preserves a series of questions posed to Lucia, whose answers are given. Lucia was captured in the town of 'Recrea' – also spelled 'Recroa' in the document and perhaps both corruptions of 'Herakleia' – though she did not know by whom. At that time she was around thirteen years old. She was aware, however, that she was one of many Greek men and women who had been captured during that particular attack. Many of these Greeks had then been sold *en masse* to Bartolomeo Lercario and Antonio Pelavicino, who had then taken them to be sold at market in Theologo/Ephesus. It was said that Iacobus de Gauterio, brother of Viollante, had bought Lucia there. At Iacobus' death, Lucia had purportedly passed to Viollante, as his sister and heir. Viollante's assertion of her right to own Lucia rested on the contention that Lucia had been sold (viz. at Ephesus) before the treaty of 6 May 1352 was

---

[43] Philotheos Kokkinos, *Logos Historikos* 31, ed. Pseutonkas, Λόγοι καὶ Ὁμιλίες, 253–4.
[44] *Liber Iurium*, ed. Ricotti, 2. coll. 603–4.

concluded, and thus that her status was in accordance with its terms. Lucia denied that she had been sold to Lercario and Pelavicino, and denied that she had been among that group taken to Ephesus: if upheld, these claims would obligate her release. The outcome is not preserved in the surviving text.[45]

The second case reveals how the terms of the treaty were understood as setting a precedent against the enslavement of Greeks. The case concerns a woman called Caly (also spelled Cali or Calli), a common Greek name of the time. Caly was enslaved, but asserted that she was Greek, and as such should have been free; however, as an enslaved person, Caly could not by law participate in legal proceedings herself directly, and so was represented by a procurator, Martinus de Gavio.[46] Martinus brought a case against Caly's enslavers, Franceschina and Bernardus de Carraria de Sextus (Sestri), on her behalf; Bernardus nominated his wife as his procurator. The extensive paperwork from the case survives: multiple sheets in the Genoese State Archive record the facts of the case and the questions posed in court in the city of Genoa over a period stretching from 18 February to 14 April 1380.

The main issue at stake was Caly's origin. Caly had been sold to Bernardus by a tailor from Chios called Ianotus (Giannotto), then living in Famagusta, which was under Genoese rule from 1374. Ianotus had sold her on the pretence that she was a Tatar, but Caly protested that she was rather a Greek from Constantinople. Moreover, her original name was not Caly but rather Tedora: she had been given a new name at the time of her sale. The contracting parties and some witnesses were all questioned to try to ascertain the truth. The questions posed indicate that it was not always easy to distinguish Greeks from others: speaking Greek, as Caly did, made it plausible that she was a Greek herself, but it did not prove it, as plenty people of other origins could speak it well, too; moreover, on Cyprus, where Caly had been, people were sold into slavery under the label of 'Bulgarians', who also spoke Greek.

Caly's origin was of key importance because it would determine her status. In her case, the treaty of May 1352 was interpreted in the widest possible terms, as meaning that all Greeks 'in the city of Genoa and its district' (*in civitate Ianue et districtu*) ought to be free. On this basis, it followed that Caly should be free, too, but only if her claim to be Greek was upheld. The documentary record ceases at the point of Caly's interrogation.[47]

---

[45] Ed. Musso and Jacopino, *Navigazione*, 230–1, No. 1; see also Barker, *Most Precious Merchandise*, 34.

[46] Balard, *Romanie génoise*, 2.797 n. 44 and refs.

[47] Ed. Balletto, 'Presenze bulgare', 174–83 (Latin), 166 (Italian summary); incomplete English translation and discussion in Barker, 'Christianities in Conflict', 61–3.

As well as specific references to the terms of the treaty of 1352, it seems to have been possible to lodge a claim against enslavement in Genoa simply on the basis of being Greek. This is seen in the case of a woman called Elena who, on 19 November 1398, contracted a man from Verona to represent her interests against Babilano Alpano, who had attempted to reduce her to slavery; the document that records her case gives her as 'formerly a maid' (*olim famula*). Elena protested that she should not be enslaved, since she was of Greek parents and the enslavement of people of Greek parentage was prohibited by law.[48] The application of this general precept has parallels in Catalan and Sicilian contexts.[49]

The exceptional position of Greeks can be seen when the success rates of their legal challenges are compared with the success rates of other Christian groups. Armenians and Romanians are known to have lodged successful claims for their freedom. Bulgarians, who were in communion with Constantinople, received mixed responses. Christians from Russia or the Caucasus, who were likely also in communion with the Greeks, do not seem to have had any luck, and the records of their claims oddly do not cite their Christianity as a reason for their release. It therefore appears that Greeks occupied the least unfavourable position among the enslaved populations of Genoa; this cannot be understood merely as a consequence of their contingently recognised shared Christianity, given the fate of connected religious communities, and should be explained, above all, as a consequence of Byzantium's diplomatic relationship with Genoa.[50]

One of the most remarkable phenomena of the Greek presence in Genoa was the existence of a Greek consul. The consulship seems to have been instituted primarily as a means of representing the commercial interests of Greek traders in Genoa. In 1434, John VIII Palaiologos asked Genoa for reciprocal privileges mirroring those held by the Genoese in Pera, including a special building (*loggia*), a consul and a justice system. The *loggia grecorum* is attested in the fifteenth century, and so is the consul. The direct evidence for the consulship is unfortunately slight and limited to a few years at the end of the fourteenth century and the beginning of the fifteenth, making it difficult to know whether there was habitually a Greek consul in Genoa or for how long this post existed. The evidence comes

---

[48] Summaries and excerpts in Verlinden, 'Orthodoxie', 450 and Otten-Froux, 'Représentation', 105 (notary Jacobinus Nepitella).
[49] See Chapter 5, *infra*.
[50] Barker, *Most Precious Merchandise*, 30–1 details the differing success rates, though I prefer a politico-cultural explanation over her attribution of them to a Genoese racialised hierarchy.

from four acts, two of 1384, one of 1390 and one of 1418, the first three of which are contained in a single notarial chartulary drawn up by Benvenuto de Bracellis. These acts reveal that the consul was not just helping traders but also people who had been enslaved by Genoese subjects.

The first act, of 19 January 1384, records how Giovanni de Alegro, notary and *consul Grecorum pro illustrisimo domino imperatore Romeorum* ('consul of the Greeks for the illustrious lord emperor of the Romans'), helped a woman called Catalina. Catalina, the daughter of Ianis of Glarentza, had been sold as a slave to a man called Geronimo Barbavayra at some unspecified place and time. With Giovanni de Alegro's help, Catalina was able to stake a legal claim to Greek identity and thereby to assert her right to freedom. This came at a price, however, and she was obliged to pay 80 Genoese *libri* (pounds of silver) to Barbavayra to settle her release. A man called Domenico Bergucio advanced 25 *libri*, who also paid 6 *libri* in legal fees; to reimburse him, Catalina agreed to work for Domenico for eight years. What is notable about this case is that Catalina was from a family that came from a town, Glarentza, outside the Byzantine Empire; de Alegro's protection therefore seems to have extended to all Greeks, regardless of subjecthood.

Giovanni di Alegro was himself Genoese, not Greek; he came from Quinto, at that time a burgh close to Genoa and now subsumed as part of the city. From other documents, it is known that he held various official notarial positions between at least 1378 and 1404, in that latter year working for the Officium Gazarie, the Genoese agency responsible for the colonisation of the Crimea. He had received his appointment from the Byzantine emperor, John V Palaiologos, while visiting Constantinople as part of a diplomatic delegation in 1382. There was at least one other consul, Giovanni Rubeo, attested in 1418.[51] The position of the consul is yet another piece of evidence for Byzantium and Genoa's diplomatic and commercial relations helping to mitigate the trafficking of Greeks by Genoese, both in the metropolis and overseas.

Byzantine Relations with the Mamlūk Sultanate

Having addressed Genoa's role in the transregional and Aegean slave trades, it is now time to turn to a less widely studied topic: the question of where Byzantium and Greeks more widely fit in the slave trading networks that served the Mamlūk Sultanate.

[51] Otten-Froux, 'Deux consuls' and 'Représentation'.

Byzantium's diplomatic relations with the Mamlūks were at their most intensive in the late thirteenth century, but they continued until the early fifteenth. At least six embassies were exchanged between the two powers in the last decades of the thirteenth century starting in 1261–2, nine in the fourteenth, and one in the fifteenth; most of them were Byzantine initiatives, and most of them are attested only through Arabic sources. The particular intensity of exchanges in the late thirteenth century was probably due to their novelty and to the new geopolitical situation, with a Byzantine emperor once more in Constantinople and a new regime presiding in Cairo. The ambassadors included traders and, on the Mamlūk side, members of the princely or legal classes, most of whom participated in only one embassy. Melkite Christians – Arabic speakers in communion with Constantinople – associated with the Patriarchate of Alexandria, were especially important because of the role they played as Greek–Arabic interpreters. While embassies are variously noted in narrative sources, and while two letters survive – one in Greek from 1349 and one in Arabic from 1411 – the text of only one actual treaty survives: that of 1281 between Emperor Michael VIII and Sultan Qalāwūn. In general, these embassies had two purposes: first, the fostering of commerce, important to both parties but especially vital for the mamlūk slave system; and second, the reinforcement of Byzantium's tutelage over the Melkite Christians of the region.[52]

Byzantium's relationship with the Mamlūks was not just diplomatic but also commercial in nature, though this latter dimension has received less attention from scholars.[53] Greek merchants are sometimes incidentally noted as having traded in Egypt in texts that have another primary concern. One example of this is found in the list of reparation claims for damages done by Byzantine naval raiders and robbers that the Genoese, represented by Nicola Spinola, sent Andronikos II Palaiologos in 1294. This claim relates how in 1290/1 a man called Ranieri Boccanegra had agreed to convey some Greek merchants from Alexandria, in return for 500 *hyperpyra*. As a form of security, Ranieri had withheld the Greek merchants' goods to the value of that sum; this, the document states, was an entirely normal practice, and the goods would have been returned once

---

[52] Mansouri, *Recherches*, 114–33; Korobeinikov, 'Diplomatic Correspondence' (including the role of the Melkite patriarchate); treaty of 1281: Holt, *Early Mamluk Diplomacy*, 118–28; letter of 1349: Canard, 'Lettre'; letter of 1411: Mansouri, *Recherches*, 163–4 (reprint of H. Lammens' 1904 translation), 265–6 (Arabic text of al-Qalqashandī).

[53] The best study is Jacoby, 'Byzantine Traders in Mamluk Egypt'; see also Mansouri, *Recherches*.

the charges had been paid in full. When the party reached Constantinople, however, a man called Kinnamos – who is given as captain of the city – imprisoned Ranieri and made his release conditional upon return of the goods. The text implies that Ranieri must have been released, but the result (it states explicitly) was that he had been unable to recoup the 500 *hyperpyra*. A claim was therefore lodged against Andronikos to that value.[54] This episode offers anecdotal evidence for the presence of Greek merchants in Alexandria in the late thirteenth century, making use of Genoese shipping to transport themselves and their wares.

Another piece of anecdotal evidence from a similar period is the hagiography of the neomartyr Michael. Michael was born in the area around Smyrna in the later thirteenth century; he was captured by a Turkish raiding party, transported to Egypt, and there became a mamlūk. Michael's life is preserved in the unusual form of an oration, composed by the prominent late Byzantine intellectual Theodore Metochites. On the basis of the text's position in its manuscript, which is probably chronologically ordered, the oration can be dated to sometime between 1305–24 (the dates of the previous and following works). The oration was apparently performed publicly, with Emperor Andronikos II in the audience. Metochites used this oration to promote Michael as a saint (he is otherwise unknown) and may have been wishing to establish a model for how a Christian should behave when captured by Muslims.[55] This text incidentally mentions that in addition to the embassy party, there were Byzantines ('Romans') present in Alexandria for the purpose of trade – unsurprisingly, alongside Italians.[56]

Two fourteenth-century bilateral agreements include clauses intended to guarantee the safety and interests of Greek merchants in the sultanate. The earlier of these is the letter exchange undertaken in 1349 between Malik Nāṣir Ḥasan and John VI Kantakouzenos, one of the clauses of which provided for the safety of Byzantine merchants in the sultanate.[57] The second is the agreement of 1385 concluded between John V Palaiologos and al-Ẓāhir Barqūq. This treaty sought to safeguard the emperor's

---

[54] 'Nuova serie', ed. Sanguineti and Bertolotto, 521 and 542 (two versions); tr. Lopez and Raymond, *Medieval Trade*, 313; Jacoby, 'Byzantine Traders in Mamluk Egypt', 250–1.
[55] Pahlitzsch, 'Eis ton neon martyra Michaēl'.
[56] Metochites, 'Oratio', ch. 8, ed. Delehaye, 676 (= *BHG* 2273); Jacoby, 'Byzantine traders in Mamluk Egypt', 251.
[57] Text in Kantakouzenos, *Historia*, IV, 38, ed. Schopen, 3.97–8; for an analysis, see Canard, 'Une lettre'; Jacoby, 'Byzantine Traders in Mamluk Egypt', 256.

subjects who were engaged in trade in the sultanate and furthermore asked for the establishment of a consul in the city of Alexandria. This request may reflect an intensification of Byzantine trade in Egypt, perhaps because of the decline of other routes formerly relied upon by the Byzantines.[58]

The hard evidence for the existence of such a consul is, on current knowledge, limited to the acts of one single notary. This is the Venetian Niccolò Venier, who worked in Alexandria between October 1420 and December 1422. This evidence survives because of the trade undertaken between Greeks and Venetians in Alexandria; the Greeks had their own Greek notaries – such as Ser Patricius, mentioned by Niccolò Venier as active in Constantinople – but their acts are now lost. Niccolò's acts attest to the presence of two *consules Grecorum*: Blaixinus Chordi (whose surname was perhaps Kordeos in Greek), who was in office in November 1421, and Stellianinus Scitara (whose surname was perhaps 'Sitaris' in Greek), who in October 1422 was noted as the former consul, probably a close predecessor of Chordi. These men were distinguished in Niccolò Venier's notarial deeds from the consul of the Cypriots, Petrus Zexomeno, who also bears a Greek name; it is therefore almost certain that the 'Greeks' in this instance mean the subjects of the Byzantine emperor rather than Greek-speaking Christians in general. The fact that these men were Greeks, in contrast to the consuls in Genoa, perhaps suggests that Alexandria was a more important market for Greeks, with a larger resident community.[59] On available evidence, it is not possible to ascertain whether Greeks from outside the reaches of the empire might have appealed to the 'consul of the Greeks' in the way they could in Genoa.

This collection of evidence suggests that Greek merchants were more or less continuously involved in commerce in the Mamluk Sultanate from its beginnings to the 1420s, and maybe beyond. When coupled with the evidence for the involvement of Greek merchants in Black Sea trade, it seems plausible that Greeks were more often active as traders than trafficked as victims along the Black Sea–Egypt trade axis. This contrasts sharply with the Black Sea–Italy/Iberia axis of trade, in which the visible Greeks were subject to trafficking rather than being active as traders.

---

[58] Ashtor, *Levant Trade*, 105 (with references); Jacoby, 'Byzantine Traders in Mamluk Egypt', 257.

[59] Verlinden, 'Marchands chrétiens' (with partial editions of notary Niccolò Venier); Jacoby, 'Byzantine Traders in Mamluk Egypt', 251–4.

Greek Captives, Cyprus and the Mamlūk Sultanate

Several literary works indicate that Greeks were enslaved in the Mamlūk Sultanate, but there appears to be almost no documentary evidence (such as notarial acts) to corroborate this claim. The fifteenth-century Veneto-Cretan merchant Emmanuel Piloti wrote a list of the various groups sold as mamlūks in Egypt, giving a representative price for each: Tatars would raise 130 or 140 Venetian ducats; Circassians 110 or 120; Greeks 90; Albanians, Slavs and Serbians (listed separately) 70 to 80.[60] To the writers of Arabic slave-buying treatises, Greeks were *Rūm*: literally 'Romans', as the Islamic world at large generally accepted the Byzantines' self-definition as *Romaioi*, something that persisted throughout the Ottoman period.[61] These Arabic manuals include racialising statements on the characteristics to be expected from enslaved people according to their origins: Greeks, for example, might be described as thrifty.[62]

The question is, however, whether the inclusion of Greeks in such treatises reflected their actual presence in the slave markets of Mamlūk Egypt and Syria, or whether their presence in these texts is merely a formality, the product of a compilatory approach that incorporated potentially outdated information found in earlier works. Certainly, Greeks feature in the characterisations of enslaved people found in the eleventh-century Persian-language *Qābūs Nāma* of Kai Kā'us b. Iskandar, which arose from a Great Seljuk context in Iran: this text also praises Greeks as thrifty, as well as affectionate, but condemns them as 'foul-tongued, evil-hearted, cowardly, indolent, quick-tempered, covetous and greedy for worldly things.'[63] Perhaps in the case of Piloti, too, the inclusion of Greeks and other Balkan peoples is misleading. In order to evaluate the possible presence of enslaved Greeks in the Mamluk Sultanate, it is necessary to turn to Latin and Greek sources.

Of the c. 2,400 references in notarial and governmental sources to Greek or probably Greek enslaved people surveyed here, only one pertains to someone who was trafficked into slavery in the Mamlūk Sultanate. This was a woman called Frossini *de nacione Grecorum*, formerly called Sophya, the daughter of the priest Georgius of Negroponte and wife of the priest Dimitrius, also of Negroponte. In Candia on 28 May

---

[60] Piloti, *L'Égypte*, ed. Dopp, 15.
[61] El Cheikh, *Byzantium Viewed by the Arabs*.
[62] Barker, *Most Precious Merchandise*, 101 (with references).
[63] Kai Kā'ūs b. Iskandar, *Qābūs Nāma*, tr. Levy, 104.

1333, Gaytanus de Romania, who lived in Candia, manumitted Frossini: the act of manumission notes that Gaytanus had bought Frossini in Alexandria, where she had promised to pay him a fee for her manumission; as she had now paid that fee, she had secured her manumission.[64] It is possible that future research in Italian archives will yield further evidence, but in the meantime, this near-silence in the face of so much evidence from elsewhere may be considered indicative. The evidence for the involvement of free Greeks in Egyptian trade, while not voluminous, is nevertheless significantly more substantial than that for enslaved Greeks trafficked there.

One reason for this imbalance may be simple evidence bias. It is plausible that Latin merchants attempted to disguise the sale of enslaved Greek Christians to Muslim buyers by doctoring the details of documents of sale or by depositing such documents separately. The late medieval papacy showed considerable concern regarding the real or potential trafficking of Christians into slavery under Muslim masters: while the enslavement of Christians by Christians tended to be discouraged, the loss of Christian souls to Islam was viewed as intolerable. If Latin traders were selling Greek Christian captives into slavery in the Mamlūk Sultanate, they would have had good reason to avoid leaving receipts.[65] Such obfuscation was clearly not deemed necessary in Latin-ruled contexts – or, at least, not always deemed necessary, as it is worth being open to the possibility that enslaved Greeks were across the board deliberately misrepresented or unrepresented in the written records of Italians and Catalans.

Another possible reason for this imbalance, however, is the role that Cyprus may have played in disrupting the Black Sea–Egypt trade axis, by providing a safe haven for runaway Greek captives. A number of Greek-language texts – *aichmalotika* and historiography – testify to the arrival there of refugees from the Romanía, while two saints' lives indicate that some of these refugees may originally have been destined for slavery in Egypt or Syria.

The concentration of Greek-language literary evidence for redemptorist practices in early fourteenth-century Cyprus is unparalleled at any other time or for any other place. This evidence, however, is largely concentrated in only two manuscripts, both from Cyprus itself and both dating to the fourteenth century. The earlier example, compiled by three scribes

---

[64] Giovanni Similiante, Archivio di Stato, Venice, Notai di Candia, DIII Busta 244, fol. 134r, No. 9; text in Verlinden, *L'esclavage*, 2.836–7, n. 395.
[65] I thank Georg Christ for this observation (private communication).

during the years 1317–20, is a remarkable survival: it comprises a chancery manual, that is to say, a reference source for people tasked with drafting documents, used by secretaries of the Lusignan regime. Its documents cover a wide array of topics including diplomacy, law, the manumission of domestic slaves, and – crucially – the redemption of captives. It is today held in the Vatican Library.[66] The second, slightly later manuscript (compiled around 1343) is a composite work containing, among other things, poems, part of Anna Komnene's *Alexiad* and the single most numerous collection of Greek-language captivity-related texts to survive from the later Middle Ages. These texts fall into two main groups: first, testimonial letters (*aichmalotika*), which are preserved in the context of collections of letter templates, some of which are related to the letters preserved in the Vatican manuscript; second, sermons, which preserve few precise details but which express concern for the fate of captives fleeing to Cyprus. This manuscript is held today in the National Library of France.[67]

Two texts in the Parisian manuscript allude to this movement of people from the Aegean to Cyprus. One of the sermons speaks of 'our brethren who have been taken captive from the Romanía by the godless Ishmaelites; how, afflicted, forcefully dragged, maltreated, oppressed in hunger and in thirst, they have been borne to our famous island, even sold off as slaves.'[68] One of the testimonials was written for a captive from the Romanía who had been sold into slavery, ransomed himself and now arrived in 'the renowned island of Cyprus.'[69]

Among those practising the redemption of captives in Lusignan Cyprus, one individual stands out: the wealthy landowner, George Lapithes. Much of what is known about Lapithes and his redemptorist activities comes from the account of the historiographer Nikephoros Gregoras, who visited

---

[66] MS Vat. Pal. gr. 367, ed. Lampros, 'Κυπριακά' (3 pts.); re-ed., with tr. and comm., Beihammer, *Griechische Briefe und Urkunden*.

[67] MS Paris. gr. 400; this manuscript has attracted renewed scholarly attention recently, having been analysed by Lauxtermann, 'Poetry and Paraenesis' and Reinsch, 'Beobachtungen'; full transcriptions of the captivity-related texts are found thus far only in Saccon's unpublished MPhil thesis, 'Ransoming Activities', and partial transcriptions (compiled independently) in Grant, 'Cross-Confessional Captivity', 1.135–40 and nn.

[68] Paris. gr. 400, fol. 42r, ed. and tr. AG (ed. Saccon, 'Ransoming Activities', 10): οἱ ἀδελφοὶ ἡμῶν οἱ ἀπὸ τὴν ῥωμανίαν αἰχμαλωτιζόμενοι ὑπὸ τῶν ἀθέων ἰσμαηλιτῶν· πῶς θλιβόμενοι, συρόμενοι, κακοχούμενοι, ἐν λιμῷ καὶ δίψει πιεζόμενοι, φέρονται εἰς τὴν περιώνυμον ἡμῶν νῆσον, πωλούμενοι ὥσπερ ἔτι (τι Saccon) ἀνδράποδα.

[69] Paris. gr. 400, fols. 146v–147r, ed. and tr. AG (ed. Saccon, 'Ransoming Activities', 18): τὴν περιώνυμον νῆσον Κύπρον παρεγένετο.

the island sometime in the years 1342 to 1347, during the reign of Hugh IV de Lusignan. Lapithes was apparently a polymath versed in Latin as well as Greek and with an interest in astronomy. He took his name from the river Lapithos, and lived in the region of Lefkosia where he was able to participate readily in courtly circles. Gregoras is effusive in his praise of the man – his wisdom, his generosity, but most of all his care for captives who were frequently trafficked there. He contributed substantial sums to their redemption, sometimes covering almost their whole ransom, and instructed others in scripture. In Gregoras's words, 'in doing this, it is as though the whole of this island is a leisure ground of charity and faith, and most of all it is the captives' freedom.'[70]

Gregoras, however, had vested interests in praising Lapithes and in idealising Lusignan Cyprus. Both men were staunch opponents of the influential Gregory Palamas and his Hesychast (that is to say, contemplative, anti-scholastic) vision of Christian orthodoxy; in 1351–4, Gregoras was imprisoned for this position. In fact, the description of Lapithes is framed as part of a description of the eastern Mediterranean by a certain 'Agathangelos' ('the good messenger'), apparently a former student of Gregoras's who visited him in prison. Agathangelos may be little more than a literary device, a 'ventriloquist's doll' through which Gregoras could criticise the Byzantine political establishment and its support of Palamism by contrasting the purportedly better circumstances under which Greek Christians lived in other places, including Lusignan Cyprus. Gregoras's description of Lapithes's activities should therefore be read with caution.[71] The passage should not be completely dismissed, however, since the evidence adduced here confirms that Cyprus did function as a refuge for captives at this time.

The evidence for the role of Cyprus as a point of disruption for the transregional slave trade is much more circumstantial. It comes from a comparative reading of the lives of two Greek saints who are said to have been trafficked in the Levantine trade system at the end of the thirteenth century. Gregory of Sinai, born near Smyrna probably in the 1250s, was captured by Turks as a young man in about 1280; he was taken to Laodikeia, probably Lādhiqīya in Syria, whence he fled to Cyprus and later entered the Monastery of St Catherine on Mount Sinai. The other was Michael, who

---

[70] Gregoras, *Historiae Byzantinae*, XXV, 8, ed. Bekker, 3.27–9, German tr. Van Dieten, 5.55–6, English tr. AG: ... ὡς εἶναι δι' ἐκεῖνον πᾶσαν ἐκείνην τὴν νῆσον ἐλέου καὶ πίστεως στάδιον, καὶ μάλιστα πάντων αἰχμαλώτων ἐλευθερίαν.
[71] Kaldellis, *Ethnography*, 148–54. For Palamas, see Chapter 3 *infra*.

has already been mentioned in connection with the evidence his martyrology offers for the presence of Greek merchants in Mamlūk Egypt.[72]

Michael was captured by Turks from his home in the land around Smyrna. From there, he was taken to Egypt, apparently shipwrecked, 'and was baptised by those ruling there according to the abominable consecration ceremonies, idolatry, and profane gibberish of Muhammad'.[73] His youth and strength led him to be received into the military as a mamlūk, but he soon conceived of the aspiration to flee. When a Byzantine embassy arrived, he donned the habit of a monk in an effort to conceal his identity, with the object of escaping with this party; then, 'the noble man was betrayed and carried off to the heathens, truly according to <God's> desire, and it is impossible to say in how so glad a manner' – in other words, that he was ultimately happy to reveal his apostasy publicly.[74] After his betrayal, Michael steadfastly professed his Christian faith; he was tempted with threats and blandishments, cast into prison in chains and sentenced to death. The miracle associated with Michael was that his mouth was heard to implore Christ's mercy even after his death. This pattern conforms to the normative structure of martyrdoms,[75] and the language is polemicised; the narrative is probably not reflective of realities among Greek mamlūks, of whom there were in any case likely perishingly few. On the other hand, the fact that there is a neomartyrdom concerning a Greek mamlūk suggests that palatine slavery in Egypt occupied a corner of the late Byzantine consciousness.

Gregory's *Life*, meanwhile, is important less for what it tells its readers explicitly about his captivity than for what may be inferred and extrapolated from it about wider networks and systems of captivity and enslavement. Gregory was from Koukoulos in the vicinity of Smyrna; this accords closely with the recurring appearance in Latin notarial sources of western Asia Minor as a key locus of captivity around the turn of the fourteenth

---

[72] For broader discussions see Pahlitzsch, 'Byzantine Saints in Turkish Captivity'; Zachariadou, 'Neomartyr's Message'; Laiou, 'Saints and Society'; Krstić, *Contested Conversions*.

[73] Metochites, 'Oratio', ch. 2, ed. Delehaye, 671: αἰχμαλωτίζεταί τε καὶ ναυαγεῖ καὶ καταβαπτίζεται τοῖς ἐκεῖσε κρατοῦσι τοῦ Μωάμεδ μυσαροῖς τελεσμοῖς καὶ θρησκεύμασι καὶ παμβεβήλοις λήροις...

[74] Metochites, 'Oratio', ch. 5, ed. Delehaye, 673: προδίδοται γὰρ καὶ συλλαμβάνεται τοῖς ἀσεβέσιν, αὐτῷ μὲν κατ' ἔφεσιν ὡς ἀληθῶς, ὁ γενναῖος, καὶ οὐκ ἔστιν ἐρεῖν, ὅπως ὡς ἡδέως εὖ μάλιστα...

[75] For the conventions of martyrdoms, see Bayrı, 'Byzantium, the Union of Churches, Bulgaria and the Ottomans', 183; cf. Zachariadou, 'Neomartyr's Message', 59–63.

century. In Laodikeia, Gregory was apparently able to attend church services while in captivity, suggesting that he was allowed a measure of mobility and autonomy. It was purportedly his and his family's mellifluous chanting during these services that brought them to the attention of local Christians and inspired the latter to ransom the captives. Importantly, Gregory travelled subsequently to Cyprus. Firstly, this implies that the 'Laodikeia' to which he was brought was that in Syria, because this port city faces Cyprus. Secondly, if the life of Michael is taken as a foil, it implies circumstantially that Cyprus may have stood in the way of a trade route that supplied the Mamlūk Sultanate with enslaved Greeks captured in the Romanía.[76]

Both of these saints' lives shed light onto some of the more opaque elements of captivity. Greek captives generally become visible as individuals only at the moments when they passed through the hands of Latin traders, when transactions were entered into the ledgers of Latin notaries. Any Greek captives who were transported across Asia Minor and Syria by land and then sold into slavery in Syria or Egypt are far less likely to be mentioned in documentary evidence. Similarly, if they were ransomed by a Greek rather than a Latin, any notarial-style documentation that would attest to that act is almost certainly lost, if it ever existed. It is possible to infer that Michael's *vita* tapped into a consciousness of Greeks from Asia Minor in the mamlūk system without uncritically accepting the constructed narrative of his martyrdom as a window onto an individual and concrete reality.

Cyprus under the French Lusignan dynasty played an important role in crusading and crusade theory in the thirteenth and fourteenth centuries. This circumstantially corroborates the hypothesis that the island became a place of refuge for slaves destined for the Mamlūk Sultanate, or that it otherwise absorbed them. Even before the fall of Acre in 1291, Cyprus was intended as a place of departure for expeditions destined for Egypt: in 1248, an Īl-Khānid embassy came to the island to offer aid to Louis IX of France in his planned crusade against the Mamlūks, though the alliance was unfulfilled and the expedition failed.[77] After 1291, as the final beachhead of Latin Christendom in the Levant, Cyprus' strategic importance grew greater still. The Lusignans' crusading activities culminated in the sack of Alexandria by Peter I in October 1365; this devastating expedition was ultimately if belatedly avenged by the Mamlūk invasion of Cyprus in

---

[76] Kallistos, 'Βίος καὶ πολιτεία . . . Γρηγορίου τοῦ Συναΐτου', ch. 4, ed. Pomjalovskij, 3–4 (= *BHG* 722).

[77] See Grant, 'Mongol Invasions', 151 and n. 90.

1425–6, which reduced the island to tributary status and resulted in the captivity of its king, Janus, for some time in Cairo.[78] Gregoras and the *aichmalotika* talk of captives coming from the Romanía to Cyprus: it is possible that Cyprus's antagonistic relationship with the Mamlūks and its centrality to the crusading movement and to Latin Europe's interests in the Levant created the circumstances that led to this trend. The ports of Mamlūk Egypt and Syria were major centres for the consumption of slaves, largely from the Black Sea; it is entirely plausible that Greeks caught up in this trade were bought and sold in the ports of Cyprus, or that they fled there from Syria, Asia Minor or Egypt; once on Cyprus, they found help from clergy to ransom themselves and their families.

One final piece of evidence for this trend, albeit more circumstantial, is the only *aichmalotikon* to record a case of captivity among Tatars of the Golden Horde. On one occasion in the late thirteenth or early fourteenth century, the Tatars attacked a place called Pyrgoi; this was probably in Thrace, though as it is a common place name meaning simply 'towers', it is difficult to identify confidently.[79] Many captives were taken during the episode; among these were two children, whose father is the subject of this letter.

The father was perhaps not captured, or else he succeeded in securing his own ransom at an early stage. At some subsequent time, he found his two children after much searching in 'the city of Chasaria', that is, a city in the Crimean Peninsula, in the house of a man called Tattaboules. 'Tattaboules' may have been the man's title rather than his personal name, perhaps referring to someone of high standing within the Tatar community.[80] The father prevailed upon Tattaboules to offer his children for redemption at 550 *aspra* (silver coins) in total, thus 275 each; in order to pay their ransom, he needed to find financial help, and hence the testimonial had been written to encourage the faithful to give him alms.[81]

---

[78] Richard, 'Chypre face aux projets de croisade'; Coureas, 'Latin Cyprus and its Relations'; Luke, 'Kingdom of Cyprus, 1291–1369' and '1369–1489'.

[79] Possible candidates include Pyrgoi: Soustal, *Thrakien*, 138 = 277; Pyrgos: ibid., 418–19 [=likely Burgas]; Külzer, *Ostthrakien*, 606–7.

[80] Chasaria: Moravcsik, *Byzantinoturcica*, 2.334; my hypothesis regarding the name is extrapolated from ibid., 2.93–4, s.v. Βούλᾶς. Beihammer's identification (*Briefe und Urkunden*, 367) of 'Pyrgoi' as modern Kazımkarabekir, around three-quarters of the way south-southeast from Konya to Karaman, is implausible on the basis of this Crimean context.

[81] 'Κυπριακά', ed. Lampros (pt. 3), 339, No. 60; Beihammer, *Griechische Briefe*, 232–3, No. 100.

The occasion that gave rise to this letter is obscure. The chronology of some of the Tatars' attacks is known. An invasion by Nogai Khan was repulsed in 1285; after his death in 1299 or 1300, a period of comparative calm ensued as the Khanate's interests moved back to the Volga region. Further attacks were launched in 1320 and 1321, with a raid of 1324 coming close to Adrianople. In 1337 they undertook one last, large invasion, meeting and fighting Turks at the Hellespont and taking a large number of prisoners from Thrace.[82] As the manuscript was written in the years 1317–20, it is possible that the *aichmalotikon* dates either to c. 1285 or (perhaps more likely) to 1320.

Why did a text describing captivity in the Golden Horde end up being copied into a Cypriot manuscript? One possible explanation is that this text travelled along the trade artery that ran from the Black Sea to Egypt and Syria via Cyprus. It is possible that the bearer had come to Cyprus seeking alms, whether upon his own initiative or as a victim of trafficking himself. Whatever the circumstances, the existence of this letter suggests that Greeks participated in some level of connectivity along this route – something that would be invisible without this letter.

Arguably, the greatest insight that the evidence of the *aichmalotika* furnishes is the shift of redemptorist activity in the Greek Christian Mediterranean from Cyprus to Crete. This seems to have happened at some point in the third quarter of the fourteenth century, since this is the time at which evidence for the redemption of captives simply vanishes from Cyprus, and begins to surface on Crete. This may have been a product of specific political, social and economic changes in the region.

In 1373–4, the important Cypriot trading city of Famagusta fell to the Genoese. The early fifteenth-century Cypriot chronicler Leontios Machairas states that when the Genoese began the invasion of the island, they mobilised the enslaved population in their favour as a temporary expedient, apparently together with peasants, thieves and murderers. According to Machairas, the Genoese gathered an army of nearly two thousand men, comprising Bulgarians, Romans (Greeks) and Tatars, with whom they conquered Paphos in the southwest.[83] Presumably, many of these people were enslaved, as these three ethnic groups represented three of the major groups of enslaved people on Cyprus at that time.[84]

---

[82] Lippard, 'Mongols and Byzantium', 208–12.
[83] Leontios Machairas, Χρονικό, [§377,] ed. Pieris and Nicolaou-Konnari, 276, ed. and tr. Dawkins, 1.358–9; cf. Arbel, 'Slave Trade', 160–1.
[84] Arbel, 'Slave Trade'; Usta, 'Evidence'.

It is important to account here for Machairas's hostility towards the Genoese, however, which might have led him to exaggerate the extent to which their allies were people of ill repute. On the other hand, the social and economic destabilisation caused by their invasion is beyond doubt. After the Genoese invasion, Lusignan Cyprus was fundamentally crippled: the crown remained trapped in a never-ending cycle of debts, so impossibly enormous that they became a legal fiction exploited by the Genoese more for diplomatic collateral than for any realistic financial gain. Famagusta acted as a sort of maelstrom for the Genoese, gradually sucking all wealth and resources out of the Lusignan kingdom, and consuming a huge proportion of Latin Levantine trade.[85]

Machairas wrote that the Genoese conquest of Famagusta was an act of divine retribution for the Cypriots' negligence with regard to refugee captives from the Romanía:

> And if you wish me to tell you how it was that Famagusta was taken, I say that this was allowed by God because of our sins. And not Famagusta only: it would have been just that they should have taken all of Cyprus as well, because of our many sins. And to tell you about it openly, first of all was the sin of the slaves. The Romanía was being ravaged, and the men were being brought over to the islands as slaves and captives (τοὺσκλάβους κὰι ἀμάλοτα [sic]), and our people treated them so hardheartedly, that they used to throw themselves down from the roofs and kill themselves, and <some> of them cast themselves into pits, and <others> hanged themselves, for the heavy torments which they made them endure, and because they were famished.[86]

It is notable that evidence for redemptorist activities on Cyprus also ceases before this time; Machairas's account may therefore reflect a real change in circumstances. It is unclear how this new situation influenced the trafficking of Greek captives to Egypt or Syria, since there is so little evidence to rely on. It is however probable that the expanding Ottoman polity was retaining many or most of the Greeks captured during its expansion into the Balkans and that the numbers being trafficked beyond the Aegean were therefore shrinking by the late fourteenth century.[87]

---

[85] Bliznyuk, 'Diplomatic Relations'.
[86] Leontios Machairas, Χρονικό, [§482,] ed. Pieris and Nicolaou-Konnari, 338–9, ed. and tr. Dawkins, 1.464–7 (quotation from 465).
[87] This hypothesis is substantiated in Chapter 6, *infra*.

Conclusion

The transregional slave trade that brought people from the Black Sea into the Mediterranean has been extensively researched and is becoming progressively better understood. The captivity and enslavement of Greeks has also received attention, but this has often been fragmentary; the main problem, however, is that scholarship has not thus far adequately framed the distinctions and intersections between these two systems.

The eastern arm of the transregional slave trade emerged in the context of the development of the Mamlūk Sultanate, the seaborne part of which was facilitated or at least assisted by the cooperation of the Byzantine Empire in 1261–2. At this early time, the slave traders seem to have been Muslims, presumably Arabs from the Mamlūk Sultanate or perhaps Persians. Genoese traders probably played less of a role in this trade than generally thought, though there can be little doubt that they became involved heavily in the Black Sea slave trade and especially in the trade routes that brought these enslaved people to Italy and Aragon–Catalonia – the western arm of the transregional trade.

At precisely this same time, Byzantium's Asian frontier was being ruptured. At some point in the last four decades of the thirteenth century, Latin traders began exporting the Greeks captured in western Asia Minor by Turks. These traders were largely Venetians and, later, Catalans rather than Genoese; the Genoese seem on the whole to have honoured their close relationship with Byzantium and to have engaged only occasionally in trafficking Greeks – something undoubtedly made easier if the Genoese are understood to have had a larger share of the Black Sea slave trade than the Venetians or Catalans.

Greeks appear to have been more often actors than victims in the transregional trade. They had cordial diplomatic and commercial relations with the Mamlūks throughout the period of the two polities' coexistence and Greeks seem very rarely to have ended up enslaved in Egypt or Syria. There is some evidence that Cyprus, the most important crusader state in the fourteenth century, became a destination for Greek refugee captives from the Aegean region, at least until the Genoese invasion of 1373–4; some of these refugees may initially have been destined for the Mamlūk Sultanate.

Overall, these two slave trades – the transregional and the Aegean – emerge as distinct in their origins but overlapping in their operation in some specific and varied ways. In the transregional trade, Greek merchants are found active in the Black Sea–Egypt arm, but not enslaved Greeks; enslaved

Greeks are found copiously in the Black Sea–Italy/Aragon–Catalonia arm, but hardly any Greek merchants. Genoese merchants, meanwhile, are found far more often in the transregional than the Aegean trade; Venetians were important to both, Catalans perhaps more important to the Aegean than transregional trade. Zachariadou's schema of the two different slave trades has thus been comprehensively elaborated and analysed here for the first time.

Part II

Social Dynamics

*The man was lamenting and saying
that they had laid waste to all his property,
And having been sold...
he had wandered around from place to place
– not of his own free will,
but compelled by godless nations...*

(MS Paris. gr. 400, f. 146v, tr. AG.)

A refugee flees from the Aegean to Cyprus in search of charity having ransomed himself from Turkish captors, early fourteenth century.

Chapter 3
Captives, Slaves and Refugees

So far in this book, the categories of captive and slave have been largely taken for granted and only briefly defined in the Introduction. The identification and differentiation of captives from slaves in a late medieval Greek context is, however, far from straightforward. Ambiguities of medieval vocabulary and the apparent mobility of many of these people also make it difficult to tell whether someone was a refugee instead of, or in addition to being a captive and/or a slave. The process of disentangling these terms and their meanings is here approached empirically, through the aggregation of a wide range of examples in Greek, Latin and Western European vernaculars. This chapter tackles first the grey areas between captivity and slavery, examining the vocabulary applied by medieval authors to each of these phenomena as well as what medieval sources can reveal about experiences of these respective conditions. It then turns to the added complication of where refugees and mobility more widely fit into these two overlapping categories of unfreedom, closing with a consideration of the trends visible in the evidence for refugees' destinations. This disentanglement helps to answer the connected question of which terms scholars should use for which conditions.

Captives or Slaves?

It is often difficult to work out whether the people mentioned in late medieval Greek and Latin texts were captives or slaves. The most common Greek terms relevant to captivity are *aichmalotos* ('captive', literally 'taken [*alotos*] by the spear [*aichme*]'), *aichmalosia* ('captivity'), *andrapodon*, ('war captive', literally 'man foot'), and their associated verbs. The standard Greek terms for slave (*doulos, sklabos*) and slavery (*douleia*) occur too, but in the context examined here they are often found in combination with terms implying captivity. *Andrapodon* is, alongside *doulos*, the term that occurs most often in late Byzantine texts. It is, for instance, the usual term in the historiographical works of John Kantakouzenos and Laonikos Chalkokondyles for a war captive who was or who would be sold into slavery.[1]

Sometimes names or epithets appear to reference the memory of captivity, but remain ambiguous for lack of context. Niketas, a copyist from Cyprus, who held the rank of lector (*anagnostes*), described himself as 'thrice-wretched' (*trisathlios*) and 'thrice-captive' (*triploechmallotos*) in a manuscript subscript of 1359/60.[2] While it cannot be ruled out that Niketas was taken captive at some point, it is perhaps unlikely that he meant by this that he had been taken captive on three occasions; rather, 'thrice-captive' is probably a further term of self-deprecation that draws on a wider discourse of captivity current on Cyprus at that time. It is therefore important to be alert to the fact that the terminology of captivity may not always have been intended literally. In 1474, a text regarding the 'Antiquities of Constantinople and the Church of Hagia Sophia' was copied by a scribe who gave his name as 'Michael Aichmalotes'; in this case, it is possible that Michael had been taken captive at the fall of Constantinople in 1453, though this cannot be known for sure.[3]

The term *aichmalotos* was also imported directly into Latin. A treaty drawn up in 1358 between Venetian Crete and the Turkish beylik of Menteşe, for example, sets up terms for the exchange of ten Cretan captives held by Prince Musa of Menteşe – one woman (*donna*), nine other 'heads' (*capita*), and a more ambiguous 'all other captives of yours' (*alia omnia emalota vestra*) – in return for twenty-four Turks of Menteşe held by Duke Pietro Badoer of Crete. Musa was obliged to investigate all the captives he held, and should he fail to send all of them in the first instance, to send any remaining prisoners forthwith.[4] This usage is evidence for the exchange of vocabulary between languages of the Aegean, where Greek, Turkish, Italian, Catalan and written Latin all intermixed.

---

[1] For a full discussion of Greek terminology in the Palaiologan period, see Köpstein, *Sklaverei*, 31–55; Rotman, *Byzantine Slavery*, 82–93, covers the ground from a middle Byzantine perspective.

[2] Ed. Turyn, *Dated Greek Manuscripts*, 127 (he copied Oxford, Bodleian, Barocci 110. ff. 1r–362v). Turyn glosses this instance as 'refugee', a gloss discussed below.

[3] Raby, 'Greek Scriptorium', 19 and 29 (Αἰχμαλώτης; MS Istanbul, Topkapı Saray GI 6); I thank Prof. Costas Constantinides for drawing this reference to my attention.

[4] Ed. Zachariadou, *Trade and Crusade*, 217–18. The neuter plural *emalota* is equivalent to the Greek αἰχμάλωτα and probably refers to a mixed-gender or unknown group; cf. 'Κυπριακά', ed. Lampros (pt. 3), 339, No. 60, where the antecedents are two children (τὰ δύο τέκνα αὐτοῦ).

In Latin, sources usually focus on the enslavement of trafficked Greek Christians rather than on their capture. When enslaved Greek Christians are mentioned in Latin documentation, they are usually called *sclavi* – 'slaves' – often without any indication of how they became enslaved. The reason for this is simple: the bulk of relevant Latin documentation comprises notarial acts of sale or manumission, or else wills in which slaves are mentioned, usually because they were being or would at some later time be manumitted. In these circumstances, the individual's legal status was key: they were mentioned in the notarial act precisely because they were, in legal terms, enslaved.

Sometimes, in documents from Catalan-Aragonese contexts, unfree Greek Christians are referred to with the terms *captivus* or the vernacular *catiu*. Here too, though, the word seems to be ambiguous: sometimes it is used apparently synonymously with *servus* or *sclavus*; sometimes it is used precisely to describe a person who has been captured but not necessarily – or not yet – enslaved. Sicilian legislation of 1310 imposed a seven-year limit upon the possession of Greek slaves who professed Latin Christianity: the subject of the legislation is 'anyone who might have purchased a captive [originating] from the aforementioned Greeks of the Romanía and taken as a slave', thus quite clearly delineating the progression from captivity through purchase to enslavement.[5]

There are various other examples from further west. In 1341, a Greek called Nicholaus was sold in Manresa, Catalonia, by Bernat Hisogoll of Puigcerda and bought by Pere Exarcell, a painter of Manresa; he was described as a *servum et captivum*.[6] In 1393, Gregory of Thessaloniki, a Greek who (remarkably) served as bishop of Aguiló in Catalonia, became involved in efforts to release Greek Christians from unfreedom in Tortosa and Mallorca; in these documents, Gregory invoked a probably inauthentic papal bull to claim that Greek Christians were not to be held as slaves; in the first case, only the term *sclaus* is used, but in the second, the two possibilities of *catius ne sclaus* are given.[7] In 1400, a man named Georgius de Grecia complained that he had been tortured in order to profess in front of a notary that he was a 'slave or captive': *servum sive captivum*.[8] In Sencelles

---

[5] *Capitula Regni Siciliae*, 1.81, Cap. 72: *quicunque de praedictis Graecis Romaniae emerit captivum, et detulerit tanquam servum* . . .
[6] Verlinden, *L'esclavage*, 1.326–7.
[7] *DOC*, ed. Rubió, 669–70, No. DCXLII; 670, No. DCXLII. The alleged papal bull is discussed in Chapter 5, *infra*.
[8] Ed. Vincke, 'Königtum und Sklaverei', 106–7, No. 109 (see also Ferrer, 'Esclaus', 188).

(Mallorca) in 1428, Jordi Verd declared that he owned a *catiu* called Mitre (Dimitrios); the same description was applied to an unnamed slave of Pere Muntaner in Marratxi.[9]

The significance of this terminology is difficult to assess. It is possible that the inclusion of the term *captivus/catiu* implied an intermediary status short of total enslavement that left open the continued possibility of redemption, though this is not entirely clear.[10] This phrasing does not seem to have parallels in documents drawn up in other Latin communities, such as Venetian and Genoese possessions, therefore suggesting that the juxtaposition of the vocabulary of captivity and slavery, often in an apparently synonymous manner, was specific to the Catalan-Aragonese sphere. There is no obvious explanation for this disparity.

The broad disparity between the Greek and Latin terminology, meanwhile, arguably reflects a difference of perspective rather than of subject. The Latin sources are the records of the enslaving society, in which slave owners were concerned to possess documentary proof of their possession and freed slaves were concerned to possess proof of their manumission. In the Greek Christian sphere, on the other hand, the primary concern of the authors of the sources was the fact of dislocation: this was the moment at which they were seized from the authors' society, and whatever happened next was a consequence of that seminal act.

People who would have been called *aichmalotoi* in Greek texts therefore often appear as *sclavi* in Latin texts, and throughout this study these *sclavi* are understood ordinarily as both slaves and captives. (There are a handful of exceptions to this rule, considered in due course.) Reading late Byzantine and early Ottoman historiography gives one the general impression that violence, conquest, captivity and dislocation were integral to the experience of the late Byzantine world.[11] Reading Latin notarial documents that record financial and/or legal transactions on a day-to-day level reveals that many Greeks were trafficked into slavery, some of whom are explicitly noted to have been captured by Turks or by Latins, such as Venetians or Catalans.[12] These are two sides of one and the same coin. Not all people captured in the later medieval Mediterranean became slaves,

---

[9] Sevillano, 'Demografia', 182.
[10] Torró, 'De bona guerra', 499 (though this discussion is about the terms 'captive' and 'slave' in opposition to one another, rather than in apposition, as here).
[11] See further Chapter 6, *infra*.
[12] Some examples have already been considered in Chapter 1, *supra*, and there are more in Chapter 5, *infra*.

nor did all slaves lose their freedom through captivity, though many Greeks did fall into both these categories during this period.

The *aichmalotoi/sclavi* equivalence is not just a hypothesis but also a general principle derived from a number of clear-cut instances. Examples have already been cited of occasions when a vendor explicitly stated before a notary that he had captured the slave in question: to recap, these include Leo (1301), captured on Samos by Filipachis de Caristo of Negroponte; Soy (1301), captured in a naval raid; Nichita Sidherocasti (1303), captured by Phylippus Bocontolo, also in the course of a naval raid; Iohannes Glafchyrno (1306), captured by Marcus Belliparo in collaboration with three Turkish galleys.[13] The second category of evidence is the appositional use of 'captive' and 'slave' in texts from Catalan-Aragonese contexts. Evidence such as this forms the basis of the equivalence drawn between *aichmalotoi* and *sclavi*.[14]

There were several ways that a captive could enter a status of recognised slavery. This is something that can be studied particularly clearly in Latin contexts in both the eastern and western Mediterranean. When a captive was sold, a document would be drawn up recording the deed. Once this document was in existence, there would be a price attached to the enslaved person; this price would affect any efforts by family members to redeem them. More broadly, once a document of sale existed, the enslaved person would have to challenge their status on the basis of the legality or illegality of their enslavement. The bases for such a challenge relied on other, external legal frameworks, and included the diplomatic context of any act of captivity, the existence of treaties making provision for captives and/or slaves and the recognition of a religious or ethnic identity as grounds against enslavement.[15]

Another route by which a person's enslavement might be legally recognised was through a declaration by the would-be enslaved individual. If no obvious paper trail existed, a trafficked person might be in a position to claim before a tribunal that there was no legal basis under which they might be deprived of their freedom. Their traffickers could try to eliminate this

---

[13] Benvenuto de Brixano, 81, No. 220; 172, No. 478; Stefano Bono, ed. Pettenello and Rauch, 251–2, No. 568; Angelo de Cartura, ed. Stahl, 221, No. 570. These examples were discussed *supra*, 40–1, 44.
[14] For Arabic terminology, see the discussion of Ibn Baṭṭūṭa and al-ʿUmarī in Chapter 6, *infra*.
[15] This theme, touched upon briefly with reference to Genoa in Chapter 2, *supra*, forms the subject of Chapter 5, *infra*.

possibility by demanding a declaration of enslaved status before a public notary. A good example of this is Georgius de Grecia, already mentioned in this chapter: a man called Dalmacius held him in chains in Castellbisbal, Catalonia, for seven years, trying to get him to confess in front of a notary that he was a 'Saracen' (and therefore a Muslim) and Dalmacius's 'slave or captive'.[16] Here, Georgius's ethnicity and by extension his religion were also at stake, but for current purposes the most important point is that Dalmacius needed Georgius to make a public declaration of his obligations to him before Dalmacius could have the necessary documentation to enforce his enslavement.

The captive/slave equivalence does not always hold in the case of Greeks, but cases where a person entered enslavement through routes other than captivity are comparatively rare. Sometimes, people sold or gave themselves into slavery to pay off debts. This was the case for a woman called Cristiana from Achaia, the northwestern Peloponnese: in Trani, southern Italy, in May 1268, Cristiana indentured herself to Sire Marthoro de Aucleno of Ragusa (Dubrovnik) for a period of ten years to cover a debt of two ounces of gold owed to a third party, Nicola Portajncase of Trani, which Marthoro had reimbursed.[17] It was also the case for Herini, who in Candia in October 1328 was pledged by her father, Georgius Papadopulo, a free man (*francus*) of 'Cavalu', to Johannes Leffa of Candia: she was to live 'as if your daughter, and to remain and live with you throughout your life'.[18] This contract uses phrasing that is shared, for example, with self-enslavement deeds from Ragusa,[19] in particular the clause stating what Herini should receive in return: food, clothing and footwear (*victum et vestitum et calciamenta*). Herini is called *filia tua anime*; this term, literally meaning a 'soul', referred in Venice to children who provided forced labour under theoretically fixed-term debt bondage contracts.[20] The comparable term *psycharion* ('little soul') appears in Greek as one among many possible terms for an enslaved person; the reference to the soul may reflect the Christian understanding, in contradistinction to the ancient Greek understanding, that enslaved people were spiritual equals of free people, despite

---

[16] Ed. Vincke, 'Königtum und Sklaverei', 106–7, No. 109 (see also Ferrer, 'Esclaus', 188).
[17] 'Neobjavljene isprave i akti', ed. Lučić, 390–1, No. 16; Krekić, *Dubrovnik*, 169, No. 9.
[18] Giovanni Similiante, Archivio di Stato, Venice, Notai di Candia, DIII B. 244, fol. 77r, No. 8: *ex nunc in vita tua do et promitto (?) tamquam pro filia tua anime ad standum et habitandum tecum in vita tua.*
[19] Skoda, 'People as Property'.
[20] Barker, 'Trade in Slaves', 118–19.

differences in corporeal circumstances.[21] Although the act does not state the reason that Herini was pledged to Johannes, it is likely, on the evidence of Cristiana, that it was because of financial hardship or debt.

Contracts of self-enslavement or enslavement by family members look very similar to some clauses of skill-based obligations. To take one example, on 16 September 1387, Nichitas Lagniti, a Greek, gave his son Michael to Domenico Zorzi, a Venetian. Just like Johannes Leffa, Domenico had to give accommodation, food and clothing to Michael, whom he was allowed to treat as if he were a slave. What distinguishes this contract from those examined above is that Michael was to learn from Domenico how to read.[22] This was not a straightforward case of destitution, but rather a means of acquiring a rudimentary education through a contractual relationship that occupied a position somewhere between an apprenticeship and slavery.

It is, thus, challenging to distinguish captivity from slavery on the basis of terminology. Differences in language (Latin vs. Greek) and perspective (society of the enslaved vs. society of the enslaver) contribute to this obfuscation, which can be in part dispelled by analysing examples where the relationship between captivity and slavery is either clearly illustrated or at least implied. In many instances, the second condition followed as a consequence of the first, but that was not always the case. From a methodological standpoint, the establishment of this relationship between captivity and slavery allows this book to discuss the captives of Greek sources and the slaves of Latin sources as belonging to the same historical phenomenon.

Experiences of Captivity

Examining terminology is a useful way of determining who may be described as a captive, but another fruitful approach is considering what an experience of captivity might have looked like. Unfortunately, there are not many detailed Greek-language narratives of captivity for the period under study here, and those that have survived were written by educated elites.[23] Historians of captivity in earlier periods of Byzantium's history are arguably in a better position in this regard due to a richer wealth and a wider range of hagiographical evidence.[24] Despite these drawbacks,

---

[21] Zepos, '«Ψυχάριον», «Ψυχικά», «Ψυχοπαίδι»', 17–20.
[22] Summary in McKee, *Uncommon Dominion*, 119 (notary N. Tonisto).
[23] For literary analysis of descriptions of captivity from across the Byzantine period, the reader is directed to Goldwyn, *Witness Literature*.
[24] Well exploited by Rotman, *Byzantine Slavery*.

however, the surviving late medieval Greek narratives provide details that can serve as points of reference for the interpretation of less detailed mentions of instances of captivity.

Perhaps the most famous example of a Greek captured in the later Middle Ages is the monk Gregory Palamas (1296–1359), archbishop of Thessaloniki. Palamas is particularly famous for his role as a leading Hesychast, that is to say, a follower of a devotional practice that used deep meditation and repetition in opposition to the scholarly modes of theology and philosophy emanating from Italy in the later Middle Ages, and which was ultimately accepted as imperial orthodoxy.[25] Palamas was taken captive near Gallipoli, where the Ottomans had recently established themselves, while on his way to Constantinople in March 1354. He wrote to his congregation in Thessaloniki describing his ensuing captivity at Pegai and Nicaea in the Ottoman beylik, which lasted for over a year. Palamas was released in the summer of 1355, perhaps ransomed by John VI Kantakouzenos or by some Serbian backers, after which he returned to Constantinople. He may have written the first part of his letter to his congregation in July 1354.[26]

Palamas's experience has attracted attention not primarily for the study of his captivity per se, but rather because his captivity led to a number of inter-religious dialogues. The circumstances of his captivity led to his involvement in a doctrinal dispute at the Ottoman court with people known as 'Chiones', described both by Palamas and by Taronites, Orhan's Armenian physician;[27] the Chiones were probably Jewish converts to Islam.[28] The details of these discussions have been discussed and contested by generations of commentators, and it is doubtful that much could be added here. Two points are worthy of note for the present purposes, however. The first is general: that

---

[25] See for example Meyendorff and Gendle, *Triads*, 1–24 (introduction), Krausmüller, 'Rise of Hesychasm', Casiday, 'John XIV (Kalekas)' and James, 'Byzantine Realpolitik'.

[26] Philippidis-Braat, 'Captivité', 109–13; Sahas, 'Captivity and Dialogue', 410–11; Laiou, 'Saints and Society', 93.

[27] The texts are in fact three in number, and have been edited and translated into French by Philippidis-Braat, 'Captivité': the letter to his congregation (136–65), Taronites's *Dialexis* (168–85), and a letter to an unknown recipient that repeats the narrative of his stay at Nicaea (186–90; no tr.). The first two were translated into English on the basis of older published Greek texts by Sahas, 'Captivity and Dialogue', and have been more recently translated by Russell, *Debate with Islam*, 385–412. Taronites is often given as being Greek, but Grierson, 'We Believe in Your Prophet', 111, identifies him as Armenian; his name might mean 'of Tarōn'.

[28] A recent article holds that they were a combination of Jews and Judaising Christians who were turning towards Islam: Balivet, 'Byzantins judaïsants et Juifs islamisés'; the bibliography of previous studies may be found in Balivet's notes.

these discussions are usually characterised as having found far more points of agreement between Christianity and Islam than they really did. Palamas's Hesychast doctrines, moreover, show no evidence of having changed as a result of these dialogues, while it is worth noting that one of the Chiones apparently hit Palamas in the face after their discussion (though to the horror of the others). The second point is specific: the mediator of the conversation with the Chiones was someone whose name is given as 'Palapanes', that is, *Balaban*, a formerly Christian slave and courtier of Orhan who acted as one of his military commanders.[29] Leaving aside the Chiones and Palamas's religious debates for now, the following remarks relate to the circumstances of his captivity, the aspect so far less explored.

Palamas relates that, upon his captivity, his captors overestimated his ability to ransom himself. He writes that 'my entire property, as one can find many who know this, consists only of what I need every day': this suggests that he would not have appeared to his Ottoman captors to be particularly rich. On the other hand, during the first week of his captivity, Palamas's captors observed that the other Christians repeatedly sought his attention. Palamas would have his readers believe, therefore, that he, despite his high office and standing, was all but indistinguishable from the other humble monks in his presence. The monks were then separated from the rest of the party on the eighth day and taken to Pegai, on the Asian side of the straits, where the captors continued to pressure them into paying money for their ransom – money which, of course, Palamas says they did not possess.[30] Keeping captives under arrest without putting them to work or selling them as slaves would have been costly; whether or not Palamas was telling the truth, it seems reasonable to accept that the wish to ransom captives quickly was a commonsense approach. The Ottomans had, in fact, already set a precedent for the capturing of senior Greek clergymen by the time they took Palamas. The life of St Dionysios relates that Theodosios, *hegoumenos* (head) of the Athonite house of Philotheou, was carried off to their capital of the time, Prousa/Bursa, on 25 March 1348. He was subsequently redeemed by the charity of coreligionists.[31]

---

[29] Grierson, 'We Believe in Your Prophet', with references.
[30] Ed. and tr. Philippidis-Braat, 'Captivité', 144–5; tr. Sahas, 'Captivity and Dialogue', 415; tr. Russell, *Debate with Islam*, 390; on this episode see also the comments of Pahlitzsch, 'Greek Orthodox Communities', 160–1. Palamas and the risk of high ransoms are also discussed in Grant, 'Gottlose Korsaren', 63–4.
[31] Metrophanes, Βίος τοῦ Ὁσίου Διονυσίου, ch. 39, ed. Laourdas, 58; Živojinović, 'Turkish Assaults', 513–14; Laiou, 'Saints and Society', 93.

In Pegai, Palamas and his companions met with a local secular community leader, called Maurozoumes. This man held the title of *hetaireiarches*, and although this position was not a high-ranking dignity by the middle of the fourteenth century, it appears that Maurozoumes was the recognisable head of the Christian community in Pegai.[32] The captives were received at a church and comforted. When Palamas describes the hospitality that the group received, he quotes from Matthew 25, which was the most frequently cited biblical chapter in clerical letters of intercession on behalf of captives. As well as making sure they had the opportunity to partake in worship, Palamas writes that Maurozoumes 'gave us shelter, and since we were naked he clothed us, and hungry he gave us food, being thirsty he gave us drink. He actually nourished us for almost three months.'[33]

The next stage of his captivity, from July 1355, was spent at Nicaea. The circumstances of this slightly later period are revealing, since Palamas implies that he had considerable freedom in what he spent his time doing, and in whose company he spent it. Palamas seems to have been aware that he would find better conditions there than in Pegai, since he used the intercession of Taronites, Orhan's doctor, to help secure his transfer there. He was able to live among the Christians in Nicaea, in the district surrounding the Monastery of St Hyacinth.[34] It has been remarked that while most Christian sources imply that Nicaea had quickly lost its Christian population, and while Christians in western Asia Minor seem almost invisible in contemporary Islamic sources, this was clearly not an accurate reflection of reality.[35] Certain Christian communities appear to have retained their integrity and continued to worship, as evident in Nicaea as in Pegai. A similar situation is implied by Kallistos's *Life* of St Gregory of Sinai: after his and his family's capture by Turks c. 1280, he was taken to Laodikeia (probably the Syrian Lādhiqīya), where he was able to attend church services despite his captivity, thanks to which he attracted the charity of the local Christian congregation.[36]

---

[32] Kazhdan, 'Hetaireiarches'.
[33] Ed. and tr. Philippidis-Braat, 144–5; tr. Sahas, 415–16; tr. Russell, 390 (quoted here): ὅς ἡμᾶς καὶ ὑπὸ στέγην ἤγαγε καὶ γυμνοὺς ὄντας ἐνέδυσε καὶ πεινῶντας ἔθρεψε καὶ διψῶντας ἐπότισε, μᾶλλον δὲ διέτρεφε μικροῦ δέοντος ἐπὶ μῆνας τρεῖς ... The importance of Matt. 25 is discussed *infra*, 116 (and 105).
[34] Ibid., ed. and tr. Philippidis-Braat, 150–3; tr. Sahas, 424; tr. Russell, 393.
[35] Pahlitzsch, 'Greek Orthodox Communities', 160–1.
[36] Kallistos, 'Βίος καὶ πολιτεία ... Γρηγορίου τοῦ Συναΐτου', ch. IV, ed. Pomjalovskij, 3–4. This text has already been discussed *supra*, 75–7.

One companion of Palamas's, Konstas Kalamares, was freed to Prousa, where he lived with 'a certain pious man' who had paid for part of his ransom. Palamas helped by raising the remaining amount of money due for his freedom. He laments the irony of the situation, and his words are worth quoting in full:

> This person had not produced the whole ransom until, by the help of God, or rather by his working a miracle, I ransomed him completely and he was free. I did not take him with me at that time, for I did not know where I would end up. But now having sent for him by letter, I the captive have a freedman as a companion and servant. Here is a situation to be added to the novelties recounted: the captive grants liberty to his fellow captive and has a freedman under his authority, when he is not yet master of himself.[37]

This passage offers insight into mechanisms of redemption and power relationships arising from charitable acts. Kalamares had secured his initial release on receipt of a down-payment; this was not, though, the full cost set for his release, and Palamas was required to make up the shortfall. Unfortunately, Palamas does not specify how he did this, but it is possible that he secured charitable donations through his own influence among local Christians in the places of his captivity. (Palamas's own ransom would almost certainly have been set at a much higher price than that of the relatively unknown Kalamares, which probably explains why Palamas was forced to remain in captivity.) Despite the fact that Palamas occupied the outwardly lowlier status of captive than Kalamares, the free man, Palamas's help had created a relationship of indebtedness on the part of Kalamares.[38] The archbishop's high social standing will also have influenced Kalamares's behaviour, whatever the monetary sums involved. Charity towards captives had biblical, patristic and legal precedents to sanction it, but it also came with the possibility of asserting a new personal, power-based relationship between redeemer and redeemed. The creation of such relationships may have been one of the motivations on account of which Greek Christians gave alms towards the freeing of captives.

---

[37] Palamas, *Epistole*, ed. and tr. Philippidis-Braat, 'Captivité', 153; tr. Sahas, 425; tr. Russell, 393–4 (quoted here; excerpt from 394).

[38] For charity and the forging of social obligations, see Stathakopoulos, 'Thoughts on the Study of Charity'. Charity is discussed further in Chapter 4, *infra*.

The case of Palamas is important for what it reveals of the circumstances of his captivity and the mechanics of his redemption. However, his account is certainly ideologically driven, and his narrative should not be accepted uncritically. It has been suggested that this account of his captivity was merely a vessel for defending his own Hesychast vision of orthodoxy: by placing himself in conversation with the Chiones, he could present his own doctrinal position as obtaining the respect of Orhan's courtiers. He may have combined various tropes of religious dialoguing in order to communicate to his congregation a message of intellectual and theological triumph.[39]

The whole episode was read entirely differently by his religious opponent, Gregoras. Gregoras wrote that Palamas was sodomised by his initial Turkish captors, and while Palamas protests that he could not pay his ransom because of his self-imposed monastic poverty, Gregoras claimed that his body was covered in concealed gold and silver. Palamas thus cast himself as spokesman of his own vision of orthodoxy to the Turks, while Gregoras portrayed him as emasculated and tainted by Islam.[40] While it is likely that Palamas and Taronites both represented Palamas's dialoguing in a way designed to reflect well on them and what Palamas stood for, it is however also likely that the events mentioned (including his captivity) all happened – though not perhaps exactly as described. Palamas's text is also surely engaged with broader discourses of captivity current in the mid-fourteenth-century Byzantine world, and to this extent its context is also far larger than the Hesychast controversy alone.

The conquest of Thessaloniki by the Ottomans in 1430 provides the context for the second narrative to be considered here. Thessaloniki had been under Ottoman rule from 1387–1403; in the context of the disruption following Tīmūr's victory over the Ottoman Sultan Bayezid I at the Battle of Ankara (1402), it was returned to the Byzantines by the Ottoman Prince Süleyman. In 1423, one year into an eight-year siege, the Byzantines ceded the city to the Venetians, hoping that the latter might be able to maintain its defence. When the Ottomans occupied the city for the second and final time in 1430, the Venetian garrison sailed away to leave the inhabitants suffer the consequences alone; since the Venetians had resisted rather than

---

[39] Kaldellis, *Ethnography*, 154–6.
[40] Nikephoros Gregoras, *Historiae Byzantinae*, XXIX, 7–9, ed. Schopen, 3.227–9; Kaldellis, *Ethnography*, 154–6. Kaldellis reads this episode in contrast to pro-Latin Gregoras's description of Lapithes (discussed *supra*, 74–5) and very favourable attitude towards the conditions of Lusignan Cyprus, interpreting this as an effort to convince his readers that he had the Latins' validation.

surrendered, Islamic law permitted the Ottomans to sack the city.[41] According to Chalkokondyles, certain inhabitants had conspired with Murad for the betrayal of the city, only to be foiled by the Venetians.[42] Chalkokondyles, born in Athens c. 1427–30, could hardly have remembered the event himself, but his sources impressed upon him that 'this was the biggest calamity suffered by the Greeks, second to none that had happened before.'[43]

John Anagnostes, in his account of the aftermath of the capture, relates that the Ottomans held 7,000 captives restrained in their tents, setting a ransom price on each person. The Ottomans told their captives that they would attain freedom if they revealed where they had hidden their property; since many had deposited their wealth in the churches or tombs, this led to the widespread destruction of these. Sultan Murad apparently expelled the soldiers of the general Sinan that had taken the city and subsequently taken up residence in its empty houses: he wished to keep the buildings for himself, and told Sinan's men that the loot and captives were reward enough for them.[44] Murad then ransomed the leading inhabitants himself, but the fate of the rest remained in the balance:

> At this point a final division of the captives took place. Those prisoners who found some means of gaining their freedom in one way or another, either by being ransomed in the manner previously mentioned, or from their own funds or from the funds of other Christians collected from various lands and cities, were released while Murad was still staying by the river Gallicus. But as for those who had no way of managing this at this time, the Turks sent them away to their own lands and districts, to be subjected to the constraints of slavery until the time when they themselves had returned home and could arrange prices for them; they could not take them with them, since they were setting out on a long journey and going to another war [that is, west towards Ioannina]. You could then have seen the victims scattered, some to the east and some to the west. Some Turks took the fathers, others the children and others again their mothers, and thus those whom nature had made one were sundered by an evil fortune.[45]

---

[41] The best discussion of Thessaloniki in the fourteenth and fifteenth centuries and of its Ottoman conquests is Necipoğlu, *Byzantium between the Ottomans and the Latins*, 39–115. The issue of resistance vs. surrender is addressed in Chapter 6, *infra*.
[42] Laonikos Chalkokondyles, *Histories*, V, 21, ed. Darkó and tr. Kaldellis, 1.388–91.
[43] Ibid., V, 22, 1.390–1.
[44] John Anagnostes, Διήγησις, 14–16, ed. Tsaras, 40–50, tr. Melville-Jones, 166–71.
[45] Ibid., 17, ed. 50–3, tr. 172–3.

This passage provides a richness of detail unusual in Palaiologan-era accounts of captivity. Christians who had enough wealth to pay their ransom immediately were, after the elites, the most likely to be freed quickly. Others would need to turn to charitable networks at a trans-regional level; this is clearly reflected in the *aichmalotika*. It is also clear that it was in the interests of the Ottomans to ransom their captives efficiently, since it was impractical and undesirable for an army on the move to support a train of non-combatants, most of whom were likely to have been women and children, assuming that the men were more likely to have been killed during the sack. A family might have been separated in the disorder of conquest and plunder – another recurring theme of the *aichmalotika*. Anagnostes's description offers a valuable foil to Palamas's narrative of his experience, in which a larger cross-section of the population is in view.

Experiences of Slavery

While narratives of captivity shed light on what happened during and immediately after an act of dislocation, there is also a wealth of information, largely in Latin sources, concerning the nature of experiences Greeks might have once they were in a state of confirmed enslavement. Much of the best evidence comes from the Crown of Aragon, a patchwork of Mediterranean territories ruled by Catalan monarchs: here, the spread of documentation is more varied than that for Venetian or Genoese contexts, including things as diverse as detailed tax records, post-mortem estate inventories and safe conduct passes. These, when combined with the more familiar notarial acts and governmental legal decisions, allow for a number of rare insights into the degree to which the diaspora of unfree Greeks under the Crown of Aragon did (or did not) integrate, both before and after manumission, into the societies that had enslaved them. This diaspora appears to have included enslaved people of unprecedentedly old age; some, after manumission, took Greek slaves of their own; there is also evidence for a continued sense of community and common identity among the diasporic community, which transcended the line between slavery and freedom. For all of these reasons, the Catalan-Aragonese evidence cannot necessarily be extrapolated to other contexts, but it is revealing in its own right of the lived experiences of a substantial number of people.

A significant source for data on the demographics of the Greek slave population on Mallorca is the enormous dossier of declarations dating from April and early May 1388, in which Mallorcans gave notice of the enslaved people in their households. Mallorca was at this time part of the

Crown of Aragon, having been an independent kingdom until its annexation in 1343–4.[46] This dossier contains mention of 385 individual Greeks, though it is probable that the real number was higher, since some owners gave incomplete declarations in other instances.[47] Frustratingly, very little detail tends to be given regarding the Greeks themselves; much more is known about their owners, since the occupation, status and/or place of residence of each is usually supplied. Slavery was evidently widespread across a large cross-section of Mallorcan society, since merchants, drapers, dyers, pharmacists, notaries and bakers (among others) all had their own slaves: in other words, members of the artisanal or professional classes. This was not dissimilar to the situation on contemporary Crete. Many of these Greeks were in *tallia/talla* or *setmaner* contracts, that is, in work-release arrangements: an enslaved person in work-release could carry out certain paid tasks (often carrying bread to municipal ovens) in return for cash; that person would then save this money with the intention of buying their freedom.[48]

While little can be said about individual Greeks, it is possible to discern trends at the level of households. First, whole families of enslaved Greeks, with parents and children living together in the same home, were not uncommon. Isabel, widow of Bernat Castayó, for example, owned Lucia together with her two (unnamed) daughters, aged thirteen and six.[49] While numerous sales are attested in the Aegean involving a pregnant mother, or a mother with a baby or small child,[50] older Greek children tend not to be found still living with their parents as they are on Mallorca. A twenty-five-year-old unnamed male slave of the pharmacist Pere Ses Eres is noted as having been the son of a Turk and a Greek, and was thus perhaps the son of two enslaved people.[51] Pericona, also called Pobleta, was the slave of Lorens de Puigperdius Bellver, aged eighteen at the time of the declaration; she was her master's illegitimate daughter (*borda*), noted to have been born 'of a certain Greek female slave' and brought up in his

---

[46] Bisson, *Aragon*, 106–7.
[47] See Hillgarth, 'Greek slave', 552, for an example.
[48] These examples are taken from the unpaginated appendix to Cateura, 'Politica'; for a discussion of these terms, see Mummey, 'Women, Slavery, and Community', 157–62.
[49] Cateura, 'Politica', appendix (unpaginated).
[50] For cases in the 1380s, see, for example, Verlinden, *L'esclavage*, 2.848 and n. 459, 2.849 and n. 461, 2.852 and n. 475, 2.852 and n. 477 (notary Manoli Bresciano, Crete).
[51] Cateura, 'Politica', appendix (unpaginated). He was one of three enslaved people whom Pere Ses Eres declared, all of whom were in work-release contracts (*en talla*) to buy their freedom.

house (*filia nutricata in domo cuiusdam serve grece dicti Laurencii*).[52] This anecdote is the briefest of allusions to a – certainly widespread but little discussed – aspect of medieval Mediterranean slavery, as all forms of slavery: the sexual exploitation of enslaved people, especially of enslaved women by male members of the household that claimed ownership over them.[53] Among these 385 individual Greeks, seven family groups and one married couple are attested.

Also striking is the old age of some of these people. Over 40% are given as being between forty to fifty years old, nearly 20% aged between sixty and eighty, while 2.8% (five individuals) are listed as being over the age of eighty.[54] By comparison, enslaved people in late fourteenth-century Genoa are estimated to have obtained their freedom on average around the age of 25 to 30, whether through manumission, redemption, escape or other means.[55] The implication of this evidence is that people might remain enslaved for life on Mallorca, whereas in Liguria a person could expect to be freed while still young. This might perhaps suggest that the influx of new slaves had declined over the fourteenth century, leading to a requirement for ageing slaves to be retained. Another piece of evidence confirms this picture of a declining population: at some point in the fourteenth or earlier fifteenth century, a brotherhood of manumitted Greeks had been established on Mallorca, meeting in the chapel of St Nicholas in the cathedral and bearing their own privileges, insignia and weapons. At some point before 1460, however, this confraternity became defunct and was taken over by Circassians. This development reflects the demographic shift away from Greeks towards Black Sea peoples discussed in Chapter 2, especially as the Circassians already had a confraternity and now had two, but it also likely reflects the gradual integration of Greek-descended people through mixed relationships.[56]

The origins of a handful of the individuals registered in 1388 are stated. A few are noted to have been purchased by Turks and/or in *Turchia* or 'the land of the Turks' (*terra turcorum*), mostly in Ephesus/Altoloco; with ten examples, this is the strongest single trend in evidence. One man, Miquel, is even said to have been purchased 'from the hands of the Turks', implying that the purchaser understood Miquel to have been 'rescued' for the sake

---

[52] Text ed. Cateura, 'Politica', appendix (unpaginated).
[53] McKee, 'Familiarity of Slaves'; Paolella, *Human Trafficking*, 167–214.
[54] Statistical break-down in Cateura, 'Politica', 135.
[55] Delort, 'Quelques précisions', 238.
[56] Juan, 'Cofradías', 572–3; Mummey, 'Women, Slavery, and Community', 84.

of Christendom.⁵⁷ This trend is suggestive of the continued importance of western Asia Minor as a centre for the exportation of Greek captives into the fourteenth century, at a time when origins in Asia Minor became apparently rarer among Greek slaves on Crete.⁵⁸ On the other hand, this may be reflective of a bias in the information declared. The prevalence of Turks and *Turchia* among the statements of origin is likely a reflection of the notion that it was less problematic to buy an enslaved Greek from a Muslim Turk than a Christian captor: owners in the second category would be less likely to declare their slaves' origins, lest that information should compromise their rights of ownership. Sometimes owners declared that they had acquired their slaves closer to home, for example in Barcelona, Montpellier or even Barbary (North Africa), while on other occasions they named the seller.⁵⁹

As well as fulfilling domestic and cottage-industry roles, enslaved Greeks in the Aragonese-Catalan sphere were exploited for skilled labour, particularly stone masonry. The most individually distinguished of these was Jordi de Déu, a native of Messina with Greek origins, who flourished in the later fourteenth century. Jordi was possibly a captive taken during the failed pro-Angevin rising at Messina in 1360–1. He was sold as a slave to Jaume Cascalls, under whom he served as an apprentice sculptor. The precise moment of his manumission is not known: he was still enslaved in 1377, and his master died in either 1378 or 1379; upon Cascalls's death, Jordi de Déu succeeded him as director of works at the Royal tombs of Poblet.⁶⁰

Jordi was one among many Greek masons serving Catalans; the rest are less well known. In June 1343, King Peter the Ceremonious, at that time asserting his control over the Kingdom of Mallorca, issued confirmation that three Greek men, Johannis Vives, Johannes Fernandi, and Jordi the stone mason (*lapicidarum*), had given their due redemption payments, and were accordingly free.⁶¹ In 1358, a post-mortem inventory was drawn up for the possessions of Pere Mates, a builder and sculptor active on Mallorca. The inventory includes notice of fifteen enslaved Greeks. Thirteen of these were male, of whom most were quarrymen (*pedrerii*), one a mason (*lapiscida*) and one a woodworker (*operarius de fusta*). All but one were fairly young, aged

---

⁵⁷ Cateura, 'Politica', appendix.
⁵⁸ Crete: Verlinden, 'Crète', 632–52 = *L'esclavage*, 2.840–68 (superseding Sakasov, 'Documents').
⁵⁹ Cateura, 'Politica', appendix. For the implications of purchase from Muslims vs. Christians, see Chapter 5, *infra*, especially 156.
⁶⁰ Rubió 'Mitteilungen', 464; Liaño, 'Jordi de Déu'.
⁶¹ Rubió 'Mitteilungen', 464.

between eighteen and thirty-five. Older (aged over forty-five and thirty-five) were his two female servants (*servas*), Cali and Arena.[62] The inventory does not state what these women's roles were, but the fact that they are not noted to have been involved in masonry work suggests that they were doing something else for their master, perhaps domestic labour.

Learning a trade was one way in which members of the Greek diasporic community on Mallorca, both free and enslaved, retained links with one another. In 1386, the three Greek boys Nicolás, Costa and Joan were captured by Venetians on Corfu. They were around fourteen years old, and as a consequence of their youth the local governor ordered that they be freed. The conditions of their release shed light on the integration of Greeks into the Mallorcan community. Their freedom was not absolute. Firstly, their movement was restricted to the island, except in the event that they should receive royal permission to leave. Secondly, they were entrusted to the care of four free Greeks, Jordi Vanover, Juan Junta, Joan Comte and Joan Pelegrí. (It is interesting to note that these Greeks were listed with surnames, perhaps reflecting their more privileged status as free- or freedmen.) Thirdly, they were given as apprentices to a tailor, a quilt-maker (*colchero*) and a carpenter, respectively.[63] While it is only a brief glimpse, this episode nevertheless suggests that Greeks might be kept together – or perhaps forced together – in groups, and it is possible that some sense of community continued among this diaspora of captives.

Once freed, some Greeks who had been enslaved on Mallorca took the opportunity to leave the island. A number of receipts for safe conduct passes survive from the year 1330. These were given both to 'Saracens' (probably Muslims from North Africa), for up to an extortionate £3 4s 6d, and to Greeks, for a comparatively tiny 6 *dineros*: this discrepancy is arguably a reflection of the trend of more lenient treatment towards Greeks than towards other enslaved groups, especially Muslims.[64] The Greeks who bought safe conduct passes numbered forty-nine individuals; they probably represent the first generation of the diasporic community of manumitted Greeks on Mallorca. This evidence speaks to the desire of some individuals to leave the society of which they had been forced to become a part.[65]

Many others, however, remained after manumission. Further notice of the considerable Greek diaspora on Mallorca comes from a series of

[62] Llompart, 'Pere Mates', esp. 116; terms glossed in Mummey, 'Women, Slavery, and Community', 155–6.
[63] Cateura, 'Politica', 130–1.
[64] The case for this discrepancy is made in Chapter 5, *infra*.
[65] Sastre Moll, 'Notas', esp. 106, 110.

receipts for the payment of the eight-*solidi* hearth tax (*monedatge*) in the northeastern village of Artà. The relevant document was drawn up in 1340 and relates to payments made three years earlier. Four Greeks are listed in the context of three transactions: Lucia, Johannes Costa and the couple Iselda and Georgius, the last of whom had died in between the payment of the tax and the drafting of the document.[66] While a number of freed Greeks evidently tried to get away from the island where they had been subjected to enslavement, others, at least for some time, made their homes there among the community. Presumably some were more readily able to leave than others.

It is remarkable that certain Greeks, once freed, even came to possess Greek slaves of their own. In 1361, Nicola, the former slave of Maymon Periç, freed his slave Mitre. Nicola, once able to participate in his own right as a free and autonomous member of the community that had once subjected him, either took the opportunity to redeem a fellow Greek through the normal means of buying and manumitting him, or else he simply wished to participate in the exploitation of unfree Greeks' labour as his own former master had once done. Another example is the Greek freedwoman Caterina, widow of the late Lorenç Balcareyns, who sold a Greek slave called Stamatis in 1372; Caterina's free status had to be confirmed following the sale.[67]

Mallorca, therefore, preserves especially rich evidence for what happened to enslaved Greeks after they were freed, or in subsequent generations; this is less well attested in contexts such as Crete or Cyprus. While some Greeks seem to have secured safe conduct passes to leave Mallorca for various destinations, some freedmen or their descendants stayed on Mallorca and practised trades; vitally, at least some continued to be identified as being Greek. It is even possible that some knowledge of the Greek language remained with this diaspora: there is a document in the Archive of the Kingdom of Mallorca dated to 1543 noting a 'Mestre Joan Grech', baker, who may have been a freedman, and who possessed two Greek books.[68] Either this man was an outlier, captured more than a century after most other Greeks known from the Crown of Aragon, or he was a descendant of a captive still distinguished as a 'Grech' several generations later.

---

[66] Gili Ferrer 'Monedatge', esp. 480–3.
[67] Mummey, 'Women, Slavery, and Community', 91–2, 94. Greeks buying and selling other Greeks in Candia: *infra*, 159–60.
[68] Hillgarth, 'Greek Slave', 554.

Captives or Refugees?

To add yet a further challenge to the interpretation of the Greek-language evidence, *aichmalotos* is sometimes glossed by scholars as meaning 'refugee'.[69] As will already be clear, mobility was a feature of captivity and enslavement in the medieval Mediterranean, but it was also a product of insecurity and conflict, including when people were not taken captive. As a result, it is often difficult to interpret the use of *aichmalotos* in texts where an instance of captivity is not explicitly described or strongly implied.

One case study that demonstrates the difficulty of distinguishing captives from refugees concerns the arrival of Greek Christians in Constantinople following the Turkish conquest of northwest Asia Minor in the first years of the fourteenth century. In the aftermath of the Battle of Bapheus in 1302, much of the Greek population in northwest Asia Minor fled over the straits to Constantinople. This is amply attested in the letters of Patriarch Athanasios I of Constantinople (in office 1289–93 and 1303–9). Athanasios took seriously not just his ecumenical leadership but also his responsibilities as bishop of Constantinople. In his second term in particular he can be seen to depart significantly from the intellectualising pursuits of his predecessors in favour of an active and reforming policy focused on the social welfare of his flock.[70] Among Athanasios's correspondence are some important pieces of evidence for his response to the arrival of Greek Christians from Asia Minor.

Firstly, a letter dating perhaps to the winter of 1304–5 records the methods by which Athanasios appealed to the *dynatoi* (the 'powerful' classes) to help these people in need. Athanasios was considering two main methods of seeking support: the first was the dispatch of a report to each of the *archontes* (secular officials) individually; the second was a semi-public reading of an open letter, which Athanasios had already drafted, to *archontes* assembled in the Palace of Blachernai. In response, the *archontes* should look after people in need over the winter and spring or else give alms.[71] The subjects of this appeal were described by Athanasios as *aichmalotos*

---

[69] Talbot, 'Athanasios', 14 n. 6, following Laurent, *Regestes*, 1.4.402, No. 1613, and Lemerle, *L'Émirat d'Aydin*, 20–1, n. 4. Bryer, 'Pontic exception', 139, explicitly follows Talbot's gloss.

[70] Talbot, 'Patriarch Athanasius', 13–14.

[71] Athanasios, *Correspondence*, ed. and tr. (slightly altered above) Talbot, 52–3, No. 22, commentary 329; cf. Boojamra, 'Social Thought', 368, and Laiou, *Constantinople and the Latins*, 90–1 and 194. On the *archontes* of the (late) Palaiologan era, see Kiousopoulou, *Emperor or Manager*, 7–8, 36–8, 50–2, 68–79.

laos polys: either a 'large group of captives' or a 'large group of refugees' – but which?

Secondly, another letter of Athanasios has been preserved that appears to have the character of an open letter. The text has been dated to one winter around the years 1305–7, so this is unlikely the text to which Athanasios had referred in his other letter; it may however be a similar text. In this later letter, the patriarch appealed directly to 'rich and poor, laymen and monks' in Constantinople, asking that they give alms according to their means to help coreligionists in need; those individuals who were being monetarily supported should be recorded by name, so that the patriarch could turn to the Emperor Andronikos II himself and ask him to make provision for those omitted. In making this appeal, Athanasios invoked Matthew 25, the most commonly cited biblical passage in texts related to captivity: in this case, the lines 'I was an hungred, and ye gave me meat' (Matt. 25:35), and its mirror-image for those who have not done good, 'Depart from me, ye cursed ... for I was an hungred and ye gave me no meat' (Matt. 25:41–2).[72] In its addressees and its invocation of Matthew 25, the letter resembles the *aichmalotika*, the testimonials written on behalf of individuals who were seeking alms to cover ransom costs. But were these people captives themselves?

In this instance, external evidence survives that suggests the translated term 'refugee' is probably to be preferred, though this term does not intrinsically rule out the possibility that some of these people had at some point been captured. Ramon Muntaner, the chronicler of the Catalan Company's exploits in the Romanía, penned a prejudicial sketch of Constantinople's response to the poverty of the Greeks who fled Asia Minor following the Battle of Bapheus. Following his account of a devastating victory by the Catalans against the Turks at Artaki/Erdek, Muntaner notes the jealousy of Michael IX Palaiologos and the Genoese. In a passage probably relating to events of the year 1303, Muntaner records how Greek Christians who had fled from Asia Minor as refugees from Turkish expansion were abandoned to poverty by the population of Constantinople: they 'were crying out in hunger and begging for bread for the love of God, and they slept among the dung heaps, and no Greek person was willing to give them anything, even though there was a large market offering all kinds of provisions'. Muntaner claims that the Catalans themselves supported over two-thousand Greek refugees as a consequence of the Byzantines' neglect.[73] However much

[72] Athanasios, *Correspondence*, ed. and tr. Talbot, 258–9, No. 102.
[73] Ramon Muntaner, *Chronicle*, tr. Hughes, 49.

Muntaner may have allowed his abject hatred of the Greeks to cloud his judgement, this picture is reasonably consistent with that found in the letters of Athanasios I for the period immediately after the Battle of Bapheus. To add further complication, it is likely that any Greek camp followers of the Catalans' would later have been sold into slavery:[74] not only are the categories of captive and refugee difficult to disentangle lexically, they were also porous and volatile in lived reality.

There may, to some extent, be a blurring of distinctions on the basis of the contexts in which captives are found. One of the most important redemptorist mechanisms in this context was the alms-seeking testimonial, which by its very nature required the bearer to travel. Most bearers of these letters seem to have been people who had secured their own freedom, but needed to recover from the financial losses thus incurred, or to ransom family members still in captivity. Sometimes, however, people still in a condition of captivity are found as alms-seekers on the move.[75] As such, Byzantine captives and former captives are frequently attested at a point when their movement was not restricted, which appears to contradict the implications of a translation of *aichmalotos* as 'captive of conflict' and assumptions about the nature of captivity. The examples of Palamas and Gregory of Sinai also point in this same direction. An *aichmalotos* was therefore usually a captive or someone who had at a recent prior time been a captive, who would often also take on the characteristics of a refugee; on certain occasions, however, it seems that an *aichmalotos* was not literally a captive, and that a figurative meaning should therefore be understood.

Another ambiguous case is that of Michael Loulloudes. Loulloudes was born sometime between c. 1276 and 1282 and is known to scholars primarily as a copyist. He lived in the city of Ephesus in western Asia Minor and was there in 1304 when it was conquered by the Turkish leader Sasa Beg, related by marriage to the house of Menteşe. The outline of Loulloudes's subsequent biography can be pieced together from his own writings, including the subscriptions he wrote into the manuscripts that he copied. In 1306, he described himself as 'most-captive (*aichmalotatos*) Michael Loulloudes, flitting to the island of Crete on account of my homeland having been captured by the godless Persians' (an archaising term for 'Turks'). In another manuscript of 1312 or 1313, he records similarly how he 'moved from Ephesus to the thrice-greatest island of Crete

---

[74] Greeks sold on Crete in 1308–9 had come from the Catalan army in northern Greece: Duran Duelt, 'Companyia', 568–71 (notary Angelo Cariolo, Candia).

[75] See further Chapter 4, *infra*.

on account of his homeland having been subjected by the Persians.' On Crete, Loulloudes was rewarded with patronage from members of the highest circles of society: he copied one manuscript upon the sponsorship of Manuel Ialinas of Candia, a Greek member of the elite, and another at the behest of Giovanni Morosini during one of his terms as Duke of Candia (1327–9 or 1338/9). By the time he arrived on Crete, Loulloudes was a lector (*anagnostes*); by 1313 he was a priest, and by Morosini's time he had ascended to the rank of first cantor (*protopsaltes*), the second most senior level of office in the Greek Church of Venetian Crete.[76]

Loulloudes used the adjective *aichmalotatos* – the superlative form of *aichmalotos* – to describe himself, and this may mean any of several things. In this chapter, three main meanings of this term have been identified: first and most basically, a captive, which may include an enslaved captive; second, a refugee – someone who has experienced involuntary displacement through war or another form of insecurity, whether or not they suffered captivity; third, someone who was in a less specific sense 'wretched', in the sense that they had suffered some kind of misfortune. Loulloudes can probably be described as a refugee, since he moved to Crete as a result of the turmoil in his home city of Ephesus. Perhaps he was also taken captive, though this is not clear. Certainly, he could have described himself as unfortunate.

For further clarification on this point, it is possible to turn once again to the single largest locus of Greek-language captivity-related texts: the important Cypriot manuscript of c. 1343 (Paris. gr. 400). The relevant texts' contents, contexts, and uses of the word *aichmalotos* and its related nouns and verbs reveal a picture that is widely corroborated by other contemporary evidence: that the primary meaning of *aichmalotos* was 'captive', but many captives became refugees in an effort to fund their ransoms, thus blurring any distinction.

Two texts in this manuscript employ comparable phrases to describe the status and movements of captives who came to Cyprus at that time. First, one of the sermons speaks of 'our brethren who have been taken captive from the Romanía by the godless Ishmaelites; how, afflicted, forcefully dragged, maltreated, oppressed in hunger and in thirst, they have been

---

[76] Turyn, 'Lulludes'; subscriptions ed. Lampros, 'Λουλούδης', 209–10: (1) αἰχμαλωτάτου Μιχαὴλ τοῦ Λουλλούδη τοῦ ἀπὸ τῆς Ἐφέσου ... μετοικισμὸν εὑρισκομένου μου ἐν τῇ νήσῳ Κρήτῃ διὰ τὸ τὴν ἐμὴν πατρίδα ὑπὸ τῶν ἀθέων αἰχμαλωτισθῆναι Περσῶν ...; (2) τοῦ ἀπὸ τῆς Ἐφέσου μετοικισμένου ὄντος ἐν τῇ τρισμεγίστῳ νήσῳ Κρήτῃ διὰ τὸ τὴν αὐτοῦ πατρίδα κρατηθῆναι ὑπὸ Περσῶν ... I thank Prof. Costas Constantinides for bringing the case of Loulloudes to my attention.

borne to our famous island, even sold off as slaves.'[77] Later on in the manuscript, one of the testimonials describes how an anonymised individual came to the author (a member of the higher clergy) from the Romanía, 'after many other captives'; his property had been destroyed, almost certainly by a Turkish group, 'and having been sold and after he had wandered around from place to place – not of his own will, but having been compelled by godless nations, he came even so far as the renowned island of Cyprus.' Somewhat confusingly, the author then states that the man had ransomed himself with a monetary payment, but was now facing a shortfall of resources – though for what, we are not told. Consequently, the captive requested and received from the author a testimonial with which he could travel around seeking alms.[78]

These passages may be broken down into narratives that involve episodes of captivity, enslavement and forced migration. The first passage evidently refers specifically to Greek Christians who were captured (*aichmalotizomenoi*) by Turkish groups in the Romanía; after their capture, they were transported to Cyprus, apparently by other people, and then sold as slaves (*poloumenoi osper eti andrapoda*). The second passage refers to another person from the Aegean region who appears to have been only one among a large group of captives, presumably also from that same region (*allous aichmalotous pollous*); he was subsequently sold, that is, into slavery (*diapratheis*), and only after that point became a refugee and came to Cyprus, where he sought charitable donations, presumably to offset the money he had been obliged to pay out for his ransom.

In the course of this process of disentanglement, some wider historical trends will become evident. Captivity was a liminal status of unfreedom that could affect any person of any status, free or unfree; because it was an 'in-between' status, it was not referred to with the same terminological precision as slavery or manumission. This makes it at times difficult to

---

[77] See 74, n. 68, *supra*.
[78] Paris. gr. 400, fols. 146v–147r, ed. and tr. AG (ed. Saccon, 'Ransoming Activities', 18): προσῆλθε τῇ ἡμῶν μετριότητι μετὰ καὶ ἄλλους αἰχμαλώτους πολλοὺς καὶ ὁ ἀπὸ τῆς Ῥωμανίας ὁρμώμενος ὁ δ(εῖνα) δακρυρροῶν καὶ λέγων, ὡς ἀπώλεσαν (ἀπώλεσεν Saccon) τὴν περιουσίαν πᾶσαν αὐτοῦ, καὶ διαπραθεὶς ἐπείπερ χώραν ἐκ χώρας ἀμείβων πλὴν οὐχ ἑκών, ἀλλ᾽ ὑπὸ τῶν ἀθέων ἐθνῶν (ἐθνῶν om. Saccon) βιαζόμενος μέχρι καὶ τὴν περιώνυμον νῆσον Κύπρον παρεγένετο. καὶ ἀργύρια δοὺς ἱκανὰ τῆς τοιαύτης πικρᾶς καὶ ἀπανθρώπου αἰχμαλωσίας ἐρρύσατο, λοιπασθεὶς ὁ τοιοῦτος καὶ ἕτερα (...?) (νομίσματα leg. Saccon) καὶ εὐπορίαν μὴ κεκτημένος δοῦναι τὰ τοιαῦτα τὴν ἡμετέραν παρεκλήτευσεν μετριότητα παρασχεῖν τῷ τοιούτῳ ἡμετέραν γραφὴν τοῦ πρὸς πάντας ἀναδραμεῖν.

say whether someone was or was not a captive, or indeed at what point a person entered or left a state of captivity and became either a slave or a free person. This question of status was answered differently depending on the perspective of the observer. Next, because medieval Greek Christian captives are often attested on the move, seeking charitable donations to raise ransom costs, captives often take on the appearance of refugees and challenge preconceptions of constraint as an integral feature of captivity. A closely related phenomenon was that many people became refugees precisely in order to avoid being taken captive, for example, in the course of an impending attack – something that makes the semantics of the word *aichmalotos* potentially even more fraught. All of these ambiguities are made doubly problematic by the fact that we have access to comparatively few first-person 'witness' narratives of captivity: instead, the historian must largely rely on texts where the voice of the captive is either undetectable or else mediated by another person.

Trends in Forced Mobility

All the people studied in this chapter had mobility as a common denominator. As the texts cited above demonstrate, this mobility was not a matter of choice but of compulsion. Before moving on from this comparative discussion of captives, slaves and refugees, it is worth highlighting some of the trends in the destinations of these people.

The destinations of Greek Christian refugees are one of the most revealing indices of non-elite social and political attitudes in the later Byzantine world. Prominent destinations are arguably markers of places that were perceived as being better locations to live than the refugees' points of origin. That is not to say, of course, that these destinations were the best of all places to be, or that they were at all times and in all ways preferable to other places; rather, the destination societies were perceived as, on balance, offering brighter prospects and/or being more practical to aim for than other alternatives.

There is a clear general trend in this demographic movement: as a rule, Greek Christians fled the expansion of the Ottomans or other Turkish groups in favour of moving to areas ruled by Latins, especially Venetians; Greek Christians did flee to Turkish groups on occasion, during times of imminent military defeats, such as sieges, but also sometimes to escape hardships at home. Sometimes, Greek Christians even seem to have fled Byzantine-ruled territory for life under Latin (again, usually Venetian) rule, apparently to escape heavy tax burdens.

A crucial caveat is that this asymmetry probably in part reflects source bias rather than historical realities. Venetian documentary sources on this period are extremely plentiful versus Byzantine or Turkish sources, and it may be that scholars are therefore disproportionately aware of refugees who settled under Venetian rule versus under other regimes. If the disparity in the evidence is indeed reflective of a historical disparity of refugee behaviour, then it would suggest that non-elites in late Byzantine society tended to favour Latin over Turkish (or even at times Byzantine) rule; this directly challenges the recent characterisation of late Byzantium by some prominent scholars as fundamentally more 'anti-Latin' than 'anti-Turkish'.[79]

One prominent route for refugees led from the Aegean region to Cyprus. To recap briefly, Greeks from the Aegean came to Cyprus to raise ransom money and may also have travelled there to escape being trafficked into slavery in the Mamlūk Sultanate.[80] The evidence for this comes overwhelmingly from the early fourteenth century, and it seems that by the conquest of the trading city of Famagusta by the Genoese in 1373–4, and all the socioeconomic instability that it caused, its importance as a destination for refugees had already ceased. The position of the route that led to Cyprus suggests that it was closely bound to wider transregional slave-trading networks.

With the exception of the Cypriot route, the movement of most refugees in the Aegean region occurred from east to west and from north to south. This reflected two overlapping trends: first, the movement of people from recently conquered or increasingly vulnerable areas of the Byzantine Empire to places further from the frontier, thus a movement generally towards the west; second, the movement of people from Turkish- or Greek-ruled territories to Latin-ruled territories, particularly those belonging to Venice.

The first trend is clearly visible in monastic documents. The peasants who worked in monastic estates were taxed, some records of which – called *praktika* – have survived. These concern the domains of the monasteries of Mount Athos in Macedonia and the Aegean island of Limnos, and they date from the period 1300–41. The names listed in the *praktika* include a number of toponymic (placename-derived) surnames. These toponymic surnames suggest, even if they cannot prove, that the named person's family was associated with the relevant place within living

---

[79] For example, Kaldellis, *Ethnography*, 168 and (less dogmatic) Necipoğlu, *Byzantium between the Ottomans and the Latins*, 286–7.
[80] *Supra*, 72–80.

memory. A person called Naxeiotes, for example, was likely to have come from the island of Naxos or to be the child or grandchild of someone who had. These figures exhibit few dramatic changes over this forty-year period, but suggest a modest level of migration from the Aegean and Asia Minor, where the greatest numbers of captives were taken in the late thirteenth and early fourteenth centuries: for example, in 1300–1, toponyms from the Aegean made up 8% of the total, 13% in 1320–1, falling slightly to 10% in 1338–41. By contrast, the figures for local, Macedonian names are between 37% and 50%, rising over time; this probably reflects the impact of the Byzantine civil wars but also stresses the localised nature of most migration. Few peasants, meanwhile, can be traced in any monastic sources as travelling from west to east in this period.[81]

Sometimes, Greek Christians fled Greek-ruled territory for Latin-ruled areas as a means of escaping straitened circumstances, especially high tax burdens. A Venetian response to demands of ambassadors sent by Manuel II, dating to 23 September 1415, suggests that a process of depopulation moving from the empire to Venetian territories was creating significant financial strain by denuding him of his taxable subjects. The emperor asked that his subjects from Thessaloniki or Constantinople who had fled to Venetian lands during the Ottoman sieges of those cities should return to their homes. Furthermore, a number of his subjects, including some sailors, had fled to Venetian territories to evade the financial burden of the rebuilding of the Hexamilion, the defensive wall on the Isthmus of Corinth; the Venetians agreed to return the sailors, but not the rest.[82] The implication is that it was cheaper and safer for imperial subjects to move to Venetian territory than to remain in Byzantine lands. It was, moreover, not only Greek Christians who sought refuge from the Turks. In 1363, the authorities at Venice assented to take in Armenian refugee families from the Black Sea region at their colonies of Methoni and Crete: this suggests that awareness had travelled far to the east of the role of these Venetian possessions as a place of safety for non-Latin Christian groups threatened by Turkish expansion.[83]

Upon the fall of Constantinople, some imperial subjects fled to the Morea, the one surviving area of the empire; in 1460, they were displaced

---

[81] Jacoby, 'Démographie', 184; Laiou, *Peasant Society*, 128–31; there is a similar discussion in Grant, 'Gottlose Korsaren', 64–6.
[82] Thiriet, *Délibérations*, 2.138, No. 1592; Necipoğlu, *Byzantium between the Ottomans and the Latins*, 72–3.
[83] Thiriet, *Délibérations*, 1.105, No. 407 (8 June 1363), 107, No. 411 (1 July 1363); text in Ἱστορικὰ κρητικὰ ἔγγραφα, ed. Theotokes, 2.1.114–15, No. 20; Vacalopoulos, 'Flight', 273.

once more, as this area in turn fell to the Ottomans, and at that time they left for Crete. These refugees, especially the clergy, were treated with concern and suspicion by the Venetian authorities, who considered them to be conspiratorial. Crete was already in cross-confessional turmoil by the arrival of the refugees: in 1452, Xiphilinos (Siphi) Vlastos, a Greek nobleman from Rethymno, attempted to organise a rebellion against the Venetians following the appointment of a pro-Church union *protopapas* in his town; in 1454 he was executed by the regime, but Venetian anxiety persisted. Greek clergy, even including pro-unionists, were understood as having the potential to form a rival community of power; such men were viewed as agents of the patriarchate, which the Venetians perceived as a competing centre of authority under both Byzantine and Ottoman rule. On 19 June 1461, the Council of Ten demanded that intelligence be gathered regarding Greeks coming to Crete from Constantinople and the Morea, with attention paid to all monks and priests.[84] The clergy were allowed, should they wish, to settle in Corfu and adjacent Venetian territories, but not anywhere else (the implication being that their other option was to leave Venetian territory entirely).[85] The importance of Venice and its overseas territories as a destination for Greek emigres continued well into the early modern period,[86] something that was rooted in the period of the crisis of captivity and the patterns of displacement that it caused.

On the other hand, the hardships of life under Venetian rule also prompted people to flee to the Turkish maritime principalities, and therefore it is important to acknowledge that the movement of refugees was not only in one direction. In 1361, for example, the Venetian Ghisi family reasserted control over the island of Amorgos, which the dukes of Naxos had tried to claim. During this dispute, the peasants of the island had moved to Crete for their safety; the Ghisi wanted them back, but the Venetian senate warned against forcing them to return: the senators were aware that the peasants would be vulnerable to attack on Amorgos and might therefore preempt the possibility by choosing to join the Turks. It is worth noting that, one century later, Amorgos had a population density of under two inhabitants per square kilometre, calculating on the basis of population

---

[84] Ed. Manousakas, Συνωμοσία, 117–18; this supersedes the summary in Lamansky, *Secrets*, 047 [sic], No. 7, whose brief sections of quoted Latin text differ slightly from Manousakas's. See also the summary of the conspiracy in Angold, *Fall of Constantinople*, 97.

[85] Ed. Manousakas, Συνωμοσία, 120. On the events of June 1461, cf. also Vacalopoulos, 'Flight', 277–8.

[86] This topic has been studied in depth by Harris, *Emigres*: for Venice, see 57–62.

figures noted by the Italian Giacomo Rizzardo in 1470; this low density almost certainly reflects the vulnerability of the island. A little after the appeal of the Ghisi, the Venetian regime offered debt settlements to impoverished former subjects who had fled to western Asia Minor and were now joining in Turkish raids against Christian territories. Similarly, in 1401, it was reported that peasants pressed into galley service preferred to cross the Aegean and join the Turkish principalities instead.[87]

The idea of a pre-empting attack or capture by Turkish groups was probably key to a number of these decisions. The historiographer Doukas explicitly presents his grandfather's choices in this way. The elder Doukas had been a partisan of Emperor John VI Kantakouzenos in the fourteenth century, for which sympathies he was imprisoned; but even after John triumphed in the civil war and became emperor in 1347, the elder Doukas chose to remain in the city of Ephesus, then controlled by the Aydınoğulları, because he predicted that the Turks would triumph. Even though his prediction was premature, it was indeed the Ottomans who triumphed in the end, and so he was ultimately correct. Doukas the historiographer lived beyond the fall of Constantinople in 1453 and in fact died during an Ottoman attack, so it must be borne in mind that he was exercising hindsight when attributing these motives to his grandfather. Whether or not his grandfather had really acted for this reason, it is plausible that it may have been an idea circulating in the fourteenth and fifteenth centuries.[88] To take a further example, during the Ottoman siege of Thessaloniki (1422–30), some of the besieged inhabitants apparently went over to the Ottomans, probably hoping to be spared the horrors of any sack, should the Venetian regime in charge of the city not make terms with the besiegers.[89]

This evidence demonstrates that Greek refugees moved both away from and towards areas that had recently been conquered by Turkish groups, though the balance of the evidence tips towards the former. People facing instability and conflict seem on the whole to have sought out safer areas of the Byzantine Empire or places under Latin, especially Venetian control; this was despite the economic hardships and social repression often experienced by Greek refugees in these places. This trend towards a preference

---

[87] Zachariadou, 'Notes sur la population', 230–1; for the population of Amorgos, see Koder, 'Topographie und Bevölkerung', esp. 232.
[88] Doukas, *Chronographia*, V, 5, ed. and tr. Reinsch, 76–9 (ed. and tr. Grecu, 44–7), tr. Magoulias, 65–6; Zachariadou, 'Notes sur la population', 229–30.
[89] Symeon of Thessaloniki, ed. Balfour, 59; Necipoğlu, *Byzantium between the Ottomans and the Latins*, 49.

for Byzantine or Latin over Turkish rule is borne out by the distribution of evidence for the redemption of captives, which forms the subject of the next chapter.

Conclusions

This chapter has explored the ambiguities of the late medieval Greek and Latin vocabulary for captives, slaves and refugees and outlined the implications of these ambiguities for the study of Byzantium's crisis of captivity as a social-historical phenomenon. The basic Greek word for a captive, *aichmalotos*, can also refer to a refugee; because captives are often found on the move, gathering ransom money, it can be difficult to decide which definition should take priority, and it may in fact be more fruitful to understand the distinction as unhelpful and, at times, false in a late Byzantine context. Greek texts tend to talk of *aichmalotoi*, rather than *douloi* ('slaves'), even when it seems that a captive was sold into slavery; this is arguably because the Greek Christian perspective was concerned foremost with the primary act of dislocation. Latin archival evidence, on the other hand, overwhelmingly talks of *sclavi* ('slaves'), because the notaries who drew up these documents were recording legally binding acts (usually sale or manumission) in which the legal status of enslavement was the primary concern. The exception to this trend is Aragonese-Catalan documentation where the terms 'captive' and 'slave' seem to have been used synonymously. This process of enquiry may appear to have highlighted more ambiguities than it has resolved, but in practice it is often possible to infer from the context on a case-by-case basis whether a person was a captive, a slave, a refugee or a combination of any two (or indeed all three) of these statuses.

Chapter 4
Methods of Redemption

This chapter explores the various ways in which Greek captives secured their freedom. It begins by considering the Church's long history of taking responsibility for helping captives. It then sets forth the main method that the Church used to assist with raising ransom costs: the wandering almsseeker's testimonial letter (*aichmalotikon*). Evidence for family members or profiteers participating in the redemption of captives is then adduced, further reinforcing the impression that redemption at this time was an overwhelmingly individual or family matter, in contrast to the organised prisoner exchanges of the Middle Byzantine period. The chapter closes by contrasting the development of redemptorist military orders in late medieval Iberia with the relative paucity of evidence for such institutional activity in the Aegean.

Ransom as Religious Duty

Helping captives was viewed as an important and virtuous act in Judaism, Christianity and Islam. Charity has a basis in all three faith traditions, and in the Middle Ages the reality of captive-taking encouraged the application and theorisation of these charitable ideals.[1] The emphasis on charity and the criticism of the rich found in the New Testament has been interpreted as a product of the historical circumstances of first-century Israel–Palestine, in which large estates were owned by absentee landlords and rented to poor tenants at exploitative rates. The hostility towards these

---

[1] For Christianity: Lieu, 'Charity'; for Judaism: M. Frenkel, 'Proclaim Liberty to Captives'; for Islam: Y. Frenkel, '*Fikāk al-Asīr*', 143–57; for all three communities: Friedman, *Encounter between Enemies* (crusading era) and Rotman, *Byzantine Slavery*, 25–81 (Middle Byzantine period).

people displayed by the members of the early Christian movement is therefore understandable.[2]

Although late medieval Greek clergy drew predominantly on the Gospels for authority on charity towards captives, relevant precepts were already present in the Old Testament. Tobit 4:10 states: 'Because that alms do deliver from death, and suffereth not to come into darkness.' A passage particularly favoured in late Byzantine texts on captivity was Proverbs 19:17, 'He that hath pity upon the poor lendeth unto the Lord; and that which he hath given will he pay him again.'[3]

In the context of helping captives, the passage most frequently and consistently invoked was Matthew 25:34–6.[4] These verses come from the parable of the sheep and the goats, during which Christ states that those who are judged worthy of sitting at the right hand of God will be those who have helped the poor, and so helped God:

> Come, ye blessed of my Father, inherit the kingdom prepared for you from the foundation of the world. For I was an hungred, and ye gave me meat; I was thirsty, and ye gave me drink; I was a stranger, and ye took me in; naked, and ye clothed me; I was sick, and ye visited me; I was in prison, and ye came unto me.

The logic of this theology of charity is that God is to be found among those whom society most rejects, or who suffer the greatest hardships; giving to those in need is therefore equated to giving to God Himself. Those who have failed to help 'the least of these my brethren' (Matt. 25:40) have therefore failed to help God, and so are judged unworthy of inheriting the Kingdom of Heaven. The implications of this belief often formed the focus for pious admonitions written in the letters of clerical advocacy for captives. This parable was particularly appropriate for writers discussing captives because it refers to various circumstances encountered by those in captivity: lack of food, water and clothing, as well as being held in prison.

The writings of the fourth-century Father, John Chrysostom, were also important for Palaiologan-era clergy when exhorting charity. Chrysostom

---

[2] Lieu, 'Charity', 15.

[3] Biblical quotations are taken from the Greek *Septuaginta*, ed. Rahlfs, and English King James Version. Byzantine texts: *aichmalotika*, considered below.

[4] The passage is cited, for example, in the *aichmalotika* of the manuscripts London, BL Harley 5624, fols. 202v–203r; Paris. gr. 400, fols. 131v–132r, 146v–147r; Paris. gr. 2671, fols. 395v–397r; Paris. gr. 2509, fols. 139v–140v; Vat. Pal. gr. 367, fol. 176r–v ('Κυπριακά', ed. Lampros [pt. 3], 339, No. 60; ed. Beihammer, *Griechische Briefe*, 232–3, No. 100).

found himself repulsed by the conspicuous consumption of the rich in the city of Antioch, and exploited the language of investment (cf. Prov. 19:17) to turn the social priorities of the rich on their head. The true investment is investment in God, which is enacted through charity, and which pays infinite dividends in the hereafter.[5] This interpretation was nothing radical, but the image of the bishop actively engaging with, and challenging, the members of his congregation is something that strongly foreshadows the reforming patriarchate of Athanasios I one millennium later.

Charity has therefore always occupied a central place in Christian thought about how to live a virtuous life. Within this wider theme, charity towards captives received considerable attention, as it did too in Islam and Judaism. Captives were particularly vulnerable, and their situation urgent, since their immediate future was uncertain. When Palaiologan-era clergymen sought to represent the plight of a captive in front of a community, they had a long cultural tradition from which to draw language and ideas.

The *Nomocanon*, the collection of Byzantine canon (Church) law, contains two extensive paragraphs of commentary on the possibilities of alienating movable wealth. Liturgical equipment or altar cloths could be sold, with the permission of the bishops, stewards and sacristans, to make up a shortfall in the money required for a ransom payment.[6] It is stressed that this is the one and only reason for which such sales or mortgages might be made.[7] Church paraphernalia may not be 'taken for debts, sold, melted down, or alienated, except for the ransom of captives'.[8] The second commentary continues this theme. It relates specifically to the movable wealth 'of the church of Constantinople': anything lying in store may be sold or mortgaged only to ransom captives.[9] There may, however, be a surfeit of valuable items in the possession of the Church, in which case this surplus should be used to provide the required funds.[10] There is also evidence from a *Novella* of Justinian (No. 65) that people in late antique Mysia were leaving real estate to the Church with the intention that the incomes of such legacies should be given for the redemption of captives.[11] In the Palaiologan period, the important fourteenth-century juridical commentator,

---

[5] See Leyerle, 'John Chrysostom on Almsgiving'.
[6] Σύνταγμα, ed. Rhalles and Potles, 108; cf. Boojamra, 'Social thought', 258 and n. 108.
[7] Σύνταγμα, ed. Rhalles and Potles, 108.
[8] Ibid.: τῶν νεαρῶν ἐπιτιμίοις ὑποβάλλει τοὺς ἱερὰ σκεύη παρὰ τὸν νόμον ἐνεχυράζοντας, ἢ πωλοῦντας, ἢ χωνεύοντας, ἢ ἐκποιοῦντας, εἰ μὴ διὰ λύσιν αἰχμαλώτων.
[9] Ibid., 109.
[10] Ibid.
[11] *Corpus Iuris Civilis*, ed. Schoell and Kroll, vol. 3, *Novellae*, 339.

Constantine Harmenopoulos, noted in his *Hexabiblos* that people who did not ransom their captive parents could be disinherited; any inheritance would pass to the local church instead, which would use that wealth for the redemption of captives.[12] In brief, there were a number of laws in the East Roman tradition that allowed for the alienation of property via the Church for the ransom of captives.

There is evidence that captives really were treated as urgently deserving of charity in Palaiologan-era Byzantium, and not just described as such in prescriptive legal texts. Archbishop Symeon of Thessaloniki (d. 1429), for example, addressed the question of alms on behalf of captives in his lengthy response to some eighty-three questions sent by Gabriel, bishop of Pentapolis. In this work, Symeon makes the remark that 'quite simply, among all the sins of the living, the ransom of captives is of greater importance than other deeds'; the reason for this is that human deeds should all be directed at releasing the soul from slavery (*douleia*) and dishonour (*asebeia*), since this equates to freeing a person from death.[13]

The word that Symeon uses for 'ransom' (*anarrysis*) is one of the terms prevalent in the *Nomocanon*. Symeon's answer is a clear Palaiologan-era representative of a tradition that spanned East Roman history. A letter of clerical advocacy written by a clergyman on behalf of a captive and copied on Crete sometime in the earlier fifteenth century articulates the same principles, in which charity towards captives is ranked 'above unction, above memorial, above feasts, above the authorities of the Church, and quite simply above anything else.'[14]

The archives of the monastery of Koutloumousiou on Mount Athos, furthermore, preserve a document that gives direct evidence for a Palaiologan-era clergyman monetising the movable wealth of the Church for the benefit of captives. In his third will, dated July 1378, the superior (*hegoumenos*) Chariton noted that Turkish raids on the Holy Mountain were resulting in the taking of prisoners. Usually, he remarks, the numbers were

---

[12] Constantine Harmenopoulos, *Hexabiblos*, V.10, ed. and Latin tr. Heimbach, 682–3. This law had roots ultimately in *Novella* 115.3.13 of Justinian, and was recapitulated in the *Basilika* 35.8.41: *Corpus Iuris Civilis*, ed. Schoell and Kroll, vol. 3, *Novellae*, 539–41; *Basilicorum Libri LX*, ed. Heimbach and Fabrot, 3.563–4.

[13] Symeon of Thessaloniki, 'Ἀποκρίσεις', ed. Migne, col. 932B (Question 72) (cited in Pahlitzsch, 'Loskauf', 133): ἁπλῶς δὲ ἐν τοῖς τῶν ζώντων ἁμαρτήμασι πᾶσιν ἡ τῶν αἰχμαλώτων ἀνάρρυσις προτιμοτέρα τῶν ἄλλων ἔργων...

[14] London, BL, Harley 5624, fol. 202v–203r, ed. AG: καὶ γὰρ ὡς ἀληθῶς, ὑπὲρ εὐχέλαια, ὑπὲρ μνημόσυνα, ὑπὲρ ἑορτάς, ὑπὲρ κτίσματα ἐκκλησίας, καὶ ὑπὲρ ἄλλο πᾶν τοιοῦτον ἁπλῶς, ἡ περὶ τοὺς ἀδελφοὺς ἡμῶν τοὺς αἰχμαλώτους ἐστὶν ἐλεημοσύνη.

low, involving two or three people, but during one raid fourteen monks had been taken. Donations for the ransom of the captives had been received, among others, from Elisabeth, widow of Stefan Dušan of Serbia, while more money had been raised by means of donations from the monastery's benefactor Vulk Branković. In order to meet the exigencies of the future, Chariton bequeathed his robes: any funds raised from their sale should be dedicated to the redemption of captives.[15]

Taken together, these various anecdotes suggest that the legal precedence given historically by the church to the ransoming of captives was still a practised reality in the Palaiologan period. These precepts may not always have been zealously followed,[16] but they were still preached, and should be understood as shaping the contexts in which clergy became increasingly important for advocacy on behalf of captives in this period.

Captives' Letters of Clerical Advocacy (*Aichmalotika*)

During the crisis of captivity, the main way that people paid for the redemption of captives was apparently by itinerant alms-seeking, often armed with testimonials written by clergy. The territorial collapse of the Byzantine Empire and its administration, particularly in Asia Minor, had increased the administrative responsibilities of the Church. The Church, while operating under severely curtailed circumstances, continued nonetheless to provide social structure and a form of local government for Christian communities.[17] These circumstances, coupled with the traditional role of clergy in the ransom of captives outlined above, made the Church the obvious focal point for redemptorist mechanisms during the crisis of captivity.

The Church's role was not limited to direct charity, but also involved the coordination of fundraising. Those affected by captivity sought to ransom themselves and their relatives by travelling around and collecting money from their coreligionists. To help these alms-seekers, clergy wrote testimonials, sometimes entitled *aichmalotika* ('pertaining to captives'). *Aichmalotika* are brief texts that outline specific instances of captivity and employ scriptural quotations to implore charity. Around a dozen such texts have been identified, mostly letters but also including a handful of associated sermons. All examples survive as copies and are usually anonymised,

---

[15] *Actes de Kutlumus*, ed. Lemerle, 135–8 (summary 134–5), No. 36; Živojinović, 'Turkish Assaults', 513.
[16] *Infra*, 103, 159–60.
[17] Hussey, *Orthodox Church*, 290; Runciman, *Great Church in Captivity*, 66–7.

intended for reference as templates. A number remain unpublished, while those in print have gone virtually unnoticed. The corpus spans the entire Palaiologan era, while analogous texts survive from the early modern period. They pertain to instances of captivity among Turks, who are usually hostilely portrayed. Many were composed and/or copied in Latin- rather than Greek-ruled contexts. The small surviving sample likely represents a mere fraction of an originally much larger literary phenomenon. The texts are vital for the detail they provide regarding redemptorist mechanisms, and for the rare glimpse they offer of the fates of non-elites.

Six examples of this genre have been published so far: one from the region of Mylasa, western Asia Minor, and dating possibly to c. 1264;[18] two in a dossier from fourteenth-century Lusignan Cyprus, one of which states that it was drafted by bishop Olbianos of Famagusta;[19] two copied on mid-fifteenth-century Crete, one of which was composed in Constantinople and the other (strictly speaking a homily rather than a letter) in Candia;[20] finally, one held at the Monastery of St Catherine on Mt Sinai, dating to the eighteenth century.[21] To these may be added the following unpublished examples: four letters and homilies in the manuscript Paris. gr. 400 (fols. 40r–43r, 131v–132r, 134r–v, 146v–147r, and 147v–148v), associated with Cyprus and dated to before the manuscript's completion in 1344;[22] one in London, British Library, Harley 5624 (fols. 202v–203r), from the late fourteenth or early fifteenth century and associated with Crete; one of obscure provenance in the fifteenth-century codex Paris. gr. 2509 (fols. 139v–140v); one lengthy letter written in the aftermath of the Conquest of Constantinople in 1453 in the late fifteenth-century codex Paris. gr. 2671 (fols. 395v–397r), and lastly another Sinaite text, Sin. gr. 1889 (fols. 296r–v), dated 1572.[23]

The *aichmalotika* usually contain four key elements: a plenary address to clergy and laity, a captivity narrative, pious admonitions and a benediction. While these four features might sometimes appear in a different order, there is sufficient structural consistency across the corpus to suggest that the

---

[18] Ed. Schreiner, 'Eine Schlacht', 612; date: Ragia, 'Turcs'.
[19] 'Κυπριακά', ed. Lampros, 155, No. 50 (pt. 2), and 338–9, No. 60 (pt. 3); ed. Beihammer, *Briefe und Urkunden*, 222–3, No. 92, and 232–3, No. 100.
[20] Ed. Mercati, 'Giovanni Simeonachis', 329–30.
[21] Ed. Amantos, 'Η αἰχμαλωσία τοῦ Νικολάου Λικινίου', 155–6.
[22] These texts have been edited and translated by Saccon in his unpublished MPhil thesis, 'Ransoming Activities'.
[23] I thank Prof. Claudia Rapp for bringing this last example to my attention. Most unpublished examples have been studied and at least partially transcribed and translated in my 'Cross-Confessional Captivity'.

aichmalotikon became a formalised genre of letter writing in the Palaiologan period. The texts were written and issued by senior clergy, that is to say, bishops, metropolitan bishops and patriarchs. Across the eastern Mediterranean, clergy copied exempla into literary manuscripts, sometimes as part of model letter collections, and other times in isolation. They belong to what might be described as a literary middlebrow: they do not belong to the world of Constantinopolitan *literati*, but neither do they contain demotic elements. They were one of the main tools of the Greek Christian world in its response to mass captivity in the thirteenth to fifteenth centuries and beyond.

The plenary address reveals that these letters were intended for the attention of a broad range of people all across Christian communities, and not exclusively Greek Christian. One text of Constantinopolitan provenance is addressed to 'archpriests, greatly honoured priests, and spiritual monks found everywhere; laymen, rulers, and the rest of God's people in Christ's name'; this fairly general list of groups is quite normal for the corpus.[24] Some letters drafted on Cyprus under the Frankish Lusignan kings, however, also appealed specifically to Latin Christian nobles. A certain Olbianos, an early fourteenth-century Greek Christian bishop of Amathous, addressed a letter that he drafted 'to all followers and worshippers of the honourable, holy, coessential, life-giving and indivisible Trinity, consisting of arch-priests, priests, monks, hieromonks, archons, knights (καβαλλαρίων), castellans (καστελλανίων), similar people, and the rest of the people in Christ's name, to both rulers and the ruled.'[25] Another contemporary Cypriot letter is addressed to clergy, knights and baileys, the last being Venetian officials residing on the island.[26] The appeal to knights, castellans and baileys suggests that Greek Christian victims of captivity could hope to receive the help of these Latin notables, despite the fact that Latins on Cyprus treated Greek Christians as second-class subjects and often traded them as slaves.[27]

Next, the section that outlines the captivity narrative is of particular interest: it reveals details of the fates of ordinary people whose lived experiences are often absent from medieval Greek texts. The narrative sections

---

[24] Mercati, 'Giovanni Simeonachis', 330.
[25] 'Κυπριακά', ed. S. Lampros (pt. 2), 155–6, No. 50; Beihammer, *Griechische Briefe und Urkunden*, ed. 222–3, tr. 298–9, comm. 360, No. 92 (here, tr. AG).
[26] Paris. gr. 400, f. 132r.
[27] On status: Coureas, *Latin Church in Cyprus*; Coureas, 'Latin and Greek Churches'; Arbel, 'Slave Trade'.

explain what had befallen the bearer and his or her family, sometimes listing people who still remained in captivity and noting the cost of their ransom. Often, these specific details have been to some extent removed: the *aichmalotika* survive in copies rather than as original letters, and it was standard in Byzantine letter-writing to remove concrete information, such as proper nouns or numbers, when letters were collected and copied.[28] Some of the *aichmalotika* note explicitly that they were either signed or sealed by their author in their original form. The involvement of senior clergymen in the redemptorist process was important because their authority gave potential almsgivers the assurance that the letter-bearer's story of captivity was true and told in good faith. The author of one letter, a metropolitan bishop, felt it necessary to add that he 'has been fully assured of, and knows precisely' the amount demanded for the ransom of a captured family.[29]

The narrative sections of the letters tend to be brief and supply few details of the sort that would allow their context to be firmly established. The letter written for a certain Demetrios by a member of an unnamed patriarch's chancery may serve as an example. The condensed narrative reveals that Demetrios and his father had made out from Thessaloniki on a boat when they were captured by some Turks. 'Demetrios So-and-so (ὁ δεῖνα) the Thessalonian here' was probably originally given his surname where the placemarker now stands. Demetrios was somehow freed – the letter does not specify how, only that it was 'by God's grace' – but his father remained in captivity. His task now was to weave his way around communities of 'God-loving and merciful Christians', collecting alms in order to free his father.[30] Across the corpus it appears that the head of the family tended, as here, to secure release first: this person, usually an adult male, would then travel around seeking charity with the *aichmalotikon* in hand to attest to his honesty. Should Demetrios have left with any ransom payments still outstanding for himself, his father's retention would have stood as surety against his defaulting; given emotional ties, a family member would have served as a far better guarantee than a deposit of material wealth.

This letter is consistent with the general picture of Turkish expansion at this time: the sea-lanes of the Aegean were prone to attack, and people

---

[28] Karlsson, *Idéologie et cérémonial*, 14–17 (I thank Prof. Dimiter Angelov for the reference).

[29] London, BL, Harley 5624, fol. 202v, ed. and tr. AG: τόσας ὅπερ ἐπληροφορήθημεν καὶ γινώσκομεν (γινόσκομεν cod.) καὶ ἡμεῖς ἀκριβῶς. (Partial ed. and tr. in Grant, 'Cross-Confessional Captivity', 1.253–4 and n. 599).

[30] Ed. Mercati, 'Giovanni Simeonachis', 330.

from Thessaloniki appear frequently as slaves in notarial acts of sale drawn up in commercial centres frequented by Latin traders.[31] Captivities like this were so widespread in the fourteenth and earlier fifteenth centuries that the letter cannot be securely dated. All that is known for sure is that the text predated 1449, the date given in the manuscript's subscript. The scribe was John Symeonakes, the leading clergyman on Venetian-ruled Crete at that point. He delivered a sermon around this time on behalf of a woman called Sophia Papadia from the nearby island of Karpathos, encouraging the assembled faithful to help her to ransom her family.[32] It is entirely possible that Symeonakes copied the letter because he was using it to inform the structure of his homily.

The third element contained in the letters comprises a meditation on the spiritual value of charity that encourages the giving of alms. These pious admonitions are structured around biblical citations: the most commonly quoted passages come from the latter part of Matthew 25 (the parable of the sheep and the goats) and Proverbs 19:17 ('He that hath pity upon the poor lendeth unto the Lord . . .'). The letters do not quote the many biblical passages that relate to captivity; this appears to be because the *aichmalotika* were understood first and foremost as letters seeking charity, of which the ransoming of captives was often understood to occupy first place. An example of this has already been quoted above, and a briefer version of this sentiment also appears in the letter drafted for Demetrios of Thessaloniki. The pious admonitions are formulaic, and it is even possible that they circulated as independent exempla, separated from the other sections of the *aichmalotika*. The register of the Patriarchate of Constantinople contains a text of this sort, copied around 1340, during the patriarchate of John XIV

---

[31] Examples: Domenico Prete, ed. Tiepolo, 23–4, No. 11 (Venice); Donato Fontanella, ed. Stahl, 243–4, No. 59 (Candia); Duran Duelt, 'Companyia', 569–71 (seven people, Candia); Državni Arhiv u Dubrovniku, Diversa notariae II, fol. 138r (Dubrovnik: summary Krekić, *Dubrovnik*, 183, No. 108); Epstein, *Speaking of Slavery*, 92–3 (Genoa); Ferrer, 'Esclaus i lliberts', 205 (Barcelona); Luttrell, 'Slavery', 94, 95, No. 21, 97, No. 32 (all Rhodes); Nicola de Boateriis, ed. Lombardo, 54–5, No. 50, 80–1, No. 76 (all Candia); Venice, Archivio di Stato, Notai di Candia, DIII B. 244, Giovanni Similiante, fol. 94r, No. 8, fol. 138v, No. 1 (all Candia); Verlinden, *L'esclavage*, 2.827, 2. 828, 2.830 (two people), 2.840, 2.846 and n. 444, 2.847 and n. 453 (two people), 2.851 (all Candia); Verlinden, 'Recrutement' 84 = 'Orthoxodie' 453 (Venice). There were also non-Greeks from the region of Thessaloniki, for example, a Bulgarian trafficked to Candia: Venice, Archivio di Stato, Notai di Candia, B9, Andrea de Belloamore, fol. 136r, No. 3.

[32] Ed. Mercati, 'Giovanni Simeonachis', 329–30.

Kalekas; this text notes the freeing of captives as a most Christian act, and quotes James 2:26: 'Faith without works is dead'.[33]

The Distribution of Testimonials

All the surviving *aichmalotika* refer to instances of captivity among Muslim groups – in most cases almost certainly Turkish groups in Asia Minor or the Balkans.[34] Not one of these texts refers to an instance of captivity among Latin Christians, despite the fact that thousands of Greek Christians suffered this fate in the thirteenth to fifteenth centuries; nor does any so much as suggest that Latins might have played any role other than potential almsgivers. Many of these texts were drafted or copied under Latin rule, and Frankish lay elites are among those to whom some *aichmalotika* from Cyprus actively appeal for help. Cyprus was the most important redemptorist haven for Greek Christians until the mid-fourteenth century: in 1369, Pierre I of Lusignan was assassinated; this was followed by a Genoese invasion in 1373–4, which led to the conquest of the important emporium of Famagusta.[35] The result was the terminal destabilisation of Cyprus' politics and economy and the transfer of redemptorist activity to Venetian Crete, a role it would retain until after the fall of Constantinople in 1453. Only one *aichmalotikon* seems to have its origins in Asia Minor, and that is the very earliest surviving example, dating from the later thirteenth century, at which time the empire was still actively campaigning in the region.[36] To this may be added the only external reference to an *aichmalotikon*, which comes from the Empire of Trebizond, also in the thirteenth century.[37] After this time, Asia Minor is conspicuously absent from the picture. This pattern fits with what is known of the movements of refugees in the same period, in which Greeks generally preferred Byzantine or Latin over Turkish rule.

It is worth noting that similar texts to the *aichmalotika* survive from Byzantium's neighbours. The Cairo Geniza, an enormous depository of documents, preserves many original letters written by, or on behalf of,

---

[33] *Register*, ed. H. Hunger et al., 192, No. 128.
[34] There is one instance of a captivity in the Crimea under the Golden Horde; the captor may or may not have been a Muslim: 'Κυπριακά', ed. Lampros (pt. 3), 339, No. 60; Beihammer, *Griechische Briefen und Urkunden*, ed. 232–3, tr. 305–6, comm. 367, No. 100 (discussed *supra*, 78–9).
[35] Edbury, *Kingdom of Cyprus*, 197–211; Bănescu, *Le déclin de Famagouste*, 8–47. The role of Cyprus as a redemptorist hub is addressed fully in Chapter 2, *supra*.
[36] Schreiner, 'Eine Schlacht'; Ragia, 'Turcs'.
[37] *Vazelonskie akty*, ed. Uspenskij, 77–9 (at 78), No. 107.

Jewish captives from across the Mediterranean. In Jewish communities, whole trains of captives would sometimes wander from one community to another, assisted by patrons such as community leaders and merchants.[38] The papyri of the Great Mosque of Damascus include an example of an alms-seeking letter written on behalf of two Muslim paupers held captive by Franks, perhaps after the sack of Nāblus in 1242 by the Knights Templar.[39] In the Greek case, testimonials for wandering captives remained important at least into the seventeenth century and perhaps beyond. Greek clergy fleeing from the Ottoman Empire travelled as far afield as Scotland and Sweden in the early modern period; they bore testimonials from higher clergy in the eastern Mediterranean and often sought to ransom family members from captivity and to carve out a living of their own in a Protestant Europe that looked favourably upon anyone who was not Catholic.[40] Perhaps this kind of document, appealing to ideals of charity rooted in the shared religion or confessional sympathies of a given community, was one that found particular importance in places where people of one religion and language were ruled by those of another. Whether these were Greek Christians ruled by Latins, Jews ruled by Muslims or Muslims ruled by Latins, in all cases, religious hierarchy and shared belief provided community structure in the absence of secular authorities of the same faith.

The *aichmalotikon* persisted as a genre for centuries after the end of Byzantium as a political entity. To give one particularly late example, Nicholas Likinios, brother of the famous doctor Andreas Likinios, was issued with one such letter in 1722. Nikolaos had been captured in the course of the Ottoman conquest of the Morea, including Monemvasia (the ancestral home of the Likinioi) in 1715. He was led captive to the island of Crete where, following a behavioural pattern at least four or five centuries old, he left his son as a hostage and set out to raise money for their ransom. Nikolaos travelled to Alexandria where he was issued with an *aichmalotikon* by the patriarch, Samuel. The patriarch's account of Likinios's tribulations, as well as an example of an *aichmalotikon*, are both preserved in a manuscript from Sinai.[41] The range of early modern analogues indicates that the *aichmalotikon* was a particular example of a wider

---

[38] Frenkel, 'Proclaim Liberty'.
[39] Mouton et al., 'Deux documents damascains', 406–20.
[40] Grant, 'Scotland's "Vagabonding Greekes"'.
[41] Amantos, 'Η αἰχμαλωσία τοῦ Νικολάου Λικινίου' (the MS is Sin. gr. 1605, fols. 159 and 194v–195v; the rubric is Ἕτερον περὶ ζητείας αἰχμαλώτων: 'Another [model letter] concerning the alms-seeking of captives').

genre of testimonials for those seeking alms for any reason.⁴² Some templates of these more general testimonials made it into printed collections of model letters: the *New Epistolary* (*Neon Epistolarion*) published in Venice in 1796, for example, contains models of 'how an arch-priest would write a letter about charity for a poor person' and 'how a metropolitan [bishop] writes a letter about charity for a monastery'.⁴³

Further Evidence for Itinerant Alms-Seeking

The practice of itinerant alms-seeking for the raising of ransoms is attested in some other Greek-language texts that broadly corroborate the mechanisms suggested by the *aichmalotika*.

The first of these is the only known external reference to an *aichmalotikon*. It is found in a thirteenth-century document from the Monastery of St John the Baptist of Vazelon, Trebizond. The acts of the monastery undoubtedly comprise the most important evidence for the social history of the Pontos region in the later Middle Ages. The document, its precise date uncertain, was drawn up at Vazelon for the hieromonk Theodoret. Theodoret records that his sister was taken captive by the Turkmens ('godless Hagarenes') and had been missing for a long time; her ransom was fixed at 850 *aspra*. Theodoret states that he 'neither carried around [lit. dragged around] an *aichmalotikon* nor sold anything'.⁴⁴ These were presumably the two main routes by which a person might be expected to raise ransom costs. This seems to be one of the earliest attestations of the use of a ransom-raising testimonial in a Byzantine context. Moreover, it is the only example from the Empire of Trebizond.

The second example does not mention an *aichmalotikon*, but it is a rare example of a description in a literary text of itinerant alms-seeking by a captive. The historiographer Nikephoros Gregoras records an anecdote dated to the second quarter of the fourteenth century, therefore dating from the heart of the crisis period, which offers further evidence of this phenomenon. The anecdote concerns a woman identified as a 'Scythian', an

---

⁴² Angelomati-Tsougaraki, 'Τὸ φαινόμενο τῆς ζητείας'.
⁴³ *Νέον Ἐπιστολάριον*, 68–71.
⁴⁴ *Vazelonskie akty*, ed. Uspenskij, 77–9 (at 78), No. 107: καὶ ἡ μία ἀδελφή μου ἡρπάγην ὑπὸ τῶν ἀθέων Ἀγαρηνῶν καὶ ἔλειψεν χρόνους ἱκανούς. εὐδοκοῦντος δὲ θεοῦ καὶ μὲ τὴν εὐχὴν τῶν γονέων μου εὑρέθη καὶ ἔπεσεν εἰς τιμὴν εἰς ἄσπρα ων΄. καὶ οὔτε αἰχμαλωτικὸν ἔσυρα οὔτε ἐπώλησα οὔτε ἄλλον τίποτε. Cf. Bryer, 'Pontic exception', 139, who references this example but does not mention the *aichmalotikon*.

archaic term probably referring to a Cuman or a Mongol from the Golden Horde.⁴⁵ Desirous of living in Constantinople, the woman married a Greek captive from Thrace whom she bought as a slave; later, she purchased that man's wife as a slave, too, thereafter taking baptism and moving to Constantinople. The man's wife, however, took the case to the patriarch: she argued that she had been wronged by the 'Scythian' woman, having lost her husband to her. The 'Scythian' woman, however, had purchased both of them and therefore had legal rights over them as their mistress; the enslaved woman thus had no cause for complaint. Ultimately, the 'Scythian' woman freed the man in recognition of their union and the fact that he was father to their children. She did not, however, free the woman, since she was obviously benefitting from her service. She promised that the Byzantine woman could buy her freedom for the cost of her purchase, after which she (the Byzantine woman) would be able to depart with her husband, and the 'Scythian' woman would keep the children. This decision was deemed just by everyone present, including the patriarch – but excluding the Byzantine woman.⁴⁶

The final turn of the story, which concerns the enslaved Byzantine woman, is of enormous importance for understanding how captives went about the business of collecting alms:

> For when the woman left the city in order to collect the purchase price, and went around her neighbours in Thrace, where she had dwelt before, she again fell into the hands of the Scythians who all of a sudden invaded Thrace, and she disappeared as a captive whereas the man henceforth continued to cohabit with the good woman of Scythian descent.⁴⁷

This anecdote presents rare and important evidence for how captivity, slavery, law and religion interacted. In this case, the legality of the enslavement outweighed questions of cultural similarity or difference. The judgement, however, was ultimately interrupted by the constant and often recurring threat of captivity.

---

⁴⁵ Shukurov, *Byzantine Turks*, 231; on ethnic terminology, see Pow, 'Nationes que se Tartaros appellant'.

⁴⁶ Nikephoros Gregoras, *Historiae Byzantinae*, XI, 5, ed. Schopen, 1.542–4, German tr. Van Dieten, 2.284–5; English tr. R. Shukurov and D. Krausmüller in Rapp et al. (eds), *Mobility and Migration*, 84–5.

⁴⁷ Nikephoros Gregoras, *Historiae Byzantinae*, XI, 5, ed. Schopen, 1.544, German tr. Van Dieten, 1.285; English tr. R. Shukurov and D. Krausmüller in Rapp et al. (eds), *Mobility and Migration*, 85.

The Individual as Ransomer

Much of the evidence considered here concerns victims of captivity taking the initiative in raising ransom costs, and clergymen responding to their needs. There is also evidence for other categories of individuals becoming involved in these processes. Three main groups are considered here: first, secular Christian elites living under Islamic rule, often officeholders of some sort; second, family members producing the money in cases where the methods of fundraising are unknown; third, ransom by third parties, whether or not for profit. Unlike in the Iberian Peninsula at the same time, there does not seem to have been a class of professional ransomers in the Byzantine world.

The Thracian city of Adrianople/Edirne is the setting for a rare piece of evidence for how a Greek layman with a community leadership role under Islamic rule might address the issue of captivity. This evidence comes in the form of a dossier of letters addressed to and written by Nicholas Isidore, *krites* of Edirne shortly after the time of the conquest of Constantinople. Nicholas Isidore's letters, curiously neglected by scholars despite being published accessibly over half a century ago, are relevant because they deal in part with advocacy on behalf of captives displaced by the Ottoman conquest of Constantinople.[48] The position of *krites* in formerly Byzantine lands did not refer so literally to a judge (the basic meaning of the Greek) as to a prominent secular individual who seems to have been the public face of the Greek Christian community in its relations with its Muslim Turkish rulers. Nicholas Isidore was someone integrated into the Ottoman imperial system, and the role that he played as advocate of the Greek Christian community presents an important point of comparison for the activity of clergymen.[49]

The dossier comprises eight letters, surviving in their original form, of which seven were addressed to Nicholas Isidore, and one written by him. Of these eight, three mention captives; the second letter is of particular interest here: it was sent by 'the suppliants of your lordship, the priests and clergymen of Gallipoli', and describes Isidore as 'the most glorious and illustrious, our sure lord and benefactor, the *archon* Isidore, judge and great *emin* [official] of the great lord'.[50] This particular letter even recalls elements of

---

[48] Ed. Darrouzès, 'Lettres de 1453'; Harris, *Emigres*, 14–15. See *PLP* #8311.
[49] Philippides and Hanak, *Siege and Fall*, 74–5.
[50] Ed. and tr. Darrouzès, 'Lettres', 80: οἱ εὐχέται τῆς αὐθεντίας σου οἱ ἱερεῖς καὶ κληρικοὶ τῆς Καλιουπόλεως, and τῷ ἐνδοξοτάτῳ καὶ περιφανεστάτῳ ἡμῶν δὲ λίαν αὐθέντῃ καὶ εὐεργέτῃ τῷ ἄρχοντι κῦρ Ἰσιδώρῳ τῷ κριτῇ καὶ μεγάλῳ ἐμμίνῃ τοῦ μεγάλου αὐθεντός. (Darrouzès maintains the eccentric original orthography.) 'Emin': often translated 'commissioner', a paid official administrator in the Ottoman Empire appointed by Sultanic decree (*berât*). See Lewis, 'Emīn'.

the clerical *aichmalotika*. It notes Isidore's repute as a prolific redeemer of captives and asks him to help someone who had been taken captive in the course of the conquest of Constantinople.[51] This letter is most interesting for the fact that it is a clerical appeal to an individual, rather than an encyclical in the manner of the *aichmalotika*. It is also important for being directed to a Greek Christian lay official who lived under Ottoman rule, since all the *aichmalotika* otherwise derive, where known, from the Latin-ruled islands of Cyprus and Crete, or else from imperial lands. Figures within Greek Christian communities were evidently able to help captives in the aftermath of the fall of Constantinople, with clergy probably taking the lead as they always had and remained legally mandated to do, but with laymen most likely bearing much of the financial cost.

When the *aichmalotika* are contrasted with the correspondence of Nicholas Isidore, we see, as it were, two sides of the same coin. These were two models for responding to Ottoman expansion – one clerical, the other lay, and both fundamentally inseparable. Nicholas Isidore's letters attest to attempts to assist fellow Greek Christians within the strictures of the early Ottoman administrative system. He was a secular leader whose power derived from the Ottomans: while he might be called upon to help those captured by the Ottomans, in his official capacity he was not in conflict with them.

Some people were sold into slavery with the explicit provision that they could be redeemed by family members, often parents, at the price of their sale. This practice is evident in Candia in the early years of the fourteenth century, when the number of captives being trafficked from western Asia Minor appears to have been at its height. Kierana, sold by a Catalan to a Candian in December 1304 and noted to have been bought in *Turchia*, was to be freed if a relative should come and offer to pay the 11½ *hyperpyra* that she cost.[52] These types of clauses are particularly common in the acts drawn up by the notary Angelo de Cartura. Maria, from Philadelphia, was sold for the same price as Kierana and with the same conditions in June 1305.[53] Georgius, sold for 25 *hyperpyra* just a few weeks later, could be redeemed by his father.[54] Although these people had been enslaved and thus left the liminal status of captivity for the more clearly defined status of slavery, these clauses suggest that these people could expect to be redeemed and therefore that their enslavement was envisaged as quite likely temporary.

[51] Ed. and tr. Darrouzès, 'Lettres', 80–1.
[52] Pietro Pizolo, ed. Carbone, 2.194–5, No. 1119.
[53] Angelo de Cartura, ed. Stahl, 29–30, No. 76.
[54] Ibid., 50, No. 128.

These clauses also limited potential exploitation in the process of redemption. Figures of political importance could reach enormous prices. Just a few years earlier, Michael Notaropoulos, son of Paulos and honoured with the dignity of *sebastos*, had been captured on the island of Kythera after rebelling against the Venetian Cretan regime. On 5 July 1301 he was ransomed by Iohannes de Molino and Andreas Cornario, both residents of Candia, for an exorbitant 6,050 *hyperpyra*.[55] At this time a male Greek slave normally cost about 14 *hyperpyra*.[56] Such redemption clauses might therefore have been a welcome mitigation in cases where people sought to buy back their captured and enslaved family members and were at the mercy of their present owners.

A number of the acts recorded by Nicola de Boateriis in Famagusta turn out, on close inspection, to be ransoms of captives half-disguised by their recourse to the standard notarial act of manumission.[57] Georgius Gisi of Tinos, for example (probably a Latin rather than a Greek[58]), was redeemed by his brother Marcus on 9 February 1361 for 140 white *bezants* (alloy coins); he had been the slave of Cosmas, son of the late Ioseph de Zibelleto, a Genoese residing at Famagusta.[59] The next month, Dimitrius Cutica similarly redeemed his nephew (*nepos*) Michalius (seemingly also known as Nicola, unless this is a scribal error), both of Negroponte, and for the same price. Here, no third party is mentioned, indicating that Dimitrius had purchased Michalius previously. Michalius recorded in the very next act that he still owed his uncle twenty *bezants*.[60]

The manumission of Dimitrius Argomatari in August 1360 may even have had a political significance, since his manumitter is given as Franceschinus Miolo the Venetian, ambassador of the house of Sanuto (or Sanudo) of the Archipelago and Negroponte to the Kingdom of Cyprus. Miolo writes that he acquired Dimitrius and whatever property he had on Cyprus at public auction in Nicosia from a certain Georginus Sichielari, given as a royal

---

[55] Benvenuto de Brixano, ed. Morozzo della Rocca, 79, No. 215; cf. 104, No. 282, where one of the ransomers, Michaele son of Giovanni Maselo, sold off his ransom profit. Fleet, *Trade*, 51–2 and n. 97 seems to be the only discussion of this incident.

[56] Wright, '*Vade, sta, ambula*', 202.

[57] Discussed in Arbel, 'Slave Trade', 158, who also notes a Jewish parallel.

[58] See *PLP* #4175 (Γίζος Βαρθολομαῖος = Bartolomeo I Ghisi, lord of Tinos and Mykonos 1259–1302) and 3952 (the former's son, Γεώργιος = Georgio I. Ghisi, *inter alia* lord of Tinos and Mykonos 1303–11).

[59] Nicola de Boateriis, ed. Lombardo, 52–3, No. 48.

[60] Ibid., 65–6, No. 60.

official in the city; Dimitrius had been among the property of another man also called Demetrius [sic]. Dimitrius was himself from Negroponte, suggesting that Miolo might have been assisting in his repatriation. From their names, it is possible that Georginus and Demetrius were both Greeks.[61] Negroponte and Tinos were both under Venice's sphere of influence; while their vulnerability was a product of Catalan and Turkish raiding, the Venetian connection might explain why Boateriis, as a Venetian notary, was involved in acts redeeming Greek slaves originating from these places. It has been suggested that he may have had a network of contacts in Negroponte in particular, thus allowing him not just to record these ransoms, but also to organise them.[62]

The acts of Nicola de Boateriis and Simeone di San Giacomo dell' Orio also record the redemptorist impulses of a man called Fetus Semitecolo. In the summer of 1362, Semitecolo freed two of his slaves, Iohannes and Dimitrius, both of the Romanía, but stipulated that they should serve him for a further year before manumission.[63] Then, on 3 April 1363, Semitecolo drew up his will.[64] He was near death and suffering from plague, but, the act states, still of sound mind. Semitecolo manumitted his own slave Petrus from Balat; he also demanded that several other people free their slaves, all seemingly Greeks – Anna from Constantinople, Costa from 'Sacrasto' (likely Karystos), and Georgius from Kalavryta; perhaps he had sold them to those owners. Furthermore, he paid the 90-*bezant* manumission fee for Michali, from somewhere in the Morea, owned by Bartholomeus de Chaneto, a Mallorcan.[65] Semitecolo was evidently troubled by the enslavement of these Greeks, and, while he still lived, wished to ensure that they would be freed.

In Chapter 1, some examples of ransom farmers in early fourteenth-century Crete and Cyprus were noted;[66] these can be supplemented by an example from Genoa a century later. On 19 May 1408, a Greek woman called Maria de Speytaigo made acknowledgement that she owed 60 *libri* to a burger of Caffa (Crimea), called Battista Spinola, since he had ransomed her from captivity among Turks and transported her from the Aegean island of Chios, then a Genoese possession, to the

---

[61] Ibid., 8–9, No. 2.
[62] Barker, *Most Precious Merchandise*, 34.
[63] Nicola de Boateriis, ed. Lombardo, 182–3, No. 169.
[64] Simeone di San Giacomo dell' Orio, summarised Otten-Froux, 44–7, No. 6.
[65] Ibid., 67–8, Nos. 39, 40, 41, 44.
[66] *Supra*, 41–2.

city of Genoa. Another man, Raffaele Frugono, agreed to reimburse Battista Spinola in return for twelve years of servitude from Maria. In this case, there was obviously a language barrier between the two men and Maria, given that another individual, Giovanni Mazurro, had to interpret between Greek and Italian. Maria would presumably have been obliged to learn Italian as quickly as possible in order to interact with her new master.[67]

In later medieval Iberia, by contrast with the eastern Mediterranean, the prevalence of captivity led to the growth of municipal, professionalised ransom practices. This is an instructive comparison. Professional ransomers were called *exeas* and *alfaqueques* on the Christian side of the frontier, the first term being borrowed from the Arabic *shīʿa* (here meaning 'companions') and the second from *al-fikāk* (redemption or liberation). Christians called the Muslim counterparts of the *exeas* by the name *almotalefe*, the origin of which is the Arabic *al-mustaḥlaf* (a person who swears to undertake a task). These professional redemptorists were useful because they had the necessary knowledge of languages and of the varying conventions of ransom law and custom in both Christian and Muslim communities. In certain Christian communities, the interlocutor would be appointed by a council and required to swear oaths of good faith. People often made a bequest in their will for the ransoming of members of their community. To the same end, a number of municipal Christian law codes legislated in favour of the conditional purchasing of Muslim slaves to raise collateral for ransom; should the ransom attempt fail, the slave would be returned to the owner from whom they had been purchased.[68] In medieval Iberia, captivity was common, and local communities accepted a responsibility for ransoming, which was carried out by experienced, paid professionals. In Greek Christian contexts, individuals took the initiative on behalf of themselves or their relatives, and clergy met them half-way. Occasionally, secular officials might provide the necessary funds or merchants might engage in ransom farming. This configuration may be described as only semi-institutionalised by comparison with the better-known contemporary Iberian context.

---

[67] Otten-Froux, 'Représentation', 102.
[68] The bibliography is extensive; see especially Brodman, 'Municipal Ransoming Law'; Brodman, 'Community, Identity and the Redemption of Captives', 241–52; Brodman, 'Captives or Prisoners'; Hopley, 'Ransoming of Prisoners'; Rodriguez, 'Financing'.

Prisoner Exchanges

By the fourteenth century, Byzantium was well acquainted with the experience of captivity. Captivity shaped the way Byzantium interacted with its Arab and Slav neighbours in the first millennium.[69] Between 896 and 911, the Arab-Muslim historiographer al-Ṭabarī lists almost annual raids launched from Muslim Cilicia into Byzantine Asia Minor and the Aegean. These were intended to generate plunder and captives.[70] The relatively well-documented nature of this period is reflected in the abundance of scholarship that has addressed it. Large-scale attacks and small-scale regional raiding were all part of the same phenomenon of broader conflict in which captives served as diplomatic pawns: prisoners would be taken and then used as a bargaining tool to bring about a temporary rapprochement between the two empires. There would then be a formal exchange, often in Cilicia, after which the process would resume. This phenomenon was the product of the centripetal force that two centres of gravity – Constantinople and Baghdad – exerted on Christian and Muslim groups respectively, as they engaged in constant conflict across a shifting frontier that extended outwards from Asia Minor into the eastern Mediterranean itself. Such a style of warfare was contingent upon the existence of two well-matched regional superpowers that acknowledged some kind of mutual political parity.[71]

The most detailed account of this process is the narrative of the sack of Thessaloniki in 904 written by John Kaminiates. The attack was led by Leo of Tripoli, a convert to Islam captured from Attaleia (Antalya, south Asia Minor). This event is described in Kaminiates's extraordinary first-hand account, apparently written as a long letter to a certain Gregory of Cappadocia. Despite the far larger volume of written evidence available for the late Byzantine versus the middle Byzantine period, first-person narratives of captivity in the manner of Kaminiates's are rare. Leo is said to have plundered the city, slaughtering many of its inhabitants and taking captive a further 22,000, most of whom were women and children. He took the captives to Crete, at that time under Muslim control and apparently acting as a centre for the exchange of Christian and Muslim

---

[69] Patoura, Αιχμάλωτοι; Rotman, *Byzantine Slavery*, 25–81.
[70] Al-Ṭabarī, *Taʾrīkh*, ed. De Goeje et al., 2154, 2185, 2186, 2200, 2250, 2251–2 and 2286–7; tr. Rosenthal, 34, 73, 74, 91, 151, 196.
[71] See Bosworth, 'Tarsus'; Garrood, 'Cilicia and the Hamdanids'; Friedman, *Encounter Between Enemies*, 33–45.

captives. Anyone not purchased on Crete (this included Kaminiates himself) was then taken to Paphos on Cyprus in order to be sold on the slave market.[72] Despite systemic geopolitical changes in the Aegean region in the intervening centuries, the centrality of Cyprus and Crete to the trafficking of captives remained into the Palaiologan period, and many of the captives of the late period came from Thessaloniki, too.

By the late period, large-scale exchanges of captives on the model of the ninth and tenth centuries had all but disappeared. The evidence suggests that the redemption of captives was very rarely mediated by the imperial centre, and instead organised on a local level by Greek Christian clergy advocating on behalf of individual captives, who were usually required to raise ransom money by their own initiative. As this redemptorist method had deep roots stretching back to late antiquity, it is possible that the great captive exchanges of the Byzantine middle period ought to be seen as exceptional and tied to the circumstances of large-scale inter-imperial warfare, and the localised clerical model of the late period as a return to normative practices, and not the other way around.[73] Indeed, there is also evidence from the middle Byzantine period indicating that smaller-scale ransoms or exchanges were common or even normal outside the imperial frontier zone.[74]

The only reference to a prisoner exchange involving Byzantium in the Palaiologan period comes from diplomatic correspondence with the Mamlūk Sultanate. These two major political entities engaged in frequent diplomacy from 1262–1411 (at least), though many of the embassies went unremarked by Byzantine historians and are known only through Arabic sources. In the thirteenth century, the Mamlūks were primarily concerned with securing access to the Black Sea slave trade; for their part, the Byzantines were sometimes concerned for the status of local Christians or, occasionally, for their commercial interests in Egypt.[75]

In 1349, the Mamlūk Sultan al-Nāṣir Ḥasan (r. 1347–1351 and 1354–1361) sent a letter to the Byzantine Emperor John VI Kantakouzenos

---

[72] John Kaminiates, *Capture of Thessaloniki*, ed. and tr. Frendo and Fotiou. Kazhdan, 'Some Questions', doubted the authenticity of the text, believing it to be a fifteenth-century redaction of tenth-century material; see the responses of Christides, 'Once Again', Farag, 'Some Remarks', and Khoury Odetallah, 'Leo Tripolites'. For Leo's origins, see John Skylitzes, *Synopsis Historiarum*, VII, 23, ed. Thurn, 182–3, tr. Wortley, 176–7.

[73] I thank Dr Max Ritter for first bringing this to my attention (private communication).

[74] For example, Rotman, *Byzantine Slavery*, 50.

[75] This has been discussed in Chapter 2, *supra*, 68–71.

(r. 1347–1354). These negotiations were precipitated by a dispute between two claimants to the Melkite Patriarchate of Jerusalem, that is to say, the patriarchate of the Arabic-speaking Christians in communion with Constantinople. One claimant, Lazarus, had been apparently wrongly deposed in favour of another, Gerasimos, the latter elected at a synod of 1341. Lazarus fled to Kantakouzenos, who used his power to champion his cause. The rapprochement was similarly sparked by persecutions of Melkite Christians in Palestine by the Amīr Shaykhū. The negotiations were also concerned with allowing Greek merchants free trade with Egypt, and addressed the reconstruction of the Church of St George in Cairo.

The letter of 1349 addressed the demands of Kantakouzenos's envoy, among which was a request for the freeing of captives 'from the land of the Romanía' held by Muslims. The sultan stressed that there was an 'ancient custom' (*synetheian archaian*) mandating the undertaking of a mutual exchange of slaves. This idea must have derived from his chancery's knowledge of ʿAbbāsid-era practices. Such a mechanism would have been a visible, dignified political gesture that put both the Mamlūk Sultanate and the Byzantine Empire on an equal diplomatic footing: this is quite unlike the local, individual clerical initiatives that otherwise characterise the later Middle Ages. It seems, however, that the exchange was not actually organised, despite the claim to precedent: the sultan noted that he had set free the captives that he held and that the ambassador had already received them.[76]

Military Orders

In the western Mediterranean from the twelfth century onwards, individuals and institutions bore the responsibility for ransoming captives. At an earlier stage, this responsibility was borne by local elites; later, this role was gradually absorbed by the redemptorist military orders, the Trinitarians and Mercedarians. From about the 1180s, private houses had opened in Iberia that were intended to serve as institutions for facilitating ransom attempts. In 1198, Pope Innocent III sanctioned the first Christian order to specialise in the redemption of captives: the Order of the Holy Trinity. This was followed sometime after 1229 with the emergence of the Mercedarians. One-third of the Trinitarians' income was to be dedicated to the ransom payments and negotiations, and the other two-thirds to their necessary expenses (food, accommodation, and so on). The Trinitarians

---

[76] Kantakouzenos, *Historia*, IV, 38, ed. Schopen, 3.97–8; for an analysis, see Canard, 'Une lettre'.

had houses in England and France as well as Iberia, but the Mercedarians remained focused on the Mediterranean coast of France and Spain and in the Balearics. The Mercedarians almost certainly played no part in the eastern Mediterranean, whereas the Trinitarians were active on a few isolated occasions, for example, during the crusade of the French King Louis IX (1248–54), when a group acted as official negotiators during his captivity.[77] There was no true equivalent of this organised, military impetus for redemption in the Levant, but the Knights Hospitaller, the Order of St John, did participate in redemptorist initiatives. At this time, based on Rhodes, the Order of the Hospitallers was the most active military order in the later medieval Aegean.

One of these initiatives appears incidentally in the Greek historiographer Doukas's narrative of the death of the important Turkish ruler Umur of Aydın in May 1348. Umur is noted to have been responsible for the construction of ships that went out to raid the Aegean islands of Naxos, Samos, Chios and Lesbos. In the Byzantine Empire, John VI Kantakouzenos had recently obtained the imperial purple following his victory in the civil war against John V Palaiologos and his guardian, Anna of Savoy. Umur set out with a fleet for Thrace and there met with Kantakouzenos's wife, Irene Asanina, since the emperor was travelling to Serbia. Umur apparently waited for the emperor for some three months, while his men raided Thrace and tried to familiarise themselves with the land, presumably with the idea that they might later try to conquer it.

While Umur was in Thrace, intelligence arrived that the Knights Hospitaller were at Smyrna, in the context of a crusade. In the time he had been absent, the Hospitallers had begun to construct a fortress dedicated to St Peter, which Doukas states was intended 'for the salvation of fugitive captives' (*phygadon aichmaloton*). Umur quickly concluded an alliance with Irene and left for his principality with a group of captives from his men's raids in tow. Once he had arrived in Smyrna, Umur launched an assault on the fortress and perished in the attempt. In the Islamic tradition, he was remembered as having died a martyr's death.[78]

Doukas also notes that the Hospitallers began construction of a further fortress at Bodrum in 1402. This fortress was dedicated to St Peter and known in Greek as the *Petronion*. The Turkish prince İlyas of Menteşe made unsuccessful attempts to prevent the construction of this fort, which

---

[77] On the military orders, see Flannery, 'Trinitarian Order' and Forey, *Military Orders*.
[78] Doukas, *Chronographia*, VII, 2, ed. and tr. Reinsch, 84–7 (ed. and tr. Grecu, 52–3), tr. Magoulias, 69. Umur is discussed further *infra*, 173–4.

was likewise to be a refuge for escaped captives. The 'escaped captives' (*phygadas aichmalotous*) who reached the fort were to be kept safe by the guards. They were then to be manumitted 'in writing, in the name of St Peter'. This structure was still intact at the time that Doukas wrote.[79] The case of the Castle of St Peter at Bodrum emphasises the strongly regionalised character of captivity and ransom in the later medieval eastern Mediterranean. Sometimes, a Latin power might take responsibility for helping Greeks captured by Turks; there is seemingly no evidence, on the other hand, for Turks sheltering Greeks captured by Latins.

The Hospitallers' role in helping Greek Christians continued after the fall of Constantinople. On 20 June 1456, an unspecified group of Christians of Asia Minor wrote to the Grand Master of the Hospitallers on Rhodes, Jacques de Milly, begging for a papal fleet to evacuate them to Hospitaller territory. These Christians sought to avoid the levying of their sons by the Ottomans for use in the janissary infantry corps – that is, the *devşirme*.[80]

It is important to note, however, that the Hospitallers did not merely redeem Greek captives but also used them for their own ends. In 1319 the knights crushed a rebellion on the island of Leros, taking nearly two thousand Greeks back to Rhodes with them. These captives supposedly amounted to all those Greeks who had not been killed. The knights refortified and garrisoned the castle.[81] Such manoeuvres may also have contributed to the unfree labour force on which the Hospitallers relied to repopulate and cultivate their domains.

It appears that the Hospitallers created a free agricultural peasantry on Rhodes through the manumission of Greek slaves. Depopulation was common in the Romanía, and local rulers sometimes made concerted moves to repopulate their lands with people from elsewhere;[82] Greek slaves may have fulfilled this role in Hospitaller domains. Chartularies preserved on Malta record a significant number of manumissions, many of which appear, on the basis of personal names or places of origin, to refer to Greeks;[83] often, it is stated that these slaves were freed by virtue of their long service. A lack of

---

[79] Doukas, *Chronographia*, XXII, 1, ed. and tr. Reinsch 222–5 (ed. and tr. Grecu, 154–5), tr. Magoulias, 122. On the fort, see de Vaivre, 'Château Saint-Pierre'.
[80] *Acta et Diplomata*, ed. Miklosich and Müller (hereafter MM), 3.291; cf. Vryonis, 'Glabas', 441–2, with tr. For the *devşirme*, see Chapter 6, *infra*.
[81] Ed. Delaville le Roulx, *Hospitaliers*, 366 (cf. Luttrell and O'Malley, *Countryside*, 36).
[82] *Supra*, 43, 112–13; *infra*, 182–92.
[83] Luttrell, 'Slavery', and Coureas, 'Manumission'. Private communication with Dr Luttrell has also helped to inform my understanding of the Hospitallers' engagement of manumitted Greeks.

slaves was also a concern: Georgius Calamia, officially a serf (his father, Micali Protutameno, was free – *francus* – but his mother, Cali tu Mangipa, a serf – *serva*), had his freedom recognised by the Master at Avignon in 1391 on the condition that he give four Greek slaves to the bailey of Kos.[84] It is probable that this was a means of ensuring that the labour pool on that island, also a Hospitaller domain, should not run dry.

The completion of the Ottoman conquest of Byzantium by c. 1460 led to a fundamentally new set of circumstances between the Hospitallers and Greek Christians by the seventeenth century. Greek merchants found favourable conditions under their new Ottoman rulers in places where they had once been priced-out by Latin merchants; Turkish raiding in the Aegean was no longer of nearly so much importance, and among the most prolific corsairs were now the Latin Christian Knights Hospitaller, now based no longer on Rhodes but at their new headquarters on Malta.[85] The Maltese archive of the Tribunale degli Armamenti preserves some examples of testimonials written in response to corsair raids that shed light on these new dynamics.

The first example concerns an act of robbery. In 1617, the Patriarch of Alexandria and future Patriarch of Constantinople, Cyril Loukaris, interceded with the Tribunale on behalf of a Christian man named Haji (that is, pilgrim) Pietro de Georgio. Haji Pietro had been robbed by Hospitaller corsairs the previous year and came before the French consulate at Saida (Sidon), modern Lebanon, to make the case that he had been unjustly robbed. The letter of intercession, written in Italian, may be the work of Loukaris himself, and not just of a secretary.[86]

The second example was drafted in 1634 and originates from the Aegean island of Karpathos. Just like Loukaris's letter of 1617, it concerns the seizure of goods rather than people. The text's origins, however, offer a precise parallel to the *aichmalotika*. Two merchants, Duca Galeazzo and Nicola, were sailing from their home island of Mytilene to Alexandria. They stopped at Karpathos to take on supplies but were there overwhelmed by three Christian corsairing vessels – a Hospitaller of Malta, a Livornese and a Sardinian. Because the legality of looting a Christian merchantman was unclear, the Livornese and Sardinian crews backed

---

[84] Ed. Luttrell, 'Slavery', 98, No. 38. Similar bargains were required of six manumitted slaves: ed. in ibid., 93; 95; 96, No. 28; 98, No. 41; 99, No. 46; Coureas, 'Manumission', 106–7, 112 (a Christian slave was explicitly required in one case).
[85] Greene, *Catholic Pirates and Greek Merchants*.
[86] Ibid., 144–5.

down; the Hospitaller, however, did not, and took almost everything. The crew approached the archbishop of the island, Ierotheos, and asked him to draft a letter of intercession that should be used for an appeal against unjust robbery. The document was written in Greek, signed and sealed by Ierotheos, and witnessed by eight other clergy, as well (apparently) as the laymen on the island. The appeal went first to the Catholic bishop of Chios, and subsequently to Valletta. It described the incident in highly emotional language, stressing the injustice of the case as an attack by Christians against Christians and being sure to note that there were no Turks on board the targeted boat.[87] The Hospitallers therefore had both positive and negative effects upon the Greek Christian community, and these effects became increasingly destructive over time.

Conclusion

Many people who were caught up in the crisis of captivity secured their redemption by themselves or with the help of others. Those seeking to ransom themselves or their families in the Palaiologan era might not have had the support of the imperial administration or of municipal institutions on an Iberian model, but they did enjoy the patronage of the Church and occasionally the help of laymen.

This help was provided on a small-scale basis. The Church suffered from impoverishment but continued nonetheless to provide social structure and a form of local government for Christian communities. Clergy helped in two main ways: through direct donations or by providing testimonials (*aichmalotika*). The *aichmalotikon* comprised a redemptorist mechanism that could function inside or outside the empire, wherever there were clergy available to compose and copy letters and a Christian population willing to donate alms. This mechanism seems to have worked particularly well in regions under Latin rule, especially Cyprus in the earlier fourteenth century and Crete in later fourteenth and earlier fifteenth centuries. Captives were ransomed either as individuals or as nuclear family units. Often, the head of the household would arrange redemption on behalf of other family members. This method relied upon personal initiative and small acts of charity.

The role of clergy in these processes was not new but had a deep history that can be traced in canon and civil law back to at least the period of Emperor Justinian I. Among the many potential objects of charity, the

---

[87] Ibid., 143–4.

ransom of captives was given particular (arguably primary) importance by these laws and associated precepts. In the late medieval period, these duties played out in two main ways: first, in the granting of testimonials to people seeking charitable donations to cover ransom costs; second (and less prominently), in the sale or mortgaging of Church property for the same reason, something otherwise usually forbidden.

Late medieval Greek Christian practices of redemption were distinctive but not unique. In the western Mediterranean, military orders emerged that took on the role of redeeming captives; this was largely absent from the eastern Mediterranean. Iberia saw the development of professional classes of ransom negotiators; in the Byzantine sphere, the nearest equivalent was a type of semi-professional ransom farming undertaken by merchants. On the other hand, the testimonials that Greek-speaking clergy wrote to help captives and their families have analogues both in neighbouring medieval societies and in the early modern Ottoman Empire – and indeed beyond. These testimonials should be understood as part of a *koine* (that is, common) redemptorist practice across western Eurasia.

Part III

Cross-Cultural Relations

*Do not be deceived in any way
and heed the words of the Franks,
because they do not in any way wish to help you,
except that they would destroy you . . .*

('Ἡ ἑλληνικὴ ὡς ἐπίσημος γλῶσσα τῶν σουλτάνων',
ed. Lampros, 63, tr. Vryonis, 'Glabas', 440.)

The Ottoman Sinan Paşa to the metropolitan bishop and nobility of the besieged Byzantine city of Ioannina, 1430.

Chapter 5
Christian Masters, Christian Slaves?

At the start of this book, mention was made of the 'three fundamental assumptions' identified by Barker as shaping medieval Mediterranean slavery: that it was legal, that it could happen to anyone anywhere, and that it was based on religious difference. That third assumption, problematised by the addition of cultural and political factors, forms the theme of the present chapter.

Broadly stated, there were three categories of identity that could be cited to prove or disprove the legality of an act of captivity or enslavement: religion, ethnicity and subjecthood. These categories overlapped to some extent, but in general the order in which the categories are given here moves in order of broadest to most specific, while the third category represents an early stage in the development of what would today be understood as international law. The categories of ethnicity and subjecthood can be found being applied increasingly in the later Middle Ages as a consequence of increasing acknowledgement of the inadequacy of distinctions of religion, precisely because conflict, diplomacy and commerce were constantly defying the apparent religious barrier. This chapter takes these three categories in turn and examines how they shaped the position of captured and enslaved Greeks under Latin masters.

Religion and Slavery

Slavery in the medieval Mediterranean was justified primarily on grounds of religious difference and not on grounds of skin colour or constructed ideas of 'race'. The generally accepted principle was that a person should not enslave another person of the same religion as them. Enslaved people were often expected to convert to the religion of their masters in time; this could help pave the way for their manumission, though it was not necessarily the case.[1]

A Muslim could enslave a Greek Christian without moral difficulty, but the issue was much more fraught when the enslaver was a Latin Christian. It was argued in the Introduction that it is anachronistic to project the modern Orthodox and Catholic Churches back into the later Middle Ages; rather, it is more accurate to think of these two groups as different traditions within the same aspirationally universal church. These two traditions had their major differences, but throughout the later Middle Ages there was a strong sense that these differences might be overcome in order to face common Muslim enemies, generally in the form of a crusade. The levels of estrangement and rapprochement between these two rites or traditions thus waxed and waned over time, something that is seen most clearly at times when the (re-)union of the Roman and Constantinopolitan Churches was being negotiated or was officially proclaimed. This ebb and flow of cross-confessional relations meant that Greek Christians were sometimes viewed by Latins as religious outsiders (and thus enslavable) and other times as religious kinspeople (and thus not enslavable).

This section considers two major strands of evidence. The first strand comprises legislation that obliged Greek Christians to become Latin Christians before they would be allowed to obtain their freedom. The question of what this religious change entailed is also addressed here. The second strand comprises evidence that the emancipation of Greek slaves was understood to go hand in hand with the proclamation of Church union between Rome and Constantinople. Together, these two strands of evidence suggest that the schism between the two Churches was sufficient for Greeks to be regarded as religiously different from Latins.

The legislation that makes up this first strand comes from the kingdoms of Sicily and Aragon, which were both ruled by members of the same Aragonese royal house after the War of the Sicilian Vespers (1282–1302). On 15 October 1310, King Frederick III of Sicily promulgated a series of constitutions in the city of Messina. These constitutions are many and wide-ranging, legislating to forbid Jewish doctors from treating Christian patients and to outlaw sorcery, to take but two examples.

This set of laws also addressed the status of Greek Christian slaves in the Kingdom of Sicily. The law understands these enslaved people as having been taken captive in the Romanía, very much in line with what

[1] *Supra*, 19–22.

is attested from notarial documents. In such cases, the enslaved person was to be freed after a period of seven years: this clause has its roots in Exodus 21:2: 'If you buy an Hebrew servant, six years he shall serve: and in the seventh he shall go out free for nothing.'[2] The use of such a precedent also suggests that Frederick and his government understood Greek Christians to be of the same people as them, presumably in contrast to the non-Christian slaves in the kingdom.

Freedom was to be granted, however, on the condition that the enslaved person should first become a Latin Christian. They must 'firmly believe and unconditionally confess the articles of faith, just as the holy mother Roman [= Latin] church believes and holds <them>, returning to the truth of the same [church], <and who> recognise <this church to be> the one and only Mistress and Ruler of all Churches.'[3] In other words, a confession of the 'correct' type of Christianity was a necessary precondition for manumission.

Reference to Frederick III's laws became programmatic. This particular clause is cited frequently in the notarial acts passed in Palermo, usually with the phrase 'according to the statutes and ordinances of our said lord King Frederick, published regarding such matters.'[4] The buyer thereby acknowledged, at least formally, that they should obtain a confession of faith and free the enslaved person within seven years. While the Constitutions of Frederick were often breached, the notarial record suggests that Greeks were the most likely to be manumitted of all the enslaved groups as taxonomised by notaries: 44 of 143 established Greek slaves on Sicily (30.1%) are attested either in manumission deeds or else mentioned in documents as freedmen (*liberti*); this compares favourably to 17.6% for 'Saracens', 17.3% for black slaves, 16.7% for Albanians and 14% for Slavs.[5] These figures emphasise the intersectional nature of religious and ethnic categories, something further elaborated in the next section of this chapter.

---

[2] I thank Dr Mark Huggins for first drawing the scriptural parallel to my attention. For the Jewish practice, see Rotman, *Byzantine Slavery*, 46–7.
[3] *Capitula Regni Siciliae*, 1.81, cap. 72. Quotation: . . . *qui firmiter credent, et simpliciter fatebuntur articulos fidei, prout sancta Romana mater Ecclesia credit, et tenet, ad veritatem redeuntes ipsius, eam unam, et solam omnium Ecclesiarum magistram et dominam recognoscant: quod tempus septenni ex eo tempore jubemus incipere, ex quo coeperint credere, et firmiter confiteri articulos fidei, ut sancta Romana Ecclesia credit, et tenet, ut superius declaratur.*
[4] Verlinden, 'Frédéric', e.g., 681: *secundum statuta et ordinaciones dicti domini nostri Regis Friderici in talibus edita.*
[5] Bresc, *Monde méditerranéen*, 1.443.

Did the confession of faith that Frederick's law demanded of Greek slaves constitute an act of conversion? It is difficult to say, but it is at least clear that the law envisages a true confessional divide between the religion of the Greek Christians and that of their enslavers. Presumably, such a confession boiled down to the usual questions, such as the inclusion of the *Filioque* clause in the Creed and the use of unleavened bread at communion; the latter part of the clause indicates (entirely unsurprisingly) that recognition of papal supremacy was vital.

On 25 November 1310, Frederick forwarded a copy of the laws to his brother James II of Aragon.[6] From this time onwards, the Crown of Aragon passed the most extensive series of legislation mitigating the captivity and enslavement of Greeks to be found in any polity, all of which is analysed in this chapter. On 28 October 1314, James promulgated a law of his own that suggests Greek slaves were already being brought to Barcelona at this early time. The law allowed the buying and selling of Greek slaves throughout the realm, but not their exportation.[7] The objective of this law was probably to protect against the possibility that these Greek Christians might end up being sold to Muslims, in which case the slaves' souls would be lost to the 'infidel'.

In continuing this discussion of the role of religion in laws governing enslavement, it is necessary to jump forward to the last piece of broad legislation enacted on the subject in the Crown of Aragon: this was the law passed by King Martin on 8 July 1401. It is notable both for being comprehensive in its treatment of non-Latin Christian groups, and for its backlash against the prevailing circumstances under his predecessor, John I, apparently far less harsh towards Christian slaves. The ordinance abolished all previous, potentially contradictory legislation, and banned officials from giving ear to slaves 'of the *natio* of the Greeks or who might be Armenians, Albanians, Russians, Bulgars, Vlachs, or of the parts or regions subject to the Constantinopolitan emperor' who proclaimed that they were free or who, upon the 'persuasions of certain people during the reign of lord King John, proclaimed their freedom and emancipation despite their masters'. Such people were to remain slaves, unless they paid their masters the price for which they were purchased – but this could not happen unless they had first showed themselves to be true 'catholics' (*et non alias quo obtinuerint in futurum ut veri catholici*), here referring to the Latin Church's aspirations to universality rather than meaning

[6] *Acta Aragonensia*, ed. Finke, 2.695–9, No. 438.
[7] Partially ed. Verlinden, 'Orthodoxie', 428.

'Catholic' in the modern sense. They would be freed only once both conditions had been satisfied.⁸

This legislation has been interpreted as the final victory of the interests of a 'municipal' slave-owning party versus an 'ecclesiastical' party that favoured less harsh laws. The latter had achieved significant traction under King John I, but the former eventually won thanks to the support of King Martin.⁹ This was not, however, a conclusive resolution of the tensions in favour of slave owners, as the promise of ecclesiastical union between the Greek and Latin Churches in 1439, plus continued diplomacy between the Crown of Aragon and Constantinople, ensured that the issue remained contested.

Supporting the claims of the Latin Church did not necessarily neutralise prejudices. A powerful example of this is the Cretan priest and scribe Michael Kalophrenas. Kalophrenas himself was imprisoned by the Veneto-Cretan authorities in 1419 for meeting Patriarch Joseph II and Joseph Bryennios in Constantinople, despite the fact that he supported union with Rome and therefore might be described as pro-Latin. His imprisonment did not end his priestly career on Crete, however, as he is attested as a priest in Candia as late as 1449. The Venetians' response to Kalophrenas's links with Constantinople is evidence for the regime's paranoia regarding Greek clergy, who were often viewed as a 'fifth column', representing interests that ran contrary to the Latins', like the refugees who came to the island after 1453.¹⁰ Kalophrenas was not himself enslaved, but he is an important figure for the history of the crisis of captivity because he copied an *aichmalotikon* into a manuscript today held in the British Library.¹¹ This text circulated on Crete, but its provenance is unknown.

Joining the Latin Church – or submitting to it, depending upon one's perspective – happened at both personal and official levels. In Chapter 1, it was mentioned that Michael VIII Palaiologos used the Church union proclaimed at the Council of Lyons in 1274 as a way of endearing himself to the

---

⁸ Ed. Kowalewsky, *Ökonomische Entwicklung*, 3.495 n. 1: [...] *servorum de natione grecorum seu qui fuerint ermines, albanesos, rossos, burgas, blaschs, vel de partibus aut regionibus Constantinopolitano imperatori subjectis se in libertatem proclamare volentium aut qui tempore dicti domini regis Johannis quorundam presuasionibus dictam proclamantes libertatem et alforiam contra eorum dominos ...*

⁹ Verlinden, 'Orthodoxie', 436–7.

¹⁰ Manousakas, 'Μέτρα'; summary in Maltezou, 'Historical and social context', 27–8. On these refugees: *supra*, 111–12.

¹¹ London, BL, Harley 5624, fols. 202v–203r; Stefec, 'Anmerkungen'. On Kalophrenas: *PLP* #10738.

papacy, and in turn (for a time at least) ensuring that the papacy would not sanction an attack on his empire by Charles of Anjou, who claimed the title of Latin emperor of Constantinople. This was not the only time that such rapprochements were attempted.

In 1339, Emperor Andronikos III Palaiologos sent an envoy, Barlaam of Calabria, to meet in secret with Pope Benedict XII in Avignon. According to a Latin account of his speech to the pope, Barlaam stated that, before a union of the churches would be possible, it would be necessary to eradicate Greek hatred of the Latins. This would require three preconditions to be satisfied: first, the French should lead a crusade against the Turks; second, indulgences should be given to anyone wishing to fight the Turks on behalf of the empire, to anyone helping to fund the war and to anyone dying in war against the Turks; third, all Greeks 'who have been sold by the Latins wheresoever they are' (*qui fuerunt venditi a Latinis ubicumque sunt*) should be freed, and no more should be sold, while any people who might buy or sell Greeks and thus fail to comply should be excommunicated.[12] This speech emphasises the extent to which Church union, military aid and the enslavement of Greeks by Latins were all tied together: the fulfilment of Barlaam's conditions would prove that the Latins really did accept the Greeks as being of one and the same religion as them, and thus pave the way for ecclesiastical rapprochement.

Such attempts continued over the following century, the primary aim of which was arguably always to secure Latin military assistance. In 1369, John V Palaiologos travelled to Rome and made a personal confession of faith to Pope Urban V, probably hoping that his subjects would follow suit and hence obtain material support from the crusading kingdoms of the Latin West.[13] Manuel II Palaiologos managed to escape from an Ottoman siege of Constantinople in 1399 in order to undertake a substantial, three-year tour of Western Europe in the hope of garnering support. After his return to Constantinople, there were yet further embassies sent to France, England, Spain and Scandinavia in the first decade of the fifteenth century.[14] Manuel's attitude to Church union is revealing: he advised his son, John VIII (r. 1425–48), that negotiations were to be used as a strategy for diplomatic leverage, to be promised but never to be followed through. John, however, ignored his advice.[15] Then, in 1413–14, Manuel Chrysoloras

---

[12] Raynaldus, *Annales ecclesiastici*, 25.161–2, No. 24.
[13] Halecki, *Empereur*; Nicol, *Church and Society*, 81 and 86.
[14] Harris, *Emigres*, 43–6; Herrin and McManus, 'Renaissance Encounters', 36–7.
[15] George Sphrantzes, *Chronicon*, XXIII5–6, ed. and tr. Maisano, 82–3.

went as Byzantine envoy to the Council of Constance upon the invitation of Sigismund, both King of Hungary and Holy Roman Emperor; Hungary was at that time the most important counterweight to Ottoman expansion on its northern frontier, and thus shared geopolitical interests with Byzantium.[16]

John VIII's envoys were courted by opposing parties in the West. In the time of his reign, Latin Christians were in dispute over whether the pope or councils held the Church's supreme authority. Those in favour of councils ('Conciliarists') were meeting in Basel in today's Switzerland and had elected their own pope, Felix V. The opposing party was headed by Pope Eugenius IV; he offered the Byzantines a council in Italy, easier to reach for a seaborne delegation than Basel, and his offer was accepted.[17]

The council opened in Ferrara in 1438 but moved to Florence in January 1439 on account of an outbreak of plague. The issues at stake were the familiar points of doctrinal and ritual disagreement: the *Filioque* clause, the doctrine of Purgatory (an innovation of the Latins), the leaven in the communion Host, and the supremacy of the patriarchal see of Rome over Jerusalem, Antioch, Alexandria and Constantinople. On 6 July 1439, a celebration of the Mass proclaimed the success of the union, but on the return of the delegation almost all the Greek signatories reneged. The sacrifice of Christian orthodoxy was too great: a people who abandoned the right and true faith could not expect to retain God's protection. Most of the union's staunchest supporters were high clergy and imperial courtiers, who often had financial interests in Latin Europe. John, suffering from gout and grieving the loss of his wife in that same year of 1439, does not seem to have devoted much energy to enforcing the union.[18]

The Byzantine delegation had voted in favour of Church union on the understanding that they would receive military aid from the West. This would include an attack on the Ottomans and provision for Constantinople's defence. In 1439, a papal bull was promulgated in support of a planned crusade, to be paid for by a tax on clergy. Finally, in 1444, an expedition was launched only to be annihilated near Varna on the Black Sea coast of Bulgaria. The broad repudiation of the Union of Florence was resented

---

[16] Herrin and McManus, 'Renaissance Encounters', 38; Gill, *Florence*, 20–1.
[17] Laonikos Chalkokondyles, *Histories*, VI, 7, ed. Darkó and tr. Kaldellis, 2.8–11; Conciliarism: Christianson, 'Conciliar Tradition'.
[18] Gill, *Council of Florence*; Nicol, *Last Centuries*, 351–9; Atiya, *Crusade*, 267; Gill, 'Freedom of the Greeks'; Ševčenko, 'Intellectual Repercussions'; Dendrinos, 'Reflections'.

by the Latins, explaining in part their delayed response. While ostensibly the direct consequence of the Church union, this crusade comprised a coalition between the Burgundians and the north Balkan kingdoms, especially Hungary, and may have had more to do with the latter's interests than Byzantium's.[19]

For the tiny pocket of imperial territory that remained in Thrace, the most immediate priority was the defence of the capital. Although the crusading fleet had formed up nearby at the Dardanelles in 1444, the army never came to Constantinople. At the city's fall in 1453, the only foreign aid that Emperor Constantine XI received was Giustiniano Longo's private company of 700 Genoese and 200 Russian archers who came thanks to the efforts of the pro-Latin Byzantine Archbishop Isidore of Kiev. These groups had pre-existing interests in Byzantium and thus their participation did not necessarily have to do with the concessions made at the Council of Ferrara-Florence.[20]

When news of the union spread in the West, the old question of the status of enslaved Greeks likewise re-emerged. In 1439, the archbishop of Valencia wrote a pastoral letter to the inhabitants of Mallorca that encouraged them to free all of their Christian slaves without distinction, because it would soon be the case that the Latins and Greeks would be members of one and the same Church. The reply of the Mallorcans combined sectarian with legal reasoning: the Greeks were nonetheless not true Christians, while it was nobody's business to deprive a slave-owner of legally acquired property.[21] Despite their objections, the Mallorcans had in fact instituted a number of mitigating measures. Each Friday, the governor was to receive petitions for freedom from slaves or from the 'advocate and procurator of the poor' (*advocat et procurador dels pobres*); this office was introduced to Mallorca by Peter the Ceremonious in 1343 and confirmed in 1372, based on an office in place at Valencia since 1337: the official was to represent the poor in legal cases, for which he would be paid from the royal treasury. Cases would be assessed within two days by a legal assembly (*audiencia*), consisting of the governor, bailiff, city judge, county judge and assessors, two members of the town council (*jurats*) and the city advocate; if a slave

---

[19] Imber, *Crusade of Varna*; Atiya, *Crusade*, 267; Nicol, *Last Centuries*, 361–3; Harris, *End of Byzantium*, 148–9.

[20] Imber, *Varna*, 27; Gill, *Florence*, 383.

[21] Kowalewsky, *Ökonomische Entwicklung*, 3.496–8, précising an unidentified document from the State Archives of Valencia, and the civil council records for 17 July 1439 in the *Libro del Abello* (location unspecified: likely Palma).

was found to have made a claim on false pretences, he or she would be subject to corporal punishment.[22]

Was there a Greek perspective on the significance of religious difference for slavery? Although it is anachronistic to speak of an 'Orthodox Church' in opposition to a 'Catholic Church' at this early time, Greek Christians did nevertheless acknowledge religious commonality with other Balkan Christians who were in communion with them. The fourteenth-century Byzantine historiographer Nikephoros Gregoras mentions that the Christians of the Balkans were agreed among themselves that they could take loot from one another but should refrain from enslaving members of the other groups. A number of archaic ethnonyms are mentioned: Thessalians, Illyrians, Triballians and Bulgarians, probably referring to the Vlachs, Albanians, Serbians and Bulgarians, respectively; the Latins, however, were not in communion with these other peoples and are not mentioned.[23] As well as rites (for example, Latin, Greek), it is therefore also useful to think in terms of communions of Christians: these two categories often overlapped but sometimes, mostly in places under Latin rule, they did not.

The religious 'us-and-them' binary of the medieval Mediterranean was therefore complicated in the case of Greeks under Latin masters in two significant ways. The first was a civic legal tradition limiting the enslavement of Greeks and sometimes other non-Latin Christians, which began in the Kingdom of Sicily and spread from there to the Crown of Aragon, ruled by members of the same family. The second was related to the question of Church union, which was intended to heal the schism between Constantinople and the West – on paper if not on the ground. As the healing of the schism symbolised the reunion of these two 'mystical limbs of Christ', it therefore followed that Greeks were clearly on the same side of the religious binary as the Latins and should consequently not be enslaved by them.

The relationship between religion, enslavement and crusades against the Ottomans emphasises the role that politics also played in this metric. Although the question of subjecthood is treated discretely later in this chapter, there is a general point that should be made here first: the existence of the Byzantine Empire as a political entity meant that Greek captives, whether or not initially Byzantine subjects, enjoyed the advocacy of the empire at the level of diplomacy; sometimes this advocacy was specifically directed at an individual or group of people, but other times, as with the examples above,

---

[22] Hillgarth, 'Greek Slave', 554.
[23] Nikephoros Gregoras, *Historiae Byzantinae*, IV, 9, ed. Schopen, 1.116; see also Köpstein, *Sklaverei*, 58.

it was a more general advocacy that probably ensured captured and enslaved Greeks enjoyed better outcomes than other Christians such as Bulgarians or Russians with whom they were in communion. It will be recalled that in Genoa, Greeks are found lodging court cases for their freedom on the basis of their origins, and being more successful than other eastern Christians; the evidence from Sicily and Aragon–Catalonia speaks to similar broad trends, for which the diplomatic clout of the Byzantine Empire, direct or indirect, is the most obvious explanation.

Ethnicity and Slavery

Under Roman law, when one sold a person into slavery, they were meant to declare the *natio* of the enslaved person. This information was often supplied, but also often omitted. *Natio* was understood in the late medieval Mediterranean as a form of taxonomy that allowed a buyer to make assumptions about the enslaved person's character: already in Justinian's time, a person's origins were understood as determining important features of their character, much like in modern constructions of 'race'. This meant that an enslaved person of a certain *natio* would be expected to have the vices and virtues of that *natio* as a whole; the value that slave-owners accorded to such information is therefore explicable.[24]

Roman law did not, on the other hand, demand that the religion of the enslaved person be declared, and this information is (as a rule) not supplied. In the section above, however, it was established that religious difference was the single most important criterion in the medieval Mediterranean for determining whether a person was enslaveable or not. The way of squaring this circle was that a person's religion was understood to be one of the characteristics that could be assumed on the basis of one's *natio*.[25] In some cases, these assumptions were probably generally correct: *Greci* and *Bulgari* were probably usually Christian (if not the 'right' type of Christian), while *Saraceni* were probably usually Muslims. In other cases, however, *natio* must have been a very poor index of religion: this was particularly pronounced in the case of people who came from the area around the Black Sea, where Tatars, for example, might be pagans or Christians.[26]

On Venetian Crete, the only guarantee of freedom was to be able to prove 'Latin' status in court, though the notion of pure 'Latinity' was problematic

---

[24] *Supra*, 14–15.
[25] As suggested by Barker, *Most Precious Merchandise*, 39–60.
[26] For Christians in the Black Sea, see Vásáry, 'Orthodox Christian Qumans and Tatars', and Grant, 'Latin Categories of Greekness'.

for obscuring the mixing of the Veneto-Cretan Greek and Latin populations. Sally McKee has observed that 'this must be one of the very first occasions in the pre-modern era when legal enslavement was ethnically and not religiously determined': because Crete's labour force in the early fourteenth century comprised so many enslaved Greek captives, it was necessary to redefine the criteria of enslavement.[27]

The Venetian regime on Crete was forced to change further social norms in order to absorb the impact of its enormous population of Greek Christian slaves. The sexual exploitation of slaves, although often passed over in silence in the documentary record, was almost certainly ubiquitous in slave-owning societies like medieval Crete. In medieval Italian societies, it was normal and considered acceptable for an unmarried man to take a concubine – that is, a sole and habitual female sexual partner who might be free or enslaved. Any children from such a union would be 'natural', that is, having more claims to rights of inheritance than 'spurious' children from casual liaisons. Married men were not meant to have affairs with slaves, but it must have happened often nonetheless.[28]

Many male masters fathered children by their female slaves. Under Roman and canon law, these children would be born as slaves. On Crete, where a colonial Latin ruling class attempted to maintain dominance over an indigenous Greek subject population and a large population of slaves (which included many Greeks captured elsewhere), this legal norm was problematic: Latin men who fathered children by enslaved people – and they were most commonly, though by no means always, Greek – needed to ensure that they had heirs, and likely also sought means by which to defend their honour. The result was that, around the turn of the fourteenth century, the law in Italian-dominated societies began to change to allow fathers to grant their children by their slaves the status of free heirs. (The mothers, however, would remain enslaved.) For example, in 1345 the Cretan magistrates forbade Pietro Porco from trying to sell his two male 'spurious' children, Dimitrios and Andronikos, born of his Greek slave Theodora. This was a product of the ubiquitous intermingling of the Latin and Greek populations on Venetian Crete.[29]

---

[27] This paragraph draws on the general ideas of McKee, *Uncommon Dominion, passim*; the quotation is from 125.
[28] McKee, 'Familiarity of Slaves'; Barker, *Most Precious Merchandise*, 77–83.
[29] McKee, 'Inherited Status'and 'Greek Women', 241. I do not agree with Barker's argument (*Most Precious Merchandise*, 83) that this may reflect an awareness of Islamic practice, under which the enslaved mothers of such children were in any case meant to be freed; factors internal to Latin societies adequately explain it.

Sometimes, enslaved Greeks staked claims for their right to freedom on the basis of ethnic identity, sometimes deliberately obscured. This practice is attested in Genoa: it will be recalled, for instance, that Elena claimed freedom from Babilano Alpano in 1398 on account of her Greek parentage.[30]

The Crown of Aragon yields further examples of this trend. In late 1400, a certain Georgius de Grecia approached King Martin I to lodge a complaint against Dalmacius (= Dalmat) of Castellbisbal. He claimed that Dalmacius 'detained him chained and fettered over the course of seven years at Castellbisbal, out of a desire to compel him to confess in a notarial act that he was of the *nacio* of the Saracens and was the slave or captive of Dalmacius.' The case was still unsettled by late 1405, when Martin stated in a second document that his court took care to know the pleas of the wretched, and that to that effect he had brought the case to the attention of Poncio Muntanerius, doctor of laws. By this time Georgius was being described as 'formerly a slave' (*olim servum*), but it is not noted when he obtained his freedom.[31] It is particularly worthy of note that Georgius was being tortured in order to give an apparently false statement of his *nacio*; once taken down in writing, a statement that he was a 'Saracen' (and therefore Muslim) would have prevented him from obtaining his freedom in the ways allowed of Greeks according to the legislation of John I (to 1401), and Martin I thereafter (from 1401). Owners and slaves alike were aware that slaves who obtained legal recognition as being Greek had, relative to all other groups apart from Latin Christians, a very good chance of obtaining their freedom on that basis.

While Dalmat's case was ongoing, in 1405, a certain Zan or Johan Dimitre was born in central Greece, the son of Michael. While still a teenager, Zan was kidnapped alongside a number of other Greeks by a group of Catalans at Patras. These Catalans were intent on selling their captives into slavery, but apparently had trouble doing so at their first stop, on Sicily. The Valencian Marti Xanxo (= Sancho) therefore took the captives to Mallorca. On 21 September 1419, aged fourteen, Zan was sold at Artà to Miquel Rotlan under the name Andreas, sometimes spelled Andreu; the sale was mediated by Daniel de Sant Martí of Valencia on behalf of

---

[30] Summaries and excerpts in Verlinden, 'Orthodoxie', 450 and Otten-Froux, 'Représentation', 105 (notary Jacobinus Nepitella); *supra*, 67.

[31] Ed. Vincke, 'Königtum und Sklaverei', 106–7, No. 109 (see also Ferrer, 'Esclaus', 188): *ipse Georgius asserit in eius Castroepiscopali per tempus septem annorum eundem Georgium detinuit catena et compedibus alligatum, volendo ipsum compellere ut fateretur cum publico instrumento se fore nacione sarracenorum atque servum sive captivum ipsius Dalmacii...*

Martí de Sa Coma of Valencia, to Miquel Rotlan, guaranteed by Antoni Castanyer, a merchant of Mallorca. Zan, however, was able to contest his enslavement on the basis that he was born to free Greek parents, and that he therefore ought to be free himself; the notary and 'procurator of the poor', Johan Sora, represented his case during the months of January–April 1426. The result of the case is not known.[32] Under the norms established by Martin I's legislation of 1401, Zan's claim to freedom would presumably have been accepted only if he could demonstrate that his capture had been illegal; otherwise, he would presumably have been required to convert to Latin Christianity and to pay the price of his sale to Miquel Rotlan in order to be freed.

One of the most extensive clusters of evidence for Greek ethnicity being cited as a means of exemption from enslavement concerns a mysterious papal bull attested only in the Crown of Aragon. It is worth tracing the full story of this bull, as it yields important insights regarding how legal claims on the basis of legislation were undertaken.

On 28 December 1381, Peter the Ceremonious (reigned 1319–87) wrote to the vicar of the town of Tortosa on behalf of a number of Greek petitioners. He noted that these petitioners were there 'under the yoke of servitude' (*sub jugo servitutis*) against their will. The Greeks wrote that Urban V had promulgated an ordinance stating that Greeks who were in captivity or slavery should be freed after seven years. 1381 appears to be the earliest date at which this controversial bull is attested; it was perhaps thought to have emerged in the wake of John V Palaiologos's confession of faith (that is, 1369 or 1370).[33] In a rather extraordinary case of concatenated transmission, the king's letter reported that the Greeks' petition stated that he himself had already published Urban's demand: 'and this very ordinance or constitution, as it is reported, appeared by order and mandate from our <men> throughout some coastal communities of our realm, disseminated by the voice of a town crier';[34] despite this, some people had not complied. Peter's wording, 'as it is reported' (*ut fertur*), suggests that he did not give or could not recall ever having given such an order, thus casting a peculiar doubt on the original papal document. If the nature of the bull should be

---

[32] Hillgarth, 'Greek Slave'.
[33] See Ferrer, 'Esclaus', 183–4 and refs.
[34] Ed. Rubió, *DOC*, 586, No. DXXXV (Rubió should have corrected the *a nativitate Domini* date to 1381, modern style: Ferrer, 'Esclaus', 184): *ipsaque ordinatio seu constitutio de nostris, ut fertur, jussu ac mandato, per aliquas civitates maritimas dominationis nostre publicata voce preconis extiterit* ...

ascertained, after investigation, to be as the petitioners had asserted, then the Greeks were to be freed in writing without delay or dispute.

The document lived on in the consciousness of Aragon into the reign of Peter's successor, John I (reigned 1387–96), but it is clear that the crown never managed to find Urban's (hypothetical) original text. In 1388, Pere de Berga, John's ambassador to Avignon, was primed to commission a papal bull – certainly from Clement VII, in office 1378–94, though he is not named in the text; this was to be modelled after that (supposedly) issued by Urban V, and would order that all the enslaved Greeks in his kingdom, especially those on Mallorca and Ibiza, should be freed. This presumably reflects the greater concentration of enslaved Greeks on the islands than on the mainland. If owners could prove that they had bought their Greek slaves from Turks, or via Christians who had bought them from Turks, then they would be compensated; this is probably because that person was perceived to have been 'rescued' from an infidel.[35] This compensation would be reckoned according to the price paid legally minus the value of services so far received, with the slave remaining a while longer in servitude to make up any shortfall. Any slaves whose owners had not purchased them from Turks had a legal right to buy their freedom. If required, it would be possible to give money to the pope and papal court in order to obtain a copy of the bull.[36]

The whole affair occurred apparently because John I himself wished to pass such legislation, but preferred to defer responsibility for it to the papacy.[37] Documents emanating from John's court in the 1390s cite the bull, but it is unclear whether John ever received the text that Pere de Berga was primed to secure. On 2 March 1388 (whether before or after Pere de Berga's request is not known), John sent an order in the same vein to the Kingdom of Mallorca, part of his composite realm. He ordained that all Greek captives should be free and considered true Christians united with the Catholic Mother Church; under no circumstances could they be required to serve retailers or traders, since they were people of free will, though they could be employed for a daily wage.[38]

The edict attributed to Urban V generated considerable friction between the secular authorities and the bishop of Barcelona, Ramon d'Escales (in office 1387–98). In 1391, the Council of One Hundred tried to prevent him

---

[35] For this notion, see Barker, *Most Precious Merchandise*, 14 and 38.
[36] Ed. Sanpere, *Costumbres catalanas*, 252–3 n. 1.
[37] Miret, *Esclavitud*, 23–4.
[38] Partially tr. Rubió, 'Mitteilungen', 466–7.

from using his sermons to proclaim the liberation of Albanians [sic] and other slaves. This would suggest that the principles found in documents that cited Urban V's purported bull were perceived to apply to other non-Latin Christians, and not just to Greeks.[39] By 1395, the text of the bull was still posing problems: on 14 August, John I wrote to Ramon d'Escales from Mallorca, telling him that he wished to have a copy of the text of the bull regarding the enslavement of Greek captives on the authority of which he had enfranchised people in his episcopal court; the king wrote that he was sending his chamberlain (*cambra*) En Bertomeu Caselles to act as his informant.[40] The court of the bishop was clearly resented for the social disruption it was causing through efforts to relieve the Greek community from the burden of slavery. For example, on 13 December 1396, Berenguer Ses-Avasses and Francesc Sa-Rovira sought redress from the Council of One Hundred for the reason that two slaves, one belonging to each, had proclaimed themselves free and fled to the episcopal palace, where they had been given an advocate and a procurator by the Church. The owners considered that they had been unjustly deprived of the labour of their slaves, and, a whole twenty years later, the dispute was still not settled.[41] On 29 December, the Council of Thirty, reviewing the situation, decided to seek a papal injunction against the bishop to prevent him from sheltering fugitive slaves; the document was to be proofed by legal experts so that the pope would have no reason to deny their petition.[42] A certain Macià Castelló took on the business of presenting this supplication to the pope at Avignon, but it is unknown if the desired injunction was received.[43] It is not unlikely that the tradition of the alleged bull of Urban V was the creation of a zealous Catalan clergyman in the mould of Ramon d'Escales sometime in, or before, 1381.

---

[39] This piece of evidence presents problems. Rubió, 'Mitteilungen', 467 n. 1, translates the document; Verlinden, 'Orthodoxie', 436, notes that his sermons encouraged freedom for Greeks, Albanians 'and other Orthodox'. The reference in both is to Arxiu Municipal de Barcelona, Libre de deliberacions de 1391 (likely *recte* Llibre del Consell), fol. 35, though this seems to be erroneous as the text is not to be found in this or related manuscripts. As Montsalvatje, *Geografía histórica*, 95, mentioned the same incident back in 1899, only without precise citation, I am inclined to believe that the document exists somewhere and is not merely a misunderstanding by Rubió repeated by Verlinden.
[40] Ed. Rubió, *DOC*, 677–8, No. DCXLIX, tr. Rubió, 'Mitteilungen', 468.
[41] Ed. Ferrer, 'Esclaus', 180.
[42] Ibid.
[43] Ibid., 181.

Further citations of the bull include two texts dated to late 1393 that concern the redemptorist activities of one Gregory from Thessaloniki, bishop of Aguiló (*un bisbe de Grecia apellat Gregori de Celonich bisbe de Aguiló*), a town in Catalonia to the northwest of Barcelona. Bearing in mind the strictures of legislation in the Crown of Aragon and Sicily, routinely demanding conversion to Latin Christianity, Gregory was certainly not a Greek Christian by the time he came to occupy his see at Aguiló, though he had quite possibly been baptised according to the Greek rite. It is clear, though, that he retained strong links among a Greek diasporic community in Aragon. Firstly, on 18 November, King John I sent a missive from Tortosa to the councillors of Barcelona: he wrote that Gregory had come before him to beg for mercy on behalf of two Greeks, a chaplain called Dimitra (a feminine-appearing Catalan version of the Greek Dimitrios) and his wife, Maria. Dimitra was Gregory's 'brother' (*un seu frare*) – probably not a biological brother, but a brother Christian (whether Dimitra was a Latin convert is unknown). Both men were at that time in Barcelona, where they were subject as captives to a citizen of the city, Guillem Sent Climent. Gregory mentions that 'the holy father through his bulls has declared that Greeks ought not be slaves or held as slaves', which, though imprecise, is obviously a reference to the tradition surrounding the legislation of Urban V, which Gregory may have understood as comprising multiple similar bulls.[44] The second of the documents provides a snapshot of Gregory acting even further afield, on Mallorca. On 21 December, King John wrote from Penyíscola to the bishop of Mallorca, Lluís de Prades. Gregory had come before the king once again, this time on behalf of a chaplain called Theodoro (similarly, whether a Latin or Greek Christian is unknown), who had two sons, Lucha and Jordi. All three had been sold as captives on Mallorca and, with an almost identical appeal to the papal decree, Gregory had begged for their release; the bishop and the city councillors, John wrote, should ensure that an outcome fitting to the law and the bull be reached.[45]

Yet further distant echoes of this bull are found. In 1457, a woman in her late thirties named Caterina attempted to claim her freedom before the governor of Valencia. Caterina had been sold as a slave on the pretence

---

[44] Ed. Rubió, *DOC*, 669–70, No. DCXLII: *e com lo sant pare per ses bolles haie declarant los grechs no esser sclaus ne per sclaus esser hauts*. Later, he refers to *la dita bolla*, suggesting ambiguity in his perception of how many documents there had been: see also the next note.

[45] Ed. Rubió, *DOC*, 670, No. DCXLII: *e com lo sant pare per ses bolles haia declarant los grechs no esser hauts per catius ne sclaus*, and later referring to *les dites bolles*.

that she was a Circassian; she, however, stated that she was a Greek from Corfu, captured by the Genoese. This was illegal, since, she alleged, Peter the Ceremonious and the popes had forbidden the sale of Greek captives. In the end, her case was dismissed because it was found that she could neither speak Greek nor describe her purported native land. The claim that she was a Circassian was upheld.[46] Martin I had annulled previous legislation on the matter of non-Latin Christian slaves, but yet, over half a century later, at least one claimant was still appealing to the supposed bull of Urban V and its purported proclamation by Peter, echoing very closely the controversial claims brought by the Greeks of Tortosa in 1381. Ultimately, this was a moot point, since Caterina's claims could be dismissed on the grounds that she was not Greek, without engaging with the contentious issue of the status of Greek slaves. As a Circassian, she might well have been a Christian, too,[47] but this group was never among those listed in the Aragonese royal edicts. It is probable that the memory of Urban V's disputed legislation died hard, despite subsequent changes to the law.

In closing this section, it is worth noting the remarkable point that certain Greeks, free or manumitted, even possessed Greek slaves of their own. Some examples from Mallorca have already been mentioned, so further examples from Candia are adduced here.[48] In 1381, a certain Maria from Thessaloniki was bought by Antonius, a *hieromonk* (both monk and priest) of the monastery of St Paul of Cofina.[49] It is possible that this was a mercy purchase, and that Antonius was engaging in the redemption of captives as championed in the Greek Christian tradition.[50] Johannes Greco, who bought Georgius of Constantinople the next year, appears to have been a Greek; with a generic surname like his, he may even have been a manumitted slave himself.[51] In 1383, there is mention of a certain hieromonk called Sofronius, of the monastery of St Anastasia of Candia, who purchased the Greek Emmanuel.[52] Once again, this may have been done with the intention of freeing him immediately, but this is uncertain. Cali Yeracarena,

---

[46] Blumenthal, *Enemies and Familiars*, 36 and 38.
[47] See Barker, 'Christianities in Conflict', for Christian slaves from the Black Sea, including Circassians, in Genoa.
[48] *Supra*, 103.
[49] Verlinden, *L'esclavage*, 2.840.
[50] The manumission that immediately follows this act, dated to the same day (ibid.: 14 May 1381) also pertaining to a Maria, might refer to the selfsame woman. Regrettably, I have not been able to verify this with reference to the manuscript.
[51] Verlinden, *L'esclavage*, 2.855 and n. 485.
[52] Ibid., 2.863 and n. 522.

who bought the Greek slave Margarita only five days later, was surely a Greek too; but the fact that she then sold Margarita after only two days to Maurus Garbarino, the chancellor of Rethymno, is a warning against assuming that all Greek Christian divines acted with the mercy to which they were exhorted.[53]

By comparison with religion, ethnicity was therefore both a parallel and subsidiary category for the taxonomising of enslaved people. The Roman law of slavery meant that Latin notaries focused on ethnicity rather than religion, but it is probable that ethnic labels were generally understood to imply a certain religious identity. In the case of Greeks, a focus on ethnicity allowed Greeks to be granted certain mitigating conditions that were not always extended to other non-Latin Christians; once again, the reason for this less harsh treatment was probably connected to (a) the political importance of the Byzantine Empire and (b) the identification of the project for the reunion of the Churches specifically with the Byzantine Empire and with Greek Christians.

Subjecthood and Captivity

Further complicating ethnic and religious categories of differentiation was the fact that some Greeks were subjects of the Byzantine emperor, but many others were not. In disputes regarding the legitimacy of enslavement, the question of whether or not someone had been legally captured was important.

In the western Mediterranean, a legal structure was developed to assert the legitimacy of capturing and selling the subjects of enemy powers. In 1276–7, a Muslim revolt broke out in the Kingdom of Valencia, probably caused by resentment at the unlawful capture of Muslims on the frontier. Because not all Muslims in the kingdom rebelled at the same time, and some did not rebel at all, a legal framework was developed that was intended to distinguish between those captives taken in the context of war and those taken in the context of peace. This framework established that a captive taken in a context of war was a legitimate captive, whereas one taken in the context of peace was not. The term used for a captive taken legitimately in a context of war was *de bona guerra*: while the term literally means 'from good war', it did not imply anything positive about the conduct of the belligerents and it did not bear the connotations that

---

[53] Ibid., 2.864. The context of the sale is unknown, and so Cali's motivations and circumstances remain mysteries.

'just war' does. The main mechanism by which the circumstances of capture were determined was through an interrogation of the captive; this was naturally problematic, since the captive could be subjected to threats or violence in order to make them confess that they were legitimately captured. In fact, the most important factor was probably that the king should have received the fifth of the value of any loot taken in conflict, to which he was customarily entitled; if an officer issued a receipt that this fifth had been paid, then the captivity was judged to have been in *bona guerra*.[54]

The development of the concept of *bona guerra* may be placed in the wider context of increasing emphasis on subjects of a polity as a corporate entity. This development took place from the thirteenth century onwards, at first largely in Italy and Iberia before spreading north through Europe. In addition to *bona guerra*, another clear manifestation of this change is the development of the law of reprisals, especially in a maritime context, and its corollary, the institution of corsairing or privateering. According to the law of reprisal, if a person committed an act of robbery and no compensation was forthcoming for the injured party, members of the injured party's political community would be allowed by their sovereign to take compensation from the accused's political community by force. This legal structure took the culpability of an individual or group of individuals and applied it to everyone who shared their sovereign. In this way, the subjecthood of an individual was understood as identifying them as part of a political entity with collective liability for the actions of its constituent members.[55] Byzantium's longstanding close contact with the Latins, meant that the law of reprisal found expression there too.[56] The growing importance of subjecthood reflects not the replacement of religious or ethnic categories with political-jurisdictional categories, but rather the introduction of a supplementary form of category.

The principles of *bona guerra* were both explicitly and implicitly applied to the status of Greeks. In the city of Marseille at the end of May 1326, a Catalan of Mallorca named Arnaud Duval bought two Greek slaves, Petro and Jorgius, from Marquet Franquer of Toulon. The day after the sale, doubt was cast (perhaps by the witnesses of the sale) as to whether the two men were indeed slaves, for which they would need to have been acquired *de bona guerra*. In response, the three guarantors agreed to insure Arnaud

---

[54] Torró, 'De bona guerra'; Blumenthal, *Enemies and Familiars*, 9–45.
[55] On reprisal and corsairing: Cheyette, 'Sovereign and the Pirates'; Katele, 'Piracy'; Mollat, 'De la piraterie'; Tai, 'Legal Status', 'Marking Water', 'Piracy' and 'Restitution'.
[56] Penna, 'Piracy and Reprisal'.

against the possibility that the slaves were not legally captured, further adding clauses of insurance against death within one year, and repossession.[57] The document does not elaborate on the precise nature of the doubt regarding the slaves' status, but other analogous cases can provide insight into how the concept of *bona guerra* might relate to Greeks.

Greeks originating from the lands of one Latin ruler might be trafficked to the lands of another. At the end of 1360, a piece of extended documentation was drawn up that details *inter alia* two disputes regarding Greek slaves taken aboard the ship *Santa Maria*. Surviving on Mallorca, this documentation had its roots in Thebes, where a series of original transactions had occurred. First, En Mateu de Moncada, the vicar-general of the Duchy of Athens and Neopatria, had written to the authorities on Mallorca to demand that two Greek slaves be either returned or else their price recompensed. This was because they had been taken aboard the *Santa Maria* without payment having been made.[58] Second, the merchants of the *Santa Maria* had purchased five Greek slaves from the region of Lepanto (Naupaktos), one of the most important harbours on the Gulf of Corinth.[59] The document states that the slaves should be freed on the grounds that Lepanto 'was and is in peace with, and within the territory of the said Duchies [of Athens and Neopatria]':[60] Lepanto changed hands often in the fourteenth century, entering Catalan control for a time in 1361.[61] In this case, subjecthood was more important than the fact that these captives were identified as Greeks.

A quarter of a century later, the Aragonese crown intervened in another case of captivity. In Montço on 7 January 1384, Peter IV responded to the petition of a certain Michael Condo, lodged on behalf of his father, Nicholo and his unnamed mother.[62] The family were Greeks of a place called 'Planes' (probably Planos on Zakynthos) in the County Palatine of Kephalonia and Zakynthos, then under the Kingdom of Naples. Michael's parents had been captured by Miquel Sabater ('Michael Sabbaterius'), a ship's captain of Mallorca, and were subsequently sold on that island. Michael and his mother bought their freedom, but Nicholo was still not free one decade after his initial capture. Michael requested that his father

[57] Mortreuil, 'Moeurs', 167–8, No. 3.
[58] Ed. Rubió, *DOC*, 325–7, No. CCXLV; see also Rubió, 'Mitteilungen', 464–5.
[59] Ibid.
[60] Ed. Rubió, *DOC*, 326: *lo qual* [Lepanto] *era e es en pau e en terra dels dits ducats*.
[61] Gregory, 'Naupaktos'.
[62] Ed. Rubió, *DOC*, 601–2, No. DLVIII; Rubió, 'Mitteilungen', 466; ed. Vincke 'Königtum und Sklaverei' 88, No. 86.

be freed: his justification was that they were not Greeks under the authority of the emperor, but rather of the County and of the Kingdom of Naples, and because of this ought not to be captured.[63] The case dragged on for much of that year, and on 24 September, in order to expedite proceedings, the king appointed Franciscus ça Garriga to assess the case anew and to ascertain whether the mother and son, having been wrongly enslaved, were due compensation for the ransom money they had paid. Though the term *bona guerra* is not used in this document, it is quite clear that this was the issue at stake: the text implies that there was a general perception that Greeks could be taken captive, but since these were subjects of the Kingdom of Naples, at that time under Charles III (r. 1382–6), either Peter was unwilling to allow the capture of subjects of a Latin Christian, or else he was keen not to aggravate Charles – though it would be Peter's son, John I, who ultimately warmed relations with the Angevins of Naples.[64]

There is also some evidence of a Byzantine emperor involving himself directly in a case of captivity. In 1419, the emperor Manuel II sent his ambassador, Paul Sofiano (= Sophianos), to Barcelona, in order to lodge a petition for the righting of injustices against imperial subjects. Sofiano explained that Petrus Loreta and a companion called Jou, whose first name is lost, had taken their ships to Damietta (Egypt), where they stole a ship. Using this vessel, they then proceeded to capture about fifty people in the Morea, whom they bore to Sicily and sold there as slaves. Sofiano appealed for their return as free persons on the basis of their Christianity (*tanquam christianas, liberas et nulli servituti subiectas*). Furthermore, Orlando of Messina had taken a Byzantine ship, while Ritzo of Trapani had sold various captured vessels in the Archipelago and in other unspecified places.[65] The participation of clergy in redemptorist processes is well attested in the Palaiologan period through the *aichmalotika*, but imperial intercession on behalf of captives is seldom encountered. In 1447 Giovanni Torcello, once the Catalans' consul at Constantinople, came before Alfonso the Magnanimous of Aragon and Naples to seek help against the Ottomans. He noted that the Byzantine emperor, John VIII Palaiologos, had complained of the depredations of Catalan pirates. Alfonso consequently ordered that

---

[63] Ibid.: [. . .] *et homines dicti comitatus et regni, quamvis sint Greci non debent captivari, cum solum in captivacione Grecorum que fieri solebat intelligerentur Greci de dominio imperatoris.* (Such appears, at least, to be the meaning of this egregiously tortuous phrasing.)

[64] Bisson, *Aragon*, 123.

[65] Partially ed. Verlinden, 'Orthodoxie', 437 n. 42; summary in Marinescu, 'Contribution', 210.

those of his Catalan subjects who engaged in piracy should deliver their Greek captives and leave imperial territory in peace.[66] These episodes suggest that Greek captives still continued to be trafficked westwards by Catalan disruptors at this late date, even though the majority of the evidence for unfree Greeks under the Crown of Aragon comes from the fourteenth century.

Conclusion

In the medieval Mediterranean, the enslavement of an individual was customarily dependent upon the existence of religious difference between the enslaver and the enslaved. In the case of Greeks enslaved by Latins, the question of whether or not a religious difference of this sort existed was a fraught one. The prospect of the reunification of the Greek and Latin Churches, combined with the prospect of crusades against Ottoman expansion, meant that Greeks were sometimes officially designated as being of the same religion as Latins, but sometimes they were not. In day-to-day life, the simultaneous presence of cultural prejudices and constant demographic mixing added yet more complexity to this relationship.

The question of ethnic identity was also invoked to determine which groups Latin Christians might enslave. Roman law, for one thing, stipulated that people selling slaves were meant to stipulate the slave's origins, and said nothing of their religion; as a result, ethnic labels such as 'Greek' or 'Tatar' came to be understood as proxies for religious identity – however unreliable. The classification of enslaved individuals by their people of origin also meant that different ethnic groups with the same religious identity were treated differently; in the case of Greeks, this was to their benefit, as they were subject to uniquely extensive mitigating legislation that limited the terms or, at times, possibility of their enslavement, especially in Genoa and the Catalan-Aragonese sphere. The main reason for these mitigating measures was probably the diplomatic clout of the Byzantine Empire and the ongoing issues of Church union and crusade, which were identified with Byzantium and with Greeks rather than with all Christians in communion with Constantinople.

This point in turn reflects the importance of a third identifying category, that of subjecthood. An 'us-and-them' binary of religion was an inadequate differential when war and peace transcended religious

---

[66] Marinescu, 'Contribution', 217.

boundaries – assuming such boundaries were clear in the first place. Ethnicity, meanwhile, did not intrinsically imply anything about a person's political allegiance: many Greeks, for example, lived under Latin rulers. Capturing the subjects of a friendly power was a politically volatile move, and in the western Mediterranean the framework of *bona guerra* was developed as a way of determining whether a captive had been taken legally in a context of conflict or illegally in a context of peace. The growing importance of subjecthood foreshadows some of the overarching ideas of diplomacy and international law today. In the later Middle Ages, however, it was one of several overlapping and often ambiguous ways of justifying or condemning acts of captivity.

Chapter 6
Turkish Conquests, Conquered Greeks

In this final chapter, the book comes full circle by returning to the history of Turkish expansion examined in Chapter 1. First, this chapter considers to what extent Greek clergy under Muslim Turkish rule could undertake their traditional role as advocates for and ransomers of captives. Then, it examines the Turkish and Arabic sources that shed light on the capture and trafficking of Greek Christians in Islamic Asia Minor, thus providing an important foil to the Latin evidence considered earlier. This chapter then turns to the impacts of Turkish conquests upon the population and demographics of western Asia Minor and the southern Balkans, following two major strands: firstly, considering the evidence for population decline as a consequence of raiding, and secondly, considering the evidence for the forced movement of population as a result of Ottoman policies of deportation, resettlement and military slavery; this in turn allows for some reflections on the possible demographic impact of the crisis of captivity upon the Aegean region.

Greek Clergy and Captives under Islamic Rule

In 1302, the Ottomans achieved a significant victory against the Byzantines at the Battle of Bapheus in northwest Asia Minor. The patriarch of the time, Athanasios I, saw the successes of the Muslim Ottomans as the result of Byzantine sinfulness and claimed in his letters that repentance combined with reform of the Church would rescue Asia Minor from its Turkish conquerors. He lamented to Emperor Andronikos that 'if everyone were to repent as much as you have, not only would the above-mentioned eastern region again attain and enjoy freedom, but it would crush the rebellious Ishmaelites and rule over their territory.'[1] His impetus for reform, however,

---

[1] Athanasios, *Correspondence*, ed. and tr. Talbot, 78–9, No. 37.

also involved a more practical element in the form of greater on-the-ground episcopal presence. Greek clergy took on increasingly important social roles in the later Middle Ages, notably – but by no means solely – the redemption of captives, but they were also quasi-political representatives of an institutional Church rooted in the imperial capital of Constantinople.

The Greek Christians who continued to live under Islamic rule in Asia Minor probably experienced reasonable tolerance so long as they did not convert to Islam and then apostatise. The Greek hierarchy, on the other hand, was viewed by Turkish rulers with more suspicion than ordinary laypeople: since they were appointed from Constantinople, they might be viewed as 'agents' of the Byzantine centre, and therefore a focal point for the Christian community, challenging or detracting from the authority of local rulers. The resulting situation was a choice between two imperfect solutions: clergy might either remain in Constantinople and hold office *in absentia* or else concede gifts – and possibly pride, too – to the local Muslim ruler in order to strike up a *modus vivendi*. Both possibilities were frowned upon by Constantinople: the first was seen by Athanasios as standing in the way of pastoral responsibility; the second was seen by the patriarchate as leading to dangerous bypasses of central authority. The higher clergy were in a difficult situation, since to preside over a see in Islamic Asia Minor without making any concessions to local rulers appears to have been impracticable.

Absenteeism meant depriving congregations of a number of services. The clergy were not only sacramental ministers but also administrators, organisers of charitable works and providers of hospitality. These activities are generally obscured by the focus of both Byzantine sources and the field of Byzantine Studies on the intellectual qualities of the Church in this period: the Hesychast controversy, the union with Rome and the considerable output of learned orations by clergy. This attention comes at the cost of an appreciation of what clergy, especially those outside the two metropoleis of Constantinople and Thessaloniki, did from one day to the next and how they achieved it. Absenteeism was a point of contention in the early fourteenth century precisely because it removed the potential of the higher clergy to do good works in the communities of their sees.

Long-term episcopal absenteeism, meaning a period over six months, was generally discouraged; if it was necessary, it required the permission of the bishop's metropolitan or of the patriarch.[2] Athanasios would have been unlikely to respond warmly to a request for absence. In a partially

---

[2] Boojamra, *Church Reform*, 110.

fragmentary letter to Andronikos, dating from 1303–5, Athanasios reflects on the bishops' absence with bitterness and despair, stressing that it would be not only just but also legally necessary for them to return to their sees: 'But they wish to live in the City; so let them divide it among themselves.'[3] These bishops, meanwhile, are unlikely to have approved of the 'rustic' Athanasios and his ascetic policies and were probably already far more pessimistic than him regarding the prospects of the empire's future in Asia Minor.[4] Athanasios's uncompromising attitude obscures the hard realism behind these men's unwillingness to take up their charges in Asia Minor: a depopulated and impoverished provincial see under potentially hostile Islamic domination was little competition for a comfortable life in the capital.

Those clergy who took up their sees in person faced an impossible dilemma, as they were servants of two masters: the patriarchate and their local Muslim ruler. Instances of these realities pepper the patriarchal register of the fourteenth century, where complaints are raised that those bishops resident in their sees acted without regard to the centre. The message found throughout the register is fairly clear and consistent: that the spread of Islam as a social and political force was intensified and accelerated by ecclesiastical absenteeism. Similar circumstances may be glimpsed in the correspondence of Matthew Gabalas, metropolitan bishop of Ephesus.

In 1329, the monk Matthew, born Manuel Gabalas, was raised by Emperor Andronikos III to the metropolitanate of Ephesus, at that time under the authority of the beylik of Aydın. Matthew spent the next decade occupying the see in name only, prevented from moving to Ephesus by the hostile circumstances there. Eventually, at some point between mid-1339 and early 1340, he made the journey to the beylik, and resided there until his deposition in summer 1351. Three relevant letters survive that were written by Matthew from his see. These texts reveal precisely those difficulties of absenteeism versus compromise that characterised clerical experiences in late medieval Islamic Asia Minor.

Matthew was clearly viewed as an 'agent of empire'. There are two indications of this: first, Umur, at that time ruler of Aydın, never agreed to meet with Matthew face to face, and instead made it necessary that he communicate

---

[3] Athanasios, *Correspondence*, ed. and tr. Talbot, 66–7, No. 32. Talbot, 'Patriarch Athanasius', 22–4, adduces further examples of the abuses of absentee clergy according to the patriarch's correspondence.

[4] Laiou, *Constantinople and the Latins*, 89.

through Hızır, his elder brother, who was in control of Ephesus but not of the beylik; second, Matthew was obliged to make a financial payment to secure his position, which was probably viewed in Constantinople as a bribe, but in Ephesus as an expression of subordination and loyalty.[5]

The situation was evidently bleak. Despite the probable suppression of Christianity in the town, there was still a congregation to which Matthew ministered. Whether or not he was exaggerating how bad the situation was, the description of his congregation in his correspondence suggests that captivity was prevalent among the Christians there:

> And the multitude of captives is a source of distress, some of whom unfortunately are slaves for the Jews, and others for the Ishmaelites. There are some among them who are of monastic or priestly calling, known to be undertaking impious service. But now, alas, those led away because of this new captivity may be reckoned in the thousands, and these from the <land> of the Romans, <and so> to what destructions of lands or cities that have occurred in the whole of eternity might these be found lesser, or indeed set beside as equal? All of these, fleeing to us <as if we were> an anchor, mourn over their misfortunes; and we, matching their lamentations for them, <but> nothing more, send them away empty-handed.[6]

The severity of Turkish raiding and the resulting enslavement of Greeks are by now familiar themes, and Matthew's letter provides a picture of how this crisis of captivity might affect the demographics of a town in a beylik of western Asia Minor. The wording of the passage suggests that the Christians who lived there included people trafficked there from elsewhere, as well, perhaps, as the residual Greek population. In describing it as 'this new captivity', Matthew is making a comparison with the biblical Babylonian captivity in order to construct for his readers a sense of its enormity. It is

---

[5] Vryonis, *Decline*, 343–8; Papademetriou, 'Turkish Conquests', 190–1.
[6] Matthew of Ephesus, *Briefe*, ed. Reinsch, 178, No. 5, German tr. 348–9, English tr. AG: προσανιᾷ δὲ καὶ ἡ τῶν αἰχμαλώτων πληθύς, ἔστιν ὧν μὲν Ἰουδαίοις, ὧν δὲ Ἰσμαηλίταις δυστυχῶς δουλευόντων. εἰσὶ δέ τινες τούτων, οἵ τῆς μοναδικῆς καὶ ἱερᾶς γνωρίζονται μοίρας ἐναγῆ διακονίαν παναγεῖς ὑφιστάμενοι. οἱ δὲ νῦν αὖ ἀχθέντες ἐκ τῆς νέας ταύτης αἰχμαλωσίας κατὰ χιλιάδας ἠριθμημένοι, καὶ οὗτοι δ᾽ ἐκ τῆς Ῥωμαίων, ποίαις ἁλώσεσι χωρῶν ἤ πόλεων ἐκ τοῦ παντὸς αἰῶνος γεγενημέναις ἤ ἐλάττους εὑρεθεῖεν ἄν ἤγουν ἴσοι παραβληθέντες; πάντες δ᾽ οὗτοι ὥς τινα καταφεύγοντες εἰς ἡμᾶς ἄγκυραν ἀποδύρονται τὰ τῆς συμφορᾶς, καὶ ἡμεῖς δ᾽ αὐτοῖς ἀντιτιθέντες δάκρυα καὶ πλέον οὐδὲν κενοὺς ἀφίεμεν.

unclear whether the 'impious service' performed by the captive monks and priests was simply domestic service to Muslim masters, or (more likely) whether Matthew meant that these people had converted to Islam.

Certain features parallel the situation in Latin-dominated lands, but other features emphasise the differences in circumstance between Turkish- and Latin-ruled communities. Matthew clearly became a focal point for enslaved Christian captives seeking help, and clergy played precisely the same role on Cyprus and Crete; in Aydın, however, Matthew appears not to have been able to give any material assistance. Indeed, no known captive's alms-seeking testimonial originates from Asia Minor, with one thirteenth-century exception, and Matthew's report might provide some explanation of the reason: this mechanism of clergy-led, community-based almsgiving presupposed the existence of a Greek Christian community with money to spare. If Ephesus's Christian population was either enslaved or now converted to Islam, at least probably impoverished, the mechanism could not have functioned. While Matthew's description may be exaggerated, its pessimism is consistent with what is known from Latin and Arabic sources about the condition of Christians in the beylik of Aydın.

The patriarchal records preserve further examples of responses to captivity, including one from Thrace in the late fourteenth century. This episode illustrates perfectly the problems created by the need felt by Christians under Islamic rule for compromise, and how these problems might directly impinge upon captives. On 5 April 1372, the Synod condemned a hieromonk and the population of Pharos, on the banks of the Bosporus north of Constantinople, for handing over Christian refugees to the Ottomans, some of whom died as a result:

> Certain Christian captives, escaping from captivity and coming to the afore-mentioned town, fled to the church of the holy great martyr and victor George, in which this man was serving as priest. When it was being demanded by the people there to lead them back to the Turks, this man not only failed to prevent their wicked resolution, but he even took part with them, and more so than anyone else. They cast these men out from the holy church and led them out in a certain rowing boat, and, having gone out with the sailors, handed them over to the Turks, while the captives beseeched them with tears to be released by them, and not to return them again to the Turks. For they knew that whenever the Turks should learn of their flight, they would exact terrible vengeance upon them and kill them; they [the people of Pharos] did not want <this outcome>, but they gave them to the Turks. [...] For having

been handed over to the Turks by them, not only did they suffer great vengeance, but some of them also died, persisting in their confession [that is, they were martyred].[7]

This document once again highlights the importance of clergy in determining the fate of captives: on the one hand, the Church was viewed as these refugees' greatest hope of safety, but on the other hand, the decisions of a local hieromonk might mean the difference between life and death for these people. It is quite possible that the hieromonk and the people of the town were acting to avoid Ottoman reprisals, since under Islamic law a besieged settlement would be allowed the option to submit for potentially more lenient terms than would be likely if the settlement resisted.[8]

This event foreshadows another, from the late 1410s, when captives and other Christians drafted into the Ottoman army deserted to Thessaloniki but were given up to Mehmed I rather than ransomed, apparently in spite of the charitable impulses of their archbishop, Symeon.[9] Moreover, one recurring trope of martyrologies from this period concerns advice from the Church authorities of Constantinople that Greeks who had converted to and then apostatised from Islam should return to the place of their apostasy. This has been interpreted as the Church abrogating responsibility for these people, fully aware that the punishment for apostasy under Islamic law was death. The Church wanted no such trouble on its hands.[10]

---

[7] MM, 1.592–3, tr. AG: ὅτι χριστιανοί τινες αἰχμάλωτοι τῆς αἰχμαλωσίας διαδράντες καὶ πρὸς τὸ εἰρημένον κάστρον ἐλθόντες κατέφυγον εἰς τὸν τοῦ ἁγίου μεγαλομάρτυρος καὶ τροπαιοφόρου Γεωργίου ναόν, ἐν ᾧ ἦν οὗτος ἱερατικῶς ἐκδουλεύων· ζητουμένων δὲ αὐτῶν παρὰ τοῦ ἐκεῖσε λαοῦ ἐπὶ τῷ πρὸς τοὺς Τούρκους πάλιν αὐτοὺς ἀγαγεῖν, οὗτος οὐ μόνον αὐτῶν τὴν πονηρὰν γνώμην οὐκ ἐκώλυσεν, ἀλλὰ καὶ κοινῇ μετ' αὐτῶν καὶ μάλιστα πρὸ τῶν ἄλλων αὐτὸς τοῦ τε θείου ναοῦ τούτους ἐξέβαλον, καὶ ἔν τινι σανδαλίῳ τούτους εἰσήγαγον, καὶ τοῖς ναύταις ἀπελθόντες πρὸς τοὺς Τούρκους παρέκδωκαν, τῶν δὲ αἰχμαλώτων καὶ ταῦτα μετὰ δακρύων ζητούντων, ἀπολυθῆναι παρ' αὐτῶν, καὶ πρὸς τοὺς Τούρκους (μὴ) πάλιν ἐπανελθεῖν, ἐγίνωσκον γάρ, ὡς ἐπειδὰν οἱ Τοῦρκοι τὴν αὐτῶν φυγὴν μάθωσι, κακῶς αὐτοὺς τιμωρήσουσι καὶ φονεύσουσι, αὐτοὶ οὐκ ἠθέλησαν, ἀλλὰ παρέδωκαν αὐτοὺς τοῖς Τούρκοις. [. . .] παραδοθέντες γὰρ εἰς τοὺς Τούρκους παρ' αὐτῶν οὐ μόνον πολλὰς τιμωρίας ἔπαθον, ἀλλὰ καί τινες ἐξ ἐκείνων ἀπέ(θανον), τῇ ὁμολογίᾳ ἐγκαρτερήσαντες. Cf. Pahlitzsch, 'Loskauf', 135–6.
[8] For the Islamic law of conquest in this period, see Runciman, *Fall*, 145, and İnalcık, 'Policy', 231.
[9] Symeon of Thessaloniki, ed. Balfour, 51; Necipoğlu, *Byzantium between the Ottomans and the Latins*, 73.
[10] Zachariadou, 'Neomartyr's Message', 61.

Clergy might also exploit to their advantage the situation that had arisen as a result of Turkish expansion. On 23 November 1381, the synod excommunicated Dorotheos, metropolitan of Peritheorion in southwestern Thrace. The reason for this action was that he had played off Ottoman authority against Constantinople's. Dorotheos was a *persona non grata* at the patriarchate, for reasons that the register does not explain. He was thrown into prison in the tower of Poroi, but escaped and fled to the Turks. With the help of the Turks, he set himself up in Peritheorion, writing back to Constantinople that he would not return to be judged by the synod. One action that is specifically mentioned in the document condemning him is his promise to the Turks that he would surrender to them any captives that had fled to him.[11] This was obviously a betrayal of the longstanding tradition of clerical advocacy for captives, and it occurred for political reasons: Dorotheos's career had been ruined, and so he turned from one master to a potential new one. Outside Constantinople, it is doubtful that the synod could do much but protest.

The retreat of the institutional Church seems to have had a detrimental effect on clerical literacy, too. In late July 1437, a Latin report on the status of the Greek Church was drawn up for the attention of the Council of Basel. It states that 'it ought to be mentioned that in many parts of Turkey one can find clergy – bishops and archbishops – who wear infidels' clothes and speak their language, and don't know how to do anything in Greek other than sing the mass, gospel and epistles. Many of them deliver their other speeches in Turkish.'[12] On Cyprus and Crete, highly literate clergy are found composing and copying letters and sermons intended to assist with the ransoming of captives, in spite of the repression of the Greek Church by the islands' Latin rulers. In Asia Minor, on the other hand, no example of such texts is found after the thirteenth century. This decline in clerical literacy will therefore have compounded the negative effects of social and political disruption upon the Church's ability to assist captives.

These cases from the patriarchal register illustrate a range of tensions that characterised ecclesiastical behaviour in Islamic-ruled territory. In these circumstances, clergy were the servants of two masters: one local

---

[11] MM, 2.37–9; Papademetriou, 'Turkish Conquests', 192.

[12] 'Terre hodierne Grecorum', ed. Lampros, 366: *Notandum est, quod in multis partibus Turcie reperiuntur clerici, episcopi et arciepiscopi, qui portant vestimenta infidelium et locuntur linguam ipsorum et nihil aliud sciunt in Greco proferre nisi missam cantare et evangelium et epistolas. Alias autem orationes multi dicunt in lingua Turcorum.*

and Muslim, the other distant and Christian; they were also subject to two laws, canon and Islamic, not to mention the importance of individual personality and ambition.

Greek Captives and Slaves in Islamic Asia Minor

Compared with seaborne routes, relatively little is known of the trade in Greek captives in inland Asia. The reason for this is an imbalance of evidence: the overwhelming majority of relevant Latin archival documents come from maritime slave-trading centres and as such tend to provide only incidental insights into inland trade. This is not to say, however, that Latin traders were absent from that inland trade: in the later thirteenth and earlier fourteenth centuries, an important trade route stretched from Ayas/Lajazzo in Armenian Cilicia (the far southeast of modern Turkey) through eastern Asia Minor to Tabriz in western Iran, and Italians are known to have been active along this artery.[13] This absence of documentation has ramifications for the study of the transregional slave trade, since it makes it difficult to assess to what extent slaves from the Black Sea and Caucasus were trafficked to the Mamlūk Sultanate across the hostile Īl-Khānate. As is so often the case with obscure historical contexts, the question that must be asked is whether the absence of evidence is reflective of the absence of a phenomenon. For traces of enslaved Greeks in Asia, it is necessary to turn instead to narrative sources, of which there are relevant examples in Turkish and Arabic as well as in Greek.

If there was one single figure central to narratives of captivity in the fourteenth-century Aegean, it was Umur of Aydın (1309–1348). The beylik of Aydın was centred on Tire and Birgi as well as Ephesus/Ayasuluk, and, in the mid-fourteenth century, was arguably more important politically and economically than the nascent Ottoman beylik. Umur's career was celebrated in the Turkish *Destān* ('epic') of Enveri; this poem, not completed until 1454 but almost certainly based on an earlier source, comprises the middle section of a larger text called the *Düstûrnâme*.[14] This poem celebrates Umur as a raider for Islam (*gazi*), and focuses almost exclusively on his religiously motivated exploits.

In 1343, the papacy proclaimed a series of military actions against Umur known as the Crusade of Smyrna. The crusaders enjoyed temporary success,

---

[13] Sinclair, *Eastern Trade*; Petech, 'Marchands italiens'.
[14] Enveri, *Destān*, ed. and tr. Mélikoff-Sayar; Lemerle, *Aydin*.

and Smyrna remained in Latin hands until Tīmūr's victorious campaign of 1402. Umur himself was killed in 1348 during an attempted reconquest, Doukas's account of which was referenced earlier.[15]

The North African traveller Ibn Baṭṭūṭa provides a Muslim outsider's perspective on Umur's actions. He describes him as 'a generous and pious prince, [...] continually engaged in *jihād* [Muslim holy war]', raiding around Constantinople and taking captives and loot; 'then after spending it all in gifts and largesse he would go out again to the *jihād*'. This, writes Ibn Baṭṭūṭa, led directly to the Greeks appealing to the pope for military aid; he understood Umur to have 'died a martyr's death' countering them at Smyrna/İzmir.[16] This was one element of Umur's character, but certainly not the only element: Umur was noted for his education in Greek; he was also John Kantakouzenos's friend, and arguably also his overlord.[17]

Clement VI's bull in proclamation of the crusade against Umur, *Insurgentibus contra fidem* (30 September 1343), emphasised only Umur's destructive raiding. It notes the Turks' naval raids on Christian-ruled lands in the Romanía, which resulted in destruction, looting, and 'what is worse, seizing the Christians themselves as booty and subjecting them to horrible and perpetual slavery, selling them like animals and forcing them to deny the catholic faith.'[18]

The bull was not incorrect: the Aydınids did indeed engage in depredations across the Romanía, and in the earlier fourteenth century were perhaps the most prolific actors in the capture of Greeks. The beylik of Aydın was a society supported by plunder and tribute that monetised its spoils – and especially captives – through a Latin-mediated export trade, though this is probably only one part of the full picture: it is likely that contemporary authors (especially the Latins and Enveri's source) focused on this element of Aydınid society to the exclusion of many other elements, for example, peaceful trade and cultural patronage.[19] This is an important caveat to bear in mind before proceeding in an analysis that foregrounds the raiding for and the trading of captives.

---

[15] *Supra*, 136–7. On the Crusade of Smyrna, see Carr, *Merchant Crusaders*, esp. 52–5, 74–8, 103–7 and 132–7.

[16] Ibn Baṭṭūṭa, *Voyages*, ed. Defrémery and Sanguineti, 2.311–12, tr. Gibb, 2.446–7.

[17] Nikephoros Gregoras, *Historiae Byzantinae*, XIII, 4, ed. Schopen, 2.648–9; Nicol, *Last Centuries*, 175, 198, 203.

[18] Tr. Housley, *Documents*, 78–9, No. 22 ('Catholic' here is not capitalised, in line with my approach); for further discussion, see Carr, *Merchant Crusaders*, 57–8.

[19] I am influenced here by Reuter, 'Plunder and tribute' (on the Carolingians).

Two of the most important testimonies for slavery and the slave trade in western Asia Minor at this time were written by outsiders, and both in Arabic:[20] they are the works of Ibn Faḍl Allāh al-ʿUmarī (1301–49) and Ibn Baṭṭūṭa (1304–1368/77). The first comprises a descriptive dossier of material on Asia Minor, written according to intelligence provided by a certain *Bilbān*, a Genoese, identified by scholars as Domenichino Doria, with whom al-ʿUmarī shared a term in prison in Egypt sometime in the decade 1328–39.[21] The latter, arguably too famous to require much introduction, comprises an extensive first-person travel narrative completed in 1357, describing a journey of epic proportions across the Islamic world; Ibn Baṭṭūṭa's travels in Asia Minor occurred back in 1332–3.[22] Both provide valuable information regarding the presence of slaves and slave markets in Asia Minor, and of enslaved Greeks in particular.

Ibn Baṭṭūṭa's remarks on enslaved Greeks offer an important complement and corrective to the Latin notarial record. At some points in his narrative, Ibn Baṭṭūṭa devotes extensive comment to these Greek slaves, while at other times he mentions quite perfunctorily his purchase of, or encounter with one. At Lādhiq/Denizli, Ibn Baṭṭūṭa observed some customs of the Greek population: they paid the *jizya*, the poll-tax levied by Muslim rulers on their non-Muslim subjects; their men wore peaked hats, and their women turbans; but Muslims, he wrote with horror, bought beautiful Greek slave-women (*al-jawārī al-rūmiyyāt*) and used them as sexual slaves (the text literally says 'gave them up to wickedness'); they were taken into the baths and there exploited with impunity.[23]

Ibn Baṭṭūṭa responded quite differently, however, to his encounter with Greeks at Birgi, then the capital city of the beylik of Aydın and under Mehmed Beg. There Ibn Baṭṭūṭa saw 'handsome figures' (*al-ṣuwar al-ḥisān*) attending the palace; when Ibn Baṭṭūṭa asked who they were, his guide, the *faqīh*, replied that they were *fityān rūmiyyūn*, a term that might mean Greek boys, slaves or pages. There were apparently around twenty of these young men, stationed in the vestibule of the palace, clothed in silk and wearing their hair down, all of which suggests that they were fulfilling a domestic

---

[20] For Turkish and Persian texts from fourteenth-century Asia Minor, see Peacock, *Islam, Literature and Society*.
[21] Salibi, 'Ibn Faḍl Allāh al-ʿUmarī': Amari, *Al ʿUmarî*. I thank Stefano Nicastro for drawing Amari's study and identification of Doria to my attention.
[22] Miquel, 'Ibn Baṭṭūṭa'.
[23] Ibn Baṭṭūṭa, *Voyages*, ed. Defrémery and Sanguineti, 2.272, tr. Gibb, 2.425.

rather than military function.[24] This episode may be interpreted as evidence that the western beyliks, at least Aydın, engaged palatine domestic slaves in a manner common to many Islamic societies.

Later, while still at Birgi, Ibn Baṭṭūṭa received from the sultan a number of gifts; the last of the list was a slave called Mīkhā'īl (Michael), whom he describes as 'a Greek mamlūk' (*mamlūk rūmī*).[25] At Smyrna (Arabic Yazmīr), at that time also under the house of Aydın, he acquired another Rūmī mamlūk as a gift from Umur, on this occasion a man named Niqūlah (Nicholas), 'five spans tall', and therefore either a child or else a person with dwarfism. It has been suggested that he might have been a captive of Umur's from a raid against Chios in c. 1330.[26] Unfortunately, the evidence is too slight to infer whether or not the use of the term mamlūk (as opposed to *fatan*, for example) should be understood to imply that Mīkhā'īl or Niqūlah had any sort of military background, or whether it simply designated him more generally as a slave. The latter is more probable: it seems from Ibn Baṭṭūṭa's description of setting out at a later point from Nicaea (Arabic Yaznīk) that his enslaved attendants – at that time one female and two male – became part of his retinue of six and probably attended to him in the manner of household slaves. This time, however, the men (possibly the two named above, though he does not specify) are called *ghilmān*, a term probably used interchangeably with *mamlūk* to designate a male as opposed to a female slave.[27] Ibn Baṭṭūṭa likely responded quite differently from his horror at Denizli to his acquisition in Ephesus (Arabic Ayā Sulūq) of a Greek virgin slave-woman (*jāriya rūmiyya*) for forty dinars – this time unnamed.[28] These three towns were all within the beyliks of Aydın or Menteşe, with Ephesus and Birgi among the most common origin points of Greek captives trafficked into slavery in Latin-dominated contexts. Ibn Baṭṭūṭa, however, seems to have been interacting mainly with Turks, and often with ruling figures: his experience was probably representative of the part of the trade that remained in western Asia Minor – far less visible, for want of notarial evidence, than the export trade.

Ibn Baṭṭūṭa's experience in Balikesir (Arabic Balī Kasrī) conforms with the testimony of his contemporary al-ʿUmarī. There, Ibn Baṭṭūṭa bought

---

[24] Ibid., ed. 2.303, tr. 2.442 (in both the French and English translations, the term 'pages' is used).

[25] Ibid., ed. 2.307, tr. 2.444.

[26] Ibid., ed. 2.310–11, tr. 2.446 (and n. 121).

[27] Ibid., ed. 2.325, tr. 2.454. The number in his retinue varied; upon his departure from Nicaea, for example, he had just lost his Turkish interpreter.

[28] Ibid., ed. 2.309, tr. 2.445.

a Greek slave-woman called Marghalīta (Margarita).[29] Balikesir was the capital of the beylik of Karası, called Marmara by al-ʿUmarī. Al-ʿUmarī mentions that the people of this beylik were constantly at war with the Greeks, and that they hunted their young men and the 'young women of the Georgians'.[30] There does not appear to be notarial evidence for Latins trading Greek slaves at Balikesir: Latins, it seems, were active either further south at Ephesus and Anaia, or else further north across the straits at Gallipoli. At least one Genoese, Domenichino Doria, however, was aware of this state of conflict and raiding for captives. Perhaps the Greek captives of Karası were dispersed across western Asian trade networks to these emporia, and perhaps some were absorbed by the internal needs or desires of the beylik – or perhaps documents of sale are yet to be discovered.

An exceptional document drafted in the beylik of Menteşe survives in the Venetian archives. The text comprises a Greek document quoted within a Latin act, and among all the documents from Western European archives employed in this book, this document is unique for being composed in Greek. In form, it is no different from its Latin counterparts, and Greek traders of the fourteenth century should probably be understood as having been very much integrated into Latin networks, living with commensurate frames of documentary and legal reference.

The Greek act was originally drawn up on 27 January 1355 to record conditions laid down by the buyer during a sale transaction. A certain Antonio de Mantello had bought the slaves Georgios Trullos (Γεώργιος ὁ Τροῦλλος) of Athens, his wife Xeni (Ξένη) and his son Chiriaco (whose name is given only in the Latin preamble) from a vendor named Georgios Athenaios (Γεώργιος ὁ Ἀθηναῖος [sic]) in Palatia, modern Balat, Menteşe.[31]

Upon making this purchase, Antonio manumitted Chiriaco and offered terms for the redemption of Georgios and Xeni. Should they serve him for five years, they would be set free upon payment of 30 florins; should they pay 46 florins before that time, they might go free early, the margin of

---

[29] Ibid., ed. 2.317, tr. 2.449. I count four slaves acquired by him in Asia Minor in all – two male and two female. As mentioned immediately above, at the time of his departure from Nicaea he had only three with him, of whom one was female; it is unclear whether he had sold or lost one of his two female slaves, or whether he in fact acquired and sold/lost more slaves that he does not mention.

[30] Al-ʿUmarī, *Bericht*, ed. Taeschner, 44, tr. Quatremère, 367: *yaqtanişu bihum min al-rūm jādhiruhu wa min al-jurz ẓibāʾuhu*. For *al-jurz* both read *kh-z-r*, 'Khazar', which is unlikely for this period and probably a copyist's error (Quatremère vowels it 'Khozars'). I am grateful to Prof. Andrew Peacock for pointing this out.

[31] Manousakas, 'Ἡ πρώτη ἐμπορικὴ παροικία'; Prinzing, 'Sklaven und Sklavinnen', 133.

sixteen florins representing the price of Xeni. Chiriaco thus ended up in a situation similar to many bearers of *aichmalotika*, and might have sought one for himself.

Georgios the Athenian was seemingly a free man from the Catalan Duchy, but it cannot be confidently inferred from this text whether he was himself a Greek or a Catalan – or indeed neither, but perhaps another Latin incomer. Unlike the slave Georgios, the notary, Michael Moschopoulos, or the witnesses Francesco Blanco, Gabriel Longgos (Γαβριὴλ ὁ Λόνγγος) and Michael Acardo, the seller Georgios is not given a family name, making it yet harder to judge. The fact that one of the contracting parties decided to employ a Greek notary does, though, suggest that Georgios the seller might have been himself a Greek (Antonio de Mantello's name suggests that he was a Latin). As Greeks are sometimes attested as selling Greeks, this would not be inconceivable.[32]

While narrating his visit to the city of Magnesia (Arabic Maghnīsīya), a domain of the beylik of Saruhan, Ibn Baṭṭūṭa reports that an unnamed male slave of his, together with another (each described as a *ghulām*), took the opportunity of contriving an escape while out to take the party's horses to water. These slaves fled towards the coast, aiming for the Genoese town of Phokaia (Ar. Fūja), which Ibn Baṭṭūṭa reckoned to be one day's journey from Magnesia. The next afternoon, a group of Turks returned the slaves; they had aroused suspicion while making their escape, and had then admitted to their plan while under duress.[33] The Genoese engaged only to a very small extent in the trafficking of Greek captives: if Ibn Baṭṭūṭa's fugitive slave and his companion were Greeks, which the context makes quite likely, then they would have had good cause to make for a Genoese emporium.

Two anecdotes from the fifteenth century provide analogous evidence. In the late 1430s, Pero Tafur, a Christian traveller from Córdoba, encountered a group of Christian captives while he was sailing through the Dardanelles; they were beckoning the ship to shore so that they might make good their escape. The captain apparently wished to ignore them (perhaps for fear of reprisals), but Tafur managed to convince him to help them. Their efforts were nearly frustrated by a group of Turks who tried to stop them, when a boat sent out from their ship with twenty crossbowmen and

---

[32] *Supra*, 103, 159–60.
[33] Ibn Baṭṭūṭa, *Voyages*, ed. Defrémery and Sanguineti, 2.313–14, tr. Gibb, 2.447–8; Ibn Baṭṭūṭa also notes that Phokaia paid an annual tribute to Saruhan in return for being left in peace.

gunmen managed to push them back. Tafur himself writes that he took an arrow to the foot during this episode, but 'it was all well done for we lost nothing and served God', making it quite clear that the act was conceived of in terms of its religious significance.[34] Some years later, George of Hungary, who wrote an account of his travails, found himself sold and resold between Adrianople/Edirne and Pergamon/Bergama, eventually ending up being the property of a farmer. George escaped on eight occasions; during the last five, he found help from Christian traders who, while still buying and selling him, did so in places that would take him closer to home. In 1458 he made good his permanent escape, and at some point in the years 1475–80 he composed his *Tractatus de moribus condicionibus et nequicia Turcorum* ('Treatise on the customs, conditions and wickedness of the Turks') back in Europe, in either Rome, Siebenbürgen or Hungary.[35] This recalls in certain respects the ransom farmers visible in archival documents, who seem to have made a business of helping Christian slaves escape from Muslim owners or dealers.

Raiding and Depopulation

This chapter has already charted the disintegration of the institutional Church in Asia Minor and Thrace in the face of Ottoman and Aydınid expansion, but this was only one element of a wider process of often violent social change. The military expansion of Turkish groups, of whom the Ottomans are the best documented, impacted whole populations.

Scholarship has identified multiple stages in the Ottomans' conquests. These stages brought new areas into the ambit of Ottoman power gradually and incrementally. Before an area was fully annexed, it would be turned into a tributary of the Ottomans, acknowledging their overlordship by paying them money. After overlordship had been asserted, the Ottomans would then begin a process of establishing a Muslim military aristocracy in the region. From the reign of Bayezid I (1389–1402), the main toolkit used to establish the new order was the combination of the *timar* (fief) and the *tahrir defter* (tax survey of fiefs). Timars were granted both to Muslim members of the conquering society and to conquered Christians who obtained privileges by surrendering to the Ottomans rather than resisting them, thus making co-operation attractive. The success of this

---

[34] Tafur, *Travels and Adventures*, tr. Letts, 150.
[35] Palmer, 'Georgius de Hungaria', drawing on the summary at 46.

method of conquest has been understood as one of the reasons why the Ottomans advanced so quickly across the Balkans in the late fourteenth and fifteenth centuries.[36]

Recent scholarship has made the case for adding a preliminary phase to this schema of Ottoman conquest. This phase has been called the '*akıncı* phase', because its main actors were raiders known as akıncıs. Akıncıs were agriculturalists or craftsmen who engaged in warfare in the Ottoman polity's frontier regions. Their origins were Christian or Muslim, nomadic, semi-nomadic or sedentary. Some must have migrated large distances, as akıncıs from Asia Minor are found in registers drawn up in the Balkans. The akıncıs were lightly-armed, mounted soldiers; they would take two horses on campaign: one hardy horse for travelling, and one fast horse for raiding. In return for their service and a yearly fee of 100 *akçe* (less than half of what some of the captives encountered in this book raised in ransom fees) the akıncıs were exempt from taxation and protected from other demands of service. These types of soldier are attested for the Balkans no later than 1400, and their mode of fighting may be assumed to have developed in Asia Minor during the previous century.

The 'akıncı phase' was a period of destruction but not of conquest. When members of the Ottoman polity began to expand into a given region, this process would begin with an extended period of raiding, for anything between 80 and 130 years. During this period, akıncıs would launch repeated attacks with the primary aim of taking captives. While many people were killed in the process of such raids, any death reduced potential profit and was thus to be avoided. The frontier lords distributed slaves among themselves, their prerogatives depending upon rank, and would seek to sell or ransom the rest. The raiders were accompanied by slave traders who acted as middlemen in the trafficking process. Skopje and Adrianople/Edirne emerge as the two most important slave markets. The frontier lords also resettled many of these captives on their land, thus repopulating desolate areas. It was only after this process of demographic exhaustion was complete that the Ottomans would move to the second and third stages of conquest, establishing overlordship and ultimately taking direct control of the region.[37]

Importantly, this primary phase of activity involved so many different actors of diverse origins that Adrian Gheorghe has argued that it would be misleading to characterise it as a phase of 'Ottoman conquest' at all. While

---

[36] İnalcık, 'Ottoman Methods of Conquest'.
[37] Schmitt and Kiprovska, 'Ottoman raiders'; Gheorghe, *Metamprphoses*.

later Ottoman chroniclers were keen to associate early military activities in the Balkans with the Ottoman dynasty, Ottoman control over the warlords who undertook these activities began to be asserted only from the last quarter of the fourteenth century, under the sultans Murad I and Bayezid I. Many of these warlords cannot in any case be traced back to the Ottoman beylik and either appear as if out of nowhere or else display associations with other polities in western Asia Minor, especially the beylik of Karası. Consequently, Gheorghe prefers to talk of the 'akıncı phase' in the Balkans not as a period of conquest but rather of 'infiltration'. Due to the heterogeneous nature of the groups who comprised the akıncıs, this infiltration was itself 'multipolar' – that is to say, that it had no single centre. It would therefore be inaccurate to imagine a co-ordinated process of expansion emanating from Ottoman 'capitals' at Bursa/Prousa or later Edirne/Adrianople.[38] This multipolar process of infiltration was one of the sociopolitical environments that shaped the crisis of captivity.

One of the *aichmalotika* appears to describe precisely this 'akıncı phase'. This *aichmalotikon* was copied into a mid-fifteenth-century manuscript containing scientific works as well as texts by John Damascene and the late Byzantine historiographer Gregoras. This manuscript's owners included Patriarch Maximus III of Constantinople (presided 1476–82) and the sixteenth-century humanist Antonios Eparchos (b. Corfu 1491; d. Italy 1571).[39] The *aichmalotikon* was copied in between scientific treatises by Nikephoros Blemmydes and Isaac Argyros. Despite being an odd insertion at this point, it is copied in the same hand as most of the manuscript, demonstrating that it was not inserted at a later point, as these letters sometimes were.

The *aichmalotikon* was written by a member of the higher clergy in response to a verbal appeal from a man who had visited him in person. This man reported how 'Hagarenes' had attacked his city and carried off captives. One of these captives was a male, probably a friend or relative, such as his father or brother; another was his wife while a third was another female, probably their daughter. Upon their captivity, these three people had been led through the region of a city that was specified in the original version of the letter, but whose name had been erased by the time this copy was made, before being taken to a region that was likewise originally

---

[38] Gheorghe, *Metamorphoses*, 141–91.
[39] 'Τύποι Βυζαντινῶν συμβολαίων', ed. Sathas, and Sathas, 'Πρόλογος', ρι΄–ρια΄; Stefec, 'Geschichte der Handschriften', 257. The text of the letter has not been published and has so far been used only in my 'Cross-Confessional Captivity', 1.274–5 and n. 648.

specified. The letter-bearer seems to have become separated from the captives, as it is said that he later discovered where they were, found them, and then gathered alms from fellow Christians to redeem them. He succeeded in ransoming the male, but the two females remained in captivity at the time of writing, for prices originally stated in the letter. The author of the letter was convinced by this story and accordingly agreed to write a testimonial for him; indeed, he may have known him already, since he states in the letter that the bearer 'is from the province of Such-and-such a place' and 'has lived a God-loving and moderate life'.

Perhaps more significant is the small amount of historical contextualisation that the text has preserved. The author situates the captivities in a pattern of raiding. First, he writes, these 'descendants of Hagar had ravaged the whole East'; in little time, however, they had also brought 'almost the whole of Europe' to heel. Each season, these people would raid both town and countryside. It was in one such raid against one city – again, originally named – that the man and two women mentioned in the letter had been taken; many others were either captured or killed.[40] While it is not possible to identify this context with certainty, it is very probable that this refers to the first or 'akıncı' phase of the Ottoman conquests in the Balkans. The reference to the 'Hagarene' subjugation of the 'East' followed by the subjugation of 'almost the whole of Europe' surely reflects the conquests by the Turkish principalities in Asia Minor, followed by the Ottomans' fast progress in the Balkans between their occupation of Gallipoli in 1352 and the disruption of their nascent empire at hands of Tīmūr at Ankara in 1402. This description of raiding fits well with the 'akıncı phase', and the letter may therefore be tentatively situated within this context and understood as a closely-informed account of this phase of conquest.

The depopulation caused by the akıncı phase of conquest is evident when considered in the light of sources and studies on the population of the late medieval Aegean region. Data relating to the desertion of villages displays a notable peak in the period under study. Within the borders of the modern Greek state and for a period stretching between the years 1000 and 1850, one study has identified 2,049 desertions of villages; this figure includes places said to have been abandoned, for example, as a result of war, and places not attested for a generation or so (thirty to fifty years) in written records. Desertion is understood in three main ways: villages that

---

[40] Paris. gr. 2509, fols. 139v–140v; partial ed. and tr. in Grant, 'Cross-Confessional Captivity', 1.274–5, n. 648.

were abandoned and, at least by the mid-nineteenth century, not repopulated; villages that were left in favour of another site nearby, usually a fortified town; and villages that had fifteen or fewer inhabitants in the early nineteenth century but seem to have been more populous at a previous point in time. These figures will not be totally reliable as they are often assumed from silences and as the volume of sources varies over time, but they yield such strong trends that even such shortcomings cannot negate their value.[41]

The trend for the period under study can be summarised as follows: desertions increased notably over the thirteenth century, yet further over the fourteenth, reduced considerably in the fifteenth and returned to low levels in the sixteenth. The later thirteenth century is estimated to have witnessed 57 desertions, an increase of more than 630 percent on the mere nine of the first fifty years. In the period 1300–1350, this figure more than doubled to 136, more than doubling once more to 322 from 1350–1400. By contrast, the fifteenth century saw only 123 desertions, fairly evenly split between its two halves (65 and 58). By the sixteenth century, this had reduced to numbers not seen since for centuries: 16 and 25, comparable to the 10 and 20 identified for the twelfth century. It is not until the time of the Greek Revolution (1821–32), a far better documented period than the later Middle Ages, that evidence for desertions surpasses that for the fourteenth century: a substantial 662 have been dated to the years 1800–50.[42]

The geographical distribution of these desertions is as important as their chronological distribution. In the second half of the thirteenth century, 66 percent of desertions occurred in the maritime regions of the Aegean and Ionian seas. This probably reflects the insecurity caused by naval raiding undertaken by Latins and Greeks; these people are documented in Venetian and Genoese compensation claim documents, which show them robbing people and taking them captive, all the while shifting between different political allegiances.[43] At this early time, it is unlikely that many Turks were yet active as sailors in the Aegean, but it is likely that comparable figures for western Asia Minor would show a high number of desertions there due to Turkish expansion. In the early fourteenth century, c. 54 percent of desertions occurred in Macedonia and Thrace and a further c. 29 percent in the northwest of Greece; the relative importance of Macedonia and Thrace remains identical for the latter half of the century.

[41] Antoniadis-Bibicou, 'Villages désertés en Grèce', 343–63.
[42] Ibid., 364 (statistics), 364–82 (relevant remarks).
[43] Ibid., 364; Grant, 'Gottlose Korsaren'; Charanis, 'Piracy'; Morgan, 'Claims Commission'.

The persistent prominence of north-central and northeast Greece reflects several notable factors: for the earlier fourteenth century, this was linked to the 'Catalan vengeance' and the Byzantine civil wars of 1321–8 and 1341–7, already mentioned in connection with the evidence for peasant migration; for the latter half of the century, it must be linked primarily to the arrival of the Ottomans. The Black Death will also have played its part from 1347, though the extent of its impact on the region is not yet well understood.[44] The decrease of desertions and the low plateau of the sixteenth century seem to represent the re-establishment of stability in the period after the Ottoman conquests, as peace returned to the region. Through all these periods, account must also be taken of factors such as bad harvests, droughts and patterns of localised migration.[45]

Conditions in the Aegean can be studied through Italian sources, too. These include population estimates made in 1470 after the Ottoman conquest of Negroponte (Euboea) and sixteenth- and seventeenth-century *isolarii* (descriptions of islands). The estimates of 1470 reveal a notable trend: islands with fewer than 1,000 inhabitants also had low population densities, while islands with more than 1,000 inhabitants had high densities. Leros, Astypalaia and Thira/Santorini had densities of a little over three people per square kilometre; in Kea and Kalymnos, for example, it was between two and three; Samothraki, Amorgos, Karpathos and Kythera had under two. By comparison, the empire of Michael VIII is estimated to have had an average population density of somewhere in the region of fifteen. It is likely that these figures reflect the tendency of inhabitants of smaller islands to seek safety on larger islands, which tended to be more agriculturally productive and therefore better protected.[46]

The isolarii, meanwhile, mention such things as the state of habitation of a given island and any attacks or natural disasters that may have affected its prosperity. When this evidence is aggregated, a pattern becomes evident whereby these islands seem to have been abandoned and then resettled at different points during the fourteenth to sixteenth centuries. Of twenty-two islands, two were abandoned in the fourteenth century: Astypalaia, in around 1340, and Tenedos, in 1383; these were

[44] Antoniadis-Bibicou, 'Villages désertés en Grèce', 364, 372–82; Tsiamis, *Plague in Byzantine Times*.
[45] Antoniadis-Bibicou, 'Villages désertés en Grèce', 364 (figures); see Laiou, *Peasant Society*, 223, 236, 254, 263, for remarks on 'catastrophic' and 'non-catastrophic' factors.
[46] Koder, 'Topographie und Bevölkerung'.

resettled in 1413 and 1438, respectively, though Astypalaia underwent a further period of desertion from 1538 to no later than 1577. Six further islands were abandoned in the fifteenth century and nine in the sixteenth, of which all but one – Ios – were deserted by 1537. The dates of resettlement show a strong trend towards the quarter-century after the Venetian victory over the Ottomans at the naval Battle of Lepanto (1571), during which period seventeen of these twenty-two islands seem to have been repopulated. A couple of the islands were resettled in the intervening period: Aïstrati in 1540 and Paros by 1563. The pattern of desertion and resettlement in the Aegean islands reflects the pattern of Ottoman conquest and settlement policy: attacks on the islands by the Turkish maritime principalities had begun in the fourteenth century; by 1566, the Ottomans had conquered the Aegean islands with the exceptions of Tenos and Crete, and in the 1570s resettled the islands of Psara, Samos and Ios with Albanian immigrants.[47]

Ottoman taxation records (*tahrir defters*) can shed yet more light on this process of repopulation. Because taxpaying heads of house were listed by name in these records, it is sometimes possible to trace the presence or absence of individuals or families between different surveys. Records related to the island of Limnos, for example, show that the Greek Diplovatatzes family left the island at some point before the tax survey of 1489 but had returned by the time the next survey was compiled in 1519.[48] In this case, too, the disruption of the conquest process prompted important locals to abandon their home, only to return once a peaceful *modus vivendi* had been established.

This evidence demonstrates that across the Aegean and further afield, the Ottomans conquered areas that were already significantly depopulated and that under their rule the population of these areas quickly recovered. There can be little doubt that the attacks of the Ottomans and their Turkish neighbours that preceded their conquests in the fourteenth to sixteenth centuries played a substantial role in this process of depopulation. There is also evidence for two other Ottoman practices that affected population and demographic profiles: first, systematically offering besieged populations the opportunity to surrender and thus save themselves from slaughter and captivity; second, transplanting or deporting individuals or whole populations by means of incentives or force.

---

[47] Hasluck, 'Depopulation'.
[48] Lowry, 'Byzantine Provincial Officials', 127–8.

Conquest and Deportation

When the Ottomans besieged settlements, they offered a choice to the inhabitants: surrender and be spared, or resist and be subjected to sack. This choice derived from legal norms developed in the early centuries of Islam that regulated war and peace. Christians (or Jews) with whom a Muslim army was at war, were first to be offered the chance to embrace Islam or submit to the poll tax (Arabic *jizya*, Ottoman Turkish *cizye*) as members of a protected community (*dhimmīs*, *zimmis*). If this offer was rejected, mercy did not need to be shown to the enemy, so long as treachery was not used. Sometimes, the resulting sacks were limited by commanders in order to avoid total destruction: Constantinople, for example, was sacked for three days in 1453.[49]

Consequently, when accounts of Ottoman conquests are examined, a pattern emerges: settlements retained Greek populations when they surrendered but were depopulated or resettled when they resisted. For example, Panidos/Banatoz and Mesene/Drizipara in Thrace surrendered to the Ottoman Sultan Murad I (reigned 1362–89) and their inhabitants were thus allowed to continue dwelling in safety. Tzouroullos/Çorlu, on the other hand, resisted until its commander was injured; it was thus stormed and apparently destroyed.[50] The examples could be multiplied, and a number of further instances are considered in detail below; the important point is that the Ottoman conquests in the Balkans left some settlements intact and others destroyed, creating an imbalance in population and labour. This imbalance will have been made even worse by the ongoing processes of emigration and depopulation, especially from and in unfortified areas.

The Ottomans addressed this imbalance by deporting people, a process called *sürgün* in Ottoman Turkish. Deportations were carried out strategically between different areas under Ottoman control in order to (re-)establish demographic balances, reinvigorate cottage industry and bring land back under cultivation. This process was regarded as vital to the good functioning of the empire: Mehmed the Conqueror described the resettlement and reinvigoration of his new capital to be the greatest struggle he had yet faced, as reflected in an endowment document in which he writes metaphorically of the progression 'from lesser wars to the mightiest war'.[51]

---

[49] Khadduri, *War and Peace*, 96–106; Runciman, *Fall of Constantinople*, 145.
[50] İnalcık, 'Policy', 234–5.
[51] Lowry, 'From Lesser Wars', 323.

The practice of deportation and resettlement in former Byzantine lands was not new. At the end of the twelfth century, the Rūm Seljuk Sultan Ghiyāth al-Dīn Kay Khūsraw I led a series of attacks along the Maeander in Karia. He achieved considerable success until halting outside Antiocheia in Phrygia on the misapprehension that the inhabitants, in fact in celebration, were making a din of arms and ready to resist him.

The sultan therefore made for Lampe, where he began a series of remarkable administrative manoeuvres. First, he ordered officials to take notes about the name and origin of all the captives he had taken, who had captured them, how much each had lost on account of their captivity and whether any relatives were still being held by any of his men; upon completion of the survey, the captives, supposedly numbering 5,000, were given back their belongings. The sultan then took the captives to the town of Philomilion and settled them in the nearby unfortified villages, even supplying grain for the cultivation of the land.

The sultan promised the captives that they would be returned to their original homes once peace between him and the Byzantine Emperor Alexios Angelos returned. Should that not come to pass, the captives were to be exempt from tax for five years and then taxed at a capped amount that would not be subject to frequent increase. The captives apparently forgot their old life within the Byzantine Empire, while their good fortune attracted yet more relatives and fellow Greeks to come and settle in the district.[52] The compilation of a detailed register plus the importance of bringing land under cultivation both anticipate the resettlement practices of the Ottomans.

The Ottoman conquest of Thessaloniki (1430) offers a well-documented and well-studied example. Thessaloniki changed hands several times in the fourteenth and fifteenth centuries, being ceded to the Byzantines after a period of Ottoman rule from 1387–1403 and then ceded to the Venetians one year into another Ottoman siege in 1423. According to Chalkokondyles, certain inhabitants had conspired with Murad for the betrayal of the city, only to be foiled by the Venetians; this conspiracy seems to have earned the inhabitants something of a concession, as many were captured, enslaved and deported rather than killed.[53]

The impact upon the population of the city was severe. Thessaloniki is reckoned to have had about 40,000 inhabitants at the time of the

---

[52] Niketas Choniates, *Historia*, ed. van Dieten, 494–5, tr. Magoulias, 272–3; Fleet, 'Economy', 238.
[53] Laonikos Chalkokondyles, *Histories*, V, 21–2, ed. Darkó and tr. Kaldellis, 1.388–91. The conquest was mentioned earlier: *supra*, 96–8.

Venetian takeover in 1423; by the time of the first surviving Ottoman tax survey of the city, that number was down to an estimated 10,414 inhabitants, of whom an estimated 4,320 were Muslim incomers.[54] Some of these were not casualties of the assault but had already left the city during the siege, either to join the Ottomans in anticipation of their victory or else to escape the siege in the short or medium term in anticipation of returning in better times; but as a Greek delegation to the Venetian regime complained in 1429, many of these who planned to return had their property destroyed – presumably looted – once they left.[55] It was likely the later sixteenth century before the population recovered from this destruction.[56]

The shell of Thessaloniki and its depleted hinterland were resettled by waves of deportation and migration. First, a thousand Turks from nearby Yenice Vardar/Giannitsa were moved to the city in about 1432, shortly after the conquest. The next waves of arrivals are visible in the tax surveys of 1478 and 1519, where they are listed by their first name, occupation and 'community' (*cema'at*), while established residents are listed by first name, patronym and 'quarter' of the city (*mahalle*). The persistence of Byzantine names for nine mahalles out of 10 demonstrates a large level of civic continuity despite the upheaval of the conquest. Of 461 taxpayers whose occupation is legible in the 1478 survey, 140 worked in the leather industry, 125 in textiles and others in shops; this distribution suggests that many of them must have come from towns and cities rather than rural areas where agriculture predominated. Toponymic surnames, including Anadoulu, Kütahyalı and Karamani, suggest that these people may have come from regions of Asia Minor recently conquered by Mehmed II. At some point in the period between 1430 and 1478, it is also likely that some of the pre-1430 population returned; this group would have included both refugees and ransomed captives.

By 1519, Thessaloniki's population had changed drastically by the arrival of an estimated 15,715 Jews who had been expelled from Spain and chose to move to the Ottoman Empire. The population was now about 29,200 and over 50% Jewish, having included no Jews whatsoever in 1478; this slight Jewish majority would remain until the Nazi occupation of Greece.

---

[54] Lowry, 'From Lesser Wars', 335–6.
[55] Going over to the Ottomans: Symeon of Thessaloniki, ed. Balfour, 59; Necipoğlu, *Byzantium between the Ottomans and the Latins*, 49; departure and destruction of property: Mertzios, Μνημεία, 78–9; tr. Vacalopoulos, 'Flight', 274–5.
[56] Vryonis, 'Ottoman Conquest of Thessaloniki'.

The arrival of thousands of Jews from Western Europe made Thessaloniki's population exceptional within the Ottoman Empire, since the sultans were careful to maintain a balance of Muslims, Christians and Jews in the other cities such as Constantinople and Trebizond.[57]

The fate of Thessaloniki was referenced by the Ottomans as a threat when trying to secure the submission of Ioannina in Epirus later that same year. Sinan Paşa offered terms to the city: churches would be saved, no mosques built, but, most importantly, the population would be spared captivity (*aichmalotismon*) and the 'tribute of children' (*piasmon paidion*). These were two different types of captivity: the first was general, and would have involved the taking, enslaving and/or ransoming of many inhabitants, as at Thessaloniki; the second was a specific form of levy for a corps of soldiers, the *devşirme*, to which this section will turn soon. In the context of Byzantine–Latin–Ottoman relations, it is notable that Sinan chose to warn the inhabitants 'not [to] be deceived in any way and heed the words of the Franks, because they do not in any way wish to help you, except that they would destroy you as they destroyed the inhabitants of Thessaloniki.'[58] Sinan wished to exploit the example of the Venetian abandonment of Thessaloniki to propagate suspicion towards the Latins, to whom the inhabitants of Ioannina might otherwise have been expected to turn for help.

It now remains to assess how the crisis of captivity fits into these contexts of depopulation and deportation. On the strength of current knowledge, it would be difficult to guess figures or relative proportions for people taken captive versus those who were killed, displaced or died of plague, but some general principles may be advanced.

First, it is clear that the southern Balkans and Aegean Islands were severely depopulated and large portions of their land abandoned by the time of their conquest by the Ottomans. It may be assumed that similar processes obtained in Asia Minor, but it is possible that migrations of Turks into the former Byzantine lands replenished more of the deficit there than in the Balkans – as reflected in the armies of 10,000 to over 40,000 attributed to the rulers of the Turkish beyliks by al-ʿUmarī upon the reports of the Genoese Domenichino Doria.[59]

Second, this population and labour deficit will have put a premium on captives. As explained in Chapter 2, the prevalence of Greeks among the

---

[57] Lowry, 'From Lesser Wars' and 'Portrait of a City'.
[58] 'Η ἑλληνικὴ ὡς ἐπίσημος γλῶσσα τῶν σουλτάνων', ed. Lampros, 63–4; tr. Vryonis, 'Glabas', 440.
[59] Discussed in Zachariadou, 'Notes sur la population', 224–5.

enslaved populations of Latin Europe declined in the later fourteenth and fifteenth centuries; at this very time, however, it is clear from Greek, Arabic and Turkish sources that Greeks were still being captured and enslaved in large numbers. A plausible interpretation of this disparity is that the Ottomans were exploiting the labour of these captives in their own territories and that comparatively few of these people were being exported. This can also be seen in the levying of non-Muslim children for enslavement, as mentioned in Sinan Paşa's letter to the inhabitants of Ioannina and explored in more detail below.

The crisis of captivity therefore continued until the consolidation of the Ottoman conquests in the southern Balkans and Aegean Sea, but as a phenomenon largely internal to the Ottoman Empire. As a result of this new situation, alms-seeking Greek captives continued to come to Western Europe in the fifteenth, sixteenth and seventeenth centuries, but Greeks are not found enslaved in these societies:[60] the geographical centre of Western European slave trading moved to the Atlantic and enslaved Greeks and their descendants vanish from view, presumably through demographic assimilation with the society of their enslavers.

Towards the end of the fourteenth century, the Ottomans began levying non-Muslim children for use as palatine and military slaves in what is known as the *devşirme*, literally 'collection' (Sinan's 'tribute of children'). This was another type of forced displacement, though one quite different in character from the examples considered above. These levied children were taken for employment as soldiers in the elite infantry Janissary corps, whose ranks had at first, from the 1360s, been filled by the one-fifth treasury tax (*pencik resmi*) due on captives taken in war.[61] The *devşirme* has usually been approached from the perspective of an institution within the Ottoman world; placing it instead in the wider picture of captivity in the later Byzantine world – after all, the context in which it emerged – has the potential to shed fresh light on some well-known sources.

It is of considerable importance in the context of the current discussion that the earliest contemporary evidence for the *devşirme* comes from a homily by a Greek clergyman, Isidore Glabas, archbishop of Thessaloniki during the years 1380–95. This sermon of Isidore's, dated to 28 February 1395, provides a polemicised, outline description of the *devşirme* and its effects upon the Christians of Thessaloniki:

---

[60] These people are studied in Harris, *Emigres*.
[61] Papoulia, *Knabenlese*; Wittek, 'Devshirme and Sharī'a'; Ménage, 'Some Notes', 'Devs̲h̲irme'; Murphey, 'Yeñi Čeri'.

I have heard the harsh decree concerning our dearest ones [...]

What would a man not suffer were he to see a child, whom he had begotten and raised ... carried off by the hands of foreigners, suddenly and by force, and forced to change over to alien customs and to become a vessel of barbaric garb, speech, impiety, and other contaminations, all in a moment? [...] Or shall he lament his son because a free child becomes a slave? Because being nobly born he is forced to adopt barbaric customs? Because he who was rendered so mild by motherly and fatherly hands is about to be filled with barbaric cruelty? Because he who attended matins in the churches and frequented the sacred teachers is now, alas! taught to pass the night in murdering his own people and in other such things? Because he who was appointed to serve the holy houses is now entrusted with the care of dogs and fowl? Because he who was raised in many and pleasing occupations and services is now forced to endure the freezing and scorching winds, and to cross rivers, mountains, precipices, and places difficult of access? ...[62]

Another key source for the early *devşirme* is the saint's life of Philotheos of Athos. Philotheos of Athos was the child of Greek refugees from Elateia, Asia Minor, who had settled at Macedonian Chrysopolis. At some time after the Ottomans had occupied northern Greece in 1371, Philotheos and his brother were taken as *devşirme* levies:

At that time a command was issued by the ruler for a levy of male children, as is customary among the Agarenes, or rather by the will of their father the Devil (John, 8:44), that despiser of good, that envious serpent, the Enemy of Christians from the beginning of time. Alas, how many among our own people were made into children of the Antichrist! Woe is me! These fine boys were taken along with the other boys who were brought to the emir. All those who had children, either two, or three or even ten, could scarcely keep one. But because the two brothers did not have kinsmen to object or resist somehow, the Agarenes took both brothers at the same time.[63]

---

[62] Isidore Glabas, Ὁμιλία περὶ τῆς ἁρπαγῆς τῶν παίδων, ed. Laourdas, 390–2; tr. Vryonis, 'Glabas', 436–7.
[63] *Life of Philotheos*, ed. Papoulia and tr. McGrath (= *BHG* 1534); quotation from ch. 2, ed. and tr. 616–19.

Miraculously, the Mother of God came to them in the image of their mother and ensured that they evaded their captivity and reached the safety of Her double monastery at Kavala ('Neapolis'). Their mother later also took holy orders at the same monastery, and all three were ecstatically reunited after the children recognised her, while she felt unable to approach them for joy.[64]

By 1395, the Ottomans were therefore demanding a tribute in young non-Muslim boys and exploiting these children as slaves – but why? Several possible reasons have been advanced: one cause internal to Ottoman institutions is the inadequacy of the Ottoman Turkmen infantry, the *yaya*, which was corrupt and difficult to manage; another, broader cause was the lack of captives available for slave labour. Given the evidence considered in this book for captivity, migration, depopulation and deportation, the idea that the *devşirme* was a response to a population and labour crisis seems very plausible. The parallel development is the disappearance of evidence for the trafficking of Greek captives to the West from the late fourteenth century onwards.[65]

Conclusions

The process of Turkish conquest at Byzantium's expense, in both western Asia Minor and the southern Balkans, caused demographic and institutional changes. The early phases of these conquests involved primarily raiding, which resulted in destruction and depopulation.

The insecure environment that this caused was unattractive to the clergy chosen to be bishops in these areas, and thus many chose to remain in Constantinople where they would be safe and comfortable; those who did take up their charges in person often faced contradictory demands from the patriarchate on the one hand, and local Muslim rulers on the other hand, the latter viewing them as political representatives of the Byzantine Empire.

Some of the Greeks who were captured and enslaved in this context were sold and exploited by Muslim masters. This side of the crisis of captivity is only peripherally documented in the Latin sources, but is to some extent illuminated by Arabic and Turkish texts. These show Greeks being

---

[64] Ibid., 618–21.
[65] Vryonis, 'Glabas', 439, lists these possible reasons but rejects the demographic explanation on the grounds that 'prisoners were abundant' at the time of the *devşirme*'s establishment.

used for domestic and perhaps also military service, especially in the context of the princely courts of the beyliks.

The impact of Turkish raiding on the population of the Aegean region was evidently devastating. This can be charted through evidence for the abandonment of settlements as well as sources that provide population figures, though it is tricky to disaggregate the effects of raiding from those of other factors such as plague, civil war or poor harvests. The result was that the Ottomans inherited severely depopulated lands and cities, though by the sixteenth and seventeenth centuries there is evidence that populations were once again on the rise in the context of peace and consequently greater security.

The Ottomans dealt with this population problem by encouraging migration and by the deportation of people. In a region where some settlements had been depopulated by conquest and others left intact thanks to their surrender, the Ottomans needed to redress imbalances of population, demographics and labour. As manpower was evidently scarce, it would have been increasingly valued, and it is probable that the Ottomans exploited the labour of the Greeks whom they captured rather than allowing them to be bought and sold by Latin merchants as they had for much of the fourteenth century. This probably also explains, at least in part, why the Ottomans instituted the levying of non-Muslim children for military slavery.

Conclusion
A Mediterranean Phenomenon

If there is one feature that distinguishes this book from most others written under the rubric of Byzantine Studies, it is surely the breadth of its geographical canvas. The exercise of tracing the phenomenon of captivity among the Greeks of the later Middle Ages has taken this book far beyond the twin metropolitan hubs of Constantinople and Thessaloniki, far beyond the Aegean region and far beyond the Byzantine Empire itself, to places ranging from Cyprus to Sicily to Valencia and almost everywhere in between. The contrast between this enormous vista and the ever-shrinking horizons of the Palaiologan polity could hardly be starker: the crisis of captivity that engulfed the Greek Christian communities of the thirteenth to fifteenth centuries was a truly Mediterranean phenomenon.

This book began in the traditional Byzantine heartlands of western Asia Minor. It traced how the westward movement of Mongols and, consequently, Turks caused a geopolitical shift in the region, pushing back the frontiers of Michael VIII's empire at precisely the time that its centre shifted from the Asian city of Nicaea to the ancestral capital of Constantinople on the European side of the Bosporus (c. 1259–61). Michael and his son, Andronikos II, took pains to reverse this process of territorial loss, as did Andronikos III later still; but despite these efforts, Turkish conquests in western Asia Minor continued, until Byzantium had become an almost entirely Balkan polity.

In the fourteenth century, these Turkish conquerors established control over important trading ports on the Aegean coast and established commercial relationships with the Italian merchants who were used to trading there. In the process of conquering Byzantine territory, the Turks had undertaken and continued to undertake many raids, battles and sieges, in the course of which they captured many Greek Christians; while some of these people were traded among Muslims in Asia Minor, a great deal of them were sold to the Italian traders who frequented the maritime emporia and thence exported to slave markets on Crete and Cyprus. It was in this way that a local geopolitical crisis developed over the course of the later thirteenth century into a regional slave trade emanating from the Aegean.

At this time, however, a larger, transregional slave trade was also taking shape. This trade was the product of broader geopolitical shifts that affected much of western Afro-Eurasia and that also originated with the Mongols. Among the regional polities that emerged in the wake of the Mongol conquests of the second quarter of the thirteenth century were the Khanate of the Golden Horde north of the Black Sea in the vast steppe areas surrounding the Volga and the Īl-Khānate in today's Iran. The Īl-Khānate established overlordship over the Seljuks of Asia Minor, Byzantium's eastern neighbours, in 1243, but were defeated in 1260 by the Mamlūk Sultanate of Egypt and Syria.

The Mamlūks were a society ruled by a class of manumitted formerly enslaved soldiers drawn from Turkic and Caucasian groups. In the context of the war with the Īl-Khānate, the Mamlūks sought to maintain their provision of enslaved soldiers by establishing good diplomatic relations with the Golden Horde, where many of these soldiers originated, and courted the cooperation of Byzantium, the polity that straddled the straits between the Black Sea and the Mediterranean and was therefore of strategic significance for this trade. The Genoese – in time, if not immediately, and never exclusively – became important intermediaries in this trade, something facilitated by newly-granted economic privileges within the Byzantine Empire. Greeks, too, found it in their economic interest to buy, sell and traffick enslaved Black Sea peoples along the route between Egypt and Crimea.

Despite the capture and enslavement of many Greeks in this period, however, very few of them seem to have been themselves trafficked along this route. This can perhaps be attributed to the role of Cyprus, ruled by a French aristocracy but peopled by many Greeks, as a point of refuge along this route, within easy reach of Mamlūk Syria. The Genoese, too, seem rarely to have captured or enslaved Greeks, something attributable above all to diplomacy with Byzantium. While this transregional trade in Black Sea slaves had certain points of overlap with the trade in Greek captives, sharing trade routes and some actors, they were distinct in both their origins and their character.

The rather loose application of the terms 'captivity' and 'slavery' in this discussion is a reflection of ambiguities of both vocabulary and descriptions of experiences in medieval texts. In Greek texts, trafficked people tend to be described as *aichmalotoi*, a term basically meaning 'captives'; in Latin texts from the same period, however, trafficked Greeks tend to appear as *sclavi*, 'slaves', and only in certain contexts (usually in the Catalan-Aragonese sphere) as 'captives', but here interchangeably with 'slaves'. In some instances, it is clear that the Greek 'captives' are the same people as the Latin 'slaves': almost all enslaved Greeks in this period entered slavery after being captured, but as most of the relevant Latin sources are legal and commercial in nature, they focus primarily on the legal and commercial issue of enslavement, while Greek sources focus on the fact of the captives' social dislocation from their community.

More confusingly still, it is evident that refugees could also be described as *aichmalotoi*. It seems that the term took on this meaning when used to describe people fleeing warfare and insecurity, though it is also possible that people were captured in such situations. People who were captured are also often found in surprisingly mobile circumstances, the main reason for which was the importance of itinerant alms-seeking for raising ransom costs. The evidence for the movement of refugees displays clear, though not uniform trends. While some Greeks chose to throw in their lots with the burgeoning Turkish principalities, more still seem to have fled away from Turkish expansion, either to safer areas of the Byzantine Empire or to areas under Italian (especially Venetian) or French rule.

Itinerant alms-seeking was probably the predominant mechanism by which Greek captives ransomed themselves in this period. In order to help people solicit donations, senior clergy wrote testimonial letters that gave the reader (or listener, if read aloud) some background information and appealed to their Christian faith as a reason for charitable impulses. This reflected both (a) the long-standing importance of the ransoming of captives among the duties of Christian clergy and (b) the Church's increasing assumption in areas no longer under Byzantine imperial control of societal roles that were previously shared with civil institutions.

The distribution of this evidence shows clear geographical emphases. In the early fourteenth century it comes overwhelmingly from Cyprus, then under the rule of the French Lusignan dynasty; then, in the fifteenth century, it comes mostly from Crete, then under Venetian rule. This distribution of evidence mirrors that for the movement of refugees, the sum total of which is perhaps surprising given the social and religious repression that Greek Christians often faced under Latin regimes.

In addition to such small-scale methods of redemption, diplomacy was sometimes used to secure the release of captives, while some people seem to have made a business out of ransoming people in return for certain financial or labour obligations. Unlike in Iberia, no new redemptorist institutions, such as military orders, ever developed in the Aegean.

In the medieval Mediterranean, the question of who could enslave whom usually rested on the identification of religious difference. Between Christians and Muslims, this difference was clear, but between Christians of different cultural or confessional backgrounds, it was often debated. Because the Church of Constantinople disagreed with that of Rome on various points of doctrine, there was an official split or schism between the two; at times this was proclaimed to have been healed thanks to diplomacy, but on-the-ground cultural differences between Latins and Greeks were too engrained for high Church politics to be translated directly into societal harmony. The result was that Greeks were sometimes proclaimed to be unenslavable or enslavable only for limited time periods. Most of the evidence for these mitigating measures comes from the Catalan-Aragonese sphere and from Genoa.

The question of whether a person qualified for such mitigating measures could be answered with reference to one or more of several categories of identification. Because Roman law demanded that an enslaved person's *natio* or people of origin be stated but not their religion, various determinants were interrogated: whether they really were a Greek or belonged instead to another ethnic group, whether they had made a profession of faith according to Latin norms, or whether they had been captured legally in enemy territory or illegally in friendly territory.

Altogether, Greeks seem to have had access to more mitigations than other enslaved groups in the Latin world. This is surely attributable above all to the continued diplomatic clout of the Byzantine Empire. In particular, the two issues of Church union and crusades against the Turks ensured that Greek East and Latin West continued to find common cause throughout the later Middle Ages. Other enslaved Christian groups such as Bulgarians, Russians or Vlachs had no such political weight behind them. Many Greeks also lived under Latin rule, making their capture a diplomatic sticking point when they were sold in the West.

The process of Turkish conquests, particularly under the auspices of the Aydınid and Ottoman polities but also by groups probably acting more independently, was violent and damaging. Greeks were enslaved and exploited in domestic contexts as well as being sold to Latins. The institutional Greek Church was in retreat in the face of collapsing resources and the impossibility of reconciling local Islamic rule with the interests of the distant patriarchate. The Christian population, too, was being diminished by raiding: many were killed, many captured and many deported to repopulate newly conquered cities; others had already fled to places such as Venice's Aegean possessions.

Ottoman expansion in Europe seems to have ushered in a new phase of the crisis of captivity. Evidence for the trafficking of Greeks by Latin traders begins to fade, but evidence for the captivity and enslavement of Greeks within the Ottoman sphere remains copious. It seems likely that substantial demographic depletion led the Ottomans to exploit the much-needed labour of captured and deported people within their own borders rather than to export them; this is seen perhaps most clearly of all in the institutionalisation of the levy of non-Muslim boys for military slavery.

This complex and wide-reaching phenomenon has not been traced before. While scholars have long been aware that Greeks were taken captive in the later Middle Ages, the sheer scale of this process, both in terms of frequency and geographic breadth, has not yet been appreciated. In order to outline this crisis of captivity among Greek Christians, it has been necessary to synthesise a huge volume of Greek, Latin, western European vernacular and sometimes also Turkish and Arabic sources. As a result, it has been possible to make this case empirically, with reference to literally thousands of cases of captivity and enslavement. From now on, captivity should be understood as one of the characteristic experiences of late medieval Greeks, both in the Byzantine Empire and far beyond.

The level of population displacement that this process caused must have been substantial. The trafficking of Greeks created a far-reaching diaspora that reached levels of considerable concentration on some islands with substantial slave economies, such as Mallorca, Crete or Cyprus. In the Aegean region itself, the forced departure of many of these captives, the movement of refugees and the arrival of a new conquering society that resettled people in depopulated areas will all have led to large population and demographic shifts. When viewed in the context of civil war and plague, this shift appears all the more catastrophic. Today, the demographic legacy of the crisis of captivity has been rendered invisible by centuries of intermarriage and intermixing, its causes, nature and extent forgotten. This book has redeemed it from oblivion.

Bibliography

Archival Documents:

—*Archivio di Stato di Palermo*

Enrico de Citella, stanza 1a, reg. 79
Giacomo de Citella, stanza 1a, vol. 77
Pellegrino de Salerno, stanza 1a, reg. 1, vols. II and V
Ruggiero de Citella, stanza 1a, vols. 76

—*Archivio di Stato di Venezia*

Andrea di Belloamore, Notai di Candia, B9
Giovanni Similiante, Notai di Candia, DIII, B244

—*Državni Arhiv u Dubrovniku*

Diversa cancellariae, XXVII
Diversa notariae II, V, and VII
Liber dotium, II

Literary Manuscripts:

London, British Library, Harley 5624
Paris. gr. 400
Paris. gr. 2509
Paris. gr. 2671
Sin. gr. 1889

Published Texts:

'1290 (anzi 1294) — Lista delle soddisfazioni e delle restituzioni da darsi come indennizzi ai genovesi', ed. G. Bertolotto, *Atti. Società ligure di storia patria* 28 (1897), 511–59.

Acta Aragonensia: Quellen zur deutschen, italienischen, französischen, spanischen, zur Kirchen- und Kulturgeschichte aus der diplomatischen Korrespondenz Jaymes II. (1291–1327), vol. 2, ed. H. Finke (Leipzig, 1908).

Acta et Diplomata Graeca Medii Aevi, Sacra et Profana, ed. F. Miklosich and J. Müller (6 vols., Vienna, 1860–90) [=MM].

Actes de Kutlumus: Nouvelle édition remaniée et augmentée: Texte, ed. P. Lemerle (Paris, 1988).

Actes des notaires génois de Péra et de Caffa de la fin du XIIIe siècle (1281– 1290), ed. G. I. Brătianu (Bucharest, 1927).

Angelo de Cartura: see *Documents of Angelo de Cartura and Donato Fontanella*.

Annales ecclesiastici, vol. XXV: aa. 1334–1355, ed. O. Raynaldus (Paris and Fribourg, 1880).

Antonio di Ponzò, *Notai genovesi in Oltremare: Atti rogati a Chilia da Antonio di Ponzò* (1360–61), ed. G. Pistarino (Genoa, 1971).

Antonio di Ponzò, *Gênes et l'Outre-Mer, 2: Actes de Kilia du notaire Antonio di Ponzò, 1360*, ed. M. Balard (Paris, 1980).

Athanasios, *The Correspondence of Athanasius I, Patriarch of Constantinople*, ed. and tr. A.-M. M. Talbot (Washington, DC, 1975).

Atti della Città di Palermo dal 1311 al 1410, vol. 1, ed. F. Pollaci Nuncio (Palermo, 1892).

Basilicorum Libri LX, ed. G. E. Heimbach and C. A. Fabrot, tr. K. W. E. Heimbach, vol. 3 (Leipzig, 1843).

Benvenuto de Brixano, *Benenuto di Brixano, Notaio in Candia, 1301–1302*, ed. R. Morozzo della Rocca (Venice, 1950).

Bullarium Romanum, vol. 4, ed. S. Franco, H. Fory and H. Dalmazzo (Turin, 1857).

Capitula Regni Siciliae quae ad hodiernum diem lata sunt, vol. 1 [no ed.] (Palermo, 1741).

Constantine Harmenopoulos, *Manuele legum sive Hexabiblos*, ed. and Latin tr. G. E. Heimbach (Leipzig, 1851).

Corpus Iuris Civilis, ed. R. Schoell and G. Kroll, vol. 3, *Novellae* (Berlin, 1895), partial tr. S. P. Scott, *The Civil Law*, vol. 16 (Cincinnati OH, 1932).

De Cartura, Angelo: see *Documents of Angelo de Cartura and Donato Fontanella*.

Diplomatari de l'Orient Catala, ed. A. Rubió i Lluch (Barcelona, 1947; repr. 2001) [=*DOC*].

Diplomatarium veneto-levantinum, vol. 1: aa. 1300–1350, ed. G. M. Thomas (Venice, 1880).
DOC: see *Diplomatari de l'Orient Catala*.
Documents inédits pour servir à l'histoire de la domination vénitienne en Crète de 1380 à 1485, ed. H. Noiret (Paris, 1892).
Documents of Angelo de Cartura and Donato Fontanella: Venetian Notaries in Fourteenth-Century Crete, ed. A. Stahl (Washington, DC, 2000).
Documents on the Later Crusades, 1274–1580, tr. N. Housley (Basingstoke, 1996).
'Documents récemment découverts datant de la fin du XIVe siècle et concernant les Bulgares de la Macédonie vendus comme esclaves', ed. I. Sakasov, *Makedonski Pregled* 7 (1932), 1–62 (in Bulgarian, with a French summary).
Domenico Prete, *Domenico Prete di S. Maurizio, Notaio in Venezia (1309–1316)*, ed. M. F. Tiepolo (Venice, 1970).
Dominicus Grimani, 'The Documents of Dominicus Grimani, Notary in Candia (1356–1357)', ed. N. Tsougarakis, *Dumbarton Oaks Papers* 67 (2013): 227–89.
Donato di Chiavari, *Notai genovesi in Oltremare: Atti rogati a Chio da Donato di Chiavari (17 Febbraio–12 Novembre 1394)*, ed. M. Balard (Genoa, 1988).
Donato Fontanella: see *Documents of Angelo de Cartura and Donato Fontanella*.
Doukas, *Chronographia: Byzantiner und Osmanen im Kampf um die Macht und das Überleben (1341–1462)*, ed. and tr. D. R. Reinsch with L. H. Reinsch-Werner (Berlin and Boston, MA, 2020), ed. and tr. V. Grecu as *Istoria Turco-Bizantină (1341–1462)* (Bucharest, 1958), tr. H. J. Magoulias as *Decline and Fall of Byzantium to the Ottoman Turks* (Detroit, 1975).
Duca di Candia: Bandi (1313–1329), ed. P. Ratti Vidulich (Venice, 1965).
'Ἡ ἑλληνικὴ ὡς ἐπίσημος γλῶσσα τῶν σουλτάνων', ed. S. Lampros, *Νέος Ἑλληνομνήμων* 5 (1908): 62–4.
Emmanuel Piloti, *L'Égypte au commencement du quinzième siècle, d'après le Traité d'Emannuel Piloti de Crète (Incipit 1420)*, ed. P.-H. Dopp (Cairo, 1950).
Enveri, Destân, ed. and tr. I. Mélikoff-Sayar as *Le Destān d'Umūr Pacha* (Paris, 1954).
Euchologion sive rituale graecorum complectens ritus et ordines divinae liturgiae, ed. R. P. J. Goar (Venice, 1730; repr. Graz, 1960).
Felice de Merlis, *Felice de Merlis, Prete e notaio in Venezia ed Ayas (1315–1348)*, ed. A. Bondi Sebellico (2 vols., Venice, 1973–8).
Geoffrey de Villehardouin, *De la Conquête de Constantinople*, trans. C. Smith in *Joinville and Villehardouin, Chronicles of the Crusades* (Hardmondsworth, 2008).

George Akropolites, *Opera*, vol. 1, ed. A. Heisenberg (Leipzig, 1903), tr. R. Macrides as *The History: Introduction, Translation and Commentary* (Oxford, 2007).

George Pachymeres, *Relations historiques*, ed. A. Failler, tr. V. Laurent (5 vols., Paris, 1984–99).

George Sphrantzes, *Chronicon*, ed. and tr. R. Maisano (Rome, 1990), tr. M. Philippides as *The Fall of the Byzantine Empire: A Chronicle by George Sphrantzes, 1401–1477* (Amherst, 1980).

Giovanni da Rocha, *Notai genovesi in Oltremare. Atti rogati a Cipro, Lamberto di Sambuceto (31 marzo 1304–19 luglio 1305, 4 gennaio–12 luglio 1307), Giovanni da Rocha (3 agosto 1308–14 marzo 1310)*, ed. M. Balard (Genoa, 1984).

Gregory Palamas, *The Triads*, ed. J. Meyendorff and tr. N. Gendle (Mahwah, NJ, 1983).

Gregory Palamas, *The Hesychast Controversy and the Debate with Islam: Documents Relating to Gregory Palamas*, tr. N. Russell (Liverpool, 2020).

Griechische Briefe und Urkunden aus dem Zypern der Kreuzfahrerzeit: Die Formularsammlung eines königlichen Sekretärs im Vaticanus Palatinus graecus 367, ed. A. Beihammer (Nicosia, 2007).

Ibn Baṭṭūṭa, *Voyages d'Ibn Batoutah*, vol. II, ed. and tr. C. Defrémery and B. R. Sanguineti (Paris, 1877), and tr. H. A. R. Gibb as *The Travels of Ibn Baṭṭūṭa, AD 1325–1354*, vol. II (Cambridge, 1959).

Isidore Glabas, ʽΙσιδώρου Ἀρχιεπισκόπου Θεσσαλονίκης ὁμιλία περὶ τῆς ἁρπαγῆς τῶν παίδων κατὰ τὸ τοῦ ἀμηρᾶ ἐπίταγμα καὶ περὶ τῆς μελλούσης κρίσεως', ed. B. Laourdas in [no ed.,] *Προσφορὰ εἰς Στίλπωνα Π. Κυριακίδην [Ἑλληνικά, supplement 4]* (Thessaloniki, 1953), 389–98.

Ἱστορικὰ κρητικὰ ἔγγραφα ἐκδιδόμενα ἐκ τοῦ ἀρχείου τῆς Βενετίας, μνημεῖα τῆς ἑλληνικῆς ἱστορίας. Θεσπίσματα τῆς βενετικῆς γερουσίας, 1281–1385, vol. 2, Pt. 1, ed. S. M. Theotokes (Athens, 1936).

John Anagnostes, *Διήγησις περὶ τῆς τελευταίας ἁλώσεως τῆς Θεσσαλονίκης*, ed. G. Tsaras (Thessaloniki, 1958), tr. Melville-Jones, *Venice and Thessalonica 1423–1430: The Greek Accounts* (Padua, 2006), 149–79.

John Kaminiates, *The Capture of Thessaloniki*, ed. and tr. D. Frendo and A. Fotiou (Perth, Australia, 2000).

John Kantakouzenos, *Historia*, ed. L. Schopen (3 vols., Bonn, 1828–32).

John Skylitzes, *Synopsis Historiarum*, ed. J. Thurn (Berlin, 1973), tr. J. Wortley as *John Skylitzes: A Synopsis of Byzantine History, 811–1057* (Cambridge, 2010).

Justinian, 'Iustiniani Digesta', ed. T. Mommsen, in T. Mommsen and P. Krueger, eds, *Corpus Iuris Civilis, Editio Stereotypa Quinta, Volumen Primum: Insti-*

tutiones recognivit Paulus Krueger, Digesta recognivit Theodorus Mommsen (Berlin, 1889).
Kai Kā'ūs b. Iskandar, *A Mirror for Princes: The Qābūs Nāma*, tr. R. Levy (London, 1951).
Kallistos, 'Βίος καὶ πολιτεία τοῦ ἐν ἁγίοις πατρὸς ἡμῶν Γρηγορίου τοῦ Σιναΐτου συγγραφεὶς', ed. I. Pomjalovskij, *Zapiski istoriko-filologičeskago Fakul'tet Imperatorskago S. Petersburskago Universiteta* 35 (1894–6): 1–64.
'Κυπριακά καὶ ἄλλα ἔγγραφα ἐκ τοῦ Παλατινοῦ Κώδικος 367 τῆς Βιβλιοθήκης τοῦ Βατικανοῦ', ed. S. Lampros, *Νέος Ἑλληνομνήμων* 15 (1921): 141–65 (pt. 2), and 337–56 (pt. 3).
Lamberto di Sambuceto, *Gênes et l'Outre-Mer, 1: Les actes de Caffa du notaire Lamberto du Sambuceto 1289–1290*, ed. M. Balard (Paris, 1973).
Lamberto di Sambuceto, *Notai genovesi in Oltremare. Atti rogati a Cipro da Lamberto di Sambuceto (3 luglio 1300–3 agosto 1301)*, ed. V. Polonio (Genoa, 1982).
Lamberto di Sambuceto, *Notai genovesi in Oltremare. Atti rogati a Cipro da Lamberto di Sambuceto (6 luglio – 27 ottobre 1301)*, ed. R. Pavoni (Genoa, 1982).
Lamberto di Sambuceto, *Notai genovesi in Oltremare. Atti rogati a Cipro da Lamberto di Sambuceto. 3: 11 ottobre 1296–23 giugno 1299*, ed. M. Balard (Genoa, 1983).
Lamberto di Sambuceto, *Notai genovesi in Oltremare. Atti rogati a Cipro, Lamberto di Sambuceto (31 marzo 1304–19 luglio 1305, 4 gennaio–12 luglio 1307), Giovanni da Rocha (3 agosto 1308–14 marzo 1310)*, ed. M. Balard (Genoa, 1984).
Lamberto di Sambuceto, *Actes de Famagouste du notaire génois Lamberto di Sambuceto (décembre 1299–septembre 1300)*, ed. M. Balard, C. Schabel, and W. O. Duba (Nicosia, 2012).
Laonikos Chalkokondyles, *Histories*, ed. Darkó and tr. Kaldellis (2 vols., Washington, DC, 2014).
Leonardo Marcello, *Leonardo Marcello, Notaio in Candia: 1278–1281*, ed. M. Chiaudano and A. Lombardo (Venice, 1960).
Leontios Machairas, *Χρονικό τῆς Κύπρου*, ed. M. Pieris and A. Nicolaou-Konnari, ed. and tr. R. M. Dawkins as *Recital concerning the Sweet Land of Cyprus entitled 'Chronicle'* (2 vols., Oxford, 1932).
Liber Iurium Reipublicae genuensis, tomus II, in *Historiae patriae monumenta* [vol. 9], ed. E. Ricotti (Turin, 1857).
Life of Philotheos, ed. S. Papoulia and tr. S. McGrath, in R. P. H. Greenfield and A.-M. M. Talbot (eds and tr.), *Holy Men of Mount Athos* (Washington, DC, 2016), 614–27.

Matthew of Ephesus, *Die Briefe des Matthaios von Ephesos im Codex Vindobonensis Theol. Gr. 174*, ed. D. Reinsch (Berlin, 1974).
Medieval Trade in the Mediterranean World: Illustrative Documents, tr. R. S. Lopez and I. W. Raymond (New York, 1967).
Metrophanes, 'Βίος τοῦ Ὁσίου Διονυσίου τοῦ Ἀθωνίτου', ed. B. Laourdas, *Ἀρχεῖον Πόντου* 21 (1956): 43–79.
Moretto Bon, *Moretto Bon, Notaio in Venezia, Trebisonda e Tana (1403–1408)*, ed. S. De' Colli (Venice, 1963).
'Neobjavljene isprave i akti XIII stoljeća dubrovačkog arhiva', ed. J. Lučić, *Arhivsk vjesnik* 13 (1970): 381–95.
Νέον Ἐπιστολάριον (Venice, 1796).
Nicola de Boateriis, *Nicola de Boateriis, Notaio in Famagosta e Venezia (1355–1365)*, ed. A. Lombardo (Venice, 1973).
Nikephoros Gregoras, *Historiae Byzantinae*, ed. L. Schopen (3 vols., Bonn, 1829–1855) and I. Bekker, tr. J. L. van Dieten as *Rhomäische Geschichte* (6 vols., Stuttgart, 1973–).
Niketas Choniates, *Historia*, ed. J. L. van Dieten (Berlin, 1975), tr. H. J. Magoulias, *O City of Byzantium: Annals of Niketas Choniates* (Detroit MI, 1984).
Notai genovesi in Oltremare. Atti rogati a Caffa e a Licostomo (sec. XIV), ed. G. Balbi and S. Raiteri (Genoa, 1973).
Notai genovesi in Oltremare: Atti rogati a Pera e Mitilene, ed. Roccatagliata (2 vols., Genoa, 1982).
'Nuova serie di documenti sulle relazioni di Genova coll'impero Bizantino, raccolti dal Can. Angelo Sanguineti, e pubblicati con molte aggiunte dal Prof. Gerolamo Bertolotto', ed. A. Sanguineti and G. Bertolotto, *Atti della Società Ligure di Storia Patria* 28 (1898): 337–573.
Pero Tafur, *Travels and Adventures, 1435–1439*, tr. M. Letts (London, 1926).
Philotheos Kokkinos, *Λόγοι καὶ Ὁμιλίες*, ed. B. S. Pseutonkas (Thessaloniki, 1981).
Pietro Pizolo, *Pietro Pizolo, Notaio in Candia*, ed. S. Carbone (2 vols., Venice, 1978–85).
Raffaele de Casanova, *Notai genovesi in Oltremare: Atti rogati a Chio nel XIV secolo dal notaio Raffaele de Casanova*, ed. L. Balletto (Bordighera, 2015).
Ramon Muntaner, *The Catalan Expedition to the East: From the Chronicle of Ramon Muntaner*, tr. R. D. Hughes and intr. J. N. Hillgarth (Barcelona and Woodbridge, 2006).
Register des Patriarchats von Konstantinopel, 2. Teil: Edition und Übersetzung der Urkunden aus den Jahren 1337–1350, ed. H. Hunger, O. Kresten, E. Kislinger, and C. Cupane (Vienna, 1995).

Ruy Gonzalez de Clavijo, *Narrative of the Embassy of Ruy Gonzalez de Clavijo to the Court of Timour, at Samarcand, AD 1403–6*, tr. C. R. Markham (London, 1859).
Septuaginta, ed. A. Rahlfs (9 ed., Stuttgart, 1935; repr. 1971).
Simeone di San Giacomo dell' Orio, 'Un notaire vénitien à Famagouste au XIVe siècle: Les actes de Simone, prêtre de San Giacomo dell' Orio (1362–1371)', summarised C. Otten-Froux, *Thesaurismata* 33 (2003): 15–159.
Spisi dubrovačke kancelarije, knjiga 1: Zapisi notara Tomazina de Savere 1278–1282, ed. G. Čremošnik (Zagreb, 1951).
Stefano Bono, *Stefano Bono, Notaio in Candia, 1303–1304*, ed. G. Petenello and S. Rauch (Rome, 2011).
Symeon of Thessaloniki, 'Ἀποκρίσεις πρὸς τινας ἐρωτήσεις ἀρχιερέως ἠρωτηκότος αὔτον', *Patrologia Graeca* 155, ed. Migne (Paris, 1866), coll. 829–952.
Symeon of Thessaloniki, *Politico-Historical Works of Symeon Archbishop of Thessalonica (1416/17 to 1429)*, ed. D. Balfour (Vienna, 1979).
'Συνθήκη Ἐνετῶν-Καλλέργη καὶ οἱ συνοδεύοντες αὐτήν κατάλογοι', ed. K. D. Mertzios, *Κρητικὰ Χρονικά* 3 (1949): 262–92.
Σύνταγμα τῶν Θείων καὶ Ἱερῶν Κανόνων, ed. G. A. Rhalles and M. Potles, vol. I (Athens, 1852).
Al-Ṭabarī, *Ta'rīkh*, ed. De Goeje et al. as *Annales*, 3 ser., vol. 4 (Leiden, 1890), tr. F. Rosenthal, *The History of al-Ṭabarī, Volume XXXVIII: The Return of the Caliphate to Baghdad* (New York, NY, 1985).
Terre hodierne Grecorum et dominie secularia et spiritulia ipsorum. De ecclesia et dominio Grecorum hic infra, ed. S. Lampros, 'Ὑπόμνημα περὶ τῶν ἑλληνικῶν χωρῶν καὶ ἐκκλησίων κατὰ τὸν δέκατον πέμπτον αἰῶνα', *Νέος Ἑλληνομνήμων* 7 (1910): 360–71.
Theodore Metochites, 'Oratio de S. Michaele martyre a Theodoro Metochita', ed. H. Delehaye in *Acta sanctorum novembris, tomus IV, quo dies nonus et decimus continentur* (Brussels, 1925), 670–8.
'Τύποι Βυζαντινῶν συμβολαίων', ed. K. N. Sathas in *Μεσαιωνικὴ Βιβλιοθήκη*, vol. 6 (Venice, 1877), 607–40.
Al-'Umarī, ed. F. Taeschner, *Al-'Umarī's Bericht über Anatolien in seinem Werke Masālik al-abṣār fī mamālik al-amṣār*, vol. I: Text (Leipzig, 1929), tr. E. Quatremère, 'Notice de l'ouvrage qui a pour titre Masalek alabsar fi memalek alamsar, Voyages des yeux dans les royaumes des différentes contrées (ms. Arabe 585)', *Notices et extraits des manuscrits de la Bibliothèque du Roi* 13 (1838): 334–81.
Urkunden zur älteren Handels- und Staatsgeschichte der Republik Venedig, ed. G. L. F. Tafel and G. M. Thomas (3 vols., Vienna, 1856–7).

Vazelonskie akty materialy dlja istorii krestjanskogo i monastyrskogo zemlevladenija v Vizantii 13–15 vekov, ed. F. I. Uspenskij (Leningrad, 1927).
'Vie de Saint Niphon, eremite au Mont Athos (XIVe siècle)', ed. F. Halkin, *Analecta Bollandiana* 58 (1940): 5–27.
William Adam, *Tractatus quomodo Sarraceni sunt expugnandi*, ed. and tr. G. Constable as *How to Defeat the Saracens* (Washington, DC, 2012).
Wills from Late Medieval Venetian Crete, 1312–1420, ed. S. McKee (3 vols., Washington, DC, 1998).

Scholarship:

Ahrweiler, H., *Byzance et la Mer: La marine de guerre, la politique, les institutions maritimes de Byzance aux VIIe–XVe siècles* (Paris, 1966).
Ahrweiler, H., 'Course et piraterie dans la Méditerranée orientale aux XIVe–XVe siècles (Empire byzantin)', in *Course et piraterie: Études présentées à la Commission Internationale d'Histoire Maritime à l'occasion de son XVe colloque international pendant le XIVe Congrès International des Sciences historiques San Francisco, août 1975*, vol. 1 (Paris, 1975), 7–29.
Amantos, K., 'Ἡ αἰχμαλωσία τοῦ Νικολάου Λικινίου', *Ἑλληνικά* 11 (1939): 151–6.
Amari, M., '*Al ʿUmarî: Condizioni degli stati cristiani dell'Occidente secundo una relazione di Domenichino Doria da Genova* (Rome, 1883).
Amitai, R., 'Diplomacy and the Slave Trade in the Eastern Mediterranean: A Re-Examination of the Mamluk-Byzantine-Genoese Triangle in the Late Thirteenth Century in Light of the Existing Early Correspondence', *Oriente Moderno* 88 (2008): 349–68.
Amitai, R., 'Between the Slave Trade and Diplomacy: Some Aspects of Early Mamluk Policy in the Eastern Mediterranean and the Black Sea', in R. Amitai and C. Cluse (eds), *Slavery and the Slave Trade in the Eastern Mediterranean (c. 1000–1500 CE)* (Turnhout, 2017), 401–22.
Amitai, R. and C. Cluse (eds), *Slavery and the Slave Trade in the Eastern Mediterranean (c. 1000–1500 CE)* (Turnhout, 2017).
Angelomati-Tsougaraki, E., 'Το φαινόμενο της ζητείας κατά τη Μεταβυζαντινή Περίοδο', *Ιόνιος Λόγος* 1 (2007): 247–93.
Angold, M., *The Fourth Crusade: Event and Context* (Harlow, 2003).
Angold, M., *The Fall of Constantinople to the Ottomans: Context and Consequences* (Harlow, 2012).
Antoniadis-Bibicou, H., 'Villages désertés en Grèce: Un bilan provisoire', in [no ed.,] *Villages désertés et histoire économique, XIe–XVIIIe siècle* (Paris, 1965), 343–417.

Arbel, B., 'Slave Trade and Slave Labor in Frankish Cyprus (1191–1571)', *Studies in Medieval and Renaissance History*, New Series, 14 (1993): 149–90.
Argenti, P. P., *The Occupation of Chios by the Genoese and Their Administration of the Island, 1346–1566* (3 vols., Cambridge, 1958).
Arnakis, G. G., 'Byzantium's Anatolian Provinces During the Reign of Michael Palaeologus', *Actes du XIIe congrès d'études byzantines*, vol. 2 (Belgrade, 1964), 37–44.
Aschenbrenner, N. and J. Ransohoff (eds), *The Invention of Byzantium in Early Modern Europe* (Cambridge, MA, 2022).
Astor, E., *Levant Trade in the Middle Ages* (Princeton, NJ, 1984).
Atiya, A. S., *The Crusade in the Later Middle Ages* (London, 1938).
Ayalon, D., *L'esclavage de Mamelouk* (Jerusalem, 1951).
Balard, M., *La Romanie génoise (XIIe–début du XVe siècle)* (2 vols., Rome, 1978).
Balard, M., Laiou, A. E., Otten-Froux, C., *Les Italiens à Byzance: Édition et présentation de documents* (Paris, 1987).
Balard, M., 'A propos de la bataille du Bosphore. L'expédition génoise de Paganino Doria à Constantinople (1351–1352)', *Travaux et Mémoires* 4 (1970): 431–69, repr. in M. Balard, *La mer Noire et la Romanie génoise: XIIIe–XVe siècles* (London, 1989), No. II.
Balard, M., 'Latins in the Aegean and the Balkans in the Fourteenth Century', in M. Jones (ed.), *The New Cambridge Medieval History*, vol. 6, c. 1300–c. 1415 (Cambridge, 2000), 825–38.
Balard, M., 'Slavery in the Latin Mediterranean (Thirteenth to Fifteenth Centuries): The Case of Genoa', in R. Amitai and C. Cluse (eds), *Slavery and the Slave Trade in the Eastern Mediterranean (c. 1000–1500 CE)* (Turnhout, 2017), 235–54.
Balard, M., 'Black Sea Slavery in Genoese Notarial Sources, 13th–15th centuries', in F. Roşu (ed.), *Slavery in the Black Sea Region, c. 900–1900: Forms of Unfreedom at the Intersection between Christianity and Islam* (Leiden and Boston, 2022), 19–40.
Balivet, M., 'Byzantins judaïsants et Juifs islamisés des «kühhân» (kâhin) aux «Χιόνες» (Χιόνιος)', *Byzantion* 52 (1982): 24–59.
Balletto, L., 'Presenze bulgare da Caffa a Genova (secc. XIII–XV)', in G. Pistarino (ed.), *Genova e la Bulgaria nel medioevo* (Genoa, 1984), 149–211.
Balletto, L., 'Schiavi e manomessi nella Chio dei Genovesi nel secolo XV', in M. T. Ferrer i Mallol and J. Mutgé i Vives (eds), *De l'esclavitud a la llibertat: Esclaus i lliberts a l'edat mitjana* (Barcelona, 2000), 659–94.
Bănescu, N., *Le déclin de Famagouste, fin du Royaume de Chypre: Notes et documents* (Bucharest, 1946).

Barker, H., 'Egyptian and Italian Merchants in the Black Sea Slave Trade, 1260–1500', PhD thesis, Columbia University (2014).

Barker, H., 'Christianities in conflict: The Black Sea as a Genoese Slaving Zone in the Later Middle Ages', in J. Fynn-Paul and D. A. Pargas, *Slaving Zones: Cultural Identities, Ideologies, and Institutions in the Evolution of Global Slavery* (Leiden, 2018), 50–69.

Barker, H., *That Most Precious Merchandise: The Mediterranean Trade in Black Sea Slaves, 1260–1500* (Philadelphia, PA, 2019).

Barker, H., 'The Trade in Slaves in the Black Sea, Russia, and Eastern Europe', in C. Perry, D. Eltis, S. Engerman and D. Richardson (eds), *The Cambridge World History of Slavery, Volume 2: AD 500–AD 1420* (Cambridge, 2021), 100–22.

Barker, H., 'What Caused the 14th-Century Tatar–Circassian Shift?', in F. Roşu (ed.), *Slavery in the Black Sea Region, c. 900–1900: Forms of Unfreedom at the Intersection between Christianity and Islam* (Leiden and Boston, 2022), 339–63.

Batlle i Gallart, C., 'Els esclaus domèstics a Barcelona vers 1300', M. T. Ferrer i Mallol and J. Mutgé i Vives (eds), *De l'esclavitud a la llibertat: Esclaus i lliberts a l'edat mitjana* (Barcelona, 2000), 265–96.

Bayrı, B. K., 'Byzantium, the Union of Churches, Bulgaria and the Ottomans through the Case Study of the Neo-Martyr George of Adrianople, 1437 (BHG 2160)', *Annuaire de l'Université de Sofia 'St Kliment Ohridski', Centre de Recherches Slavo-Byzantines 'Ivan Dujčev'* 95 (2006): 183–91.

Bayrı, B. K., *Warriors, Martyrs, and Dervishes: Moving Frontiers, Shifting Identities in the Land of Rome (13th–15th Centuries)* (Leiden, 2020).

Becker, B. N., 'Life and Local Administration on Fifteenth Century Genoese Chios', PhD thesis, Western Michigan University, Kalamazoo (2010).

Bees, N., 'Συμβολὴ εἰς τὴν ἱστορίαν τῶν μονῶν τῶν Μετεώρων', *Βυζαντίς* 1 (1909): 191–331.

BHG: see Halkin.

Beihammer, A. D., *Byzantium and the Emergence of Muslim-Turkish Anatolia, ca. 1040–1130* (London, 2017).

Bisson, *The Medieval Crown of Aragon: A Short History* (Oxford, 1991).

Blanchet, M-H, 'L'Église byzantine à la suite de l'Union de Florence (1439–1445) de la contestation à la scission', *Byzantinische Forschungen* 29 (2007): 79–123.

Bliznyuk, S. V., 'Diplomatic Relations between Cyprus and Genoa in the Light of the Genoese Juridical Documents: ASG, Diversorum Communis Ianue, 1375–1480', in A. D. Beihammer, M. G. Parani and C. D. Schabel (eds), *Diplomatics in the Eastern Mediterranean 1000–1500: Aspects of Cross-Cultural Communication* (Leiden and Boston, MA, 2008), 275–92.

Blumenthal, D., *Enemies and Familiars: Slavery and Mastery in Fifteenth-Century Valencia* (Ithaca, NY, 2009).
Bongi, S., 'Le schiave orientali in Italia', *Nuova Antologia* 2 (1866): 215–46.
Boojamra, J. L., *Church Reform in the Late Byzantine Empire: A Study for the Patriarchate of Athanasios of Constantinople* (Thessaloniki, 1982).
Boojamra, J. L., 'Social Thought and Reforms of Athanasios of Constantinople (1289–1293; 1303–1309)', *Byzantion* 55 (1985): 332–82.
Bosworth, C. E., 'The City of Tarsus and the Arab–Byzantine Frontiers in Early and Middle ʿAbbāsid Times', *Oriens* 33 (1992): 268–86.
Brand, C. M., 'The Byzantines and Saladin, 1185–1192: Opponents of the Third Crusade', *Speculum* 37 (1962): 167–81.
Bresc, H., *Un monde méditerranéen. Économie et société en Sicile, 1300–1450*, vol. 1 (Palermo, 1986).
Brodman, J. W., 'Municipal Ransoming Law on the Medieval Spanish Frontier', *Speculum* 60 (1985): 318–30.
Brodman, J. W., 'Community, Identity and the Redemption of Captives: Comparative Perspectives across the Mediterranean', *Anuario de Estudios Medievales* 36 (2006): 241–52.
Brodman, J. W., 'Captives or Prisoners: Society and Obligation in Medieval Iberia', *Anuario de Historia de la Iglesia* 20 (2011): 201–19.
Brutails, A., *Étude sur l'esclavage en Roussilon du XIIIe au XVIIe siècle* (Paris, 1886).
Bryer, A. A. M., 'Greeks and Türkmens: The Pontic Exception', *Dumbarton Oaks Papers* 29 (1975): 113–48.
Bryer, A. A. M., 'The Roman Orthodox World (1393–1492)' in J. Shepard (ed.), *The Cambridge History of the Byzantine Empire, c. 500–1492* (Cambridge, 2009), 852–80.
Bryer, A. A. M. and H. W. Lowry (eds), *Continuity and Change in Late Byzantine and Early Ottoman Society. Papers Given at a Symposium at Dumbarton Oaks in May 1982* (Birmingham and Washington, DC, 1986).
Cameron, A., *Byzantine Matters* (Princeton, PA, 2014).
Canard, M., 'Une lettre du Sultan Malik Nâṣir Ḥasan à Jean VI Cantacuzène (750/1349)', *Annales de l'Institut d'Etudes Orientales de la Faculté des Lettres d'Alger* 3 (1937): 27–52, reprinted in M. Canard, *Byzance et les musulmans du Proche Orient* (London, 1973), No. X.
Carr, M., *Merchant Crusaders in the Aegean, 1291–1352* (Woodbridge, 2015).
Carr, M. and A. C. Grant, 'The Catalan Company as a Military Diasporic Group in Medieval Greece and Asia Minor', in G. Christ, P. Sänger and M. Carr (eds), *Military Diasporas: Building of Empire in the Middle East and Europe (550 BCE–1500 CE)* (Abingdon and New York, 2022), 176–93.

Casiday, A., 'John XIV (Kalekas), Byzantine Theology-cum-Politics and the Early Hesychast Controversy', in F. Olivie (ed.) *Le patriarcat oecuménique de Constantinople aux XIVe–XVIe siècles: Rupture et continuité* (Paris, 2007), 19–35.

Cateura Bennasser, P., 'Política, guerra y esclavitud: Cautivos griegos en la Mallorca de 1388', *Asociación Hispano–Helénica, Anuario de 1989* (Athens, 1991), 123–66.

Charanis, P., 'Piracy in the Aegean during the Reign of Michael VIII Palaeologus', *Annuaire de l'Institut de philologie et d'histoire orientales et slaves* 10 (1950): 127–36.

Cheyette, F. L., 'The Sovereign and the Pirates, 1332', *Speculum* 45 (1970): 40–68.

Christianson, G., 'Introduction: The Conciliar Tradition and Ecumenical Dialogue', in G. Christianson, T. M. Izbicki and C. M. Bellitto (eds) *The Church, Its Councils, and Reform: The Legacy of the Fifteenth Century* (Washington, DC, 2008), 1–24.

Christides, V., 'Once again Caminiates' "Capture of Thessaloniki"', *Byzantinische Zeitschrift* 74 (1981): 7–10.

Chrysostomides, J., 'The Byzantine Empire from the Eleventh to Fifteenth Century', in K. Fleet (ed.), *Cambridge History of Turkey, Volume 1: Byzantium to Turkey, 1071–1453* (Cambridge, 2009), 6–50.

Chrysostomides, J., 'Venetian Commercial Privileges under the Palaeologi', *Studi Veneziani* 12 (1970): 267–356, repr. in C. Dendrinos and M. Heslop (eds), *Byzantium and Venice: 1204–1453. Collected Studies by Julian Chrysostomides* (Aldershot, 2011), No. III.

Cluse, C., 'The Role of the Slave Trade in the *De recuperanda* Treatises around 1300', in R. Amitai and C. Cluse (eds), *Slavery and the Slave Trade in the Eastern Mediterranean (c. 1000–1500 CE)* (Turnhout, 2017), 437–69.

Constantelos, D. J., *Byzantine Philanthropy and Social Welfare* (New Brunswick, NJ, 1968).

Constantelos, D. J., *Poverty, Society and Philanthropy in the Late Mediaeval Greek World* (New York, 1992).

Coureas, N., 'The Latin and Greek Churches in Former Byzantine Lands under Latin rule', in N. I. Tsougarakis and P. Lock (eds), *A Companion to Latin Greece* (Leiden, 2015), 145–84.

Coureas, N., *The Latin Church in Cyprus, 1195–1312* (Aldershot, 1997; repr., Abingdon, 2016).

Coureas, N., 'Latin Cyprus and Its Relations with the Mamluk Sultanate', in A. J. Boas (ed.), *The Crusader World* (London and New York, 2016), 391–418.

Coureas, N., 'The Manumission of Hospitaller Slaves on Fifteenth Century Rhodes and Cyprus', in J. Schenk and M. Carr (eds), *The Military Orders, 6.1: Culture and Conflicts in the Mediterranean World* (London, 2017), 106–14.

D'Amia, *Schiavitù romana e servitù medievale: Contributo di studi e documenti* (Milan, 1931).

Daniel, C.-N., 'Coping with the Powerful Other: A Comparative Approach to Greek–Slavonic Communities of Rite in Late Medieval Transylvania and the Banat', PhD Thesis, Central European University (Budapest, 2014).

Darrouzès, J., 'Lettres de 1453', *Revue des études byzantines* 22 (1964), 72–127.

Dashdondog, B., 'The Black Sea Trade in the 13th–14th Century that Changed the Political Balance in the Near East', *Golden Horde Review* 7 (2019): 283–94.

Delaville le Roulx, J., *Les Hospitaliers à Rhodes jusqu'à la mort de Philibert de Naillac (1310–1421)* (Paris, 1913).

Delort, R., 'Quelques précisions sur le commerce des esclaves à Gênes vers la fin du XIVe siècle', *Mélanges d'archéologie et d'histoire* 78 (1966): 215–50.

Demacopoulos, G. E., *Colonizing Christianity: Greek and Latin Religious Identity in the Era of the Fourth Crusade* (New York, 2019).

Dendrinos C., 'Reflections on the Failure of the Union of Florence', *Annuarium historiae conciliorum* 39 (2007): 135–52.

De Vaivre, J.-B., 'Essai de chronologie des campagnes de construction du château Saint-Pierre (Bodrum, Turquie)', *Comptes rendus des séances de l'Académie des Inscriptions et Belles-Lettres* 153 (2009): 601–22.

Dincer, A., '"Enslaving Christians": Greek Slaves in Late Medieval Cyprus', *Mediterranean Historical Review* 31 (2006): 1–19.

Dölger, F., *Regesten der Kaiserurkunden des oströmischen Reiches von 565–1453, 3. Teil: Regesten von 1204–1282* (2nd ed., ed. P. Wirth, Munich, 1977), *4. Teil: Regesten von 1282–1341* (Munich and Berlin, 1960), and *5. Teil: Regesten von 1341–1453* (Munich and Berlin, 1965).

Du Cange, C. du Fresne, *Glossarium mediae et infimae latinitatis*, ed. I. Favre (10 vols., Niort, 1883–7).

Duran Duelt, D., 'La Companyia catalana i el comerç d'esclaus abans de l'assentament als Ducats d'Atenes i Neopàtria', in M. T. Ferrer i Mallol and J. Mutgé i Vives (eds), *De l'esclavitud a la llibertat: Esclaus i lliberts a l'edat mitjana* (Barcelona, 2000), 557–71.

Duran Duelt, D., 'Els mallorquins a la Romania (segles XIII–XVI)', in *El Regne de Mallorca: cruïlla de gents i de cultures (segles XIII–XV)* (Palma, 2008), 241–55.

Duran Duelt, D., 'Los Ducados de Atenas y Neopatria en el comercio regional e internacional durante la dominación catalana (siglo XIV) II: el comercio de larga distancia a través del observatorio de Barcelona y Mallorca', *Estudios bizantinos* 7 (2019): 85–118.

Edbury, P. W., *The Kingdom of Cyprus and the Crusades, 1191–1374* (Cambridge, 1991).

Ehrenkreutz, A., 'Strategic implications of the slave trade between Genoa and Mamluk Egypt in the second half of the thirteenth century', in A. L. Udovitch (ed.), *The Islamic Middle East, 700–1900: Studies in Economic and Social History* (Princeton, NJ, 1981), 335–46.

EI², EI³: see *Encyclopaedia of Islam*.

El Cheikh, N. M., *Byzantium Viewed by the Arabs* (Cambridge, MA, 2004).

Encyclopaedia of Islam, Second Edition, ed. P. J. Bearnam, T. Bianquis, C. E. Bosworth, E. van Donzel, W. P. Heinrichs et al. (12 vols., Leiden, 1960–2005, online) [=*EI²*].

Encyclopaedia of Islam, Third Edition, ed. K. Fleet, G. Krämer, D. Matringe, J. Nawas and E. Rowson (Leiden: 2007–, online) [=*EI³*].

Epstein, S. A., *Speaking of Slavery: Color, Ethnicity, and Human Bondage in Italy* (Ithaca, NY, 2001).

Epstein, S. A., *Purity Lost: Transgressing Boundaries in the Eastern Mediterranean, 1000–1400* (Baltimore, 2006).

Farag, W. A., 'Some Remarks on Leo of Tripoli's Attack on Thessaloniki', *Byzantinische Zeitschrift* 82 (1988): 133–9.

Favereau, M., 'The Golden Horde and the Mamluks', *Golden Horde Review* 5 (2017): 93–115.

Ferrer i Mallol, M. T., 'Després de la mort. L'actuació d'algunes marmessories a través d'un manual del notari barceloní Nicolau de Mediona (1437–1438)', *Analecta Sacra Tarraconensia* 71 (1998): 281–325.

Ferrer i Mallol, M. T., 'Esclaus i lliberts orientals a Barcelona. Segles XIV i XV', in M. T. Ferrer i Mallol and J. Mutgé i Vives (eds), *De l'esclavitud a la llibertat: Esclaus i lliberts a l'edat mitjana* (Barcelona, 2000), 167–212.

Ferrer i Mallol, M. T., and J. Mutgé i Vives (eds), *De l'esclavitud a la llibertat: Esclaus i lliberts a l'edat mitjana* (Barcelona, 2000).

Flannery, J., 'The Trinitarian Order and the Ransom of Christian Captives', *Al-Masāq* 23 (2011): 135–44.

Fleet, K., *European and Islamic Trade in the Early Ottoman State* (Cambridge, 1999).

Fleet, K., 'The Turkish Economy, 1071–1453', in K. Fleet (ed.), *Cambridge History of Turkey, Volume 1: Byzantium to Turkey, 1071–1453* (Cambridge, 2009), 227–65.

Fleet, K. (ed.), *Cambridge History of Turkey, Volume 1: Byzantium to Turkey, 1071–1453* (Cambridge, 2009).
Forey, A., *Military Orders and Crusades* (Aldershot, 2001).
Fossati Raiteri, S., 'Schiavitù nelle colonie genovesi del Levante nel basso medioevo', in M. T. Ferrer i Mallol and J. Mutgé i Vives (eds), *De l'esclavitud a la llibertat: Esclaus i lliberts a l'edat mitjana* (Barcelona, 2000), 695–716.
Frankopan, P., 'Byzantine Trade Privileges to Venice in the Eleventh Century: The Chrysobull of 1092', *Journal of Medieval History* 30 (2004): 135–60.
Frenkel, M., '"Proclaim Liberty to Captives and Freedom to Prisoners". The Ransoming of Captives by Medieval Jewish Communities in Islamic Countries', in H. Grieser and N. Priesching (eds), *Gefangenenloskauf im Mittelmeerraum: Ein interreligiöser Vergleich* (Hildesheim, 2015), 83–97.
Frenkel, Y., '*Fikāk al-asīr*. The ransom of Muslim Captives in the Mamlūk Sultanate', in H. Grieser and N. Priesching (eds), *Gefangenenloskauf im Mittelmeerraum: Ein interreligiöser Vergleich* (Hildesheim, 2015), 143–57.
Friedman, Y., *Encounter between Enemies: Captivity and Ransom in the Crusader Kingdom of Jerusalem* (Leiden, 2002).
Fynn-Paul, J., 'Empire, Monotheism and Slavery in the Greater Mediterranean Region from Antiquity to the Early Modern Era', *Past and Present* 205 (2009): 3–40.
Garrood, W., 'The Byzantine Conquest of Cilicia and the Hamdanids of Aleppo, 959–965', *Anatolian Studies* 58 (2008): 127–40.
Geanakoplos, D. J., *Emperor Michael Palaeologus and the West* (Cambridge, MA, 1959).
Geanakoplos, D. J., *Constantinople and the West: Essays on the Late Byzantine (Palaeologan) and Italian Renaissances and the Byzantine and Roman Churches* (Madison, WI, 1989).
Gheorghe, A., *The Metamorphosis of Power: Violence, Warlords, Akıncıs and the Early Ottomans (1300–1450)* (Leiden, 2023).
Gili Ferrer, A., 'El monedatge d'Artà de l'any 1337', *Bolletí de la Societat arqueològica Lul·liana* 56 (2000): 477–88.
Gill, J. S., *The Council of Florence* (Cambridge, 1959).
Gill, J. S., 'The Freedom of the Greeks in the Council of Florence', *Birmingham Historical Journal* 12 (1969–70): 226–37.
Gioffrè, D., *Il mercato degli schiavi a Genova nel secolo XV* (Genoa, 1971).
Goldwyn, A. J., *Witness Literature in Byzantium: Narrating Slaves, Prisoners, and Refugees* (Cham, 2021).
Grant, A. C., 'The Mongol Invasions between Epistolography and Prophecy: The Case of the Letter "Ad flagellum"', c. 1235/6–1338', *Traditio* 73 (2018): 117–77.

Grant, A. C., 'Book Review: *That Most Precious Merchandise: The Mediterranean Trade in Black Sea Slaves, 1260–1500*', *Al-Masāq* 32 (2020): 357–60.

Grant, A. C., 'Cross-confessional Captivity in the Later Medieval Eastern Roman World, c. 1280–1450', PhD thesis, University of Edinburgh (2 vols., 2021).

Grant, A. C., 'Scotland's "Vagabonding Greekes"', 1453–1688', *Byzantine and Modern Greek Studies* 46 (2022): 81–97.

Grant, A. C., 'Gottlose Korsaren in der spätmittelalterlichen Ägäis', in R. Hank, H. Leppin and M. Plumpe (eds), *»Alle, die mit uns auf Kaperfahrt fahren«: Piratengeschichten auf den Meeren der Welt* (Frankfurt and New York, 2023), 49–72.

Grant, A. C., 'Captives, Slaves, and Latin Categories of Greekness', in N. Gaul (ed.), *The Post-1204 Byzantine World: New Approaches and Novel Directions* (Abingdon, forthcoming).

Greene, M., *A Shared World: Christians and Muslims in the Early Modern Mediterranean* (Princeton, 2000).

Greene, M., *Catholic Pirates and Greek Merchants: A Maritime History of the Mediterranean* (Princeton, 2010).

Gregory, T. E., 'Naupaktos', in A. P. Kazhdan et al. (eds), *The Oxford Dictionary of Byzantium* (3 vols., Oxford, 1991), 1442–3.

Grierson, R., '"We believe in your Prophet": Rumi, Palamas, and the Conversion of Anatolia', *Mawlana Rumi Review* 2 (2011): 96–124.

Grieser, H., and N. Priesching (eds), *Gefangenenloskauf im Mittelmeerraum: Ein interreligiöser Vergleich* (Hildesheim, 2015).

Hadjinicolaou-Marava, A., *Recherches sur la vie des esclaves dans le monde byzantin* (Athens, 1950).

Halecki, *Un empereur de Byzance à Rome* (Warsaw, 1930; repr. London, 1972).

Halkin, F. (ed.), *Bibliotheca Hagiographica Graeca* (3 vols., Brussels, 1957; 1 vol., Brussels, 1984) [*BHG*].

Harris, J., *Greek Emigres in the West, 1400–1520* (Camberley, 1995).

Harris, J., *The End of Byzantium* (New Haven, 2010).

Harris, J., *Byzantium and the Crusades* (2nd ed., London, 2011).

Harris, J., 'Constantinople as City-State, c. 1360–1453', in J. Harris, C. Holmes, and E. Russell (eds), *Byzantines, Latins and Turks in the Eastern Mediterranean World after 1150* (Oxford, 2012), 119–40.

Harris, J., 'The Patriarch of Constantinople and the Last Days of Byzantium', in C. Gastgeber, E. Mitsiou, J. Preiser-Kapeller, and V. Zervan (eds), *The Patriarchate of Constantinople in Context and Comparison* (Vienna, 2017), 9–16.

Hasluck, F. W., 'Depopulation in the Aegean Islands and the Turkish Conquest', *The Annual of the British School at Athens* 17 (1910–11): 151–81.

Hazard, H. W. (ed.), *The Fourteenth and Fifteenth Centuries*, in K. M. Setton (gen. ed.), *A History of the Crusades*, vol. 3 (Madison WI, 1975).

Heng, G., *The Invention of Race in the European Middle Ages* (Cambridge, 2018).

Herrin, J. and McManus, S. M., 'Renaissance Encounters: Byzantium Meets the West at the Council of Ferrara-Florence 1438–39', in M. S. Brownlee and D. H. Gondicas (eds), *Greek East and Latin West* (Leiden, 2013), 35–56.

Hershenzon, D., *The Captive Sea: Slavery, Communication, and Commerce in Early Modern Spain and the Mediterranean* (Pennsylvania, 2018).

Hill, G., *A History of Cyprus, Volume 2: The Frankish Period, 1192–1432* (Cambridge, 1948).

Hillgarth, J. N., 'A Greek Slave in Majorca in 1419–26: New Documents', *Mediaeval Studies* 50 (1988): 546–58.

Holt, P. M., *Early Mamluk Diplomacy (1260–1290): Treaties of Baybars and Qalāwūn with Christian Rulers* (Leiden, 1995).

Hopfgartner, L., 'Altologo', in [no ed.,] *Miscellanea storica ligure* 2 (Milan, 1961), 99–110.

Hopley, R., 'The Ransoming of Prisoners in Medieval North Africa and Andalusia: An Analysis of the Legal Framework', *Medieval Encounters* 15 (2009): 337–54.

Housley, N., *Documents on the Later Crusades, 1274–1580* (Basingstoke, 1996).

Hussey, J., *The Orthodox Church in the Byzantine Empire* (Oxford, 1986).

Imber, C., *The Crusade of Varna, 1443–45: Crusade Texts in Translation* (Aldershot, 2006).

İnalcık, H., 'Ottoman Methods of Conquest', *Studia Islamica* 2 (1954): 103–29.

İnalcık, H., 'The Policy of Mehmed II toward the Greek Population of Istanbul and the Byzantine Buildings of the City', *Dumbarton Oaks Papers* 23 (1969–70): 229–49.

Jackson, P., *The Mongols and the West, 1221–1410* (Harlow, 2005).

Jacoby, D., 'Phénomènes de démographie rurale à Byzance aux XIIIe, XIVe et XVe siècles', *Études rurales* 5–6 (1962): 161–86.

Jacoby, D., 'The Rise of a New Emporium in the Eastern Mediterranean: Famagusta in the Late Thirteenth Century', Μελέται και Υπομνήματα (Ίδρυμα Αρχιεπισκόπου Μακαρίου III), 1 (1984), 145–79, repr. in D. Jacoby, *Studies on the Crusader States and on Venetian Expansion* (Northampton, 1989), No. VIII.

Jacoby, D., 'Byzantine Traders in Mamluk Egypt', in A. Avramea, A. Laiou, and E. Chrysos (eds), *Byzantium, State and Society. In Memory of Nikos Oikonomides* (Athens, 2003), 249–67, repr. in D. Jacoby, *Latins, Greeks and Muslims: Encounters in the Eastern Mediterranean, 10th–15th Centuries* (Aldershot, 2009), No. IX.

James, L. J., 'Byzantine Realpolitik and the Effects of Hesychasm upon the Eastern Church following the Council of Florence–Ferrara (1438–1445)', *The Patristic and Byzantine Review* 11 (1992): 67–76.

Jotischky, A., 'Ethnographic Attitudes in the Crusader States: The Franks and the Indigenous Orthodox People', in K. Ciggaar and H. Teule, (eds), *East and West in the Crusader States: Context — Contacts — Confrontations III: Acta of the Congress Held at Hernen Castle in September 2000* (Leuven and Dudley, MA, 2003), 1–19.

Juan, R., 'Cofradías de libertos de Mallorca', *Boletín de la Sociedad Arqueológica Luliana* 34 (1975): 568–84.

Kaldellis, A., *Hellenism in Byzantium: The Transformations of Greek Identity and the Reception of the Classical Tradition* (Cambridge, 2007).

Kaldellis, A., *Ethnography after Antiquity: Foreign Lands and Peoples in Byzantine Literature* (Philadelphia, 2013).

Karlsson, G. H., *Idéologie et cérémonial dans l'épistolographie byzantine: Textes du Xe siècle analysés et commentés* (Uppsala, 1962).

Katele, I. B., 'Piracy and the Venetian state: The Dilemmas of Maritime Defense in the Fourteenth Century', *Speculum* 63 (1988): 865–89.

Kazhdan, A. P., 'Some Questions Addressed to the Scholars Who Believe in the Authenticity of Kaminiates' "Capture of Thessalonica"', *Byzantinische Zeitschrift* 71 (1978): 301–14.

Kazhdan, A. P., 'Hetaireiarches', in A. P. Kazhdan et al. (eds), *The Oxford Dictionary of Byzantium* (3 vols., Oxford, 1991), 925.

Kedar, B. Z., 'Segurano-Sakrân Salvaygo: Un mercante Genovese al servizio dei sultani Mamalucchi, c. 1303-1322', in C. M. Cipolla and R. S. Lopez (eds), *Fatti e idee di storia economica nei secoli XII-XX. Studi dedicati a Franco Borlandi* (Bologna, 1976), 75–91, reprinted in B. Z. Kedar, *The Franks in the Levant, 11th to 14th Centuries* (Aldershot, 1993), No. XXI.

Khadduri, M., *War and Peace in the Law of Islam* (Baltimore, 1955).

Khoury Odetallah, R., 'Leo Tripolites – Ghulam Zurafa and the Sack of Thessaloniki in 904', *Byzantinoslavica* 56 (1995): 97–102.

Kiousopoulou, T., *Emperor or Manager: Power and Political Ideology in Byzantium before 1453*, tr. P. Magdalino (Geneva, 2011).

Koder, J., 'Topographie und Bevölkerung der Ägäisinseln in spätbyzantinischer Zeit: Probleme der Quellen', *Byzantinische Forschungen* 5 (1977): 217–34.

Koder, J., 'Überlegungen zur Bevölkerungsdichte des byzantinischen Raumes im Spätmittelalter und Frühneuzeit', *Byzantinische Forschungen* 12 (1987): 291–308.
Kołodziejczyk, D., 'Slavery in the Atlantic and the Black Sea', in F. Roşu (ed.), *Slavery in the Black Sea Region, c. 900–1900: Forms of Unfreedom at the Intersection between Christianity and Islam* (Leiden and Boston, 2022), 418–42.
Köpstein, H., *Zur Sklaverei im ausgehenden Byzanz* (Berlin, 1966).
Korobeinikov, D. A., 'Diplomatic Correspondence between Byzantium and the Mamlūk Sultanate in the Fourteenth Century', *Al-Masāq* 16 (2004): 53–74.
Korobeinikov, D. A., 'Raiders and Neighbours: The Turks (1040–1304)', in J. Shepard (ed.), *The Cambridge History of the Byzantine Empire, c. 500–1492* (Cambridge, 2009), 692–728.
Korobeinikov, D. A., *Byzantium and the Turks in the Thirteenth Century* (Oxford, 2014).
Korobeinikov, D. A., 'The Formation of Turkish Principalities in the Boundary Zone: From the Emirate of Denizli to the Beylik of Menteşe (1256–1302)', A. Çevik and M. Keçiş (eds), *Menteşeoğulları Tarihi* (Ankara, 2016), 65–76.
Kowalewsky, M., *Die ökonomische Entwicklung Europas bis zum Beginn der kapitalistischen Wirtschaftsform, III: Englische, deutsche, italienische und spanische Wirtschaftsverfassung in der zweiten Hälfte des Mittelalters* (Berlin, 1905).
Krausmüller, D., 'The Rise of Hesychasm', in M. Angold (ed.), *The Cambridge History of Christianity, Volume 5: Eastern Christianity* (Cambridge, 2006), 101–26.
Krekić, B., *Dubrovnik (Raguse) et le Levant au Moyen Âge* (Paris, 1961).
Krstić, T., *Contested Conversions to Islam: Narratives of Religious Change in the Early Modern Ottoman Empire* (Stanford, 2011).
Külzer, A., *Tabula Imperii Byzantini, 12: Ostthrakien (Eurōpē)* (Vienna, 2008).
Laiou, A. E., *Constantinople and the Latins: The Foreign Policy of Andronicus II, 1282–1328* (Cambridge, MA, 1972).
Laiou, A. E., 'The Palaiologoi and the World around Them (1261–1400)', in J. Shepard (ed.), *The Cambridge History of the Byzantine Empire, c. 500–1492* (Cambridge, 2009), 803–33.
Laiou-Thomadakis, A. E., *Peasant Society in the Late Byzantine Empire: A Social and Demographic Study* (Princeton, NJ, 1977).
Laiou-Thomadakis, A. E., 'Saints and Society', in E. A. Laiou-Thomadakis (ed.), *Charanis Studies: Essays in Honor of Peter Charanis* (New Brunswick, 1980), 84–114.

Laiou-Thomadakis, A. E., 'The Byzantine Economy in the Mediterranean Trade System; Thirteenth–fifteenth Centuries', *Dumbarton Oaks Papers* 34–5 (1980–1): 177–222.

Laiou-Thomadakis, A. E., 'The Greek Merchant of the Palaeologan Period: A Collective Portrait', Πρακτικὰ τῆς Ἀκαδημίας Ἀθηνῶν 57 (1982): 96–132, repr. in A. E. Laiou-Thomadakis, *Gender, Society and Economic Life in Byzantium* (Aldershot, 1992), No. VIII.

Laiou-Thomadakis, A. E. (ed.), *Urbs Capta: The Fourth Crusade and Its Consequences* (Paris, 2005).

Laiou-Thomadakis, A. E., 'Priests and Bishops in the Byzantine Countryside, Thirteenth to Fourteenth Centuries', in D. G. Angelov (ed.), *Church and Society in Late Byzantium* (Kalamazoo, MI, 2009), 43–57, repr. in A. E. Laiou, *Economic Thought and Economic Life in Byzantium* (Farnham, 2013), no. VIII.

Lamansky, V., *Secrets d'État de Venise* (St Petersburg, 1884).

Lampe, G. W. H., *A Patristic Greek Lexicon* (Oxford, 1969).

Lampros, S., 'Μιχαὴλ Λουλούδης ὁ Ἐφέσιος καὶ ὑπὸ τῶν Τούρκων ἅλωσις τῆς Ἐφέσου', *Νέος Ἑλληνομνήμων* 1 (1904): 209–12.

Laurent, V., *Les Regestes des actes du Patriarcat de Constantinople*, vol. 1: *Les actes des patriarches*, Fasc. 4: *Les Régestes de 1208 à 1309* (Paris, 1971).

Lauxtermann, M. D., 'Parasinus graecus 400: Poetry and paraenesis in Cyprus', *Revue des études byzantines* 79 (2021): 149–81.

Lemerle, P., *L'émirat d'Aydin, Byzance et l'Occident: Recherches sur 'La Geste d'Umur Pacha'* (Paris, 1957).

Leopold, A., *How to Recover the Holy Land: The Crusade Proposals of the Late Thirteenth and Early Fourteenth Centuries* (Aldershot, 2000).

Lewis, B., 'Emīn', in *Encyclopaedia of Islam, Second Edition*, ed. P. J. Bearnam, T. Bianquis, C. E. Bosworth, E. van Donzel, W. P. Heinrichs et al. (12 vols., Leiden, 1960–2005, online).

Leyerle, B., 'John Chrysostom on Almsgiving and the Use of Money', *The Harvard Theological Review* 87 (1994): 29–47.

Liaño Martínez, E., 'Jordi de Déu, un artista siciliano al servicio de Pedro el Ceremonioso', *Aragón en la Edad Media* 14 (1999): 873–86.

Liddell, H. G., R. Scott, H. S. Jones, and R. McKenzie, *A Greek–English Lexicon* (Oxford, 1940).

Lieu, J., 'Charity in Early Christian Thought and Practice', in D. Stathakopoulos (ed.), *The Kindness of Strangers: Charity in the Pre-Modern Mediterranean* (London, 2007), 13–20.

Lindner, R., 'Anatolia, 1300–1451', in K. Fleet (ed.), *Cambridge History of Turkey, Volume 1: Byzantium to Turkey, 1071–1453* (Cambridge, 2009), 102–37.

Lippard, 'The Mongols and Byzantium, 1243–1341', PhD Thesis, Indiana University (Bloomington, IN, 1984).
Livi, R., *La schiavitù domestica, nei tempi di mezzo e nei moderni: Ricerche storiche di un antropologo* (Padua, 1928).
Livingston, A. A., 'Grifon "Greek"', *Modern Language Notes* 22 (1907): 47–9.
Llompart Moragues, G., 'Pere Mates, un constructor y escultor trecentista en la "Ciutat de Mallorques"', *Boletín de la Sociedad Arqueológica Luliana* 34 (1973): 91–118.
Lopez i Bonet, J. F., 'Un fruit de l'expansio mediterrànea. Esclaves Gregues a Mallorca a mitjan segle XIV i la triple mutilació juridical: Nació, estat i gènere', *Congreso de Historia de la Corona de Aragón* 18 (2004): 1459–518.
Lowry, H. W., '"From Lesser Wars to the Mightiest War": The Ottoman Conquest and Transformation of Byzantine Urban Centers in the Fifteenth Century', in A. A. M. Bryer and H. W. Lowry (eds), *Continuity and Change in Late Byzantine and Early Ottoman Society. Papers Given at a Symposium at Dumbarton Oaks in May 1982* (Birmingham and Washington, DC, 1986), 323–38.
Lowry, H. W., 'Portrait of a City: The Population and Topography of Ottoman Selânik (Thessaloniki) in the Year 1478', *Diptycha* 2 (1980–1): 254–93, repr. in H. Lowry, *Studies in Defterology: Ottoman Society in the Fifteenth and Sixteenth Centuries* (Istanbul, 1992), 47–64.
Lowry, H. W., 'The Role of Byzantine Provincial Officials following the Ottoman Conquest of their Lands', in *Studies in Defterology: Ottoman Society in the Fifteenth and Sixteenth Centuries* (Istanbul, 1992), 123–30.
Luke, H., 'The Kingdom of Cyprus, 1291–1369', in H. W. Hazard (ed.), *The Fourteenth and Fifteenth Centuries*, in K. M. Setton (gen. ed.), *A History of the Crusades*, vol. 3 (Madison WI, 1975), 340–60.
Luke, H., 'The Kingdom of Cyprus, 1369–1489', in H. W. Hazard (ed.), *The Fourteenth and Fifteenth Centuries*, in K. M. Setton (gen. ed.), *A History of the Crusades*, vol. 3 (Madison WI, 1975), 361–95.
Luttrell, A., 'Argos and Nauplia: 1311–1394', *Papers of the British School at Rome* 34 (1966): 34–55.
Luttrell, A., 'Crete and Rhodes: 1340–1360', *Acts of the III International Congress of Cretological Studies* (Athens, 1974), 2.167–75, repr. in A. Luttrell, *The Hospitallers in Cyprus, Rhodes, Greece and the West, 1291–1440* (London, 1978), No. VI.
Luttrell, A., 'John Cantacuzenus and the Catalans at Constantinople: 1352–1354', in Asociación Nacional de Bibliotecarios, Archiveros y Arqueólogos (eds), *Martínez Ferrando, archivero: Miscelánea de estudios dedicados a su*

memoria (Barcelona, 1968), 265–77, repr. in A. Luttrell, *Latin Greece, the Hospitallers and the Crusades, 1291–1440* (London, 1982), No. IX.

Luttrell, A., 'Slavery at Rhodes: 1306–1440', *Bulletin de l'Institut historique belge de Rome* 46–7 (1976–7): 81–100, repr. in A. Luttrell, *Latin Greece, the Hospitallers and the Crusades: 1291–1400* (London, 1982), No. VI.

Luttrell, A., 'The Latin East', in C. Allmand (ed.), *The New Cambridge Medieval History, vol. 7, c. 1415–c. 1500* (Cambridge, 1998), 797–811.

Luttrell, A., and G. O'Malley, *The Countryside of Hospitaller Rhodes, 1306–1423: Original Texts and English Summaries* (London and New York, 2019).

Madden, T. F. (ed.), *The Fourth Crusade: Event, Aftermath, and Perceptions* (Aldershot, 2008).

Maltezou, Ch., 'The Historical and Social Context', in D. Holton (ed.), *Literature and Society in Renaissance Crete* (Cambridge, 1991), 17–47.

Maltezou, Ch., '"Ἕλληνες καὶ Ἰταλοί ἔμποροι στήν Ἀναία τῆς Μικρᾶς Ἀσίας (ἀρχές 14ου αἰ.)', in A. D. Angelou, C. N. Constantinides, E. Jeffreys, and N. M. Panagiotakis (eds), *Φιλέλλην. In Honour of Robert Browning* (Venice, 1996), 253–63.

Mango, C., 'Chypre carrefour du monde byzantin', *XVe Congrès international d'études byzantines, rapports et co-rapports, V. Chypre dans le monde byzantine, 5. Chypre carrefour du monde byzantin* (Athens, 1976), repr. C. Mango, *Byzantium and Its Image: History and Culture of the Byzantine Empire and Its Heritage* (London, 1984), No. XVII.

Manousakas, M. I., *Ἡ ἐν Κρήτῃ συνωμοσία τοῦ Σήφη Βλαστοῦ (1453–1454) καὶ ἡ νέα συνωμοτικὴ κίνησις τοῦ 1460–1462* (Athens, 1960).

Manousakas, M. I., 'Μέτρα τῆς Βενετίας ἔναντι τῆς ἐν Κρήτῃ ἐπιρροῆς τοῦ Πατριαρχείου Κωνσταντινουπόλεως κατ' ἀνέκδοτα βενετικὰ ἔγγραφα (1418–1419)', *Ἐπετηρὶς Ἑταιρείας Βυζαντινῶν Σπουδῶν* 30 (1960–1): 85–144.

Manousakas, M. I., 'Βενετικὰ ἔγγραφα ἀναφερόμενα εἰς τὴν ἐκκλησιαστικὴν ἱστορίαν τῆς Κρήτης τοῦ 14ου–16ου αἰῶνος (πρωτοπαπάδες καὶ πρωτοψάλται)', *Δελτίον τῆς Ἱστορικῆς καὶ Ἐθνολογικῆς Ἑταιρείας τῆς Ἑλλάδος* 15 (1961): 149–233.

Manousakas, M. I., 'Ἡ πρώτη ἐμπορικὴ παροικία τῶν Βενετῶν στὰ Παλάτια (Μίλητο) τῆς Μ. Ἀσίας (Ἕνα ἑλληνικό ἔγγραφο τοῦ 1355) (πίν. 67)', *Δελτίον τῆς Χριστιανικῆς Ἀρχαιολογικῆς Ἑταιρείας* 3 (1964): 231–40.

Mansouri, M. T., *Recherches sur les relations entre Byzance et l'Egypte (1259–1453) d'après les sources arabes* (Tunis, 1992).

Marcos Hierro, E., 'The Catalan Company and the Slave Trade', in R. Amitai and C. Cluse (eds), *Slavery and the Slave Trade in the Eastern Mediterranean (c. 1000–1500 CE)* (Turnhout, 2017), 321–52.

Marinesco [= Marinescu], C., 'Notes sur les Catalans dans l'Empire byzantin pendant le règne de Jacques II, 1291–1327', in [no ed.,] *Mélanges d'histoire du Moyen Âge offerts à M. Ferdinand Lot par ses amis et ses élèves* (Paris, 1925), 501–15.

Marinescu, C., 'Contribution à l'histoire des relations économiques entre l'Empire byzantin, la Sicile et le royaume de Naples de 1419 au 1453', in International Congress of Byzantine Studies (ed.), *Atti del V Congresso Internazionale di Studi Bizantini. Roma 20–26 settembre 1936. I. Storia–Filologia–Diritto* (Rome, 1939), 209–19.

Markl, O., *Ortsnamen Griechenlands in "fränkischer" Zeit* (Graz and Cologne, 1966).

Martin, M. E., 'The Venetian–Seljuk Treaty of 1220', *The English Historical Review* 95 (1980): 321–30.

Mas Latrie, L., *Histoire de l'Île de Chypre sous le règne des princes de la maison de Lusignan* (3 vols., Paris, 1850–61).

McKee, S., 'Greek Women in Latin Households of Fourteenth-Century Venetian Crete', *Journal of Medieval History* 19 (1993): 229–49.

McKee, S., 'The Revolt of St Tito in Fourteenth-Century Venetian Crete: A Reassessment', *Mediterranean Historical Review* 9 (1994): 173–204.

McKee, S., *Uncommon Dominion: Venetian Crete and the Myth of Ethnic Purity* (Philadelphia, PA, 2000).

McKee, S., 'Inherited Status and Slavery in Late Medieval Italy and Venetian Crete', *Past and Present* 182 (2004): 31–53.

McKee, S., 'Domestic Slavery in Renaissance Italy', *Slavery and Abolition* 29 (2008): 305–25.

McKee, S., 'The Familiarity of Slaves in Medieval and Early Modern Households', in C. Schmid, S. Hanß, and J. Schiel (eds), *Neue Perspektiven auf mediterrane Sklaverei (500–1800)* (Zürich, 2014), 501–14.

Ménage, V. L., 'Devs̲h̲irme', in *Encyclopaedia of Islam, Second Edition*, ed. P. J. Bearnam, T. Bianquis, C. E. Bosworth, E. van Donzel, W. P. Heinrichs et al. (12 vols., Leiden, 1960–2005, online).

Ménage, V. L., 'Some Notes on the "devshirme"', *Bulletin of the School of Oriental and African Studies* 29 (1966): 64–78.

Mercati, G., 'Di Giovanni Simeonachis, Protopapa di Candia', *Miscellanea Giovanni Mercati*, vol. 3 (Vatican City, 1946), 312–41.

Mertzios, K., Μνημεία μακεδονικής ιστορίας (Thessaloniki, 1947).

Miquel, A., 'Ibn Baṭṭūṭa', in *Encyclopaedia of Islam, Second Edition*, ed. P. J. Bearnam, T. Bianquis, C. E. Bosworth, E. van Donzel, W. P. Heinrichs et al. (12 vols., Leiden, 1960–2005, online).

Miret i Sans, J., 'La esclavitud en Cataluña en los ultimos tiempos de la edad media', *Revue Hispanique* 41 (1917): 1–109.
Mollat, M., 'De la piraterie sauvage à la course réglementée (XIVe–XVe siècle)', *Mélanges de l'Ecole française de Rome. Moyen-Âge, Temps modernes* 87 (1975): 7–25.
Montsalvatje y Fossas, F., *Geografía histórica del condado de Besalú* (Besalú, 1899).
Moravcsik, G., *Byzantinoturcica II: Sprachreste der Türkvölker in den byzantinischen Quellen* (2nd ed., Berlin, 1958).
Morgan, G. 'The Venetian Claims Commission of 1278', *Byzantinische Zeitschrift* 64 (1976): 411–38.
Mortreuil, P., 'Moeurs et institutions marseillaises au Moyen Âge. L'esclavage', *Revue de Marseille et de Provence* 4 (1858): 153–74.
Moschonos, N. G., 'Der Sklavenmarkt im östlichen Mittelmeerraum in der Palaiologenzeit', *Südost-Forschungen* 65–6 (2006): 28–49.
Mouton, J.-M., J. Sourdel-Thomine and D. Sourdel, 'Deux documents damascains touchant au rachat de captifs détenus par les Francs', *Archiv für Papyrusforschung* 59 (2013): 406–20.
Mummey, K. D., 'Women, Slavery, and Community on the Island of Mallorca, ca. 1360–1390', PhD thesis, University of Minnesota (2013).
Mummey, K. D., 'Enchained in Paradise: Slave Identities on the Island of Mallorca, ca. 1360–1390', in J. Watkins and K. L. Reyerson (eds), *Mediterranean Identities in the Premodern Era: Entrepôts, Islands, Empires* (Farnham, 2014), 121–38.
Murphey, R., 'Yeñi Čeri', in *Encyclopaedia of Islam, Second Edition*, ed. P. J. Bearnam, T. Bianquis, C. E. Bosworth, E. van Donzel, W. P. Heinrichs et al. (12 vols., Leiden, 1960–2005, online).
Musso G. G., and M. S. Jacopino, *Navigazione e commercio genovese con il Levante nei documenti dell' Archivio di Stato di Genova (secc. XIV–XV)* (Rome, 1975).
Necipoğlu, N., *Byzantium between the Ottomans and the Latins: Politics and Society in the Late Empire* (Cambridge, 2009).
Neocleous, S., 'Byzantine-Muslim Conspiracies against the Crusades: History and Myth', *Journal of Medieval History* 36 (2010): 353–74.
Nicol, D. M., *Meteora: The Rock Monasteries of Thessaly* (London, 1963).
Nicol, D. M., *Church and Society in the Last Centuries of Byzantium (Birkbeck Lectures, 1977)* (Cambridge, 1979).
Nicol, D. M., *The Despotate of Epiros, 1267–1479: A Contribution to the History of Greece in the Middle Ages* (2nd ed., Cambridge, 1984).
Nicol, D. M., *The Last Centuries of Byzantium, 1261–1453* (2nd ed., Cambridge, 1993).

Nystazopoulou, M. G., *Ἡ ἐν τῇ Ταυρικῇ Χερσονήσῳ πόλις Σουγδαία ἀπὸ τοῦ ΙΓ' μέχρι τοῦ ΙΕ' αἰῶνος. Συμβολὴ εἰς τὴν ἱστορίαν τοῦ μεσαιωνικοῦ ἑλληνισμοῦ τῆς νοτίου Ῥωσίας* (Athens, 1965).
ODB: see *Oxford Dictionary of Byzantium*.
Otten-Froux, C., 'Deux consuls des Grecs à Gênes à la fin du 14e siècle', *Revue des études byzantines* 50 (1992): 241–8.
Otten-Froux, C., 'La représentation des intérêts byzantines en Italie', *Byzantinische Forschungen* 21 (1996): 99–109.
Oxford Dictionary of Byzantium, ed. A. P. Kazhdan et al. (3 vols., Oxford, 1991) [=*ODB*].
Pahlitzsch, J., 'Byzantine Saints in Turkish Captivity in 14th century Anatolia', in G. Christ, F. J. Morche, A. Beihammer, S. Burkhardt, W. Kaiser, and R. Zaugg, *Union in Separation: Diasporic Groups and Transcultural Identities in the Eastern Mediterranean (1100–1800)* (Rome, 2015), 219–28.
Pahlitzsch, J., 'The Greek Orthodox Communities of Nicaea and Ephesus under Turkish Rule in the Fourteenth Century: A New Reading of Old Sources', in A. C. S. Peacock, B. De Nicola, and S. N. Yıldız (eds), *Islam and Christianity in Medieval Anatolia* (Farnham and Burlington, VT, 2015), 147–64.
Pahlitzsch, J., 'Zum Loskauf von griechischen Gefangenen und Sklaven in spätbyzantinischer Zeit. Formen und Akteure', in H. Grieser and N. Priesching (eds), *Gefangenenloskauf im Mittelmeerraum: Ein interreligiöser Vergleich* (Hildesheim, 2015), 123–41.
Pahlitzsch, J., 'Slavery and the Slave Trade in Byzantium in the Palaeologan Period', in R. Amitai and C. Cluse (eds), *Slavery and the Slave Trade in the Eastern Mediterranean (c. 1000–1500 CE)* (Turnhout, 2017), 163–84.
Pahlitzsch, J., 'Eis ton neon martyra Michaēl', in D. Thomas (ed.), *Christian–Muslim Relations 600–1500: A Bibliographical History* (Brill Online, 2020).
Palmer, J. A. B., 'Fr. Georgius de Hungaria, O.P., and the *Tractatus de moribus condicionibus et nequicia Turcorum*', *Bulletin of the John Rylands Library* 34 (1951): 44–68.
Paolella, C., *Human Trafficking in Medieval Europe: Slavery, Sexual Exploitation, and Prostitution* (Amsterdam, 2020).
Papademetriou, T., 'The Turkish Conquests and Decline of the Church Reconsidered', in D. G. Angelov (ed.), *Church and Society in Late Byzantium* (Kalamazoo MI, 2009), 183–200.
Papoulia, B. D., *Ursprung und Wesen der "Knabenlese" im Osmanischen Reich* (Munich, 1963).
Patoura, S. *Οἱ αἰχμάλωτοι ὡς παράγοντες ἐπικοινωνίας καὶ πληροφόρησης (4ος-10ος αἰ.)* (Athens, 1994).

Peacock, A. C. S., 'The Saljūq Campaign against the Crimea and the Expansionist Policy of the Early Reign of 'Alā' al-Dīn Kayqubād', *Journal of the Royal Asiatic Society* 3 ser., 16 (2006): 133–49.

Peacock, A. C. S., 'The Seljuk Sultanate of Rūm and the Turkmen of the Byzantine Frontier, 1206–1279', *Al-Masāq* 26 (2014): 267–87.

Peacock, A. C. S., B. De Nicola, and S. Nur Yıldız, *Islam and Christianity in Medieval Anatolia* (Farnham, 2015).

Peacock, A. C. S., *Islam, Literature and Society in Mongol Anatolia* (Cambridge, 2019).

Penna, D., 'Piracy and Reprisal in Byzantine Waters: Resolving a Maritime Conflict between Byzantines and Genoese at the End of the Twelfth Century', *Comparative Legal History* 5 (2017): 36–52.

Petech, L., 'Les marchands italiens dans l'Empire Mongol', *Journal Asiatique* 250 (1962): 549–74.

Philippides, M., and W. K. Hanak, *The Siege and the Fall of Constantinople to the Ottoman Turks in 1453: Historiography, Topography and Military Studies* (Farnham, 2011).

Philippidis-Braat, A., 'La captivité de Palamas chez les Turcs: Dossier et commentaire', *Travaux et Mémoires* 7 (1979): 136–65.

PLP: see 'Trapp'.

Pow, S., '"Nationes que se Tartaros appellant": An Exploration of the Historical Problem of the Usage of the Ethnonyms Tatar and Mongol in Medieval Sources', *Golden Horde Review* 7 (2019): 545–67.

Preiser-Kapeller, J., 'Liquid frontiers. A Relational Analysis of Maritime Asia Minor as Religious Contact Zone in the 13th–15th century', in A. C. S. Peacock, B. De Nicola, and S. Nur Yıldız (eds), *Islam and Christianity in Medieval Anatolia* (Farnham, 2015), 117–46.

Prinzing, G., 'Zu Sklaven und Sklavinnen im Spiegel des Prosopographischen Lexikons der Palaiologenzeit', in A. Berger, S. Mariev, G. Prinzing, and A. Riehle (eds), *Koinotaton Doron. Das späte Byzanz zwischen Machtlosigkeit und kultureller Blüte* (Berlin, 2016), 125–48.

Prinzing, G., 'Byzanz', in H. Heinen, et al. (eds), *Handwörterbuch der antiken Sklaverei*, vol. 1 (Stuttgart, 2017), 468–86.

Queller, D. E., T. K. Compton, and D. A. Campbell, 'The Fourth Crusade: The Neglected Majority', *Speculum* 49 (1974): 441–65.

Queller, D. E., *The Fourth Crusade: The Conquest of Constantinople* (2nd ed., Pennsylvania, 1997).

Quirini-Popławska, D., 'The Venetian involvement in the Black Sea slave trade (fourteenth to fifteenth centuries)', in R. Amitai and C. Cluse (eds), *Slavery and the Slave Trade in the Eastern Mediterranean (c. 1000–1500 CE)* (Turnhout, 2017), 255–98.

Raby, J., 'Mehmed the Conqueror's Greek Scriptorium', *Dumbarton Oaks Papers* 37 (1983): 15–34.
Ragia, E., 'Les Turcs en Asie Mineure occidentale et la bataille de Mylasa: 1079/1080 ou 1264?', *Revue des études byzantines* 63 (2005): 217–24.
Rapp, C., M. Kinloch, D. Krausmüller, E. Mitsiou, I. Nesseris, Ch. Papavarnavas, J. Preiser-Kapeller, G. Rossetto, R. Shukurov, and G. Simeonov, *Mobility and Migration in Byzantium: A Sourcebook* (Göttingen, 2023).
Redford, S. and Leiser, G., *Victory Inscribed: The Seljuk Fetihnāme on the Citadel Walls of Antalya, Turkey* (Istanbul, 2008).
Reinsch, D. R., 'Einige Beobachtungen zur zypriotischen Handschrift Parisinus Graecus 400', *Travaux et Mémoires* 24 (2020): 197–208.
Reuter, T., 'Plunder and tribute in the Carolingian Empire', *Transactions of the Royal Historical Society* 35 (1985): 75–94.
Richard, J., 'Le Casal de Psimolofo et la vie rurale en Chypre au XIVe siècle', *Mélanges d'archéologie et d'histoire* 59 (1947): 121–53.
Richard, J., 'Le Royaume de Chypre face aux projets de croisade', *Comptes rendus des séances de l'Académie des Inscriptions et Belles-Lettres* 153 (2009): 857–63.
Rodriguez, J., 'Financing a Captive's Ransom in Late Medieval Aragon', *Medieval Encounters* 9 (2003): 164–81.
Roşu, F. (ed.), *Slavery in the Black Sea Region, c. 900–1900: Forms of Unfreedom at the Intersection between Christianity and Islam* (Leiden and Boston, 2022).
Rotman, Y., *Byzantine Slavery and the Mediterranean World*, tr. J. M. Todd (Cambridge, MA, 2009).
Rubió i Lluch, A., 'Mitteilungen zur Geschichte der griechischen Sklaven in Katalonien im XIV. Jahrhundert', *Byzantinische Zeitschrift* 30 (1929–30): 462–8.
Runciman, S., *The Great Church in Captivity: A Study of the Patriarchate of Constantinople from the Eve of the Turkish Conquest to the Greek War of Independence* (Cambridge, 1968).
Runciman, S., 'Teucri and Turci', in S. A. Hanna (ed.), *Medieval and Middle Eastern Studies, in Honour of Aziz Suryal Atiya* (Leiden, 1972), 344–8.
Runciman, S., *The Sicilian Vespers: A History of the Mediterranean World in the Later Thirteenth Century* (Cambridge, 1958, repr. 1992).
Runciman, S., *The Fall of Constantinople, 1453* (Cambridge, 1965, repr. 1990).
Saccon, L., 'Ransoming activities in the 14th century eastern Mediterranean: The evidence of the Parisinus Graecus 400', M.Phil thesis, University of Oxford (2019).

Sahas, D. J., 'Captivity and Dialogue: Gregory Palamas (1296–1360) and the Muslims', *The Greek Orthodox Theological Review* 25 (1980): 409–36.

Salibi, K. S., 'Ibn Faḍl Allāh al-ʿUmarī', in *Encyclopaedia of Islam, Second Edition*, ed. P. J. Bearnam, T. Bianquis, C. E. Bosworth, E. van Donzel, W. P. Heinrichs et al. (12 vols., Leiden, 1960–2005, online).

Saint-Guillain, G., 'Venetian Archival Documents and the Prosopography of the Thirteenth-Century Byzantine World: Tracing Individuals Through the Archives of a Diaspora', in G. Christ, F. J. Morche, A. Beihammer, S. Burkhardt, W. Kaiser, and R. Zaugg, *Union in Separation: Diasporic Groups and Transcultural Identities in the Eastern Mediterranean (1100–1800)* (Rome, 2015), 37–79.

Sanpere y Miquel, S., *Las Costumbres catalanas en tiempo de Juan I* (Gerona, 1878).

Santschi, E., *Régestes des arrêts civils et des mémoriaux (1363–1399) des archives du duc de Crète* (Venice, 1976).

Sastre Moll, J., 'Notas sobre la esclavitud en Mallorca "el libre de Sareyns e de Grecs de lany de M CCC XXX"', *Mayurqa* 21 (1985–7): 101–19.

Sathas, K. N., 'Πρόλογος', in K. N. Sathas, *Μεσαιωνική Βιβλιοθήκη*, vol. 6 (Venice 1877), δ΄–ρις΄.

Saunders, J. J., 'The Mongol Defeat at Ain Jalut and the Restoration of the Greek Empire', in J. J. Saunders, *Muslims and Mongols: Essays on Medieval Asia*, ed. G. W. Rice (Christchurch, NZ, 1977), 67–76.

Savvides, A. C. G., 'Some Notes on the Terms Agarenoī, Ismaelītai and Sarakenoī in Byzantine Sources', *Byzantion* 67 (1997), 89–96.

Savvides, A. C. G., 'Can We Refer to a Concerted Action among Rapsomates, Caryces and the Emir Tzachas between AD 1091 and 1093?', *Byzantion* 70 (2000): 122–34.

Schein, S., *Fideles crucis: The Papacy, the West, and the Recovery of the Holy Land, 1274–1314* (Oxford, 1991).

Schmitt, O. J. and M. Kiprovska, 'Ottoman Raiders (Akincis) as a Driving Force of Early Ottoman Conquest of the Balkans and the Slavery-Based Economy', *Journal of the Economic and Social History of the Orient* 65 (2022): 497–583.

Schreiner, P., 'Eine Schlacht bei Mylasa im Jahre 1079/1080? Ein Beitrag zur Erforschung der Region von Milet', in *ΕΥΨΥΧΙΑ. Mélanges offerts à Hélène Ahrweiler*, vol. 2 (Paris, 1998), 611–17.

Sciascia, L., 'Schiavi in Sicilia: Ruoli sociali e condizione umana', in M. T. Ferrer i Mallol and J. Mutgé i Vives (eds), *De l'esclavitud a la llibertat: Esclaus i lliberts a l'edat mitjana* (Barcelona, 2000), 527–45.

Setton, K. M., *The Catalan Domination of Athens, 1311–1388* (Cambridge, MA, 1948; repr. London, 1975).

Setton, K. M., 'The Catalans in Greece, 1311–1380', in H. W. Hazard (ed.), *The Fourteenth and Fifteenth Centuries*, in K. M. Setton (gen. ed.), *A History of the Crusades*, vol. 3 (Madison WI, 1975), 167–224.
Ševčenko, I., 'Intellectual Repercussions of the Council of Florence', *Church History* 24 (1955): 291–323.
Sevillano Colom, F., 'Demografía y esclavos del siglo XV en Mallorca', *Bolletí de la Societat Arqueològica Lul·liana* 34 (1973–5): 160–97.
Shepard, J. (ed.), *The Cambridge History of the Byzantine Empire c. 500–1492* (Cambridge, 2009).
Shukurov, R., *The Byzantine Turks, 1204–1461* (Leiden, 2016).
Sinclair, T., *Eastern Trade and the Mediterranean in the Middle Ages: Pegolotti's Ayas–Tabriz Itinerary and its Commercial Context* (Abingdon and New York, 2019).
Skoda, H., 'People as Property in Medieval Dubrovnik', in G. Kantor, T. Lambert, and H. Skoda (eds), *Legalism: Property and Ownership* (Oxford, 2017), 235–60.
Soustal, P., *Tabula Imperii Byzantini, 6: Thrakien (Thrakē, Rodopē und Haimimontos* (Vienna, 1991).
Stantchev, S. K., *Spiritual Rationality: Papal Embargo as Cultural Practice, 1150–1550* (Oxford, 2014).
Stathakopoulos, D., 'Introduction: Thoughts on the study of charity in the Byzantine Empire', in D. Stathakopoulos (ed.), *The Kindness of Strangers: Charity in the Pre-Modern Mediterranean* (London, 2007), 1–13.
Stefec, R., 'Anmerkungen zu kretischen Kopisten der ersten Hälfte des 15. Jahrhunderts', *Codices Manuscripti*, 85–6 (2012): 38–52.
Stefec, R., 'Zur Geschichte der Handschriften des Francesco Patrizi und des Antonios Eparchos', *Nea Rome* 9 (2012): 245–60.
Stello, A., 'Caffa and the slave trade during the first half of the fifteenth century', in R. Amitai and C. Cluse (eds), *Slavery and the Slave Trade in the Eastern Mediterranean (c. 1000–1500 CE)* (Turnhout, 2017), 375–98.
Stouraitis, Y., 'Is Byzantinism an Orientalism? Reflections on Byzantium's Constructed Identities and Debated Ideologies', in Y. Stouraitis (ed.), *Identities and Ideologies in the Medieval East Roman World* (Edinburgh, 2022), 19–47.
Tai, E. S., 'Restitution and the Definition of a Pirate: The Case of Sologrus de Nigro', *Mediterranean Historical Review* 19 (2004): 34–70.
Tai, E. S., 'Marking water: Piracy and Property in the Premodern West', in J. H. Bentley, R. Bridenthal and K. Wigen (eds), *Seascapes: Maritime Histories, Littoral Cultures and Transoceanic Exchanges* (Honolulu, 2007), 205–20.
Tai, E. S., 'The Legal Status of Piracy in Medieval Europe', *History Compass* 10 (2012): 838–51.

Tai, E. S., 'Piracy', in J. B. Friedman and K. M. Figg (eds), *Trade, Travel and Exploration in the Middle Ages* (repr., London 2017), 490–2.

Talbot, A.-M. M., 'The Patriarch Athanasius (1289–1293; 1303–1309) and the Church', *Dumbarton Oaks Papers* 27 (1973): 11–28.

Thesaurus Linguae Graecae ® Digital Library, ed. M. C. Pantelia, University of California, Irvine: http://www.tlg.uci.edu.

Thiriet, F., 'Venise et l'occupation de Ténédos au XIVe siècle', *Mélanges d'archéologie et d'histoire de l'Ecole française de Rome* 65 (1953): 219–45.

Thiriet, F., *Régestes des déliberations du Sénat de Venise concernant la Romanie* (3 vols., Paris, 1958–1961).

Thiriet, F., 'La situation religieuse en Crète au début du XVe siècle', *Byzantion* 36 (1966): 201–12.

Thiriet, F., *Délibérations des assemblées Vénitiennes concernant la Romanie: 1160–1363* (2 vols., Paris, 1966–1971).

Torró, J., '"De bona guerra". El ambiguo estatuto del cautivo musulmán en los países de la Corona de Aragón (siglos XII–XIII)', in M. Fierro & F. García Fitz (eds), *El cuerpo derrotado. Cómo trataban musulmanes y cristianos a los enemigos vencidos (península ibérica, ss. VIII–XIII)* (Madrid, 2008), 435–83.

Trapp, E., R. Walter, H.-V. Beyer (eds), *Prosopographisches Lexikon der Palaiologenzeit* (Vienna, 1976–2000) [=*PLP*].

Tria, L., 'La schiavitù in Liguria (ricerche e documenti)', *Atti della Società Ligure di Storia Patria* 70 (1947): 1–253.

Tsiamis, C., *Plague in Byzantine Times: A Medico-Historical Study* (Berlin and Boston, 2022).

Turyn, A., 'Michael Lulludes (or Luludes), a Scribe of the Palaeologan Era', *Rivista di studi bizantini e neoellenici* 10–11 (1973–4): 3–15.

Turyn, A., *Dated Greek Manuscripts of the Thirteenth and Fourteenth Centuries in the Libraries of Great Britain* (Washington, DC, 1980).

Usta, A., 'Evidence of the Nature, Impact and Diversity of Slavery in 14th Century Famagusta as Seen through the Genoese Notarial Acts of Lamberto di Sambuceto and Giovanni de Rocha and the Venetian Notarial acts of Nicola de Boateriis', MA Thesis, Eastern Mediterranean University, Famagusta [Gazimağusa] (2011).

Uzunçarşılı, İ. H., *Anadolu beylikleri ve Akkoyunlu, Karakoyunlu Devletleri* (Ankara, 1937).

Vacalopoulos, A., 'The Flight of Inhabitants of Greece to the Aegean Islands, Crete, and Mane during the Turkish Invasions (Fourteenth and Fifteenth centuries)', in A. E. Laiou-Thomadakis (ed.), *Charanis Studies: Essays in Honor of Peter Charanis* (New Brunswick NJ, 1980), 272–83.

Van Tricht, F., *The Latin* Renovatio *of Byzantium: The Empire of Constantinople (1204–1228)*, tr. P. Longbottom (Leiden, 2011).

Vásáry, I., 'Orthodox Christian Qumans and Tatars of the Crimea in the 13th–14th Centuries', *Central Asiatic Journal* 32 (1988): 260–71, repr. in I. Vásáry, *Turks, Tatars and Russians in the 13th–16th centuries* (Aldershot, 2007), No. XVI.

Verlinden, C., 'Esclaves du Sud-Est et de l'Est européen en Espagne orientale à la fin du Moyen Âge', *Revue historique du Sud-Est européen* 19 (1942): 371–406.

Verlinden, C., 'Esclavage et ethnographie sur les bords de la mer Noire', *Miscellanea historica in honorem Leonis van der Essen* (Brussels and Paris, 1947), 287–98.

Verlinden, C., 'La colonie vénitienne de Tana, centre de la traite des esclaves au XIVe et au début du XVe siècle', in [no ed.,] *Studie in Onore di Gino Luzzatto*, vol. 2 (Milan, 1950), 1–25.

Verlinden, C., *L'esclavage dans l'Europe médiévale* (2 vols., Ghent, 1955–1977).

Verlinden, C., 'La Crète, débouché et plaque tournante de la traite des esclaves aux XIV et XV siècle', in [no ed.,] *Studi Amintore Fanfani*, pt. 3 (Milan, 1962), 591–669.

Verlinden, C., 'L'esclavage en Sicile au bas Moyen Âge', *Bulletin de l'Institut historique Belge de Rome* 35 (1963): 13–114.

Verlinden, C., 'Traite des esclaves et traitants italiens à Constantinople', *Le Moyen Âge* 69 (1963): 791–804.

Verlinden, C., 'Orthodoxie et esclavage au bas Moyen Âge', in [no ed.,] *Mélanges Eugène Tisserant*, vol. 5, pt. 2 (Vatican, 1964), 427–56.

Verlinden, C., 'L'esclavage en Sicile sous Frédéric II d'Aragon 1296–1337', in [no ed.,] *Homenaje Jaime Vicens Vives*, vol. 1 (Barcelona, 1965–7), 675–90.

Verlinden, C., 'L'esclavage dans le royaume de Naples à la fin du moyen âge et la participation des marchands espagnols à la traite', *Anuario de historia económica y social* (1968): 345–401.

Verlinden, C., 'Le recrutement des esclaves à Venise aux XIVe et XVe siècles', *Bulletin de l'Institut historique Belge de Rome* 39 (1968): 83–202.

Verlinden, C., 'L'esclavage dans le péninsule ibérique au XIVe siècle', *Anuario de estudios medievales* 7 (1970–1): 577–91.

Verlinden, C., 'Venezia e il commercio degli schiavi provenienti dalle coste orientali del Mediterraneo', in A. Pertusi (ed.), *Venezia e il Levante fino al secolo XV. Atti del 1 Convegno internazionale di storia della civiltà veneziana (Venezia, 1–5 giugno 1968)*, vol. 1 (Venice, 1973), 911–29.

Verlinden, C., 'La traite des esclaves dans l'espace byzantin au XIVe siècle', in. M. Berza and E. Stănescu (eds), *Actes XIVe Congrès international d'études byzantines*, vol. 2 (Bucharest, 1975), 281–4.

Verlinden, C., 'Marchands chrétiens et juifs dans l'État mamelouk au début du XVe siècle d'après un notaire vénitien', *Bulletin de l'Institut historique Belge de Rome* 51 (1981): 19–86.

Verlinden, C., 'La esclavitud en la economía medieval de las Baleares, principalmente en Mallorca', *Cuadernos de historia de España* 67–8 (1982): 123–64.

Verlinden, C., 'Aspects de la traite médiévale au Levant vus à travers les sources italiennes. 1. Diachronie de la traite des esclaves tartares. 2. L'activité de traitant d'esclaves d'un marchand vénitien à Constantinople (1436–1439)', *Bulletin de l'Institut historique Belge de Rome* 53 (1983–4): 123–58.

Verlinden, C., 'Encore la traite des esclaves et les traitants italiens à Constantinople', *Bulletin de l'Institut historique Belge de Rome* 59 (1989): 107–20.

Vincke, J., 'Königtum und Sklaverei im aragonischen Staatenbund während des 14. Jahrhunderts', *Gesammelte Aufsätze zur Kulturgeschichte Spaniens* 25 (1970): 19–112.

Vryonis, S. Jr., 'Isidore Glabas and the Turkish Devshirme', *Speculum* 31 (1956): 433–43.

Vryonis, S. Jr., 'Seljuk Gulams and Ottoman Devshirmes', *Der Islam* 41 (1965): 224–52.

Vryonis, S. Jr., *The Decline of Medieval Hellenism in Asia Minor and the Process of Islamization from the Eleventh through the Fifteenth Century* (Berkeley and Los Angeles, CA, 1971).

Vryonis, S. Jr., 'The Ottoman Conquest of Thessaloniki in 1430', in A. A. M. Bryer and H. W. Lowry (eds), *Continuity and Change in Late Byzantine and Early Ottoman Society. Papers Given at a Symposium at Dumbarton Oaks in May 1982* (Birmingham and Washington, DC, 1986), 281–322.

Wittek, P., *Das Fürstentum Mentesche: Studie zur Geschichte Westkleinasiens im 13.–15. Jh.* (Istanbul, 1934).

Wittek, P., 'Devshirme and Sharī'a', *Bulletin of the School of Oriental and African Studies* 17 (1955): 271–8.

Woodhouse, S. C., *English–Greek Dictionary: A Vocabulary of the Attic Language* (London, 1910).

Wright, D. G., '*Vade, sta, ambula*: Freeing Slaves in Fourteenth-Century Crete', *Medieval Encounters* 7 (2001): 197–237.

Yudkevich, J., 'The Nature and Role of the Slave Traders in the Eastern Mediterranean during the Third Reign of Sultan al-Nāṣir Muḥammad b.

Qalāwūn (1310–41 CE)', in R. Amitai and C. Cluse (eds), *Slavery and the Slave Trade in the Eastern Mediterranean (c. 1000–1500 CE)* (Turnhout, 2017), 423–36.

Zachariadou, E. A., *Trade and Crusade: Venetian Crete and the Emirates of Menteshe and Aydin (1300–1415)* (Venice, 1983).

Zachariadou, E. A., 'The Catalans of Athens and the Beginning of the Turkish Expansion in the Aegean Area', *Studi Medievali*, ser. 3, 21 (1980): 821–38, repr. in E. A. Zachariadou, *Romania and the Turks (c. 1300–c. 1500)* (London, 1985), No. V.

Zachariadou, E. A., 'Σχετικὰ μὲ τὴν χρονολόγηση τοῦ θρήνου τῆς Ἀθήνας (1329)', in [no ed.,] *Ἀφιέρωμα στὸν καθηγητὴ Λίνο Πολίτη* (Thessaloniki, 1978), 25–8, repr. in ead. *Romania and the Turks (c. 1300–c. 1500)* (London, 1985), No. VI.

Zachariadou, E. A., 'Holy war in the Aegean during the Fourteenth Century', in B. Arbel, B. Hamilton, and D. Jacoby (eds), *Latins and Greeks in the Eastern Mediterranean after 1204* (London, 1989), 212–25.

Zachariadou, E. A., 'The Neomartyr's Message', *Δελτίο Κέντρου Μικρασιατικῶν Σπουδῶν* 8 (1991): 51–63.

Zachariadou, E. A., 'Notes sur la population de l'Asie Mineure turque au XIVe siècle', *Byzantinische Forschungen* 12 (1987): 223–31; repr. in Zachariadou, *Studies in Pre-Ottoman Turkey* (Aldershot, 2007), No. III.

Zepos, P., '«Ψυχάριον», «Ψυχικά», «Ψυχοπαίδι»', *Δελτίον τῆς Χριστιανικῆς Ἀρχαιολογικῆς Ἑταιρείας* 10 (1981): 17–28.

Živojinović, M. 'Concerning Turkish Assaults on Mount Athos in the 14th Century, Based on Byzantine Sources', *Orijentalni Institut u Sarajevu, Prilozi za Orijentalnu Filologiju* 30 (1980): 501–16.

Index

absenteeism of bishops, 167–8
Aegean region, 3, 183–5; *see also* individual islands
aichmalotika (alms-seeking testimonials), 9–10, 13, 21, 139
   and *akıncıs*, 181–2
   and Byzantine campaigns, 33–4
   and distribution, 124–6
   and itinerant alms-seekers, 126–7, 196
   and narrative, 119–24
   and refugees, 104–5, 106
   and Tatars, 78–9
akıncıs, 180, 181, 182
Albanians, 72
Alexandria, 69–71, 73, 77
Alexios I Komnenos, Emperor, 32
Alexios III, Emperor, 27
Alexios IV, Emperor, 27, 28
Alexios Philanthropenos, 34
Alexios Strategopoulos, 29
Alfonso Fadrique, 47, 48, 49
Alfonso the Magnanimous, King, 163–4
ʿAli Beg, 31
alms-seeking testimonials *see aichmalotika*
Amorgos, 112–13
Andreas Cornario, 130

Andronikos II, Emperor, 31, 33, 34
   and Catalans, 44, 45, 46
   and Genoese, 63–4
   and Ottomans, 166, 168, 194
Andronikos III, Emperor, 51, 148, 194
Angelo Cariolo, 46
Angelo de Cartura, 40, 43, 44
Angeloi dynasty, 27
Angelus de Riço, 41
Angevin dynasty, 30, 45
Anna Komnene
   Alexiad, 74
Antalya, 32
Antonio de Mantello, 177–8
Antonios Eparchos, 181
apostasy, 167, 171
apprenticeships, 102
Aragon, Crown of, 98–9, 162–3
   and ethnicity, 154, 155–6
   and slavery legislation, 144, 146–7, 151
Armenians, 67, 146
Arnaud Duval, 161–2
Astypalaia, 43, 184–5
Athanasios I, Patriarch, 104–5, 106, 166–8
Athanasios of Meteora, St, 47–8
Aydın, 18, 33, 48–9, 169–70, 175–6
   and Umur, 136, 168–9, 173–4

'Ayn Jālūt, Battle of, 54
Ayyūbids, 28, 55, 57

Baldwin of Flanders, Emperor, 28
Balikesir, 176–7
Balkans, 1, 2, 29, 151, 180–1
Bapheus, Battle of, 34, 39, 44, 166
Barker, Hannah, 58
  That Most Precious Merchandise, 6
Barlaam of Calabria, 148
Barqūq, Sultan, 56, 70–1
Bayezid I, Sultan, 179, 181
Benedict XII, Pope, 148
Benvenuto de Brixano, 39–40
Berenguer of Entenca, 45
Berke, 54
Bernard de Castigelo, 50
Biachinus Belo, 41
Bible, the, 94, 105, 116, 123, 145, 169
Black Death, 2, 184
Black Sea, 3, 21, 195
  and Genoese, 30, 55–7
  and Venice, 61–2
Blaixinus Chordi, 71
Bodrum fort, 136–7
bona guerra, 160–2
bondage, 38
Boniface of Montferrat, 28
Bosporus campaign, 64–5
Bulgarians, 8, 67, 197
Byzantine Empire, 1, 2, 3, 4, 16–17
  and advocacy, 151–2
  and the Church, 149–50
  and collapse, 30–4
  and Genoese, 55–6
  and infighting, 27–8
  and Mamlūks, 68–71
  and Ottomans, 51, 166–7, 187
  and prisoner exchanges, 134–5
  and scholarship, 7, 8
  and subjecthood, 163–4

Caffa, 55, 56
Cairo Geniza, 124–5
Çaka, 32
Candia (Heraklion), 2, 15, 50–1, 61–2, 159–60
canon (Church) law, 2, 117
captivity, 2–5, 6, 7–8
  and *aichmalotika*, 119–27
  and Byzantine campaigns, 33
  and Catalans, 45, 46–7
  and categories, 22–3
  and context, 58–61
  and Crete, 38–41, 44
  and Cyprus, 72–80
  and experiences, 91–8
  and Genoese, 61–8
  and geography, 194
  and individual ransoms, 128–32
  and Islamic rule, 169–79
  and Ghiyāth al-Dīn Kay Khūsraw I, 187
  and Ottoman conquests, 189–90, 198
  and prisoner exchanges, 133–5
  and raids, 181–2
  and refugees, 104–9
  and religious duty, 115–19
  and sources, 10–11, 13
  and status, 108–9
  and subjecthood, 162–4
  and terminology, 85–91, 195–6
  and war, 160–2
Catalans, 2, 17, 87
  and Crete, 38, 42–3
  and ethnicity, 154–5
  and piracy, 163–4
  and the Romanía, 44–52
Catholics, 20, 144, 146–7
Chalkidiki, 45
Chariton, 118–19
charity, 2, 95, 115–19, 123–4
Charles III of Naples, King, 163
Charles of Anjou, 30, 32, 148

children, 63–4, 153, 190–2
Chioggia, War of, 62
Chiones, 92–3
Christians, 6, 94
  and Islam, 57–8, 92–3
  and Jews, 19
  and ransomers, 132
  see also Greek Christians; Orthodox Christians
Church, the, 20, 115
  and *aichmalotika*, 119–20
  and Ottomans, 197
  and ransom payments, 117–18
  and union, 144, 147–51
  see also clergy
Circassians, 14, 72, 159
Clement VI, Pope, 174
Clement VII, Pope, 156
clergy, 2, 4, 10, 166–73
clerical advocacy see *aichmalotika*
Conciliarists, 149
concubines, 153
Constantine XI, Emperor, 150
Constantine Harmenopoulos, 117–18
Constantinople, 1, 4, 150
  and Byzantines, 30–1
  and Catalans, 46
  and Fourth Crusade, 28
  and judicial court, 51–2
  and Macedonia, 29, 30
  and Nicaea, 54
  and Ottomans, 167
  and refugees, 104–5
  and sacking, 186
conversion, 19–20, 92, 143–4, 145–6, 155
  and Islam, 57, 167, 170, 171
corsairs, 5
Council of One Hundred, 156–7
Council of Thirty, 157
Crete, 2, 4, 195, 196
  and captives, 86
  and crisis, 38–44
  and ethnicity, 152–3
  and Michael Loulloudes, 106–7
  and notaries, 12
  and refugees, 112–13
  and religion, 21
  and Venetian control, 29
  see also Candia (Heraklion)
Crimean Peninsula, 32, 78
crusades, 2, 4, 144, 173–4
  First, 32
  Fourth, 28
  Fifth, 55
Cyprus, 2, 5, 107–8, 195, 196
  and *aichmalotika*, 121, 124
  and crisis, 34–8
  and Greek captives, 72–80
  and refugees, 110
Cyril Loukaris, 138

Dalmacius of Castellbisbal, 154
Dalmau Sunyer, 46
Damietta, 55
debt, 90–1
depopulation, 182–5, 198
deportation, 186–92, 197–8
desertions, 182–5
Despotate of Epirus, 29, 51
devşirme ('collection' of non-Muslim children), 190–2
Dimitrius Argomatari, 130–1
diplomacy, 30, 63, 74, 143, 151, 195, 196–7
  and Aragon, 147
  and Mamlūks, 134
  and subjecthood, 165
Dorotheos, 172
Doukas, 113, 136–7
Duchy of Athens, 45, 46, 47, 50, 51

Egypt, 3, 4; see also Mamlūks
embargoes, 57–8
Emmanuel Piloti, 72

INDEX 235

enslavement *see* slavery
Ephesus, 35, 40, 65–6, 106–7, 113
  and Matthew, 168–70
Epirus, 29, 51
ethnicity, 14–19, 59–61
  and slavery, 152–60, 164
Eugenius IV, Pope, 149

Famagusta, 35, 36–7, 79–80
families, 99–100
Felix V, Antipope, 149
Ferran Ximenes of Arenos, 45
Fetus Semitecolo, 131
fiefs, 179–80
Filioque clause, 4, 20, 146
forced mobility, 109–14
Franceschinus Miolo, 130–1
Franciscus de Brurbin, 50
Franks *see* Latins
Frederick III of Sicily, King, 45, 144, 145–6
freedom *see* manumission

Galata, 30, 55
Gallipoli, 43–4, 45
Gautier II of Brienne, Duke of Athens, 45, 51
Genoese, 2, 5, 195
  and Black Sea, 55–7
  and Cyprus, 79–80
  and Greek captives, 61–8
  and Macedonia, 29, 30
  and notaries, 12–13
  and ransoms, 131–2
  and slave ethnicity, 59
George of Hungary, 179
George Lapithes, 74–5
George Mouzalon, 34
Georgius de Grecia, 154
Georgius Musseri, 43
Gheorghe, Adrian, 180, 181
Ghiyāth al-Dīn Kay Khūsraw I, Sultan, 187

Giovanni de Alegro, 68
Giovanni Orsini, 51
Giovanni Quirini, 43
Giovanni Similante, 50
Giovanni Torcello, 163–4
Giustiniano Longo, 150
Golden Horde, 54–5, 195
Grand Catalan Company, 44–5, 46
Greek Christians, 1–5
  and *aichmalotika*, 9–10, 125
  and Aragon, 146–7
  and *bona guerra*, 161–2
  and Byzantine Empire, 151–2
  and captivity context, 58–61
  and Catalans, 45–7, 50–1
  and the Church, 150–1
  and Crete, 38–44
  and crusades, 28
  and Cyprus, 36–7
  and ethnicity, 154–9
  and forced mobility, 109–14
  and Genoese, 61–8
  and Hospitallers, 137
  and Ibn Baṭṭūṭa, 175–7
  and Islamic rule, 167, 170–1
  and Latins, 148
  and legislation, 8
  and Mallorca, 49–50, 98–100, 101–3
  and Mamlūks, 72–80
  and mitigations, 197
  and Ottomans, 179–80, 189–90, 194–5
  and refugees, 105–6
  and religion, 20–2
  and Sicily, 144–6
  and slave ownership, 159–60
  and slave terminology, 87–8
  and sources, 10–11
  and subjecthood, 162–3
  and taxonomy, 15–16
  and terminology, 17

and Turks, 100–1
Greek consul, 67–8, 71
Gregory, bishop of Aguiló, 158
Gregory Palamas, 75, 92–6
Gregory of Sinai, 48, 75, 76–7, 94
Guillelmus Simon, 50
Guy de Lusignan, 36

Halmyros, Battle of the, 45
Hesychast, 75, 92, 93, 96, 167
Hızır, 169
Hospitallers *see* Knights Hospitallers
Hülegü, 54
Hungary, 149, 150

Iberia, 3, 132
Ibn Baṭṭūṭa, 174, 175–7, 178
Īl-Khānate, 54, 55, 57, 195
İlyas of Menteşe, Prince, 136–7
Innocent III, Pope, 28, 135
Iohannes de Molino, 130
Isaac II, Emperor, 27, 28
Isaac Argyros, 181
Isaac Komnenos, 35
Isidore Glabas, 190–1
Isidore of Kiev, Archbishop, 150
Islam
  and capitivity, 166–73
  and charity, 115, 117
  and Christianity, 92–3
  and slavery, 173–9
  see also Muslims; Ottoman Empire
Italy, 3, 59
itinerant alms-seeking, 126–7

Jacobus Raynaldus, 50
Jacques de Milly, 137
James II of Aragon, King, 146
Jews, 19, 115, 117, 125, 188–9
Johannes Çoli, 50
John I of Aragon, King, 146, 147, 156, 157, 158

John II of Thessaly, 47
John V Palaiologos, Emperor, 34, 70–1, 148
John VI Kantakouzenos, Emperor, 65, 70, 113, 134–5, 136
John VIII Palaiologos, Emperor, 67, 148–9
John Anagnostes, 97–8
John Chrysostom, 116–17
John Damascene, 181
John Kaminiates, 133–4
John Kantakouzenos, 86
John Symeonakes, 123
John Tarchaneiotes, 34
Joseph II, Patriarch, 147
Joseph Bryennios, 147
Justinian I, Emperor, 139

Kai Kā'us b. Iskandar
  Qābūs Nāma, 72
Karpathos, 138–9
Knights Hospitallers, 136, 137–9
Knights Templar, 35
Konstas Kalamares, 95
Koutloumousiou monastery, 118–19
krites, 128

Lamberto di Sambuceto, 12–13, 36–7, 42
Laonikos Chalkokondyles, 86, 97
Latins, 2–3, 4, 10
  and Cyprus, 35
  and 'Greek' label, 16
  and Mongols, 55
  and religion, 20, 21, 22, 144
  and slave terminology, 87
  and terminology, 17
  see also Church, the
leavened bread, 4, 20
Leo of Tripoli, 133–4
Leonardo Marcello, 39
Leontios Machairas, 79–80

Lepanto, 162, 185
literacy, 172
Louis IX of France, King, 77, 136
Lusignan dynasty, 5; *see also* Cyprus
Lyons, Council of, 147–8

Macedonia, 3, 29, 45, 183
McKee, Sally, 153
Mallorca, 49–50, 162
   and the Church, 150–1
   and ethnicity, 156–7, 158
   and slaves, 98–100, 101–3
Malta, 138
Mamlūks, 3–4, 5, 195
   and Acre, 36
   and Byzantine relations, 68–71
   and Cyprus, 72–80
   and Genoese, 55–6
   and Golden Horde, 54–5
   and Ottomans, 176
   and prisoner exchanges, 134–5
   and slave ethnicity, 59
Manfred of Sicily, 30
Manuel II, Emperor, 111, 148
Manuel Chrysoloras, 148–9
manumission, 10, 12, 13, 20, 22
   and Crete, 44
   and Cyprus, 36–7
   and ethnicity, 154
   and Mallorca, 102–3
   and Mamlūk elite, 54, 195
   and Sicily, 145
Manzikert, Battle of, 31–2
Martin I, Emperor, 154, 155, 159
Martin IV, Pope, 30
Martin of Aragon, King, 146, 147
Matthew (Manuel Gabalas), 168–70
Maurozoumes, 94
Maximus III of Constantinople,
   Patriarch, 181
Mehmed the Conqueror, 186
Melkite Christians, 69, 135

Menteşe, 18, 48, 49, 86, 106, 136–7, 176–7
Mercedarians, 135–6
mercenaries, 44–5
Michael (neomartyr), 70, 75–7
Michael Angelos, 29
Michael IV Autoreianos, Patriarch, 29
Michael VIII Palaiologos, 1, 29–30
   and Charles of Anjou, 32
   and the Church, 147–8
   and Constantinople, 54, 55
   and Mamlūks, 69
   and Ottomans, 194
   and Turkmens, 31, 32–3
Michael IX Palaiologos, Emperor, 34
Michael Kalophrenas, 147
Michael Loulloudes, 106–7
Michael Notaropoulos, 130
Milan, Treaty of, 39
military orders, 2, 135–9, 140, 173–4
mobility *see* forced mobility
monasteries, 110–11, 118–19
Mongols, 31, 54, 195
Morea, 111–12
Muhammad Beg, 31
Murad I, Sultan, 97, 181, 186
Musa of Menteşe, Prince, 86
Muslims, 6, 19
   and *aichmalotika*, 125
   and Christians, 57–8
   and Greek slaves, 144
   and ransomers, 132
   and Valencia, 160
   see also Mamlūks
Mylasa, 33–4

Naples, 163
al-Nāṣir Ḥasan, Sultan, 70, 134–5
natio, 14–15, 152, 197
Navarrese, 45
Neopatras, 45, 47, 50
Nicaea (Nikaia), 1, 29, 31

Niccolò Venier, 71
Nicola Gripioti, 41
Nicola Spinola, 69
Nicola de Boateriis, 130, 131
Nicola de Corron, 50
Nicholas Isidore, 128–9
Nicholas Likinios, 125–6
Nikephoros Blemmydes, 181
Nikephoros Gregoras, 74–5, 126–7, 151
Nomocanon, 117, 118
notaries, 12–13, 15–16, 36–7
Nymphaion, Treaty of, 55

old age, 100
Orthodox Christians, 20, 21, 144, 149
Osman I, Sultan, 34
Ottoman Empire, 1, 3, 5
　and Byzantine collapse, 34, 51
　and Chiones, 92–3
　and conquests, 186–92, 194–5
　and Greeks, 138
　and raids, 179–85, 197–8
　and ransoms, 128–9
　and Thessaloniki, 96–7
　see also Islam

Paganino Doria, 64, 65
Pahlitzsch, Johannes
　'On the Ransom of Greek Captives and Slaves in the Late Byzantine Period. Forms and Actors', 8
papacy, 21–2, 57–8, 73
　and bulls, 155–9
　see also Benedict XII; Clement VI; Clement VII; Eugenius IV; Felix V; Innocent III; Martin IV; Urban V
Paul Sofiano, 163
peasantry, 38, 79, 110–13, 137
Peloponnese, 3; *see also* Morea
Pera *see* Galata
Pere de Berga, 156
Pero Tafur, 178–9
Peter III of Aragon, King, 30

Peter IV of Aragon, King, 162–3
Peter the Ceremonious, King, 101, 150, 155–6
Philip of Swabia, 27
Philotheos of Athos, 191
Pietro Badoer of Crete, Duke, 86
Pietro Pizolo, 40, 41
Philotheos Kokkinos, 64
Phylipo de Millano, 41
Phylippus Bocontolo, 41
praktika (tax records), 110–11
prisoner exchanges, 133–5
Purgatory, 20

Qalāwūn, Sultan, 69

race, 18–19; *see also* ethnicity
Ragia, Efe, 34
raiding, 1, 5–6, 59, 113, 133
　and Catalans, 44–5
　and corsairs, 138
　and Crete, 43–4
　and naval, 30, 32, 41, 69
　and Ottomans, 169, 179–85
　and Turks, 48, 52, 118–19
　and Umur of Aydın, 136, 173–4
Ramon d'Escales, 156–7
Ramon Muntaner, 105–6
Ranieri Boccanegra, 69–70
ransoms, 2, 5, 139–40
　and *aichmalotika*, 125
　and Crete, 41, 42
　and individuals, 128–32, 133
　and Ottomans, 97–8
　and Palamas, 93
　and religious duty, 115–19
redemption, 5, 9–10, 196–7
　and Cyprus, 73, 74–5, 79
　and family members, 129–30
　and military orders, 135–9, 140
　see also aichmalotika; ransoms
refugees, 36, 73, 104–9, 110–14, 196
religion, 19–22

and duty, 115–19
and ethnicity, 152–3
and slavery, 143–52, 164, 197
see also Christians; Islam; Jews
repentance, 166–7
reprisals law, 161
Rhodes, 137
Richard I of England, King, 35–6
rites, 21–2
Roberto of Naples, 51
Roger of Flor, 44, 45, 46
Romanía, 15, 27–30, 44–52, 67, 137
Rome, 16
Rubió i Lluch, Antonio
    Diplomatari de l'Orient Catala, 7
Rūm, 31, 32
Russians, 8, 67, 197
Ruy Gonzalez de Clavijo, 41

Saccon, Lorenzo
    'Ransoming Activities in the 14th
    Century Eastern Mediterranean', 8
Saladin, Sultan, 55
Salvetus Pezagnus, 42
Saracens, 14–15
schismatics, 4, 20
scholarship, 6–8
Scotland, 125
self-enslavement, 90–1
Segurano Salvaygo, 57
Seljuks, 31–2
Serbians, 72
sexual exploitation, 153
Sicily, 30, 59–60, 144–6, 151
Sigismund of Hungary, Holy Roman
    Emperor, 149
Simeone di San Giacomo dell'Orio,
    131
Sinan Paşa, 189, 190
Sinope, 32
skilled labour, 101–2
slavery, 2–5, 6, 7–8
    and Catalans, 45, 46–7, 50–1

and categories, 22–3
and Crete, 38–43
and Cyprus, 36–8
and ethnicity, 14, 15–16, 59–61,
    152–60
and experiences, 98–103
and Genoese, 55–7
and Islamic rule, 173–9
and Mallorca, 49–50
and Muslims, 57–8
and race, 18–19
and raids, 180
and redemption, 129–30
and religion, 19–20, 143–52
and repopulation, 137–8
and sources, 10–11, 13
and terminology, 85–91, 195–6
Slavs, 11, 72
Smyrna, 173–4
stone masonry, 101–2
Stefano Bono, 40
Stellianinus San Scitara, 71
subjecthood, 151, 160–5
Sweden, 125
Symeon of Thessaloniki, Archbishop,
    118
Syria, 3, 4

Taronites, 92, 94
Tatars, 56, 59, 72, 78–9, 152, 164
taxation, 110–11, 185
Theodore Laskaris, Emperor, 29
Theodore Metochites, 70
Theodoret, 126
Thessaloniki, 28, 133–4
    and Ottomans, 96–7, 167, 171,
    187–9, 190–1
Thessaly, 3, 45, 47–9
Thira (Santorini), 43
Thrace, 3, 45, 150
    and desertions, 183, 186
    and Islamic rule, 170–1, 172
timars, 179–80

Tīmūr, 174
Tommaso Ottone, 64
trade networks, 2–4, 173
trafficking, 3–4, 195–6
   and Genoese, 61–8
   and tribunals, 89–90
transatlantic slave trade, 15, 18, 19
Trebizond, 29, 126
Trinitarians, 135–6
Turkmens, 31, 32–3
Turks, 1, 2–3, 4–5, 148
   and Byzantine campaigns, 33
   and Catalans, 48–9
   and Crete, 40–1
   and slave purchases, 100–1
   and terminology, 17–18
   see also Ottoman Empire

al-'Umarī, Ibn Faḍl Allāh, 175, 177
Umur of Aydın, 136, 168–9, 173–4
unfreedom *see* captivity; slavery

unleavened bread, 4, 146
Urban V, Pope, 148, 155–7, 158, 159

Valencia, 46, 63, 150, 154–5, 160
Venetians, 2, 5, 28–9
   and Black Sea, 61–2
   and Lepanto, 185
   and notaries, 12
   and refugees, 111
   and Seljuks, 32
   and Thessaloniki, 96–7, 187–8
Verlinden, Charles, 7–8
villeins, 39
Vlachs, 8, 11, 14, 197

William of Adam, 57

Zachariadou, Elizabeth
   Trade and Crusade, 6, 7
Zan Dimitre, 154–5
Zara (Zadar), 28

EU representative:
Easy Access System Europe
Mustamäe tee 50, 10621 Tallinn, Estonia
Gpsr.requests@easproject.com